MW00770811

My Word Is My Bond

My Word Is My Bond

Voices From Inside The Chicago Board of Trade

ARLENE MICHLIN BRONSTEIN

John Wiley & Sons, Inc.

Published by John Wiley & Sons, Inc., Hoboken, New Jersey.

Published simultaneously in Canada.

For general information on our other products and services or for technical support, please contact our Customer Care Department within the United States at (800) 762-2974, outside the United States at (317) 572-3993 or fax (317) 572-4002.

Wiley also publishes its books in a variety of electronic formats. Some content that appears in print may not be available in electronic books. For more information about Wiley products, visit our web site at www.wiley.com.

Library of Congress Cataloging-in-Publication Data:

My word is my bond: voices from inside the Chicago Board of Trade / [interviewed by] Arlene Michlin Bronstein.

p. cm.

Based on transcripts of interviews conducted for a documentary video which celebrates the 160th anniversary of the Chicago Board of Trade (CBOT).
ISBN 978-0-470-23898-1 (cloth)
1. Chicago Board of Trade–History. 2. Futures market–United States–History. 3. Chicago Board of Trade–Officials and employees–Interviews. 4. Investment advisors–United States–Interviews. 5. Floor traders (Finance)–United States–Interviews. I. Bronstein, Arlene Michlin, 1949- II. CME Group. III. Title: Voices from inside the Chicago Board of Trade.
HG6024.U6M9 2008
332.64'4092273–dc22 2007052396

Printed in the United States of America

10 9 8 7 6 5 4 3 2 1

For Jack and Esther

The Most Valuable Commodity: Wonderful Parents

Contents

Foreword

Experience is a great teacher. A financial exchange like the Chicago Board of Trade should be regarded as a learning institution of the highest caliber. For 160 years, men and women have devoted their professional lives to this venerable financial organization—writing the extensive rulebook of auction market fundamentals along the way, continually honing their risk transference skills, and ultimately delivering a venue for global financial opportunity. Lessons taught here would be difficult to duplicate in any academic environment.

Reflecting a collective memory spanning nearly 100 years, the pages of this book are filled with thought-provoking interviews with some of the most influential members of the Chicago Board of Trade. Their words convey the importance of issues such as the need for transparency in the markets, the effect of world events on the financial landscape, and the essential role of integrity in business.

Though not always frictionless, their innovations, explorations, and strong opinions have contributed significantly to the greater good of the exchange. When you consider that these are people who literally have seen and done it all in the futures industry, their wisdom is not only insightful, but incredibly valuable.

In today's global environment, ever-changing geopolitical and economic trends continue to create a growing need for risk management and hedging tools. To better serve this evolving financial marketplace, the Chicago Board of Trade and the Chicago Mercantile Exchange completed a historic merger in July 2007. By forging a single entity, CME

Group, we have begun to write the next chapter in our industry. Going forward, it's imperative that we listen to the voices of the past as we shape our collective future.

Terrence A. Duffy
Executive Chairman
CME Group, Inc.

Preface

On the top of the Chicago Board of Trade Building in the heart of the city's financial district is a statue of Ceres, the Roman goddess of grain. Although Ceres is a symbol of the exchange's 160-year connection to the business of agriculture, to many of the denizens of the LaSalle Street canyon she represents much more. Her stalwart presence has witnessed economic booms, financial depressions, droughts, floods, and wars. Through every period of history, she has stood tall and proud, an icon not only of the exchange, but of Chicago as the risk management capital of the world. The irony is that Ceres is faceless—without eyes, nose, or mouth—and yet she embodies the people who on a daily basis confront the markets with searching eyes, a nose for business, and the necessary mouth and voice to conduct their transactions.

My Word Is My Bond: Voices from Inside the Chicago Board of Trade was created to give that rooftop icon a face and the added attraction of a personality. In the course of reading the 21 interviews in this book, you will experience the exchange through the eyes of people who have witnessed nearly 100 years of history. You will find a nose to sniff out the truths from the high and low points of this venerable institution. These collective chronicles will give a voice to Ceres, to tell the stories that will animate her and the history of this unique business.

The idea for this book came after the production of an hour-long documentary that celebrates the 160th anniversary of the Chicago Board of Trade (CBOT). Twenty-one voices from the CBOT were chosen to represent the depth and breadth of the trading experience. The interviews were conducted from April through June 2007, just prior to the CBOT vote to merge with the Chicago Mercantile Exchange. The participants span a wide range of ages. They tell the Board of Trade story from diverse angles, which include a historical perspective of world activities and a market perspective of how this financial institution has not only survived, but thrived.

The founding fathers on that spring day, April 3, 1848, could never have imagined that their progeny would one day shed the mantle of membership and become shareholders. In fact, many of the exchange's contemporary members could not believe in either the possibility or the profitability of such a change. They were wrong. Sometimes the unimaginable need not be forbidding. Sometimes change is not only necessary, but good.

The CBOT demonstrates the ability of permanence and change not just to coexist, but in fact to perpetuate a strong institution. Reading this book, you will get a sense of the motivation and drive of the men and women who have devoted their lives to serving the marketplace. You will read their firsthand accounts describing the vagaries of being market makers during the Dickensian "best of times and worst of times" on the trading floor of the CBOT.

These 21 individuals have all worked in the same place and performed similar jobs, while having very different viewpoints on that experience. What they do share is a love of the exchange and an unshakeable belief in the importance of honesty and integrity in their everyday work and their lives beyond the CBOT. They are all givers in the best sense of the word, volunteering in and out of their workplace. They have an abiding allegiance to the exchange and have nurtured it through its many changes. As Charles Darwin said, "It is not the strongest of the species that survives, not the most intelligent, but the one most responsive to change."

Although change has been a hallmark of the CBOT, it never has come easily. The exchange has always been made up of rugged individualists who possess strong opinions on how things should be run. Through these stories, you will learn firsthand about the many courageous pioneers. You will be able to experience the difficult process of trying to balance the security of continuity with the opportunities of traveling a different road, moving from trading agricultural commodities to financial interest rate–based instruments. You will be given an inside look at how the members and staff of this great institution developed these new contracts, and as a result enhanced not only the livelihoods of its members, but also the livelihoods of market participants and consumers in the agricultural and financial industries throughout the United States and around the world.

Perhaps it was prescient that Ceres, placed on the rooftop in 1930, is without facial features. Now it is no longer necessary to stand in a pit, to see fellow traders eye to eye. It is no longer necessary to yell out orders or to flash hand signals to denote that a transaction has taken place. Because of computers, trading has become a near-faceless experience. Yet as the business continues to evolve, it becomes so much more diverse, interesting, and profitable than it was in its original conception. But what hasn't changed is Ceres. Her image is timeless. She remains a talisman, her creation commissioned by those entrepreneurial traders to ensure good fortune to all who should come under her featureless gaze down the LaSalle Street canyon and into the heart of Chicago's financial district.

In some sense, this book represents the last word on the exchange and its history. It was written to shed light on the inner workings of the CBOT, a unique institution whose unprecedented innovations and leadership have spawned a global financial industry. No longer is there a single entity known as the Chicago Board of Trade. In 2007, the CBOT was acquired by the Chicago Mercantile Exchange. In their merged form, they have created a new company called CME Group, Inc. Together they are the world's largest and most diverse exchange. Their future together is an exciting new chapter in the world of commodities and finance.

Acknowledgments

In the best sense, this book was a collaborative effort. From its very inception, there were many people who made this book possible. First, thanks have to go to Bernard W. Dan, who was president of the Board of Trade when I brought to him the idea for doing a video history about the exchange. Having worked his entire career in the financial arena, Bernie was well aware of the significant contributions the CBOT and its members had made to make Chicago the risk management capital of the world. His enthusiasm and willingness to back this project brought about a chain of events that produced a historical documentary video. This book is based on interviews from those taped sessions.

Once Bernie had signed on to this project, he turned to the exchange's Corporate Communications Department, led by the very capable Maria Gemskie. As managing director, Maria was instrumental as our liaison to the various parties who made this book possible. Most important, she brought in the CBOT's senior editor Barbara Z. Kodlubanski to oversee the video and the book. Barb's 24 years of experience with the exchange added to the depth and breadth of this project. She not only managed the day-to-day activities, but was essential in providing content and editing.

Production Craft in Chicago, Illinois, headed by Dawn Arnold, was hired to produce the documentary. I was assigned to conduct the interviews. Dawn did an exceptional job of organizing this monumental task. She was ably assisted by an extremely talented team: Jim Skvaril, Dan Wood, Bob Schordje, Jason Fowler, Tim Troy, Tom Pinchuk, and Risé

Sanders. From those taped interviews, written transcripts were created that were responsible for the content of this book.

The design of this book was expertly produced by Allen Stebbins of Stebbins Graphic Design in Woodstock, Illinois. It was his vision that packaged the material into this fine historical document. William Valicenti of Quad Graphics in Anaheim, California, was hired to take the photographs for the book. He is a very gifted man who brought his skilled eye to each portrait. His additional photographs of the building and the hand signals are extraordinary and help to preserve the historical accuracy of the book.

A special thank you to Bill Falloon of John Wiley & Sons for taking on this project. We were lucky that Bill came on board for both the video and the book. Bill is a noted CBOT historian and author of the book *Market Maker: A Sesquicentennial Look at the Chicago Board of Trade* (CBOT, 1998).

I'd also like to thank Billy Assimos of Ceres Café for finding the much-needed chocolate brownies during the hectic days of shooting at the CBOT building.

Neither the book nor the video would have been successful without the incredible participation of each of the interviewees. They gave many hours to this project: from pre-interviews to the taped interviews to the follow-up chapter edits and their suggestions for improving the content. Each adds a significant gift to the history of the exchange, and it was an honor to work with all of them.

And last, but certainly not least, I want to thank my husband, Keith Bronstein, for being my living resource to the historical information and economic content that makes this book so special. His knowledge, insight, and personal experience were invaluable throughout every detail of this project. He is an incredible human being and not a day goes by that I am not in awe of his intelligence and kindness. My life is so blessed to have him, and our children, Scott and his wife Liza, Jaime, and Hawkeye, and our granddaughters Cameron, Dylan, and Zoey by my side.

Arlene Michlin Bronstein

CHAPTER 1

Scaling Great Heights

Patrick H. Arbor

As a man who loves climbing mountains, Patrick H. Arbor has been well suited to face many uphill challenges. From his early childhood, growing up in an unstable family followed by four years at the Catholic–run Mercy Home for Boys and Girls, Patrick dreamt of living the life of a high-powered, successful executive.

After graduating from high school and attending Loyola University, he began looking for ways to fulfill his goal of being successful while doing good deeds. Even as a young man, he developed great character, strength, and personal discipline. He abstained from alcohol, tobacco, and caffeine. His addictions, if one could call them that, are for physical fitness, traveling, mountain climbing, and great devotion to family. Patrick Arbor allowed the adversity of his young life to motivate him to become a successful, respected leader.

Following his graduation from Loyola University, he started out as a teacher of algebra and economics at Sullivan High School in Chicago.

Although he enjoyed the process of helping young people learn, he became disillusioned with the school system. This led him to pursue a career in politics and business. By the early 1960s, he was married and raising two young children in Harwood Heights, Illinois. At the time, it was an unruly village, filled with taverns and gambling establishments. He seized an opportunity to change the small village when he was elected to the job of mayor. Under his administration, he was able to close down the gambling places and have the liquor establishments conform to normal hours.

In an effort to make a better living, he began looking for a more lucrative business opportunity. He answered a blind ad in the newspaper and began working at the Jefferson State Bank. From this experience he learned the banking business. After two years, he answered another blind ad and found a job at the Chicago Board of Trade (CBOT) for Uhlmann Grain. Although he initially worked as a back-office employee, it wasn't long before he found his way into the trading pits.

Unfortunately, his first attempt at success at the CBOT didn't last very long, as he lost a lot of money and had to sell his membership and find a life off the floor. While working for a construction company, he heard that membership prices had fallen and he decided to give it one more shot. This time he would call on his exceptional discipline to make this job work.

In a matter of months, Mr. Arbor began his ascent in this field of dreams. The 1970s heralded the great bull markets in grains. He traded well and began working his way through the committee system at the exchange. Having made up his mind that he wanted to be part of the fabric of this great institution, he devoted his time to making a difference by participating in a number of committees such as the Executive Committee and Board of Directors of both the Board of Trade Clearing Corporation and the National Futures Association (NFA).

In 1980, these experiences led him to the Board of Directors, where he participated in the leadership of the exchange. He helped lead the exchange through the harrowing days of the Crash of 1987, oversaw the building of a new agricultural floor (completed in 1982) to relieve overcrowding, and was instrumental in relieving the CBOT of the onerous lease on the building at 444 West Jackson Boulevard. He championed and oversaw the construction of a new financial floor in 1997. In addition, he spent a great deal of time as a spokesperson for the exchange as a global ambassador.

Serving as the longest-running chairman in the exchange's history (six years from 1993 to 1998), Patrick Arbor has been an advocate for innovation, expansion, and integrity. He has been a reliable source for the media on all things related to the Chicago Board of Trade. He has been a major proponent of the move toward an initial public offering (IPO) for the CBOT and a big supporter of the merger with the Chicago Mercantile Exchange (CME).

Mr. Arbor is proud to have been a part of the glorious 160-year history of the Chicago Board of Trade and looks forward to the continued growth of the CME Group Inc.

President Bill Clinton appointed Patrick to the Western Newly Independent States (WNIS) Enterprise Fund Board of Directors in October 1994. His numerous board positions include Chicago's Mercy Home for Boys and Girls, the Mission of Our Lady of Mercy, Catholic Charities of the Archdiocese of Chicago, and the Illinois Facilities Fund.

Previous board appointments include the Executive Committee and the Board of Trustees of Loyola University of Chicago; the United States Association for the United Nations High Commissioner for Refugees; First State Bank & Trust Company of Park Ridge, Illinois; London Investment Trust (LIT), PLC; United Financial Holdings, Inc.; and the United Community Bank.

At present, Patrick serves as a director of First Chicago Bank & Trust Co., a billion-dollar bank holding company, and of Merriman Curhan Ford & Co., an American Stock Exchange (Amex)–listed company. He is a principal of the trading firm Shatkin Arbor.

The author of numerous articles on finance in leading professional and academic journals, and a veteran mountain climber who has scaled many of the world's tallest peaks, Pat Arbor is a lifelong resident of Chicago and has three children and six grandchildren.

****

First, I would like to explore some of your personal story.

I grew up on the west side of Chicago and graduated from Saint Mel High School. I came from a mixed family; by that I mean my mother was Irish and my father was Italian. There was irresponsible drinking on the Irish side of the family, so as a result I've never had a drink of alcohol in my life. I matriculated at Loyola University, graduating in 1958 with a bachelor's degree in science and commerce and minors in education and mathematics. With that background, I decided to teach at the high school level. I taught for two years at Sullivan High School at 6636 North Bosworth Avenue.

After those two years, I decided to enter the business world. I literally answered a blind ad in the newspaper to work for a bank that I had never heard of before. As a result, I went to work for the Jefferson State Bank. I worked for a man named Bernie Feinberg, who taught me everything I know about business. I like banking; I like money and finance, and I really cut my teeth there. Bernie was a great mentor and a great leader.

In the two years I worked at the bank, I was doing a lot of work down on LaSalle Street. I was delivering securities back and forth, depositing securities for payment and bringing checks back to the bank. I became interested in the world of finance and decided to seek my fortune on LaSalle Street. Once again, I answered a blind ad in the newspaper for a company I had never heard of before, called Uhlmann Grain.

Although I didn't know it at the time, Uhlmann Grain was the Rolls-Royce of the futures industry. They were trying to broaden their product mix into securities, and I was hired as a back-office trainee. I received a marvelous introductory education working with Uhlmann Grain. My first boss at the Board of Trade was Fred Uhlmann. Fred and his father, Richard Uhlmann, along with John Benjamin, ran this marvelous company, and they were gracious in sharing their business acumen with me.

After a couple of years working there, I decided to go into business for myself, but I really didn't know what to do. I was thinking about a seat on the Board of Trade and I was also thinking about buying a currency exchange. There was a currency exchange for sale at Laramie Avenue and Chicago Avenue on the west side of Chicago. The price for the currency exchange was $15,000. At the same time, the Board of Trade seat was about $11,700. So it was kind of a flip of a coin, biased by the fact that the Board of Trade seat was cheaper. So I purchased the seat on the Chicago Board of Trade.

How did you finance that?

Bernie Feinberg lent me the money at the Jefferson State Bank, and I paid him back in a couple of years, because my first soiree in the soybean market wasn't so good. I lost money for the first six months and actually throughout the first year. Finally, after a couple of years, I started to make some money and I paid him back.

Can you remember your first day down on the floor?

My first day on the trading floor was very intimidating. I had no idea what to do. It was about 1965. Bernie Feinberg's friend, Ernie Kahn, introduced me to Henry Shatkin. Henry accepted me as a client, took me down on the floor, and introduced me around the pit. I had no idea what to do. The first thing I did was to buy one contract of soybeans, which proceeded to decline for the next couple of days. I think I was out about $800, and that was comparable to the end of the world to me.

Can you describe what the people were like on the floor at that time?

The people at that time, in my opinion, were more of the gentleman type. This is particularly compared with the traders we see today. Men wore jackets, shirts, and ties. They came dressed properly, had manners, and conducted their affairs with great civility. There was a great amount of humor at the Board of Trade, too.

Give me some examples.

There was one great example. In the 1980s, we had a customer trading through us at Shatkin Trading named Vic Proeh. Vic wore a toupee. One day after wearing the toupee for all of those years, he decided he didn't want to wear it anymore. So very appropriately, he waited until 9:29:30 A.M. to enter the pit, 30 seconds before the grain opening, to make his toupeeless debut. He knew he was going to suffer some kind of heckling. As he was a customer of Shatkin, one of the members yelled out, "That Shatkin will take anything for margin." So that elicited a lot of laughs.

I am sure it did. Can you talk about some of the legends at the CBOT, both people you had heard about and people you knew personally?

There have been many legends at the Chicago Board of Trade. During my era there were Ralph Peters, Eddie Wilson, and Gene Cashman, who stood out as some of the great speculators. Then there were outstanding traders: Red Rose, Lee Stern, Henry Shatkin, Jordy Glassman, and the Cashman family. I think that Gene Cashman was the most legendary trader.

What made these people stand out?

I think it was a mixture of courage, the magnitude of risk they took on, and then a certain dose of discipline.

How does discipline play into trading?

In my opinion, the cornerstone, the bedrock of trading, is discipline. It is the ability to take a loss. It's the ability to trade within your means, to know how much money you can afford to lose. It's the discipline not to add to a bad trade. Just like in real estate, where it's location, location, location, in our industry, it's discipline, discipline, discipline. And I think the best example of that is probably Lee Stern. Lee Stern always knew how to take a loss. I watched him. If he had a trade that was no good, he would take a loss.

It's hard to walk away.

Very difficult. You're fighting many things. You're fighting the loss of money, first of all. You're also fighting your ego, the fact that you made a mistake; and to overcome those two things requires an awful lot of discipline.

Sometimes even with discipline, things don't work. People think about the Board of Trade as a place where everybody makes it, but I think you've had a personal experience when that wasn't true. Tell me about that.

I'm an example of one who did not make it the first time. A number of my colleagues didn't make it the first time, either. I joined the Board of Trade in 1965 and by 1968 I was done. I was there only three years. I had a couple of good years and then I had one bad year. I lost most of my money and I had to leave the Board of Trade. Now at that time, everyone was having trouble at the Board of Trade. I didn't realize that. Later I heard that a lot of people were having trouble because the markets had low volatility. There wasn't much going on.

It was because of those times that the Board of Trade started the Chicago Board Options Exchange (CBOE). And it was because of those times that the Board of Trade started financial futures products. The exchange realized that we had to broaden our diversity beyond the agricultural products. Now that was before the great Russian markets of the 1970s occurred, because no one could foresee them at that time. In 1968 and 1969, things were very lean at the Board of Trade. The volumes were down, markets were slow, and people were having a hard time making money.

So what happened to you?

I left the Board of Trade and had a series of jobs. The final job I had on the outside was working on construction. I worked as an ironworker and I was a rod buster. I was tying rebar together and we were putting it on the top two floors of the telephone building at the corner of Federal and Harrison. I could look across Eisenhower Expressway and see Ceres on top of the Board of Trade building and I said, "Please, please let me go back there. I'll be a good boy. I'll behave. I will have discipline." And it turned out that's the way it worked out.

How?

The memberships were trading at $31,000 and then they suddenly went down to about $17,000, which was where I had sold mine in 1968. And I figured if I went and talked to Bernie Feinberg, I could probably borrow some more money. Fortunately, he agreed. Then I went and talked to Henry Shatkin, who had been my clearing firm, and he encouraged me to come back.

But by the time I got the money together and applied, memberships had shot back up to $31,000. In those days you had to wait two months before you could buy a membership, so I couldn't just run in—*carpe diem*, seize the day—and buy the one for $17,000. I had to wait until I was approved two months later. Bernie was going to lend me $20,000. That left me $11,000 short. So I went to Henry Shatkin, and Henry wrote me a check for $11,000. I'll never forget that for the rest of my life, because that was the difference between me being here today and not being here today. It would be like lending me $11 million today. I paid him back in a week and a half!

How were you able to do that?

It was just one of those fortuitous things. I came back in August of 1970 and the first week it was kind of quiet. The second week we had a fungus corn blight market; this fungus was attacking the corn crop. All of a sudden the corn market heated up, and I was in corn. On Monday, the corn was limit up and Tuesday they were calling "Limit up," too, and I thought two days in a row might be a little bit too much. I was inclined to sell some corn, but not a whole lot.

Then the market opened up limit bid to about three lower. There was a broker across the pit named Marshal Smith, and he was bidding limit up. We made eye contact and I said, "Sold." I had no idea how much I was going to sell, and by the time I went over to check the trade limit up, we were still counting how many to buy, it was about 340 stuff (340,000 bushels), which was a big trade at the time. By the time I wrote it down, I was scared to death. The market was three cents lower. I started buying in a short position from John Morris, as I recall, about four cents lower and the market went down from there on. But I was happy, because I made $12,500 in that trade.

Fantastic. That's what the business is all about. Tell me about how integrity plays into your business.

Integrity is the cornerstone of the business. To be good at the business you need discipline, but the glue, the cement, the structure of the Board of Trade is integrity. In Latin we say *meum pactum dictum*. It means "my word is my bond." It's a wonderful place to do business, because you can trust. There's no contract, not even a handshake—just a nod of the head, a wave of the hand, or a verbal acknowledgment that you made the trade.

How about the word 'tradition'?

Tradition plays a big part in it. One of the best traditions was handed down from the old-timers, the senior citizens of the Board of Trade, to the newer traders. They would teach and mentor the young people on the dos and don'ts of the CBOT. Many times it would be done politely, even with civility, as I mentioned before, but it would be done in a way that you certainly received the message of proper conduct in the pit and honoring the trade.

Can you tell me somebody who was a mentor to you?

Henry Shatkin has been a mentor to me. He used to always use that Pinocchio line, "Always let your conscience be your guide," and I think that served me well over the years.

What was the first lesson that you learned?

The first lesson I learned that really worked was to take a loss. Equally important was the early lesson I learned about the value of camaraderie: the network, the spirit of helping each other at the Board of Trade. We had that when I started and we still have it here today.

I was lucky to be in the good graces of Henry Shatkin and have him help me. Since that time, I have taken his lead and helped many other people. It is rewarding to think that I have passed on that tradition to other people, and I think those people have brought other people to the exchange. It is a fine culture of people helping people helping people. It's what has made the Board of Trade great.

There is an expression that you learned as a young trader.

Yes. "It's better to emulate than innovate." In other words, I think it's always better to start out copying someone who has been successful than try to do it yourself.

When I first came to the Board of Trade, I looked around. I looked at the speculators, and there were some successful speculators, but there were many speculators who were not successful. I looked at the brokers. There were many brokers who were successful, but then there were some brokers who weren't as successful. I looked at the scalpers, and some of them were pretty successful and some of them not so successful. But to me, the spreaders always seemed to be successful. They seemed to drive the nicer cars. They had the nicer homes. They had better lifestyles. So I tried to copy the spreaders and emulate their success.

Part of the success of the Board of Trade happens in an arena of self-regulation. Why would that be important?

Self-regulation is important because we know best how to regulate our business. It's in our best interest to regulate our business, because if we keep the bad apples out and if we keep the good business practices in, we will keep this business strong in the future. It's better for us to do it than someone who does not understand our business.

For six years you were the chairman of the Chicago Board of Trade. I believe that makes you the longest-running chairman ever. You've seen firsthand how self-regulation affects your industry. Why do you feel it works so well?

One of the great honors of my life was to serve as chairman of the Chicago Board of Trade. In fact, it was probably the greatest honor of my life to serve as chairman of this magnificent institution. I was proud of the way we self-regulated ourselves, and I was proud of the fact that we self-regulated our member firms and our members. I think we did it admirably. We did it with transparency. We did it with integrity. We did it with honesty. And we also had other layers of regulation overseeing us, like the Commodity Futures Trading Commission (CFTC), and our own self-regulatory agency, the National Futures Association (NFA). However, we felt we did it best.

How did you deal with the CFTC?

There were times when the Board of Trade didn't necessarily see eye to eye with the CFTC. The CFTC was looking to create regulation and authority where, in my opinion, it wasn't necessary.

An example would be the risk-based capital rules. The CFTC imposed 6 percent capital requirements on customer segregated funds, regardless of whether the money was employed or not employed. So if customer seg funds were all in cash, a company still had to maintain 6 percent capital of those customer seg funds. If there's no risk, then there should be no need for a risk-based capital adjustment. That would be an example of how the CFTC didn't fully understand our business.

In 1989, we had a terrible event occur at the Board of Trade. There was an undercover sting operation, and it was a horrible time for our industry. Many friends of mine, many customers of ours, were caught up in this horrendous time. The FBI had these undercover moles on the floor of the Board of Trade. They were trying to entrap people into doing things wrong. Were there some things done wrong? Absolutely there were some things done wrong, but many of the violations were akin to parking meter offenses and not major criminal acts.

Because of this investigation, the CFTC, the newspapers, and the world kind of looked at the Board of Trade in a bad light. And my answer to that was: If you had taken a look at the wrongdoing at the Board of Trade, it was less than one-quarter of 1 percent of our member population. In the Catholic religion there were 12 apostles. The Lord himself had a doubter, a denier, and a traitor. Three out of 12—that's a 25 percent failure rate for the Lord himself. If we had less than one-quarter of 1 percent, I think we did pretty well.

Great story. Speaking of that, what does that say about the character of the Board of Trade?

The character of the Board of Trade is one of the pillars of strength of our exchange. The character is really a measure of our membership, and our membership is a wonderful, diverse group of people. We come from all walks of life. We have MBAs from Harvard. We have sons of Italian immigrants who were butchers. We have educated people, uneducated people, professionals, doctors, dentists, and lawyers. But through it all, the character of all of these men and women is pretty much the same. There is desire for success and the ability to take risks, all with great love and pride in the Board of Trade.

The CBOT is home to a diversified population with shared values and goals. They're people of honor. They're people of courage. They're people of conviction. They're people who know how to take a risk and want to be in business for themselves. They embody the American spirit of entrepreneurship. These are people who come to the CBOT, every day, to try to carve out a living with a card and a pen.

I think that's really the character of the Board of Trade: rugged individualists who are willing to contribute back to the exchange, too, by serving on committees, serving on all forms of governance at the Chicago Board of Trade. It's a wonderful fraternal experience.

How do you explain that fraternal spirit when these people go into the pit every day and join in the rough-and-tumble experience?

I think that's just the nature of competitiveness. It's almost akin to a sporting event. Most men, and many women, love to play sports. They compete head-to-head all day long. They compete with great enthusiasm for winning. However, at the end of the day, they realize that they have a lot in common and they can leave the daytime competitive arena and can socialize at night.

Can you give me an idea why there aren't more women down there?

The first female member of the Board of Trade was Carol Ovitz. I think that was around 1970 or 1971. She is a wonderful woman, kind of small, and never really made it big in the pit. The pits are something akin to a sporting event. It's like playing a game of basketball or a game of football. There certainly is a locker-room mentality in the pit. It just doesn't bode well for a woman.

A good example is my own family. My daughter, Colleen, still feels a little bad that I never allowed her to come to the Chicago Board of Trade floor. My son, Michael, was here. He is a member of the Board of Trade and a member of the Chicago Mercantile Exchange, and my daughter always felt that she was kind of discriminated against. My daughter was employed at Northern Trust Bank. She had a nice suit on. She ate in a nice cafeteria every day with gentlemen, and I did not want her here. It's very difficult for a woman to be on the floor, because of a woman's size, the level of a woman's voice, and the rugged nature of the pit.

With the advent of computer trading, maybe screen-based trading will encourage more women to participate.

Computer trading has democratized the process. There's no difference when you're in front of a computer screen. With a keyboard and a mouse, it doesn't matter if you're six feet or five feet tall, a former baseball or basketball player or a five-foot-two woman; it makes no difference. If you have the same agility and the same discipline, then the screen treats you equally.

How important are the changes that have taken place?

They're very important. These changes are going to carry the CBOT and the CME into the next generation. Both of these exchanges are going to experience even greater success, because as good as a broker is, as good as a trader is, there are only so many trades an individual can make in that pit during a given day, per minute.

For example, a good broker may be able to execute five or 10 trades in a minute, if he's working rapidly. And a good trader can do only maybe five or 10 trades at most in a minute. But a computer can do an infinite number of trades and expand the whole world beyond the pit, beyond the customer base to the world, through the Internet. I know it's going to lead to exponential growth in trading, and I support it fully.

One of the people who was in the forefront of the computer age was Ray Cahnman. How were his views accepted?

I know Ray Cahnman well. Ray was a customer of ours. He came down on a Ginnie Mae permit and was trading Ginnie Maes. I was in charge of monitoring his account. Quite frankly, we had a sheet of trades that was as thick as the Chicago phone book that I couldn't understand.

It was just difficult for us to analyze the accounts. Ray knew what he was doing, but we couldn't understand what he was doing. This was back in the 1980s before we had computers. He was one of the first ones to understand the complexity of the Ginnie Maes, and later on the 30-year bond and 10-year note spreads. Ray Cahnman is probably as close to a genius as one can find. From the beginning, he supported the use of computers and electronic trading. I know he's trading around the clock.

Why did it take the Board of Trade so long to understand that computers might be a good thing?

It dawned on me back in the 1990s, when I was chairman of the CBOT. One of the many things I accomplished was to forge a link between the Board of Trade and Liffe (London International Financial Futures Exchange) in London to trade the bund contract. Chairmen had tried this before me and were not successful in forging such a link.

Jack Wigglesworth, chairman of Liffe, and I had a good relationship. With his help, I was able to create this link where Liffe traded the bund contract during London hours, and we were going to trade them here during Chicago hours. We were going to link them and have them cross margined, and they were going to be fungible. At that time, Liffe controlled about 90 percent of the bund trading.

In 1991–1992, Eurex, an all-electronic exchange in Frankfurt, started trading the bund contract in Germany electronically, with a bunch of computers and a bunch of servers. If I had heard Jack Wigglesworth say it once, he had said it at least a dozen times: "There would be no way the Germans would be able to take the bund contract away from Liffe, because there were more people employed in financial services in the city of London than there were in the whole city of Frankfurt, Germany."

Unfortunately, Jack was wrong, because Eurex came into Chicago with its computer screens. Customers liked trading electronically. The Eurex system was good. The markets were deep and liquid, and in very short order the Eurex decimated the Liffe, completely took the bund contract volume away.

That was an eye-opener for me. I didn't like it. I didn't like seeing the pits shut down and the trades going electronic. I didn't like losing my hair, either, but there's not much I can do about either one.

And then what happened?

I realized we had to do something here very quickly. We had lost the bund contract to Eurex. Eurex was talking about trading our financial products electronically, and, quite frankly, we didn't have the right systems operating. So we then forged a link with Eurex to try to work with them to start trading these contracts electronically.

When you became chairman, you had three goals. Can you tell me each of the goals and how they were met?

I ran for chairman in December of 1992. I ran on a platform of three goals: One was to increase profitability for members. The second was to build a new trading facility. And the third was to provide more access for our customers.

Trying to build more profitability for our members was one of my priorities. I wanted to reduce the exchange fees that members had to pay. I think we reduced them from two cents to one and a half cents, to trade more profitably for the members. Another cornerstone of my chairmanship was championing the building of the new trading facility.

Billy O'Connor, who was a great chairman, tried to have this passed the year before. We all realized that we needed this trading floor. This was before electronic trading. Eurex was just starting, so no one, at that time, had any idea that Eurex was going to do what it ended up doing. It was before the computer, before the Internet. Things happened very rapidly in the 1990s technologically. It was just a pivotal time.

When I took office in 1993, the first thing I did was start a referendum to pass a member vote to build a new trading floor. It passed two to one. We were going to build a $180 million facility. Dave Brennan chaired the new trading floor facility committee, and we constructed it under budget and on time. It's a 60,000-square-foot, state-of-the-art trading floor large enough to house a Boeing 747. We were off to a great start.

Unfortunately, technology has rendered that room basically obsolete, but maybe some good things will come from that with our merger with the CME. The plan would be to move the CME's agricultural products that are still traded open outcry to the CBOT.

My third goal was to increase access for our exchange customers. We knew that the more order flow we could bring here cheaper and quicker, the more trading opportunities and profit opportunities there would be for our members, member brokers, and our traders. To do that, I encouraged the electronic order entry by routing orders electronically from off-site locations through the Electronic Clerk (EC).

The orders came from the brokers' desks into the pit, and they also used headsets. Allowing brokers and clerks to use headsets to receive the transmission of orders from the customers into the pit made it more friendly for the customers to bring their orders to the floor.

Those were the three goals I wanted to achieve: increasing trading profits for the members, building a new trading facility, and increasing customer access. I fulfilled them all.

So I'd say you had a very successful tenure.

It was successful. We had six great years. It may be hard to believe, but 1998 was the last year the Chicago Board of Trade was the world's largest futures exchange. It all changed in 1999, and all because of one word. That one word was technology. That year, Eurex took over the number one spot in the world.

So this great legacy the Board of Trade had for 150 years was all changed by an exchange that was only eight or nine years old. Eurex became the leader because it was offering its products to its customers electronically and the Board of Trade was still offering our products to our customers through the open outcry method. I loved that method. I grew up with that method. It's wonderful. But there's just not much you can do about the advent of technology. It's changing the world.

What do you think will happen?

I am confident the future of our exchange is going to be glorious. I am confident the Board of Trade is moving in the right direction. I am confident Charlie Carey is doing a great job with the board of directors, moving the trade more electronically. I think that the merger with the Chicago Mercantile Exchange will be an outstanding achievement.

As we expand our customer base, I believe the Board of Trade will have a more glorious future than ever, but it's going to attract a new type of trader. It's going to be computer-type traders. It's going to be teams of traders—cadres of traders working together to develop algorithms, technology systems, and communication networks.

This new technology will afford many new job opportunities. There will be a need for programmers, network administrators, technicians, all kinds of technologically savvy people. What I see as a problem is that it's not going to be individual traders like before. It's going to be a team effort, where people are working together to develop trading programs.

Do you think it takes away the face-to-face workday?

Yes, it does. It's definitely going to take away the face-to-face work experience. I think it already has. This is true not only around this building, but around the Chicago area. You're seeing more proliferation of trading arcades and trading rooms. But one thing you do notice is they all want to be close to the server. They don't want to be remote, because they're dealing in nanoseconds. They're dealing in split seconds, so the closer they can be to this host server, the better it is for them. It's like a race. The one who gets there first is probably going to get the best chance at the trade.

So there will still be clusters of traders around the exchanges, but they won't meet on the floor. They might meet in the restaurants, or in the bars, or in the hallways. But you're never going to have that great trading-room mentality like we had before.

Do you think there's any room for pit trading?

I don't think so, not in the future. It will take some time for some of these products to move electronically, but human beings just cannot do what computers can do.

What is your take on commodity and derivative options trading?

Paul McGuire was a longtime, successful member and a great chairman of the CBOT. He was a smart, respected man, but he did not like options. He thought options would be the ruin of the CBOT. He was right on so many other things, but he was wrong on this. The interesting fact is that Paul was not alone in his opinion. People were afraid of changes.

But options have been a great, great product line for the Chicago Board of Trade. We introduced agricultural options in the early 1980s, and they've been very successful. And, of course, our financial options are also very successful. Interestingly enough, most of those options are still traded in the pit, although I've noticed in the past couple of months that this is slowly starting to change.

I see the percentages traded on the screen growing up in the financial options. It's going to take a little time for the algorithms, the technology, the programmers and the mathematical computations to catch up, but they will. They will eventually have options on the screen like they have futures, bonds and 10-year notes on the screen, too.

Can you discuss the importance of interest rate futures?

As I said earlier, back around 1970, the Board of Trade was not doing very well. Our products were pretty narrowly based in the agricultural complex. So the Board of Trade started to diversify. We started trading options on equities at the CBOE in 1973. But they really began working on it in 1969. Around that time, there was a young PhD out of California named Richard Sandor. It was his theory, based on his doctorate dissertation, that if we traded interest rate futures the way we trade pork bellies, or soybeans, or corn, we could provide valuable price discovery and hedging for the financial markets.

A lot of people thought it was a crazy idea. They said it wouldn't work, because interest rates for a long time had been very, very stable. During the 1950s, interest rates hardly moved at all. In the 1960s, they started to move a little bit, but almost nobody envisioned the breakdown of the Bretton Woods Agreement, going off the gold standard, and the Russians' grain purchases. Almost no one could imagine that oil prices were going sky-high and that the subsequent inflation would cause this gyration of interest rates. Fortunately, the Board of Trade did see this possibility. They engaged Richard Sandor to come to Chicago and work for the exchange and develop an interest rate contract.

The first contract was the Ginnie Mae contract, and the rest was history. If the Board of Trade hadn't done that, the Board of Trade would be nothing more than a second-rate exchange. Today, financial products account for 82 percent of our business. So the introduction of financial futures has made the Chicago Board of Trade successful.

What are some of the new products on the horizon?

I think new products are always difficult to introduce. We've tried many of them. We tried insurance and many other types of contracts. In my opinion, the emission allowance contracts are going to be of great value in the future. Under the direction of Richard Sandor, the Chicago Climate Exchange is leading the way in trading rights to make our planet carbon neutral.

Yesterday, the Supreme Court ruled against the Bush administration, saying the government has the right to regulate emission laws on some automobiles. They don't get it in Washington yet, but someday soon they will. Today the United States and Australia are the only holdouts from the Kyoto Protocol agreement. However, I think there will soon be a mandate in this country for some kind of emission allowance standards, and at that point you'll start seeing trading of these emission allowance credits. And I believe that this market solution to solve environmental problems is a sensational idea.

I think trading in water could be a great product, too. Natural resources of all kinds are the products of the future that we could trade. Another product that has been tried, but hasn't worked so well, is bandwidth. Bandwidth could be a product we could be trading someday. The world was laced with bandwidth for Global Crossing and WorldCom. The world, of course, never used much of that cable, because it was overlayered throughout the world. But as Thomas Friedman said in his book *The World Is Flat*, the bad news is the world has been oversupplied with fiber-optic cable, but the good news is it's there. It exists. As the demand catches up with the supply, I think we could be trading in bandwidth, and even perhaps in microchips or DRAMs (dynamic random-access memories).

Those are unique thoughts. I want to go back a little bit to discuss your role in the Crash of 1987. I'd like you to be the eyewitness.

On Monday, October 19, 1987, the Chicago Board of Trade Board of Directors had traveled to New York for a board meeting. The stock market was a little shaky at that time, because on Friday there had been a storm that ravaged parts of England and caused the market to go down sharply, some 100 points, both in London and in New York. But no one ever could have imagined what happened on that Monday the 19th.

The directors at the CBOT had been split up into different groups. My group was with Goldman Sachs. Others went with Morgan Stanley. A few CBOT member firms were trying to understand more what these other member firms did. They wanted to talk to these member firms about how we could help them with our product line at the CBOT. It was like a marketing trip in conjunction with the board meeting.

As we sat in the boardroom at these trading rooms in New York, we watched the market go down, closing down 509 points. Everyone thought the world was coming to an end—that some apocalypse was going to happen. Even though the board meeting was still supposed to go on in New York, they sent Don Andrew, who was on the executive committee and me back to Chicago, in case something happened on Tuesday. They felt there might be a need for some authority at the Chicago Board of Trade.

By the following morning, Karsten "Cash" Mahlmann, who was the chairman at the time, canceled the meeting and the board of directors came back to Chicago. Everybody was waiting with an anxious breath to see what was going to happen on that Tuesday. The market had been so severely damaged and so had the markets around the world. They were all collapsing and cascading down.

So Tuesday morning came and the market opened sharply lower again. I think the Dow Jones Industrial Average was around probably

2,200 at the time and it went down to 2,100, down to 2,000, down 200 points right off the bat. We were clustered up in Tom Donovan's office—Cash, myself, and Don and we were all watching very carefully what was going on. We had a contract here called the MMI; the Maxi contract we called it. This was an index that mirrored the Dow Jones contract. It had about a 90 to 94 percent correlation with the Dow, as I recall it, but as the market kept collapsing that Tuesday, panic set in.

The special systems just couldn't function. They couldn't handle the overflow, and they shut down. Then the Amex shut down. Then the CME shut down and the CBOE shut down. And it left only our little market, the Maxi contract, open. That was a small contract relative to most of these contracts, but it was a contract that was trading. We used to trade 5,000 to 7,000 contracts a day at the time. We were on the phone in Tom's office with the CFTC, the Federal Reserve, the Treasury, various other government agencies, and other exchanges. Nobody knew what to do.

However, I had an idea. I kept saying, "Let's keep this market open. These stocks are trading somewhere. The market is trading. You may not like the price, but at least there's a market, and I believe, in free markets for free men, that we should keep these markets open." So as I was arguing with my colleagues to keep the market open and we were having discussions with the regulators and the other exchanges and I was just about to lose when the market stopped going down. It stopped at around 1,700 and rallied 200 points.

We were not the only ones watching this contract because it was the only market open. It was the only one with any transparency. As it turned, one of our members, Blair Hull, had stepped in and bought the bottom of the market. Little by little, the other markets started to open and stability returned to the markets. So some would say he's the man who saved Western civilization.

It's a wonderful story, because it speaks so much about the character of the Chicago Board of Trade and the ability of the exchange to make a difference in the economy.

Yes, it does. The Board of Trade has always had an important place in the economy of the United States, whether it be price transparency for farmers or price transparency for the mortgage brokers, for the bankers, or for the interest rate traders. We think that the prices we provide here are a very good barometer, an accurate barometer, of exactly what the prices of commodities, or interest rates, or stock indexes should be. If you don't like it, you can always sell it or buy it, depending upon your view. But we think we've done very well over the years and we're going to continue to do well in the future.

Describe the exchange's global reach.

The exchange's reach certainly extends throughout the world. For instance, I'm on a bank board in Ukraine, Moldova, and Belarus. I travel to Eastern Europe once or twice a year and the wheat traders in Ukraine buy and sell off the prices at the Chicago Board of Trade.

So it doesn't make any difference if you're in China, Ukraine, or Keokuk, Iowa; if you want to know the price for corn, you look at the price of corn at the CBOT. Our prices are used as benchmarks throughout the world. Our global reach is extensive, and the CBOT has done a very good job of marketing itself by publishing different brochures in different languages and disseminating them throughout the world.

Do you want to comment on the IPO?

I fully support the IPO. I tried to do it when I was chairman in 1997 and 1998, when Jimmy Hines and Rob Moore presented me with an idea of converting our Project A member-partnership into a corporation and conducting an IPO. I thought they were off balance for about 24 hours, until I spoke with a few investment bankers. The investment bankers at Montgomery Securities in San Francisco and William Blair in Chicago loved the idea.

After doing a lot of work and going to my executive committee, I brought the investment bankers to the CBOT. They were waiting in the anteroom of our directors meeting, and I tried to get them into the boardroom. I knew if I had the investment bankers make a presentation, the board of directors would have a fiduciary responsibility to act on it.

However, there was a motion to table. A motion to table is nondebatable, and I wasn't even able to allow them to enter the boardroom. I had to excuse myself from the board meeting and express my regrets. And they were very nice. They said, "We understand. Many times there's sellers' remorse." It was the right idea, probably at the wrong time.

In retrospect, it's much better that it happened the way it did. If that had happened when I introduced the concept of an IPO, we would have been the first exchange to go public. But in all honesty, I think it was better to wait until now, because I think the valuations are greater now than they would've been then.

So I think the IPO is a good thing. It takes the Board of Trade into a new era. We're in a corporate culture now as a for-profit organization.

We're going to be run like a business should be, not like a membership or fraternal organization, which had served us well for a long time. In the modern-day era of corporations you can't operate that way, because a corporation could raise money in the capital markets for investment capital, expenditures, and technology. A membership organization can't do that. And with a shareholder group having more responsibility, more economic decisions based on profit motives rather than what's good for the members, and so forth, I think it's going to drive the Chicago Board of Trade to even greater success, albeit with a different base—not so much members as much as shareholders.

Can you comment on the possible merger?

I fully support the merger between the Chicago Board of Trade and the Chicago Mercantile Exchange. I tried to do it when I was chairman. Many chairmen attempted to amalgamate with the Chicago Mercantile Exchange. It was a long-sought-after dream by both exchanges, so I fully support the merger.

The merger between the CBOT and the CME makes a lot of sense, because we have a great commonality in customer base. We have some commonality in products. Where the Board of Trade dominates in the long end, the Chicago Mercantile Exchange dominates in the short end, so there could be some margin cooperation there. The CBOT has the grains, the corn, and the wheat. The CME has the meats. The meats have to feed off the corn and the grains, so there's some synergy there. I think by merging these two great exchanges that two plus two could add up to five, because it'd be accretive; there would be a reduction of staff and back-office expenses and a combination of technology systems. I fully support it. I think it's a great idea.

What do you think will be the significance of this merger?

The significant thing is that from 1848 to 1998, a span of 150 years, the Board of Trade reigned as the number one, largest futures exchange in the world. The combination of the Chicago Board of Trade and the Chicago Mercantile Exchange will unite these two great exchanges under one exchange that will create the largest exchange in the world, and restore this great history to Chicago where it rightfully belongs.

How would you compare mountain climbing to being a trader?

They're both uphill battles. Climbing a mountain requires a great sense of discipline, a great sense of preparation, a great sense of staying healthy, a great sense of staying hydrated, but mainly being prepared. At the Board of Trade, I think, those same requirements are essential.

This is a personal question. Are you still part owner of the barbershop here?

Yes, I am, along with Ernie Karmin, Dave Goldberg, and Henry Shatkin. Vic Lala took over the barbershop when his brother Joe died and they were at 328 LaSalle. They moved over to the Insurance Exchange building at 175 West Jackson, and then the rent was raised there, so they moved over to the CBOE building. And Vic came to the four of us and said, "Look, I want to keep this barbershop for the members of the Board of Trade, but it was $60,000 to move the barbershop." He asked if we would each kick in $15,000. So we all did. And I think Ernie Karmin and I go there for haircuts. I think Henry and Dave go elsewhere. So at least we get a free haircut.

You've given so much to the Chicago Board of Trade. What would you like your legacy to be?

When I think of all the things I did at the Board of Trade, the one thing that I was probably the most proud of was disengaging us from the onerous lease on the building at 444 West Jackson Boulevard. I suppose the crowning achievement was the building of the trading facility, a 60,000-square-foot modern state-of-the-art trading floor.

You certainly were an important part of the history of the CBOT. Why do you think this institution has lasted for almost 160 years?

This great institution has lasted nearly 160 years because of our stalwart membership. We have a membership that has strength, intelligence, staying power, and pride. We have a commitment to make the Board of Trade grow. It's the membership that makes this institution outstanding and strong

CHAPTER 2

A Dream Fulfilled

Keith D. Bronstein

After graduating from the University of Wisconsin–Madison with a bachelor of arts in history and economics, Keith D. Bronstein headed straight for the Chicago Board of Trade. Being a member of the exchange had been a dream of his since he started working summers as a clerk for a few of the exchange firms. With the help of his uncle, Lee B. Stern, who cosigned his bank loan, Keith became a member in 1970 for $30,000.

From clerk to broker to independent speculator, all roads at the CBOT have been explored by Mr. Bronstein. Continuing his education after hours at the University of Chicago, he adopted Milton Friedman's economic ideas. He employed them in his approach to the way markets' price discovery mechanisms would work.

From 1973 to 1983, Keith served as vice president of Lee B. Stern and Company. During this period, he charted markets and serviced customers as a floor broker and trader. In 1983, he joined Tradelink LLC, where he remains to this day in the position of director. At that company, while continuing to trade a proprietary account, he developed market trading groups, brought about the return of metals trading, and began an environmental fund to trade sulfur, CO_2, and other environmental products.

During his tenure at the Chicago Board of Trade, Keith headed numerous committees. He was the youngest member to serve on the exchange board of directors. He was a governor of the Chicago Board of Trade Clearing Corporation and chairman of the Business Conduct Committee. He volunteered his time to many other groups such as the Soybean Committee, Soybean Products, New Products, and the Marketing and Education Committee. He taught classes for the exchange for new members on the rules and regulations of the CBOT and market strategy. He has also lectured at Northwestern University in the Kellogg School of Management on exchange-traded derivatives.

Mr. Bronstein is a member of many other exchanges: the Minneapolis Grain Exchange, the Chicago Climate Exchange, the Chicago Climate Futures Exchange, and the Commodity Exchange in New York. He was also a member of the International Monetary Market and the MidAmerica Commodity Exchange.

Being a member of the Chicago Board of Trade for over 35 years, Keith is often called upon to share his market opinions. He has been quoted in such publications as the *Chicago Tribune*, *Crain's Chicago Business*, *Grant's Interest Rate Observer*, the *New York Times*, and *Barron's*. He has served as an economic and environmental adviser to many U.S. senators and state governors.

As a man devoted to improving the environment and the human condition, Keith has served on the boards of many like-minded companies. These include American Ecology, Electronic Recyclers, and SLIL Biomedical. He has also volunteered his time for many organizations such as the University of Wisconsin Foundation, the Board of Visitors at the University of Wisconsin Medical School, and the Highland Park Hospital Foundation. He served on the Glencoe Park District for six years, two of those as president. He is also very supportive of the Leukemia/Lymphoma Society, the Northwestern Memorial Hospital Foundation, and the Lynn Sage Cancer Research Foundation.

Keith has been married for 36 years and has three children, Scott and his wife Liza, Jaime, and Hawkeye, and three granddaughters.

****

Tell me how you first heard about the Chicago Board of Trade.

I heard about the Board of Trade from my uncle, Lee Stern, who was like a father to me. Lee was a longtime member of the CBOT. As a little boy, I was brought here as a guest and found it exciting and cool. When I was 14, he got me my first job at the CBOT. I worked for Dan Rice and John McCarthy and H. Hentz and Company and Hayden Stone. Later, I worked for Lee B. Stern and Company. I did this all as a teenager.

What made you want to be a part of this industry?

I thought it was a way that I could be my own boss and earn a good living. For me it was very exciting. It was all about economics, and since the time I was very young, it was a subject that had interested me. At one point a little bit later, as I learned more about things that had transpired at the CBOT, I found out that during the Great Depression many members of the Board of Trade had done very, very well. My high school textbooks had taught that during the Depression, everything went down and it was such an awful time. Yet there were people at the CBOT who were able to be very prosperous during that time, because after initial price busts in the early 1930s there were bull markets in grains. That kind of noncyclical opportunity at any time, opened a world of possibilities for me. I found the concept very intriguing.

How did you buy your membership?

I graduated from college and borrowed $30,000 from the Continental Bank. I had to have my uncle Lee Stern cosign the note through his company, Lee B. Stern and Company. He was my clearing member.

How long did it take you to pay that back?

I'm not exactly sure. I think that I borrowed the money and bought the membership in December of 1970. I didn't start working full-time until June of 1971, after I graduated from college. I probably paid it back in the fall of 1972 or very early in 1973.

Did you work full-time as a trader?

I worked as a trader during trading hours. After the close, I worked two jobs as a clerk for different firms. I cleared trades, which I had been doing since I was 14 years old. I started clearing trades when things were all done by hand, really by hand. And so I continued to clear trades and trade and work as a floor broker, and I was also attending graduate school at the University of Chicago at night.

Can you tell me about the clearing process at that time?

During this era, at the end of the day, each clearing firm would collect its trading cards from the trading floor and bring them to its office.

There would be somebody who would sit at a keypunch machine, and the feedback was all of these punch cards. Somebody would enter all of the trades, all of the information on the trading cards that came up from the trading floor, into a keypunch machine, and it would now come out in basically holes that had been punched in digital cards. And when all of our firm's cards were punched, somebody would take them to the office of the Chicago Board of Trade Clearing Corporation.

The clearinghouse was located on the fourteenth floor of the Board of Trade. You'd take the cards there; you'd hand in the cards, and they were inserted into huge mainframe computers. Every firm's cards would come there, and the cards would ideally match up. Now, of course, there were always outtrades, so there were some cards' trades that didn't match. You would wait until the run was in. If it was a busy day, we might wait until three o'clock or 3:30. On a quiet day, we'd go back to the clearinghouse at about 2:45 P.M. and wait around for the run to be in. Then we would see what kind of outtrades existed.

This became a small social event. People would be standing around and smoking, and men would be making passes at the few women who were there. It was a different environment. I was always the youngest person around, and it was interesting to observe. Most of the people who were operating as clerks were of a different economic stratum than the members. Many of these clerks, including myself, looked forward to the opportunity to become an exchange member. Being a clerk was a different culture, although an important part of the greater exchange milieu.

Anyway, the run would come in and then you would take your printout that showed what your outtrades were. You'd take them back to your office and you'd call the firms with which you had the outtrades to discuss them and see if they could be resolved on the phone. After that process went on, then you'd readjust the punch cards and take them back to the Clearing Corporation, and they'd have a second attempt at clearing the unresolved trades. Those trades still not resolved were handled the next morning. Someone like me had to be there very early with the sheet that showed what trades were still unresolved.

I'd pull out the individual trading cards from the traders who had unresolved trades, and I'd go down to the exchange floor. I'd look for my broker or my trader to try to get the trade resolved, and I'd look for the person from the firm our trade was out with, to resolve it with them.

Did it always work out?

It had to. By definition, all the trades had to be cleared when the market opened the next morning, though often there were arguments about these things. Sometimes they literally couldn't be resolved, so you'd agree to disagree. One side or the other would enter their trade under protest. Then that transaction would automatically go to one of the exchange's regulatory committees to be resolved at a later date. They would choose a time when both parties could present their case. Usually, if there were monetary differences we'd settle up by check the same day, or if there were quantity differences, they might trade it out in the marketplace. If there was really a dispute that couldn't be settled, then later, it would end up being resolved by a committee.

Tell me about your first day trading in the pit.

The first day that I traded in the pit, it was really kind of a bizarre experience for me. As I said, I'd been at the Board of Trade since I was a little kid, so I knew almost everybody, but they all seemed to be my grandfather's age. There were a handful of men like my uncle, Lee Stern, who were probably in their late thirties or early forties. Other than that, everybody there was elderly. I had spent my time working at the CBOT calling them Mr. So-and-So. Now I was a member and supposedly on equal standing, but I sure didn't feel that way at first. It was hard to break the habit of saying "Mister," because now I was supposed to refer to them by their first names. I was sure that they were looking at me like, "What is this kid doing in here?" So there was really some discomfort with that generational thing in the beginning.

When you first came down, what did you trade?

When I started, I wanted to trade soybeans, and it was a little hard to break into the soybean pit. Silver was a new market, and there was an opportunity with a couple of guys who were doing silver arbitrage. There were some price inefficiencies between New York and Chicago, and so they asked me to help them out.

I did that for only a few months. Then there was an opportunity in the soybean pit and I just jumped at it. When I was just a kid working summers in the pit, I heard someone say, "Look, soybeans are the major leagues. If you can trade soybeans, you can trade anything. But if you can trade anything, you can't necessarily trade soybeans." I really believed that was true, so I decided I'd better learn to trade soybeans.

Tell me about some legendary figures on the floor at that time.

There were different figures in terms of being legendary. There was a blind man who traded from the side of the pit and had his Seeing Eye dog with him at all times. He used to call me Aramis, because he knew when I was around by the cologne I wore at the time. There were a number of former pro athletes like George Seals, Glenn Beckert, George Altman, and Johnny Musso who were very successful broker/traders. They were all great gentlemen and fun to have around. The floor has always had many interesting figures.

Of course one of the greatest traders was Lee B. Stern, and I say that without any bias. He was somebody whose mind was literally like a computer, before most people knew what computers were. He would make high-frequency, complex transactions. He had the ability to see the short-term trades and where the market was going, and he was able to capitalize on these trades in high volume. He was, and still is, amazing.

There was Julius Frankel, who was a big customer of mine. He was the most wonderful man. Julius was from my grandfather's era. He fit well in that role. He was one of the greatest speculators of all time, but to look at him, you would have no idea of his prominence. In stature, he was a little man of German descent and walked with a limp. He often wore a fedora, always wore a suit, and yet was simply brilliant as a speculator. One day, Julius and I went out to lunch and he had a particularly good trade going on. We went to his club and were having lunch when some other men walked into the dining room. I didn't know who they were, but one of them was Julius's stockbroker.

The man came over to our table. Julius takes his hand and pulls him down toward the table, and he says, "Pally"; Julius called everybody "Pally"; that was his expression. He says, "Pally, you have to find me some good new stocks to buy." He spoke with that heavy German accent, which I can't possibly duplicate. This fellow looks at me with an expression of exasperation and says, "He owns every stock on the New York Stock Exchange; how can I possibly find a new stock to buy?"

Julius was quite a guy, and it was an honor to know him. Having had him as my customer was very special. Before I worked for him, Julius had been the customer of a firm called John Morris and Company for a long, long time, and John Morris, who was of Julius's generation, had retired. When John retired, Julius came to me and said, "I want you to take my account." I was flattered, but kind of taken aback, and I said, "That's very nice, but why do you want me to take your account, considering my lowly stature?" He said, "Because I know you're someone I can trust," and that was the most important thing to him. So, it was very cool and I felt quite honored.

There were other great speculators, like Billy and Eddie O'Connor. They had an amazing ability to bring all of this information about crops together and evaluate it, and it was almost as though they had a script for how things would play out during the entire crop year. They would initiate these long-term positions and put them in deferred months and hold them for an extended period of time. It was like putting all your eggs in one basket and then watching the basket until all the eggs would hatch into big chickens! They were just brilliant at being able to do that.

My dear friend Richard Stark from Iowa was mentored by the O'Connor brothers and he has been very successful, having learned from their trading examples. He is a banker and a farmer, as well as being a brilliant speculator. One of Richard's other mentors was Dick Frymire. Dick was an amazing man. He came from an agricultural background. I would describe Dick's mind as being like putting together a Rubik's cube. He had the ability to see and understand how everything was related to everything else all the time. So he would put together these complex transactions "of long this and short that" and "short this and long that." Then he would look at it after two days, and everything had gone in his direction, and then he'd know exactly when to take it off.

Dick had remarkable patience and remarkable insight. I remember one year, I was excited about buying wheat and selling corn. I went to Dick and started talking about that transaction, and he liked the idea and he liked the reason that I was proposing it. So I put the trade on, and I was losing money and a few days went by and I was losing more money. Then I started averaging down, which was never a good idea, and I put on more of the trade. I'd be talking to Dick a couple of times a day; he'd say, "No, no, I love it. Yeah, it's terrific. You're right, you're right, you're right." I finally said to him after a couple of weeks like this, "Do you have any of this trade on?" He said, "No, because it wasn't the right time to do it."

Several days after that, he walked into the soybean pit and said to me, "I'm going to buy some wheat and sell some corn. You want to go do it for me?" Because I was his broker, I put it on for him. That, of course, turned out to be the low day on the entire trade, and it was an enormous winner. He had a way of understanding everything about the market and seeing how everything fit together. Like I said, I describe that as a Rubik's cube.

Would you describe Paul Maguire as having a similar, unique trading genius?

Absolutely. Paul was a brilliant intellectual and came across like the stereotype of the "absentminded professor." Paul had the ability to put together combinations of seemingly unrelated commodities and securities and make a trade out of these combinations that would be dazzling in its accuracy and profitability.

How about Herman Magged?

Herman Magged was a broker and a wonderful guy. He was one of my uncle Lee Stern's best friends. When I started trading, there was something big going on. I don't remember what it was, but there was some kind of political controversy that was going to restrict free trade or something, and people were agitated and saying that the Board of Trade was not going to make it.

Herman was standing there and he started telling me that when he was a teenager he was working as a runner on the floor. At that time, there was this older member who was a broker, who said to him, "Son, don't think you're going to make a career out of this, because they're going to shut this place down before your twenty-first birthday." Herman, who was probably 60, said to me, "So, remember. That was 40 years ago when somebody said that to me, so don't listen to any of that." I always have thought about his wisdom when the Board of Trade has been "at risk" for one reason or another.

He also was very encouraging to me in another way. When I started trading, there was a guy in the pit who for some reason didn't like me. He was kind of a gruff and imposing physical type of person, and was often in fights in the pit. When I started trading as a member and I was trading in the soybean pit, he'd be spreading from month to month, and he would go past me, and every time he went past me, it was like a basketball game where you're getting elbowed. He'd inadvertently, so to speak, knock the cards and pencil out of my hand. When I started filling orders, he knocked my deck out of my hands, which was really a pain because you'd have to pick all the orders up and re-sort them. He literally was doing this all day, every day. I was trying my best to ignore it, but it was not easy.

Then one day, Herman said to me, "Look, there's only one way to put an end to this, and you're going to have to put an end to it, because you can't work in this environment." I said, "Well, how do I put an end to it?" He said, "Tomorrow morning, when the opening bell rings, whatever's in your hands, drop it. Be standing next to him, and when you drop everything, turn around and punch him right between his eyes as hard as you can. He's going to go down like a ton of bricks. I don't care if you break his nose; it doesn't matter. But that'll change it!" I was really uncomfortable with that thought. I am basically a nonconfrontational type of man and I certainly never contemplated such a move as part of my career.

So I thought about it all night. The next morning, I'm getting ready for the opening and this guy happens to be standing right next to me, and already he's jostling me. I decide that I'm really going to have to go through with this. And so the bell rings, and I drop my cards and my pencil on the floor and I turn around, and I hit him with everything I've got between the eyes. He goes down and his head hits the step of the pit behind him.

At first there was kind of a shock in the pit, and then the few people standing right in the area began to applaud. Then the guy stands up, collects his things, jumps up, and starts bidding for soybeans as though nothing ever happened. Not only did he never touch me again, but when we'd be walking across the floor and kind of crossing each other's path, he would step away. He never really spoke to me, but he also didn't try to abuse me any longer.

It's a rough business.

It was a different kind of business, yes.

Tell me about the common themes that some of these legends shared.

I think there are a couple of common themes; the most important being that they were very transparent in what they did. These were people who were willing to share their knowledge and their insights with the people around them. I've learned so much that became such an asset to me, just from being in the milieu of being able to talk to men like Dick Frymire, Eddie O'Connor, Julius Frankel, Gene Cashman, and the McKerr brothers.

I learned a lot from Rotchy Barker, who had an amazing understanding of risk versus reward. He was able to structure trades in a way that the risk was always manageable and yet the profit potential was great. There are many other terrific traders, but these leaders were always willing to share what they thought about the market. You could walk up to them, even if they barely knew you, and say, "What do you think?" and they'd tell you what they thought and why. And then some days, they'd be nice enough to ask you with genuine interest what you thought. But the point is, there was that kind of transparency and a shared experience.

I think the other thing that they all had in common was that they did their own work. They were brilliant traders or brilliant speculators or a combination of the two, but it was all because of them. They did their own research, whatever that research was, and it was varied from person to person. They did their own studying. They evaluated prices themselves. If they looked at charts, they looked at those charts and they analyzed the information all by themselves.

Without trying to romanticize the past, if you look at the big reputation, famous Wall Street traders of today, they have cadres of researchers—hundreds of MBAs surrounding them crunching numbers and applying all this science to markets. Looking back on the men that did all this work themselves, I just have a lot more respect for their accomplishments.

Tell me about their integrity and the role that integrity plays at the Chicago Board of Trade.

Integrity was and is everything. Think about it: trading at the Board of Trade has always been done without even a handshake. You just acknowledged in the pit with a hand signal that you had made a trade with someone, and that was it. Most of the time, there wasn't any question about those trades. Occasionally there were mistakes; those were the outtrades. But as far as not standing behind your trade or not acknowledging that you made that trade when in fact you did, the whole business was built on implicit honesty. It is a business that, without integrity, never could have existed.

The few people who did come through the CBOT over the years who didn't have that quality of integrity didn't last, because they couldn't. People pretty much caught on to them quickly and then there was no one for them to trade with and they were gone.

Do you see that word applying today?

I think integrity has to apply today; I don't think there's any choice. It's different today, because trades are not acknowledged just across a room with hand signals. Trades are done principally electronically, but without integrity, there's no foundation for any business.

What was the first lesson that you learned?

I would say that the first lesson that I learned was to make sure that you were well prepared. You had to have a good sense of what was going on in the market, but also enough knowledge to think critically about what the market was doing. I learned that you had to respect price, because price never lies. I quickly found out the importance of always, always, knowing enough so that you can think critically about what the general public is saying about anything, and decide if, in fact, they're right or wrong.

Speaking of right and wrong, when there are situations that need governing at the CBOT, this is generally handled by the members. How do you think self-regulation works in the industry?

The self-regulatory mechanism of the Board of Trade and the Chicago Mercantile Exchange (CME) here in Chicago is critical to their success, and something that can't ever be replicated or necessarily improved upon in the future. The self-regulatory mechanism has the elegance of having highly skilled, highly trained people who are making their livings in the markets working along with very capable, intelligent, well-trained exchange employees, who are completely objective about everything they see. So the member provides the guidance whenever the exchange regulatory employee may have a problem.

It is a marriage that you just can't replicate, because the members are the people who are involved in these regulatory committees. You can't hire people like this, because they're too well paid in their regular jobs as traders. They are doing it because they really care about the institution and care about the markets and care about their careers, and they want the Board of Trade to continue to thrive. They are willing to give their time for no pay and apply their expertise and knowledge that they have for the greater good. Government bureaucrats can't possibly accomplish that. They're never going to be as well trained, and they're never going to be as capable. In most cases, if they were, they would have been in the private sector.

You served on some of these committees during the time of the Russian grain embargo. Tell me how self-regulation worked.

I was on the board of directors of the CBOT during the Russian grain embargo. We received a call as directors one Sunday in the late afternoon. We were told there was going to be an emergency session of the directors. So we all came down to the exchange and we were told that President Carter had put an embargo on a Russian grain sale made the previous week. I think because of our knowledge of markets—because all of us in that room were involved in the markets—we understood the implications of this. Needless to say, it was pretty profound.

However, at the same time we also understood the importance of the market staying open, of price being arrived at in the free market, and of the transparency of these transactions. So while there were financial repercussions down the road later, the exchange opened as scheduled and the market was allowed to trade.

I think because the board of directors were exchange members and traders and owners of firms, they clearly understood that keeping the markets open was the right thing to do. Weeks after this occurrence, the Department of Agriculture and the Treasury Department worked out some arrangements with some of the firms that had been financially disabled by the cancellation of their trades.

When you served on the Business Conduct Committee, there was the unraveling of the silver market. Tell me about that.

The silver market had gone on an unprecedented price explosion in late 1979. It's something that had been building for several years. In 1980, the price peak was reached early in the year, I think in January, at $50 an ounce. Silver had come from $3 an ounce. There had been some questionable activity that had taken place that had promoted the extent of the price rise. It was something beyond what the normal supply and demand for the metals would have justified. It involved a number of different individuals and companies. It was pretty much out of control and it wasn't going to take long for the bubble to burst.

Silver was coming out of everybody's ears. I had a personal experience with this. I was driving to work very early in the morning, on a bitterly cold January day, as they tend to be in Chicago. I was listening to the radio and heard there were lines of people standing on the west s ide, outside a metals smelting company.

People were standing out there at 5:30 in the morning, even though the factory didn't open until much later. They had their silverware with them, because they were bringing silver cups and spoons and forks and knives to this factory to melt them down to get the money for the silver, because silver was so obscenely priced. I heard this and was just astounded by it, and decided I wanted to see it for myself.

Talk about seeing the free market really work! I drove over because I knew where this facility was located, and sure enough, even though it was 18 degrees below zero, there were people standing outside in a line. There were mothers with their kids before it was time to go to school. I saw grandparents standing there, holding bags and boxes filled with silver. When I got to work that morning, I knew unequivocally that was it for the silver squeeze; it was over. I was right.

Soon there was a liquidity crisis, which developed essentially throughout the financial system, because there were major brokerage firms that were involved in one way or another, leveraging the transactions of the individuals and companies that were involved in trying to get the price of silver to go higher.

The Board of Trade, between our committee structure and the Clearing Corporation that we worked hand and glove with, was able to handle the crisis pretty much in-house. At the time, I was chairman of the Business Conduct Committee and I was also on the board of directors of the Clearing Corporation. I was working as a liaison between the two financially responsible entities. Over time, we helped these firms to recover.

It took months to work out of these positions and come up with the margin that they needed to handle the financial side of this. Had this just been handled by government bureaucrats, I don't believe it would've been handled properly. The markets wouldn't have stayed open, and the crisis would have wreaked a great deal of havoc in the United States' financial system.

History will blame this on the participants who owned the silver, but equally at fault were the brokerage firms that were willing to take on the risk of backing these transactions. The firms could clearly see that these positions were beyond the realm of the norm. The financial intermediaries, motivated by greed without responsibility, facilitated the development of this fiasco.

If we fast-forward to the Enron market disruption, it was the same types of firms and the same over-the-top greed that were involved. This can be said of today's subprime lending fiasco. The difference between these financial crises was the brilliance of the exchange mechanism of daily mark-to-the-market clearing and transparency versus the others' barely visible off-balance-sheet nature. I believe that is why the silver problem was contained to the direct participants and why these other market events became much more systemic crises.

Tell me about the role of the Clearing Corporation.

The Clearing Corporation is the independent third party that is the counterparty to all transactions. The idea of a Clearing Corporation is one of the things that make exchange-traded derivatives the wonderful thing that they are, because the counterparty is always guaranteed. So I can make a trade with somebody and I don't have to worry about whether that person has the credit, has the money, or is going to stand behind the trade, because the Clearing Corporation is this independent third party that is the counterparty to all these trades. I think that the vitality of the exchange-traded market is there because of the existence of the Clearing Corporation.

Let's talk about the character of the Board of Trade.

I think that the character of the Board of Trade can best be described by the fact that this was a business that you could start for yourself, literally with just a card and a pencil. Then, through your own hard work and initiative and through any one of a number of different venues—one could be a scalper or a spreader or ultimately a speculator or a floor broker—you could build a wonderful life for yourself and your family.

One of the traditions of the Board of Trade, back when I started and still today, is that there are many extended families. We have multiple generations that prove that from father to son to uncles and cousins, this is a place to make a wonderful living. I think that part of it speaks to the innovation of the culture—the trading culture that developed here in Chicago at the Board of Trade. That culture and innovative spirit spread out from the CBOT and really goes all around the world.

Can you explain what a speculator is?

A speculator is someone who evaluates a price structure and will take a position because they believe an asset is either priced too low or priced too high. The thing that differentiates a speculator from a gambler, which is a question that's often asked, is a speculator is assuming an existing risk. A gambler creates the risk for the sake of the gamble.

As a specific example, let's take the farmer who grows corn. There is an implicit risk in the corn that's grown. The farmer is exposed to the price risk after he's grown the corn. If you are a corn miller, you are exposed to the price risk of corn because you haven't bought it and you have to mill it. If you are someone who has a company that feeds hogs, chickens, and cattle, you're exposed to the mixed feed price risk, so there's this entire trail throughout the economic pyramid of price and supply risk.

These risks are not necessarily matched by time. That's where the Board of Trade came from in the 1800s. At that time, a farmer would harvest grain and bring the grain to the river, because he had to bring it someplace where there was the means of transportation, so it could be taken to the population centers of the East. The farmer would bring all the grain at once, and clearly prices were very depressed. The grain would be taken to the East and be consumed over a period of months, and all of a sudden in May, June" and July in Boston, prices would surge because the grain stores had been depleted.

So the idea of the Board of Trade was that here was a way for the grain to not depress the price at harvest time. You could sell your grain forward and have a contract for it and extend it during the course of the entire year. There also wouldn't be implicit shortages or much higher prices later in the year. None of this figures in gambling.

There is absolutely no risk in the Chicago Cubs playing a baseball game. There's no risk on the victory or the loss of the baseball game other than to the players. At the track, horses run. If they run so people can bet, then again, the risk has been created for the sake of the gambler. I think that's the distinction between gambling and speculating.

Do you think that the CBOT is a model for a worldwide price discovery mechanism?

The Board of Trade has a tradition of possessing a special culture. We have grown up with a culture of believing in and manifesting an egalitarian, open, what we used to call "auction market" on the floor. There is still an auction market even though the market is principally electronic. This provides open information that is available to all. There's always the best bid and best offer, so it really is an egalitarian system and that's always going to resolve at the best price.

When you resolve at the best price, if you think of it in commercial terms, in essence you're passing on that efficiency downstream. So, for example, if we get the most efficient price for corn, at the end of the day, all of prices of the people who have these risks throughout the channel of the corn-feeding cycle will be more reasonable, because we've been able to arrive at the most efficient price at any given time. That applies to any of the derivatives we trade, whether they're credit market derivatives or equity derivatives or anything else.

How important is the role of innovation?

I think that Chicago has been the home of innovation and will continue to be the home of innovation. It goes back to that idea of our special culture. We're always looking for ways to do things and create markets that can service a need. When it's been attempted to create a market where no need was being served, that market failed. The markets that have succeeded have been answering a need.

As we moved from grains to securities options with the creation of the Chicago Board Options Exchange (CBOE), Treasury instruments, foreign exchange, stock indexes, and now the very exciting platform in biofuels and clean air and water; these are all things where there's an economic need. We create contracts, standardized contracts, to satisfy that need. By creating these standardized contracts in an open, transparent way, we make it possible for those who really need to use them to always get the best competitive price for their need.

You originally traded soybeans and silver. Are there new products that are attracting you?

I am working with Pete Steidlmayer and Burt Gutterman on a multi-tiered trading vehicle called the X-Concept. We conceived this idea many years ago and launched it at the CBOT, but it was too complicated to attract the needed volume. We've now patented the essence of the program, retooled it, and feel it is almost ready to be publicly listed.

Right now, I think the available products that are attracting me are mostly related to the environment and, to some extent, to the way the environment interacts with agriculture. From time immemorial, farmers in the United States—for that matter, all over the world—have grown food. As we go forward in time, it is my contention that farmers are going to be growing food, fuel, and possibly even environmental remediation. This is because as farmers learn to use practices where they sequester methane to generate electricity, we will use less natural gas.

They can sequester carbon, and that carbon can be literally exported either to U.S. industrial centers or even around the world. There are industrial centers that haven't been able to reduce their carbon emissions. As we live in a carbon-constrained world, the market will be the place to overcome rapid climate change. We can effect change in that area, because there is already a need.

Tell me more about trading sulfur and carbon.

Sulfur trading and carbon trading are fairly new. They come out of the concept of cap and trade, where we're dealing with the environment as a scarce resource. We've taken the concept of a crop. Every year there's a wheat crop, so now every year there's a sulfur crop and every year there's a carbon crop. We've taken that concept of a crop, and we are trading that crop so those who need it can purchase it and those who have an excess of it, or are the producers of it, if you will, are able to sell it.

The effect is that we can lower the cap every year. We're doing that in the United States in sulfur right now, and hopefully nationwide we'll be doing it in carbon very soon. Since we lower that cap every year, everyone wins. The consumer wins, the environment wins, and the industrial emitter of greenhouses gases also wins, because those who can, within their businesses, reduce their emissions beyond what the minimum requirement is now have something they can monetize, which is the surplus reduction.

Those with the best of intentions, but who still can't reduce their emissions as far as they need to, now have a marketplace where they go out and purchase the additional requirements. Therefore they don't have to worry about shutting down a plant or turning off the power to my house.

Do you think that can really work?

I definitely think it's going to work. It spurs innovation. By following this model, we spur innovation throughout the economy and society. So now we have a whole world developing biofuels, as I mentioned before, and ethanol and biodiesel. These are innovative products that grew out of the fact that we still have a dependency on foreign oil and a pollution mentality by virtue of burning these fossil fuels.

The marriage of innovation to the markets is a very important concept. We understand that we have a dependency on petroleum-based products that come from around the world. Too often this dependency comes from nations that are hostile to us. At the same time, we produce too many carbon and sulfur emissions and so we're responsible for degrading our environment.

With the advent of transparent auction markets in greenhouse gases, we've put a price on environmental responsibility everyone can see. We all know there is a profit opportunity in solving these problems. Farmers respond with carbon-constraining techniques and leasing their land to wind farm developers to generate clean electricity. Others apply scientific initiatives vigorously to solar development. Of course, there are great strides being taken in the development of biofuels.

Another innovation was the creation of the CBOE. What do you see as its importance?

I remember that the notion about the CBOE was the genius of its creators: the O'Connor brothers, Billy and Eddie; Paul McGuire; Larry Bloom; Corky Eisen; Harry Brandt; David and Bobby Goldberg; and a few other members of the Chicago Board of Trade. They were creating something for the benefit of the exchange members, because it was going to be something that was countercyclical.

It was their contention that if the grain markets were dull, quiet, or not active, the CBOE would provide Board of Trade members with the opportunity to trade something else that was completely uncorrelated.

In this case it meant equity options?

The idea for this exchange has had an interesting effect on the equity world. Equity options had been trading in the United States for decades, but they'd been traded in dealing rooms and investment banks, where there was no price transparency, there was no anonymity, and the price discovery mechanism was so weak that you didn't know whether you were paying too high a price or selling at too low a price, and you didn't know what other competitive bids and offers might exist. The CBOE changed all of that. It brought it out into the daylight, and consequently the equity option business grew profoundly. I think it contributed to the growth of the entire equity world as well.

Talk about the significance of the interest rate futures.

The creation of the interest rate futures market was the genius of Richard Sandor. He's the father of interest rate futures along with many other things. The creation of the interest rate futures market permitted our credit-based economy to grow profoundly. I am convinced that much of the growth our economy has enjoyed over the past 25 to 30 years would not have happened had interest rate futures not existed. Once again, the CBOT brings transparency to the marketplace. Now we could price interest rates in a public market where everybody could see what the price was, and everybody could competitively participate in being either a borrower or a lender.

Once that happened, innovation kicked in and mortgages began to be priced off of government securities, which are trading at the CBOT. Then people began to collateralize auto loans and a myriad of other products. But the point of the matter is, we live in a credit-based world that would never have evolved to the point that it got to today, and the economy would never have grown to the levels that the economy has grown to today, without the creation of that product.

Were you there when the bond pits opened?

I was there the first day they started trading. I never actively traded in the Treasury pits. I traded those products, but I did it through brokers. I was either on the grain floor and entered orders over the phone to those markets or, when I moved to the office and stopped coming down to the floor altogether, I was just entering orders to those pits.

Let's talk about some of the events that happened in the world and affected the floor of the Board of Trade. For example, talk about the assassination of Martin Luther King Jr. in 1968.

I was in college when Dr. King was assassinated, and I don't know that it affected the markets all that much; however, I remember the day very well. During all my college vacations, I would work at the exchange. This unfortunate tragedy happened during my spring break. I was at the CBOT working as a clerk so people at the firm where I was working could have some time off.

What I remember most profoundly about it was that everybody was very shaken up. The city was in chaos. The mayor instituted some kind of curfew. I don't remember the details, but I know I was at the CBOT, and I couldn't go to the train station to go home. I wasn't the only one. There were a number of people like me, clerical people, around the exchange in the same position. We all congregated on the top floor of the CBOT, which at the time was empty. We looked to the west and south, and we saw what looked like the city burning down.

It is a memory I've never been able to shake. I mean, it certainly shaped part of my life in thinking about how could we have gotten to this place where we're burning down our city? It wasn't happening just in Chicago, either. It was a very profound, personal memory. I stayed there all night and worked the next day and then finally got to go home.

How about the crisis in Chernobyl in 1986?

I think the Chernobyl event was kind of a wake-up call to people involved in markets. Putting aside the human casualties, which were terrible, what we learned in markets is that you can't go to sleep on price discovery. That day we learned that it's always like a tinderbox; there can always be an event that can profoundly change things.

I watched the markets explode the day after Chernobyl. Some of the smartest people at the CBOT got trapped in horrible positions. They lost enormous amounts of money because it was an unknown. What did it mean that a nuclear reactor blew up? Are all the Russian people going to die? Is all the Russian food supply going to be contaminated for a thousand years? So the market responded profoundly.

The lesson I took away from that is that you never discount the unexpected and you never go to sleep on a position. I learned that you can't say to yourself, "Oh, this has to be that way." I wasn't the only person who learned that lesson.

Can you think of any other events that happened outside of the Board of Trade that affected markets?

The stock market Crash of 1987 certainly affected markets at the Board of Trade. The Board of Trade was not a leading stock market, but we saw a spectacular rise in Treasury prices in what was called the "flight to quality". We saw a meltdown of grain prices, which was completely irrational. Grains were in an oversupplied bear market, and the fact that on stock market crash day, grain prices melted down, was a lesson as well. They, too, recovered, but once again, you saw fear and people reacting and you saw the people selling what they could sell.

Do you think that the markets are influenced by political events such as the election of different presidents?

Traditionally, it's been best for market activity when there have been loose money policies. That was typically identified with Democratic presidents. That's the historical perspective on it. I don't think that rule really holds true any longer. I think that, essentially, governments are in the business of trying to avoid economic weakness, not that that's a bad thing; it's just a fact. Consequently, more debt and printing of more money seem to be consistent with the political philosophies of both parties. The only real partisan difference might be in tax policy, where one party might be more pro-growth than the other.

However, the biggest enemy to free markets and to free men is government interference in trade. If either party adopts policies of restricting free trade, or a president who restricts free trade imposes embargoes and uses trade as a weapon, not unlike what the Organization of Petroleum Exporting Countries (OPEC) does, then that will be not just deleterious to the markets, but also to the fabric of free society.

Let's talk about some of the products you helped to create for those free markets to use.

I was always stimulated by the concept of new products. I was chairman of the New Products Committee while I was a director. I was particularly interested in the evolution of the products I had a great deal of passion for. I was chairman of the Soybean Committee and we rewrote the soybean contract. I was always involved in the rewriting of contracts, like the agricultural contracts, because it was important to keep them current. Things shifted, things changed, and we had to make our contracts relevant to those changes.

When I started, most of the grain was delivered at elevators in Chicago. There are almost no grain elevators in Chicago at all any longer. Now the deliveries are in Toledo and in shipping stations down the Mississippi River. That's the way transit works, so that's the way our contracts are designed.

How about the electronic metals market?

It became obvious to me the metals market in New York wasn't functioning at a level consistent with what the marketplace deserved. They were floor-based at a time when electronic trading was emerging in elsewhere. They weren't particularly responsive to their customer needs.

With the wholehearted support of CBOT President Bernie Dan, we got a mini-gold and a mini-silver market launched at the Chicago Board of Trade, and we made it an electronic contract. It began to succeed, because that's what customers really wanted. Once we saw the need, we went ahead and listed what we call full-size metals contracts, which perfectly matched the size of the New York contracts. Our market grew to having the greater market share, and the New York markets are now virtually 100 percent electronic as well.

You've been off the floor now for 20 years. Tell me about the transition from being in the pits to the screen.

I made that transition long before there was electronic trading. I did it because I was getting increasingly interested in multiple markets that were trading at multiple exchanges in different places. At the time, the way the communication structure of the world was organized, if you were standing in the soybean pit, which I did much of the time, or perhaps in the corn pit, it was very difficult to have a position in Treasuries or have a position in foreign currencies or have a position in cotton or have a position perhaps in a number of different stock options, because you didn't have ready access to execution if you wanted to change that position or add to it. You also didn't have access to a very good information flow. There were a few little Reuters machines around the floor of the Board of Trade, and there were people lined up to read the news. So, that was the point in time when I decided I needed to work out of an office, so that I could have more information available to me all the time.

Do you think it's good that people trade 24/7?

I think that it's changed the business a great deal. I think that for somebody who's watching their own account, it's made for longer days and longer nights and maybe less family time. I think about when I was raising a family, if there had been 24-hour trading seven days a week, it would've really affected the interaction I had with my young children and my wife. On the other hand, it's an ongoing flow of news, and markets are allowed to provide equal price discovery in various time zones. I certainly don't think it's a bad thing, especially in corporate structures.

For the economy as a whole, I think it's a very good thing. For example, our firm trades 24/7. Now I can go to sleep, but we have people who are assigned to those different time zones. They are watching the markets and are able to watch my position or the firm's position. It has created more jobs, and I have great respect and appreciation for the people who watch the overnight markets.

Does it speak to the globalization of markets?

There's no question it speaks to globalization of markets. I think that it demonstrates that the vitality and the innovation and the transparent egalitarian markets are birthed here in Chicago; they continue to blossom here in Chicago, and the successful exchanges around the world have adopted our way of doing business. The Chicago exchanges' embrace of 24/7 markets has profoundly facilitated the globalization of financial and commodity markets.

The Board of Trade has gone through many changes in the past 10 years. Can you talk about the external pressures that have motivated the Board of Trade to make the extreme changes?

I think that the external pressures were market-based pressures, and as people who were making our livings in markets, it's something that we should have understood. Eventually we came to understand this, but we were slow on the uptake. The fact of the matter is, electronic trading was coming and the Board of Trade was slow to embrace it. That created a problem because we really struggled with how slow we were to embrace it.

We had a period of leadership that was particularly slow in embracing change—change in the electronic trading world, change in clearing—and it really put us behind. Luckily, we got a new chairman, Nick Neubauer, at that juncture. He stepped in at the right time and really understood we needed to change how we did business. He provided a couple of years of leadership that helped us get over the hump. Once we embraced that change, we became a leader again.

Reflecting on members who understood and maximized the opportunity presented in this transition, two men rise to the top of my list: Les Rosenthal and Ray Cahnman. Les was a great trader. He was a particularly innovative exchange member and former CBOT chairman. Les took his company, Rosenthal Collins Group, and so fully embraced the transition to electronic trading for his customers that his firm grew into an industry titan.

Ray Cahnman embraced technology very early. He aggressively became perhaps the greatest trader/market maker in the exchange's history. Ray is always able to not just embrace change but, in fact, anticipate change and maximize every opportunity it provides. He has been enormously successful. He sees "the road not taken" and certainly enjoys the challenges of traveling in new directions.

What do you see as the CBOT's effect on the world economy?

I think that we are a leader in terms of demonstrating to world economies how they can function most effectively and efficiently. We show them how to provide their consumers with the lowest prices and their producers with the highest prices. By the way, those two things are not mutually exclusive, because when you have efficient markets, a producer who understands how the market works is going to maximize his return, and a consumer who understands how the market works is going to maximize his return.

What do you predict will be the future of trading?

I am confident that trading will continue to grow, and it will grow profoundly. I think the environmental products probably have spectacular growth ahead of them. It wouldn't be a surprise to me if environmental products are the largest-volume nonfinancial products trading on exchanges in the future. The Board of Trade will certainly participate in this trading through our agricultural markets.

I think that another thing that we'll see is much more concentrated electronic trading—short-term concentrated trading by large firms. Markets will always provide opportunities for somebody in the intermediate and in the long term. There will be opportunities for someone who sees a price discrepancy and is going to take advantage of it.

I think short-term trading, the intraday, minute-to-minute trading, is going to become increasingly difficult for the individual, because there are just too many large pools of capital with too many PhDs and very fast computers that are parsing a limited amount of data and kind of chopping it up.

I'm very optimistic about trading, volume, the future of the exchanges, and the intermediate- and longer-term trader. For the very short-term traders, it's going to become a much more difficult world.

Where do you think future competition is going to come from?

I think that exchange competition is very healthy, and there will be exchange competition, because there are other exchanges around the world looking opportunistically at the industry. If the merged Board of Trade/CME ever became abusive of the kind of power that they had by being such a strong institution, other exchanges would rise up to try to find a way to take advantage of that.

I think the over-the-counter market is the big risk. The OTC market is the danger and not just to the exchange. It's a danger to the world economy. The OTC market is all dressed up wearing Armani suits. They want to take the marketplace back to where it was in the nineteenth century: no transparency, no anonymity. You come in, here's the price, big price spreads, and no counterparty risk for them. They want to create an environment where they can take the counterparty risk, port it off to some sham kind of third-party clearing member, a clearing corporation, to take the risk away from them. I think the over-the-counter market will be profoundly competitive, and they'll use their political influence and their vast wealth to further their goals at the expense of public markets. I think it would be tragic if they were able to succeed.

Do you think the IPO had an effect on the Board of Trade's future?

In my opinion, the IPO was great for the Board of Trade's future. The IPO put the Board of Trade in a profit mode. It removed whatever remaining remnants there might have been of an old boys' club, a transition that many older institutions all over America had to make as well. It made the Board of Trade realize that we had to take our products and compete in the world or else not survive. I think it was a great thing for the exchange. I would say the current leadership at the CBOT, with Charlie Carey, Bernie Dan, the board of directors, and the administrative staff, has been outstanding.

Let's discuss the CBOT merger with the CME.

I see it as a win-win-win all the way around. I think that members of both exchanges win, the city of Chicago wins, the state of Illinois wins, and the United States wins because of the ability of that marketplace to be the most efficient, most innovative, most dynamic marketplace in the world. It would certainly become the envy of the world, because exchanges around the world are trying to emulate us. This merger would assure us of continuing to be in that position.

You say it's good for the city of Chicago. What is that relationship?

I don't know the exact numbers, but the city of Chicago derives thousands of jobs from this industry. It also has thousands of consumers who get their income from this industry, so it's a very, very important thing to the city of Chicago.

Where do you see your personal place in the new marketplace?

I think I'll probably continue to do pretty much what I'm doing now. I always like to look for new ideas and price inefficiencies and places where maybe no one's looking right now. So I'll continue to do that.

How about old traditions in a new era for the exchange?

The dominant old traditions, being honesty and integrity, I don't think are just old traditions. I think they're something that should be in every business—past, present, and future.

What do you think the Board is going to look like in 10 years? Will there still be a trading floor?

As for what the floor will look like in 10 years, I have my own personal hopes that date back more than 10 years. At that time, we could start to see the coming of electronic trading. I suggested and begged and pleaded to the administration that we maintain the floor trading culture without having the floor trading as a means of exchange. I'm not saying that this won't happen; maybe it will.

In other words, for those who have a Board of Trade membership, what they now call a trading right, why can't we take the facility in this building and set up kiosks or desks or pods and provide members with that space and with phones and computers and anything else they might need to trade? It would then be almost exactly like it was 50 years ago, when you could walk on the floor of the exchange, and I could walk up to my friend Rotchy and say, "Hey, what do you think of the July/December wheat spread?" Well, the difference is that in those days, we'd walk into the pit and trade the July/December wheat spread. Why not be able to go to a workstation and just trade the July/December wheat spread, but still have that shared information, shared psychology, the ability for younger people to interact with people with more knowledge, experience, and success in order to learn?

I'm hoping that the Board of Trade will adopt that model going forward. I still think it makes sense, as the trading culture creates a sense of community. This would certainly encourage the industry's continued growth. The building is here, the technology is here, and I think it would open an absolutely spectacular new chapter for the exchange.

Wouldn't it also provide more transparency than you can get with the electronic trading?

The transparency of electronic trading is on the screen. I think what's missing is this ability to share information among market participants. The marketplace becomes more proprietary, and it becomes increasingly difficult to be an individual entrepreneur if you work for some mega investment bank; you're on a big trading floor where you can chat with lots of people about the market. If you're sitting in a small office and you're 28 years old and just learning and there are 10 other

28-year-olds just learning, who really helps you grow? Who helps you understand and learn and get some of these lessons that only experience can provide? So I think that the transparency of information will benefit; the transparency of price already exists.

Last question: What would you like your legacy to be to the Chicago Board of Trade?

I've been at the Board of Trade my whole adult life. When I think in terms of a legacy, I think about my feelings toward the exchange. I'd say that each and every day, I have thought about the Chicago Board of Trade and what I could do to assure its continued vitality and its continued leadership. I have focused on the exchange's continued success and its continuation as a bastion of opportunity. So I guess I'd like my legacy to be that the Chicago Board of Trade lives on in its new form integrated with the CME. I would like it to experience a healthy future with those principles of integrity and honesty continuing to survive and thrive for today's shareholders, customers and tomorrow's generations.

CHAPTER 3

Integrity–The Basis of All Trade

Bernard P. Carey

Bernard Peter Carey was born in 1916. He grew up in a house filled with market talk and interest in business. This was not a surprise, considering his father, Peter Bernard Carey, not only was a hardworking member of the Chicago Board of Trade, but also served three terms from 1932 through 1934 as president of the exchange.

Despite this strong exposure to the world of futures trading, the young Bernard Carey's first career thoughts took him in a different direction and led him to join St. Mary of the Lake Seminary upon his graduation from Quigley High School. However, after a number of years at the seminary, he decided that the priesthood was not his calling. He finished his formal education at Spring Hill College in Mobile, Alabama, where he earned a bachelor of arts in English literature. After graduation, he did a brief stint with Electro-Motive Company, which was a subsidiary of General Motors. By 1940, he decided to follow his father's footsteps to the Chicago Board of Trade.

This important career decision was interrupted in 1941 when he was drafted into the U.S. Army. In 1942, he transferred to the U.S. Army Air Force in England, subsequently flying 25 combat missions over Germany as part of the Eighth Air Force unit. For his courage and accomplishments, he received four Air Medals and the Distinguished Flying Cross. While Bernard was still serving his country in Europe, his father left the CBOT because price ceilings interrupted his trading and made it difficult to make a living. Peter Carey then became sheriff of Cook County. He died in that position at the age of 56.

After the war, Bernard went back to work at the CBOT and married Alice "Tek" Durkin. They had four children: Mary, Bernard Jr., Paul, and Martha. While raising them, he became very active at the CBOT, serving on the Business Conduct and the Executive committees. It was his mission to try to keep the exchange out of the hands of the government and have it remain a self-regulating institution.

While working toward this goal, Bernard served on the board of directors. He was the second vice chairman, then first vice chairman, and finally, following his father's lead, he became CBOT Chairman for three consecutive years from 1963 through 1965. During his tenure, he successfully kept the exchange from being subjected to a transaction tax. In 1973, he became the first chairman of the Business Conduct Committee for the Chicago Board Options Exchange.

Bernard Carey has spent his life as a trader and ardent supporter of the Chicago Board of Trade. He is proud that his children have experienced trading at the exchange; currently, there are three generations of Careys trading: his son, Bernard Jr., and Bernard's two sons, Bernard and Paul, and two grandchildren, Michael and Emily. He is also a proud uncle of Charles P. Carey, the last chairman of the Chicago Board of Trade and the current vice chairman of CME Group Inc., the new company resulting from the merger of the Chicago Mercantile Exchange and Chicago Board of Trade.

The Carey family has honorably served the CBOT for more than a century, representing the finest examples of integrity and tradition.

****

Let's talk about your life and contributions to the Chicago Board of Trade. Going back a little bit, did you have a large family?

I had two brothers and one sister.

Tell me about your parents; let's talk about you mom first.

Well, she was about five foot one, a great pianist and a wonderful lady. My mother always regretted I wasn't called Peter.

Really? Why?

Oh, the oldest son and all that. My father was Peter Bernard and I'm Bernard Peter.

Describe your father.

Well, he was a great, big guy. He was six foot two. He went to high school, but that's all. At the turn of the century, going to college was pretty rare.

How did he discover the Chicago Board of Trade?

He got a job as a clerk and worked that way for a number of years. Finally, he borrowed some money and became a member in 1920.

How much did his seat cost?

I am not exactly sure; it was probably about $5,000. His family gave part of the money to him. He had some from savings and the rest his mother and father gave him.

What did he trade?

Mainly, he traded wheat. At the time, we didn't have many things to trade. The Board of Trade didn't introduce soybean trading until 1936, I think it was, and it didn't become popular until 1940. But the big trade was wheat.

Was he always in the building on LaSalle Street?

Yes, but they had an older building that they tore down and built this present building in 1930. The older building was only a nine-story building and this one was, at one time, the tallest building in Chicago. It's a 42- or 43-story-high building. Of course, now it's dwarfed by other taller buildings.

What's your earliest memory of being on the floor as a little boy?

I was probably about 12 years old and my brother was 10, and we stopped there on our way to summer camp. Right after the visit with my father on the floor of the Board, we got on a train and went to northern Wisconsin for camp.

What did you think when you saw it for the first time?

I had no idea what to think. There was a lot of noise and I didn't understand what it all meant.

When did it occur to you that you might want to work at the CBOT?

After I got out of college. I was in the seminary studying for the priesthood for seven years, and finally I decided it wasn't for me. Then

I went into the senior year at Spring Hill College, which was located in Mobile, Alabama. It was a Jesuit school and I graduated from there.

After graduation, I didn't come to the Board of Trade right away. It was late in 1939 and I had another job. My father thought that the business was going to be very robust in the coming years, though, so he bought me a membership for $1,900. I became a member in January of 1940 and I'm still there.

In the 1930s, your dad was president of the CBOT. I heard that he met President Franklin Roosevelt at one point. Could you tell me about that?

Yes, it was when Roosevelt was the president-elect. My father had an appointment with him and went down to Indianapolis. Roosevelt had a bad leg, so he was in bed when my dad came for the visit. Roosevelt let my father come in and sit on his bed and talk to him. My dad asked him directly, "Well, what are you going to do about the Board of Trade?" And Roosevelt said, "Nothing." And so my father rejoiced at those words, but it wasn't true. The first thing Roosevelt did was set up the Commodity Exchange Authority (CEA).

What was that?

They were going to regulate trading and then examine it for fair trading practices. The Board of Trade already did that on its own, but the government wanted an agency on hand to oversee the business.

How long did the CEA last?

It lasted until the 1970s and then changed to the Commodity Futures Trading Commission (CFTC), which is a more exact title for what they were doing than before.

How did your father feel about that government intervention?

Of course he was against all these government organizations. He felt that the Board carried sufficient rules and regulations to govern itself.

Do you remember any other stories that your dad told you?

Well, he and a committee from the Board went down to Washington. It was shortly after Roosevelt took office. He went with five members from the Agriculture Committee. At that meeting, my father noticed many of the other guests wearing these Phi Beta Kappa pins on their lapels. And he didn't miss many tricks. He asked one of his people, "What are those things they're wearing?" And the fellow explained that they were Phi Beta Kappa insignia keys.

My dad asked, "Where do you get them?" And the guy responded that the best place was a pawnshop, because the insignia keys had gold in them. My dad told one of his staff that he'd like to pick some up for the men on the committee from the CBOT. And so the next time the committee walked in, they had the Phi Beta Kappa insignia on, too.

He sounds like he was a very clever man.

He was, especially for only being a high school graduate.

I understand he was involved in the discussion of a transaction tax at the time.

Yes. I don't know much about that because it was before my time. There have been various attempts since then, including by the City of Chicago. The mayor threatened to put a tax on our trading, and the Board came back at him and said, "Well, if you try to put on a tax, we'll just move over to Gary and have our exchange there."

Tell me some of the things he taught you about the industry?

In particular, I remember him talking about trading. He said that in trading, it's always the hardest thing to let a profit run. It is against human nature. You want to grab onto a profit, instead of letting it run like it's supposed to. And he said you've got to trade in accordance with your own financial situation. Don't do more than you can pay for.

Did he teach you to trade? Was he your mentor?

Yes, he was. I stood alongside him in the pit. Of course, I couldn't emulate what he was doing and the numbers he was doing it in, but he told me about it: letting profits ride, taking losses and not getting discouraged. He said it was most important to keep your discipline.

Did those lessons apply to the way you traded?

Oh, yes. Always!

Was the $1,900 you paid for your membership in 1940 a lot?

Well, looking back it was. At the time, it seemed a good price, and my father staked me to it. Soon after that, when we got in the war, and I remember, our trade fell off to nothing. A membership in 1942 sold for $25. Because of price ceilings, there was no trade in wheat or corn or oats. The only thing that was trading was rye.

What did you do during the years when there was very little trade?

You made do with what you could. Then I was drafted into the U.S. Army and I didn't have to worry about trading. But when we did, we just got along with trading in rye. And it wasn't very good.

How long were you in the Army?

I served for four years. I got in the U.S. Army Air Force and flew missions over occupied Europe out of England. That took me about nine months. Then I was in a transport outfit and I went down to North Africa and Italy, and then back to the United States. But altogether, I was in the service four years.

After the war, you came back to the Board of Trade. Had the markets gotten better?

Not right away, but they did eventually. I got out in late 1945. Then 1946 was pretty dry, but by 1947 we had a good market. That was when we shipped a lot of grain to Europe, which was still reeling from the effects of war. That gave us a big trading opportunity, especially in wheat.

What do you say about people who think that everybody at the CBOT makes a lot of money?

They're very naive. It simply isn't true. People need good market judgment and discipline. Not everyone has that. Most of the traders are interested in short-term movements, not long-term movements. You need a lot of experience. I can't explain it, except that you develop a feeling for the market and you've got to trust your feelings. The longer you are down there, the better feeling you get.

I mean, the discipline applies whether you're a big trader or a small trader, whether you trade off or you don't trade off on it. But you always have to have the discipline. You've got to keep in mind what your bankroll is, how much risk you can stand, and then act accordingly.

How does integrity play into the Board of Trade?

Integrity is the basis of all trade, but especially in the pits. While it seems like it is a bedlam of confusion down there with all the shouting, it really isn't bedlam at all. For people who have been around, they generally know what's going on. Lots of times there is confusion about who did what and how much. But, you've got to trust people down there.

How important is the idea of mutual trust?

You just have to have it. You trade with a number of people every day. They're shouting and there's confusion. Somehow everybody has to stand behind their own trade. If you don't, you get a bad reputation and word spreads like wildfire. So there's very little of that going on.

Tell me some of the companies you worked for.

I didn't work for anybody; I worked through people. I was an individual trader. First it was my father who cleared trades, so I traded through him. Then I traded through a firm called C.J. Whiteman for many years. When they went out of business I switched to Goldberg.

Can you tell me something about your time as chairman? Was there any challenge to that?

Plenty. It was during my term that this guy Anthony De Angelis pulled his scam. It caused us a lot of trouble, but we got out of it all right. Tino De Angelis was a clever crook. He had a tank storage facility in New Jersey on the ocean that supposedly held vegetable oil, like cottonseed oil or soybean oil. Apparently, he had gotten rid of the soybean oil and I guess he didn't report it. In order to make it look like he hadn't done anything, he filled his tanks with water. Finally, they caught up with him.

According to John Gilmore, you single-handedly saved the industry during that time.

Well, thank you, Mr. Gilmore. I know we spent a lot of time on it, and we came out of it all right.

When you think back to your tenure as chairman, what are some of the things that you accomplished?

Previously, a man in the storage and shipping and trading business didn't have to register his firm with the Board of Trade. As long as he was a member, he was not required to register his firm. But we closed the gap on that one and made it obligatory to register your firm, even if you were a member. Having to register your firm with the Board of Trade helped in discovering any false transactions that existed in the delivery system and storage system.

What about the role of being a self-regulatory industry?

Well, it's very important. If the government took over the regulatory powers of the CBOT, I'm convinced it would not run as well as it does right now. They simply don't know what the members of the CBOT know, and so they wouldn't be adequately informed as to the importance or unimportance of certain events. I think there's a worldwide confidence in the fairness and honesty of the dealings of the CBOT.

Do you think other industries look to the CBOT for price discovery?

Oh, they look for price discovery, that's for sure. And of course, the big commercials use it for hedging purposes—buying hedges or selling hedges. Exporters will use the futures market for a buying hedge. They will make a deal in the future based on the price now and buy against any future price rise by buying a futures contract to protect themselves against a price rise.

On the other side, the storage people will sell a futures contract against their holdings to protect against a price drop. That's the way the futures market contributes to the overall stability of the grain trade.

Do you remember when the farmers used to bring their products to the floor of the Board of Trade?

The farmers didn't bring them in; the railroads brought them in. The farmers would sell to an elevator that was located out in the country, and the elevator would put the product in railroad cars and the cars then would come into the Chicago yards. They would take samples out of the cars and bring them to the floor of the Board of Trade.

Can you tell me how they displayed the prices of trades?

They used to mark up the price changes with chalk on a blackboard. Then in the 1950s that changed. Instead of having guys walking up and down on walkways, writing prices down with a piece of chalk on a blackboard, the prices all showed up mechanically and it was much more efficient. They'd get up there faster and were easier to read, too, because they would put the prices in red and green. The electronic price board was much better and faster, and it was welcomed.

Would you describe yourself as a speculator?

I was a speculator. It might be defined as a person who holds on to a position longer than a day trader. And I would do a little speculating and some day trading. A speculator assumes a risk that's inherent in the marketing of a product, while a gambler creates the risk.

You mentioned you traded wheat. Were there any other products that you traded?

I traded soybeans. They were introduced to the trading floor in 1936, and for four years there were only one or two guys in the pit. There was no interest in the soybean contract at all. In 1940, it caught fire and it's been a major contract ever since. All the commercial houses decided they had to use the futures market to hedge their products.

Do you think that there are going to be some new futures products coming up?

I don't know exactly, but I hear talk that there's going to be futures in weather forecasting. That's risk enough for you!

What about the importance of interest rate futures?

Well, that was a new product and it went over big. I didn't understand it at first, but now it is very understandable and you can see why a futures market would come into play there.

Let's talk about the memories that you have of some historical events. What happened when the government put price ceilings on after World War II?

The government had put on price ceilings until after the war and ceased them shortly after the war so that the market could reflect the true value of the commodity. When they took their price ceilings off, it helped the Board of Trade's volume of business immensely. The theory was that price control would hold inflation down. It didn't work very well. It held the price of the commodity down, but not inflation.

Did they think to do it again during the Korean War?

Yes, they did. They put ceilings on prices, but that lasted only a couple of years.

Do things in the outside world affect trading?

Oh, yeah, like the time Russia had that big accidental nuclear explosion in the Ukraine; that had an effect. We didn't know the extent of the thing. We knew that it happened and there were a lot of rumors flying around. Initially, we thought that all the crops in Russia would be destroyed, but they weren't. So after the initial reaction of a big price boom, it faded away. The damage wasn't nearly what they originally thought it to be.

How do things like war affect trading?

World War II started in 1939. I became a member in 1940, and in May of 1940 the Germans made the big breakthrough in France. When France folded, our markets plunged. They went sharply down. They eventually recovered, but that was the initial reaction to that.

I remember wheat, which I was trading and my father was trading. It broke the limit of 10 cents when it first came out. Then the next day, before the opening, my dad told me that it was going to open lower, but it would probably bounce back. He advised me that I should buy or sell for myself a little bit on the first. I'd been down there just five months and I was really a novice.

But I did do what he said and I grabbed a small amount. I got an immediate five-cent profit, which meant about $250. I took it right away. I bumped into him about an hour later and he said, "What'd you do?" And I told him. He said, "Is that all you're going to do?" I said, "Hey, I worked for $250 for five months for General Motors and I just made that same amount in five minutes. I'm going to keep it." He got a real kick out of that.

Can you remember the lowest and the highest you ever traded wheat?

Yes, $0.66⅝ was the lowest and nearly $8 was the highest.

How about soybeans?

Well, the lowest was somewhere around $2, and the highest was about $16.

How about corn; did you ever trade corn?

Oh, sure. The highest and lowest? The lowest was around $0.20 a bushel and the highest was around $2.

Do you see the CBOT trading things other than food products?

Oh, yes. I think it's going to happen. I don't understand why the ethanol futures contract isn't trading more than it does, but who knows? I guess the commercials don't want to use it, but they will.

What do you think about the future of trading on the floor?

I think the floor trading will persist. It's a great means to create liquid markets.

And what's your take on trading by computer?

Oh, it's coming. It's coming along big now.

What did you think when the Board of Trade had an initial public offering (IPO), and the membership became shareholders?

For a long time I didn't know what to make of it, but I do think it makes the buying and selling of memberships as shareholders easier to do than formerly.

Would you tell me about the day of the IPO?

I was invited to ring the opening bell for that day. After the bell ringing, we went down on the floor and watched the trading begin in the Chicago Board of Trade stock.

There have been three generations of Careys who have served as heads of the Chicago Board of Trade. Tell me how you feel about the job your nephew Charlie Carey is doing.

He's a well-informed kid and he's a kid who works hard and I'm proud of him.

I've heard you described as a man of great intelligence and great strength and a man who made other people want to do their very best. How would you like people to remember you?

We never got paid for anything that we did, so I would like people to think of me as a person who gave his time and abilities with generosity.

I thank you for generously sharing your stories today.

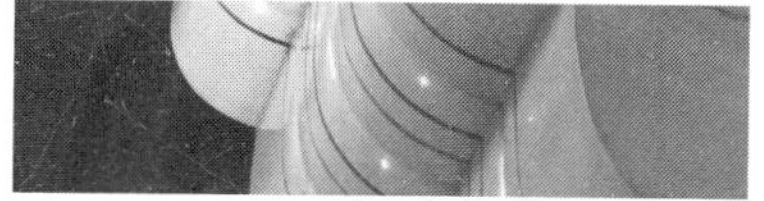

CHAPTER 4

A Family Legacy

Charles P. Carey

Charles Peter Carey has spent his entire life connected to the Chicago Board of Trade. Although there are many families who shared the title of "member" at the CBOT, there are no other families that can claim the title of chairman three times over.

Charles Peter Carey follows in the footsteps of his grandfather, Peter Bernard Carey, who from 1932 through 1934 held the position of president, a precursor to the current role of chairman; and his uncle, Bernard Peter Carey, who was chairman from 1963 through 1965.

A lifelong resident of Chicago and graduate of Oak Park River Forest High School, Charlie attended Western Illinois University in Macomb, where he received a degree in business administration with a minor in finance. In 1976, he began his futures trading as a member of the MidAmerica Commodity Exchange. In 1978, he became a member of the Chicago Board of Trade.

Charlie was reelected on March 2, 2005, to serve a second consecutive two-year term as chairman of the Chicago Board of Trade. In addition, he served on the board of directors for 11 years, including terms as vice chairman, first vice chairman, and full member director.

Prior to being chairman, Charlie Carey also served the CBOT as a member and officer of many committees. He was a member and served as the first vice chairman of the CBOT Executive Committee, was a member and served as chairman of the Finance Committee, and was a member of the Human Resources Committee. In addition, he was committee chairman of Margin, Regulatory Oversight, Rules, Exchange Business Plan Implementation, and Operations. He also has served as vice chairman or co-vice chairman of Business Conduct, Floor Traders, Task Force on Government Securities, and T-bond Evening Session committees. Further, Charlie has served as a member of Trading Facility Task Force, as well as the Joint Venture, New Products Executive Launch, Regulatory Compliance, and Strategic Planning committees.

During his three-term tenure as the chairman of the Chicago Board of Trade, the CBOT has achieved consecutive annual volume records. He spearheaded the move of the CBOT from a nonprofit, member-owned organization to a for-profit, New York Stock Exchange–listed public company. He also played a pivotal role in the CBOT's merger with the Chicago Mercantile Exchange in 2007 to create CME Group Inc., the world's largest and most diverse futures exchange.

For his record of excellent service in the industry and his humanitarian efforts, Charlie Carey has been honored with many special awards. In 2006, he received the Ellis Island Medal of Honor by the National Ethnic Coalition of Organizations Foundation, Inc.; NECO provides a valuable service by recognizing the contribution that our immigrant ancestry has made to the spirit and fabric of the United States.

That same year, he was the recipient of the Rerum Novarum Award, created by Pope Leo XIII in 1891 to highlight the relationships among government, business, labor, and the Church. It paid particular attention to the condition of the working class. The award honors lay men and women who support and promote the Catholic social teaching and is given to the person who exemplifies the ability to honor the dignity of human beings and human labor, upholding the right to organize and the right to a living wage.

In 2007, Mr. Carey was presented a Lifetime Achievement Award by the Anti-Defamation League, whose mandate is to secure justice and fair treatment for all citizens alike and to end discrimination. In May of 2007, he received the Distinguished Alumni Award from Western Illinois University, the highest honor bestowed on an alumnus.

In his spare time, Charlie is an avid sports fan, and the president of the Chicagoland Sports Hall of Fame. This organization provides scholarships for underprivileged youths.

Mr. Carey is married and has three children.

****

How did you first hear about the Chicago Board of Trade?

I heard about the Board of Trade because my father worked here. So, when other kids were asking their fathers what they did for a living, I asked my father what he did for a living. He said he was a grain trader at the Chicago Board of Trade. It was a little difficult and challenging to explain to my friends, because they all had fathers who were firemen or policemen or worked in an office.

What is your first recollection of seeing the floor?

I can remember taking a train ride with my mother on the Rock Island train down to the old LaSalle Street station and walking across to the Chicago Board of Trade. The CBOT had an observation deck above the trading floor and we actually watched the end of trading one day. I can remember being up there and watching prices flash on the board and watching this big ring of men standing around, and I was really having a hard time comprehending what they were doing in that big ring.

When did you know that you wanted to go into the business?

I was always very interested in it, but, as most people will tell you, it's kind of a complicated business to understand. It wasn't until I graduated from college that I decided that I wanted to try trading for a living at the Chicago Board of Trade. I'd always had a great interest in the business and I wanted to follow in my father's footsteps. But it was when I got out of college that an opportunity came up and I took advantage of it.

What was that opportunity?

Actually, the first opportunity to get into trading was when I purchased a membership at the MidAmerica Commodity Exchange, where they traded smaller contracts. They used to call them "job lots" when they traded them here on the Chicago Board of Trade. And at one time, it was called the Open Board of Trade, but they renamed themselves the MidAmerica. We traded the smaller increments and it was a great training ground for new traders.

You said one of the reasons you came to the CBOT was because of your father. Another reason was that your grandfather had been chairman of the CBOT. Can you take us way back into your Board of Trade family history?

My grandfather, Peter B. Carey, passed away about 10 years before I was born, but I heard a lot of stories about him. In fact, when I first joined the exchange, there were some old-timers still trading who had come to the Board of Trade in the 1930s to trade wheat. My grandfather started out in 1903 as a messenger. He ended up becoming a member. He left the business for a while, and in 1920 he came back and in 1932 was elected chairman of the Chicago Board of Trade. So I grew up in a house full of Board of Trade stories.

Can you tell me if you remember hearing anything from your father about the days when his father was in the business?

My dad's name was also Charlie Carey, and he was kind of young when his dad was at the CBOT. My uncle, Bernard Peter Carey, was the oldest boy and he joined the Chicago Board of Trade in 1940. His father was still trading at the time. He was able to spend some time with his father and meet some of his father's friends and learn from the experienced old-timers about the markets and about how the Chicago Board of Trade worked.

I've grown up on the stories from my Uncle Bernard and from my father, Charlie, and from their friends. So I was able to put together a lot of stories over the years just from sitting around after playing golf or having a dinner or a drink. I absorbed the history of the Carey family at the Chicago Board of Trade over time.

Could you share some of those stories with us?

There are a lot of them. My grandfather came down here in the 1920s, when they had some volatility. It was the Roaring Twenties, and the Chicago Board of Trade was part of that. Seats traded at $64,000 in 1929 before they went down to $25 during World War II. My grandfather's first go-round at the exchange was a little difficult. The second time, he was much more successful. I am very proud of the fact that he served as chairman. I've gotten to know a lot about what he did through the CBOT archives and reading about his chairmanship.

In 1932, Peter B. Carey was called upon to testify in front of Congress about a transaction tax. The government was always looking for ways to get more money. It's interesting that it happened again in 2003 and 2005. And I think in 2007, we'll be testifying about the transaction tax and what a burden it is for this type of business. It's kind of an interesting tie through history.

Can you tell me about some of the legends that your dad told you about?

My father, Charlie, started trading in 1948. He talked about the soybean markets in the 1950s, and the impact of the Korean War. He liked to talk a lot about a gentleman by the name of Lawrence Ryan. Larry Ryan was a famous trader who came down here from modest beginnings and became a very successful trader. They loved to talk about the 1953 and 1954 soybean markets, when soybeans doubled in price. Prices went from $2.00 to $4.25. That $4.25 high was not exceeded until 1972 or 1973. So I've heard about the cycles that take place in commodity trading directly from the people who were here for more than one cycle. They saw 20-year cycles. Larry Ryan was a big trader.

There are a lot of legendary traders. I've met Richard Dennis through friends. He was probably one of the most legendary traders in the 1980s and is still very involved in our markets. He is not a presence on the floor like he was at one time, but he was written up in *Business Week* and other publications in the 1970s as one of the new breed of traders.

I actually got to meet a fellow by the name of Joe Dimon. Anybody who's over 60 or 70 years old knows who Joe Dimon was. He came from the South, where his father was mayor of a small town in Georgia. Joe was a man who, rumor had it, had amassed a fortune of about $14 million in the 1954 bean market. Whether that was true or not, who knows? Then it was rumored that he lost it all two to three years later. The Board of Trade seat at the time cost about $3,000.

I had dinner with his partner, Ralph Root. Ralph was a gentleman who made a small fortune trading in stocks when he was at Rutgers University. He was a real character, and his roommate's father was head of National Distilleries. When President Franklin Roosevelt repealed prohibition, that stock went from $5 to $55 a share and Ralph made $250,000, which was a fortune during the Depression.

Ralph had been a member of the New York Stock Exchange. He left there because of the Depression and came to the CBOT around 1936 to trade wheat. That was about the time of the dust bowl and there were big opportunities in the wheat market.

There were other fascinating tales about people in our business. For example, in the 1940s, there was an investigation in which three big-time traders were called to Washington to answer a congressional investigation about a boatload of rye that happened to have sunk in Lake Michigan. They were accused of sinking the boat to create a corner in rye.

These are the types of stories that I've heard from people who actually were involved in the stories or were very close to the stories. A pastime of mine is collecting these stories and passing them on. You'll never wear me out. I can tell these stories for hours about the characters and the people and the trades and the human element of this great institution.

Give me some more examples of that human element.

I had a great friend by the name of Joe Grogan. He never married, so the Board of Trade was pretty much his life. The markets in the 1960s didn't provide very many opportunities. There was not a lot of volatility, so the traders spent a lot of time reading the newspaper and waiting for something to happen that would provide them with the kind of volatility and volume that could become profitable.

One of the great stories about Joe involved the time he was trading soybeans and there was a limit up soybean market. He was trying to decide whether he should stay long on soybeans or spread them off against another month. Well, the decision was made for him when certain back months were taken off the limit.

Suddenly it was like a cattle herd panic. Joe ran down to sell the one option that had come off the limit, so that his trade was no longer profitable and he went back up to the top option. In the meantime, a scuffle broke out. His shoe flew off and he was walking around in his stocking feet trying to get his trade done. Soybeans went from limit up to limit down in a matter of minutes, because somebody had changed a report—a weather report or something like that. I still can picture Joe finishing the trading day, looking for his shoe at the bottom of the soybean pit.

It's a very volatile place to be.

Oh, absolutely, and it could get physical from time to time. If somebody was tall or had a booming voice, they had an advantage in the open auction market. With electronic trading, that doesn't exist. Now it's a completely different profile of trader that's successful. But at that time, a physical presence was a valuable asset. From time to time you felt like you were in a football game. People were getting knocked down and tackled. One broker might have an order and 10 people would want to get to that order, and suddenly the traders would be pushing and shoving to participate in a particular transaction. I was involved in it sometimes. It was always fun for me, being an old football player. I knew how to move in a crowd.

Who were some of your mentors?

Well, I'd say my Uncle Bernard was somebody that I spent a lot of time with. My father, while he was alive, was a mentor, too. Unfortunately, he passed away in 1977, but I spent two or three years with him just talking about the markets and he gave me historical perspectives. He'd talk about grain companies. He'd talk about good buying and bad buying. He would describe the kind of people who had market savvy, and he really tried to teach me all the pitfalls and all the dangers of trading.

My father taught me that you have to have a certain discipline and you have to have a certain understanding. If you don't, you can fall for these traps, and it's going to be very expensive. He told me that I should always be alert, that I should make sure to always study the market. He said every trader should make sure that they are studying the participants in the market and have a firm understanding of the fundamentals. It was important to understand about structure getting overbought or oversold and who's participating.

I learned my first lessons from my father, and those are lessons that I've never forgotten. They have provided me with fond memories of him and his link to his era of the 1950s and the 1970s. At that time we had the Russian wheat sale in 1972. We had a $12 soybean price in 1973. We had big markets going on because the world markets had opened up. Nixon had taken us into Russia and China. These types of events were changing the face of the world. The Board of Trade was participating in those changes and shaping the way the world was going to deal with agricultural needs. I was learning in a somewhat different environment. But some things don't ever change, and that's the human element and human nature.

Tell me about some of the other lessons that you learned.

There's an old saying: Fear and greed drive markets. When I was first trading, I was sitting in a coffee shop with Ralph Root and he gave me two books and said that I should read them. One was Edwin Lefèvre's *Reminiscences of a Stock Operator*, which was supposedly a book about Jesse Livermore, a famous stock trader in the 1920s. The other was Charles Mackay's *Extraordinary Popular Delusions and the Madness of Crowds*, which is a book that reminds us not to get caught up in the crowd. Do your own thinking. Be independent. Think on your feet. Do your own analysis. Don't just go along, because the crowd is not always right and if you don't have your own game plan and your own discipline and your own approach to the market, you're not going to be successful.

Not following the crowd is a good idea, but many people follow their families into this business. Why do you think there are so many trader families down here?

I think that if you're close to your parents, a lot of times, whatever business they are in, you'll also be drawn to it. If you have a close relationship with your father, then most likely you would want to go to work with him. I don't care if he's selling automobiles or running his own business.

This business is certainly not for everybody, but my father loved it and we've got a great history here. It was definitely a factor that drew me into it. Also during that time, the business was expanding. There was more and more opportunity for guys like me than there ever had been in prior years. So aside from the family tradition, the opportunity was also there.

There are many families working together at the exchange. They know firsthand what it is like. They know there are good years. They know the bad years can be tough. I think it was tougher on the traders than on their families. As children we didn't know whether it was good or bad. But we did know some years were better than others by whether there was a new car in the driveway or whether we were taking a nice vacation or staying home. We knew it was a boom-and-bust business. Back then it was a grain-trading club, and it was a much smaller business up until the 1970s, 1980s, and 1990s.

The marketplace became diversified into financial derivatives with different types of products, and today the world seems much smaller. Technology, telecommunications, all those advances have fed right into the Chicago Board of Trade and helped us to remain an important pricing mechanism and pricing vehicle for the rest of the world.

Are there other members of your family who are at the CBOT?

Yes. I have a younger brother, James. He was a bond broker for many, many years and now he's filling orders in the corn pit. He's been a member since 1980. We were able to scrape up enough money to get him an associate membership, so he went to the bond pit. At the time, we really weren't sure how it was going to fare, but about six years later it was the biggest product success that the exchange had ever seen. Treasury rate and interest rate futures, which include 30-year bonds and 10- and 5-year Treasury notes, became one of the biggest complexes we have. It still drives the greatest amount of volume for the exchange, but with our transition to electronic trading it has changed the face of our business.

When your family gets together, do they talk about the Board of Trade?

I talk about business with my brother, and we talk about opportunities and about markets and market participants and trends. All those things are relevant to his future and to my future. So yes, we do discuss it, but we try not to overwhelm the rest of the family with it and try to talk more about sports.

How about the idea that you had three generations being chairman of the Chicago Board of Trade? That's quite a link.

It is; but it certainly wasn't planned. When I joined the exchange, being chairman was not something I even thought about. I viewed the office as being for all these older guys who were really smart. I had a lot of respect for them.

The first time I was brought into the exchange governance process was by a chairman named Tom Cunningham. He was chairman in 1983 and 1984. He asked me to serve on the Membership Committee. I said, "I don't know, Tom. I don't think I have time for that stuff." And he said, "Oh, no, we want you to do this, and we think you'd be good." I said, "Well, I'm honored. Okay, I'll do it." And then Bobby Goldberg was the next Chairman, and he asked me to serve on the Floor Governors Committee, which I did.

When Cash (Karsten) Mahlmann asked me to serve on the Business Conduct Committee, I think he took a risk putting me on that committee, because a lot of people didn't feel that I was seasoned enough or qualified enough. As part of that committee, I ended up involved in one of the biggest cases ever. It was the Ferruzzi case that resulted in an emergency action in July of 1989.

The Ferruzzi Group was an Italian conglomerate involved in the grain market. Ferruzzi had taken a very large position in futures in 1989, which turned out to be a mistake, because the cash market didn't do what they had expected. So, to try to make up for it, they attempted to corner the market. The Board of Directors took emergency action. A hearing and trial process followed. It went on for a long time; the Board of Trade was sued, and I think the litigation just ended in the past two or three years.

Ferruzzi clearly wasn't playing by the rules, and the committee found that to be true and eventually the courts agreed. To be able to see that process was absolutely fascinating; it went from an exchange hearing committee to a courtroom environment. It's similar to a court proceeding and you've got people giving testimony and court reporters. And there were boxes and boxes of documents. I don't know how many rooms were filled with grain orders in the cash market and grain orders in the futures market. They were reviewing all this documentation to tie the activity together and determine whether what Ferruzzi was doing was economically sound business or were abusing their hedge status.

I don't know if people remember the whole background story, but Ferruzzi almost won the America's Cup in 1992, and the person who was running the company at the time was a gentleman by the name of Raul Gardini. He was eventually charged with fraud in his own country, and they found him dead from an apparent suicide in his Milan apartment in 1993. The Board of Trade took a lot of criticism, and the farmers were angry—they thought that our action resulted in lower prices for them. But we stood our ground, and over time the truth came out.

That was a hard time in the history of the CBOT.

It was very difficult, because at the same time the FBI sting was taking place, which is something that I think we would all like to forget. Soybean traders were charged. At the time, my feeling was that it should have been handled administratively by the Commodity Futures Trading Commission; anyway, they were looking to investigate the integrity of our markets.

Regardless of the result of certain court proceedings, we showed that our process here does have integrity. Otherwise people wouldn't use these markets. People come here voluntarily. They aren't forced to come here. If we're not the best price, if we're not the most liquid market, if we don't provide the most transparent price, people will not use these markets. We understand the value of enforcing our own rules.

That was definitely one of the toughest times for the leaders of the exchange. I was still on the Business Conduct Committee, but not a board member. Still, I could see the strain that was put on the directors.

I think having been on the floor and knowing the people involved, I had a better understanding about the things that were alleged. I think the allegations were a little bit over the top, but they ended up prosecuting the cases and unfortunately individuals ended up going to jail. It was hard to see people you trusted and did business with face those kinds of difficulties in their lives.

You talk about the word 'integrity'. Does it play a key role in your business?

It's probably the biggest driver of our success. We have an open process, one of integrity, whether it's the firm taking the order, whether it's the guarantee at the clearing corporation, or whether it's the fact that since we started the business in 1848 there's never been a default. Every day it is two traders, trading face-to-face in the pit, honoring their trades. Some days it's so hectic you can't even recall all of them, yet the trades are honored.

By the next day, if there's any dispute, it's resolved between the two principals and the business goes on. Now that's honesty. That's integrity. That's trust. And that's what allowed so many transactions to take place instantaneously, because it's the principles that stand the test of time. Now the trades take place on an electronic trading platform and they match immediately. So that integrity that really creates the value proposition continues.

Would you say that integrity works hand in hand with the idea of self-regulation?

Self-regulation is something that has always existed here, and it's even more important to us now as a publicly traded company. We've always self-regulated, and you've always had people who would not tolerate any type of behavior that was not aboveboard as far as the customer was concerned, as well as the other traders. It was self-regulated because the traders stood in the ring and they were able to police the transactions. Everyone in close proximity observed the activity. If something was going on, it didn't take long for the word to get out that somebody was not playing by the rules. Those people were dealt with severely.

The whole self-regulation model has also been part of our success, because if the funds were not there, if there was a question about a clearing member's ability to make good on the trades or if an individual on the floor was not providing the best price for his customer, they'd be dealt with swiftly. The members knew what was going on, because they were here every day and were witnesses to the behavior. It was a process that worked well and has served our institution very well.

Why do you think so many people would want to volunteer for jobs that are involved with self-regulation?

That's a good question, because it's a difficult job, acting as a policeman to your own colleagues. But I think so many people volunteer because they understand how important it is and they take their responsibility very seriously.

How do you think the Board of Trade has changed since you first came to the exchange?

It has changed, but it's always changing. The biggest change I've seen is electronic trading. The business has gotten so big and the membership has grown. It was a small, some would say grain-trading club in the 1940s, 1950s, and 1960s. Then suddenly in the 1970s, the business exploded. Whether it was because of the Chicago Board Options Exchange that was founded by the leaders of the Board of Trade or the listing of the Ginnie Mae futures contract, which eventually led to an interest rate complex, or whether it was stock index futures, all these innovations brought in a lot more participants. It changed the membership. It wasn't quite as clubby. It was a much bigger business. It was something we weren't accustomed to, but we dealt with it. It provided tremendous opportunity and it provided a tremendous service to the users of the marketplace.

You talk about it being a clubby kind of atmosphere. Can you talk about the different types of people that are on that floor?

We've had all types of members: everything from Harvard Business School graduates to people who haven't finished high school. A lot of people started as clerks and worked their way up. Actually, that was pretty much a formula for a lot of members. When I first got here, the concentration of membership was mostly Chicago people, but that has changed now. We attract the attention of the world. It's kind of a melting pot, and that's the kind of diversity I witnessed around here.

Probably one of the most famous traders was Julius Frankel, who came from another country later in his life and became a very successful grain trader. He made his fortunes when he was 60 or 70 years old. He was a fixture when I first got here. We've also had many athletes. I heard stories about John Barrett, whose grandson happens to be a very good friend of mine. John played football against Jim Thorpe, and he was a longtime corn broker and worked for Dan Rice. I believe Paddy

Driscoll, who was a famous athlete, was here. Fast-forward to the 1970s, when we had athletes like Glenn Beckert and George Seals and George Altman who joined this exchange.

What would you say is the secret to success on the floor?

We already talked about the importance of a physical presence, but most of the people who are successful here are disciplined. Having an athletic background could help, but it is no guarantee. The people who succeed are self-motivated, driven individuals who really enjoy the competitive environment that this business provides.

How do you respond to the people who say, "Everybody who comes down to the CBOT makes it"?

I would have to disagree. You don't hear the stories about the people who come, try, and leave. This business isn't for everybody. It's a true test. And if you don't have a certain passion for markets, you're not going to be successful here. You're going to be marginal. It's not just about the money. It's about the passion. It's about the competition. It's about challenging yourself daily, because if you're not willing to do that, this is not the place for you.

People who love trading want to do it all day and all night. Tell me what happened when the CBOT tried night trading.

I was part of night trading. Electronic trading really hadn't arrived yet. It was still just a vision. It was a political hot potato. I recall John Conheeney, a director from Merrill Lynch, losing an election because he made an innocent remark in a speech about "black boxes" in the future, predicting the future success of electronic trading over open outcry.

Night trading started in the spring of 1987. It was a way of serving the markets in Asia. It provided hours of competitive trading they previously didn't have. Before night trading, to hedge their risk they had to go directly to a bank, and those markets were not transparent. They couldn't do their business easily. It was similar to bonds or Ginnie Maes in the early days. By opening this market up at night, they went from these big, wide bid and offer spreads the customers had to pay to a very narrow bid and offer spread. I think it lasted a total of 10 years; by that time electronic trading on Project A, the CBOT's first electronic trading system, became the preferred method of trading at night. The exchange ended open auction night trading around late 1996 or early 1997.

As electronic trading was embraced, it was apparent that there were better ways to handle business in the evening. Once you had viable electronic systems that could handle the business and had the confidence of the users, it was clear that it was better to provide that type of access than to provide the trading floor.

Until the advent of a viable electronic trading system, night trading provided a lot of opportunity. We were there when the bombing in the first Iraq War started, when Saddam Hussein invaded Kuwait. That event had a big reaction in the market. I remember going to dinner that night with Charlie DiFrancesca, Joe Grogan, Richard Dennis, and I think Richard's brother, and Jack Kotz. I was living downtown at the time and I offered Richard Dennis a ride home. He got in my car and saw that I had a car phone and said, "Do you mind if I make a call?" He called the market with two minutes to go and started selling thousand lots of bonds, because he heard about Saddam Hussein invading Kuwait. He's sitting in my front seat and I think if I was still down on the floor, I would be filling those orders and making some money. That was history.

Then, sometime in March that year, when the United States finally did start Operation Desert Storm and the Iraqis left, there was some dramatic volatility in the marketplace that evening as well. The outlet was there and people could basically hedge the risk. They could balance their positions, and the marketplace was open to allow people to do whatever they needed to do in light of the international risk that was taking place. It's the safety valve. It's the outlet for people to hedge and manage risk and "get to the sidelines," as we like to say. If the markets were not open, they wouldn't be allowed to do that. So it was good. It was very valuable.

Do you think that with the advent of computer trading, where people can trade 24/7, that same thing is happening, but more in people's homes than on the floor?

It's not just in homes. It's in institutions, too. Nobody can work 24 hours a day. You have to sleep sometimes. It is changing the profile of the market. People have access to the market 24 hours a day, and there's a lot of commerce taking place outside of our borders, and we want to try to capture that by keeping our markets open.

So whether it's customers in Europe, Asia, Japan, China, India, the Middle East, Dubai, or other places in the world, people can access our markets 24 hours a day. As a result there are a lot of moves taking place. As recently as a month ago, we had a big move in the stock market in China and it spilled over into the opening in New York. So these are truly global markets and you have to be open to serve the needs of the customers or they are going to find another outlet.

Where do you think your major competition will come from in the next few years?

It's happening right now. We've always had competition with over-the-counter markets. We are trying to provide a better product. We also have international exchanges that are going to compete with us. You have Euronext linking up with the New York Stock Exchange. Clearly, they're going to list stocks in both markets so that they can take advantage of the disparities in regulations. But they're also very vocal about entering into the derivatives market, which could mean a lot of different things. I would expect that when they look at the Chicago Board of Trade and the markets that we have here in the United States, they may be looking to list.

Who knows who the next player is going to be? On March 15, 2007, a new exchange called ICE (Intercontinental Exchange) made a bid for the Chicago Board of Trade, which kind of slowed down the merger process between the Chicago Mercantile Exchange and the Board of Trade. So the competition is out there. It's global. The next wave may be Asia or Latin America. You don't know.

One of the most important things that we have to offer at the CBOT is integrity. Whether it's clearing, whether it's rules and regulations from the CFTC or the SEC, these markets are safeguarded. People feel secure in these markets. So, the competition will come, no doubt about it. What we have to do is remain a low-cost provider and maintain deep liquidity pools. That's what's driven the success here, and that's what is going to drive our success in the future. We have to be prepared for competition at all times, because these markets are big and there's a lot of opportunity here.

Let's go back in time and talk about the impact of the flood of 1992, not only on the physical structure, but on the economy.

I was serving on the Board of Directors and we were informed that our basement was flooding. Then suddenly it was on the news that there was a construction company that was driving pylons in the river and they had pounded one through the top of a tunnel. These were the old coal tunnels and garbage tunnels that served the city of Chicago, and I was very familiar with them because in college I worked for Pat Nash at Nash Brothers Construction. I had worked in those tunnels, and we'd had to go down and move pumps around and dig out.

Commonwealth Edison had put together a generating plant out on Roosevelt Road to serve all the new buildings in the Loop. You had the

Sears Tower that opened somewhere around 1973 and that had all these demands for power. Some of the engineers figured they could run all the conduits with all these massive electricity pipes going through there. That was what the construction company I worked for did. I knew from experience there was a coal tunnel that had been there since the 1930s, and with the opening in the tunnel, water was able to rush into the CBOT. It got within a foot of our telephone switch which would have been devastating. Thank goodness it didn't get there. We were lucky.

When we were in the board meetings, I would describe my job at the construction company, where the tunnels went and how they were used, and what we did when we were down there. We spent a lot of time over a few days deciding what to do. We went to shortened hours and it became apparent our markets actually had an impact on New York. The actual cash trading slowed down when we had to close trading.

By the time we were able to reopen, it became apparent at that time that there was a strong link between the futures contracts traded here and the cash markets in New York. It affected everybody's market. It even affected 30 South Wacker, where the Chicago Mercantile Exchange is located, even though they were not affected directly as we were. Anyway, it showed what an impact the Chicago Board of Trade had throughout the world and especially on the New York markets.

Can I take you back to the Crash of 1987?

Well, I remember corn prices in the $1.80s. We had a big sell-off late in the day, because the stock market was selling off. There had been some chatter about trade disputes between the United States and some European countries, so I think that unnerved the market. Then there was something taking place at the time called portfolio insurance. People would begin to sell, and the lower the market went, the more they'd sell, and we had a tremendous break in the securities markets. It led to liquidation all over the place.

About the same time, we were in a down market for the bonds, and during night trading it became apparent that Alan Greenspan knew exactly what to do. The Federal Reserve reacted beautifully and they opened the spigots. Suddenly the Fed was lowering the rates dramatically to respond to what had taken place in the market. It was the perfect response. He had obviously done his homework, going back to the 1930s and analyzing what was done wrong in 1929.

We had an immediate 10 to 12 point rise in the bond market in a matter of 48 hours. It was unprecedented volatility for the time. It was challenging to manage that risk. I was merely an independent trader and a floor broker. I know that when I walked in to do the outtrades and we didn't have the same kind of technology and efficiencies in 1987 that we have today, I was looking for a purchase of some bonds that I had done the night before for a customer and they hadn't shown up yet. I said, "That's going to be serious. If we don't find this one, it's a couple of million dollars." But the trade was honored. The individual on the other side called me and said he remembered the trade.

It goes back to what I was saying about the integrity of our markets. The fact of the matter is, it was a time of amazing volatility. We never witnessed anything like that, but the markets were there to allow people to rearrange their risk and move their portfolios around, and that is what the Board of Trade is here for.

What about things like the war in Iraq? Does that have any bearing on the markets?

The Gulf War, the United States' initial incursion in Iraq in the early 1990s, created some volatility, some uncertainty, and the need for the people to move to the market and adjust their positions accordingly. With the media covering everything there is very little doubt about what is happening in the world. The war in Iraq really doesn't create the kind of volatility we have seen in the past. What we've seen as a result of this war is rising oil prices. The oil prices are driving a big change in this industry: renewable fuels, ethanol, biodiesel, wind power, solar power, and things we don't trade yet, but maybe someday we will.

Anyway, that's kind of the indirect effect that has been taking place in the Middle East and that has changed the entire agricultural economy that we serve. We've seen some dramatic price moves in corn and soybeans, but not so much in wheat, because it's not really used as much. But we've seen a big, big change in agricultural prices. There are other influential factors like China and India raising their quality of life, but the war in Iraq itself and all the instability in the world, and in the oil-producing nations, have really driven a big change here in this agricultural economy.

Let's talk about the opening of the new agricultural floor.

It was 1982 and it was another one of those political situations that are never simple around here. I think that there were some cost overruns. In the 1970s, they bought a parking lot behind the Board of Trade, but the first plan was voted down and then the second plan was voted up. Finally we moved into this new building in February 1982. I think everybody will tell you the thing that they remember most is how the noise was deafening. On the old floor, the sound was absorbed. On the new floor there was a big design flaw and you couldn't hear anything.

That was an early problem, but the floor has served us well. Then we had to expand beyond that. In 1997, we opened another trading floor. We actually built a new trading facility on LaSalle that houses the Treasury complex, the Dow Jones Index, and options trading on those products. With the merger, CME products will be trading in that room as well. So I've seen two floors open since I've been a member.

The agricultural floor is named for Eddie Mansfield. Can you tell me about him.

Everybody who came down to the floor of the CBOT knew and respected Eddie Mansfield, who was the guard of the front door. Eddie knew everybody's name. He knew my father's name. He knew my grandfather's name. He told me stories all the time about my grandfather, Peter B., bringing famous baseball players down to visit the Chicago Board of Trade. My grandfather had a friend from the South Side who was the third-base coach for the Yankees. That was in the 1920s during the era of Babe Ruth, Lou Gehrig, and all these famous baseball players. Herb Pennock, who was a hall of fame pitcher, came to visit, and Eddie was so thrilled to talk about all these great athletes who came to the Board of Trade.

Eddie was there when we came down as kids, and he was there when we came in as members. He was our one constant. What a charming individual and what a link to the past. I think he started in the 1920s down here, and everyday that you walked on the floor of the Board of Trade you were always glad to see Eddie Mansfield standing there. So the leadership at the time decided to name the trading floor after him, and I think we're all very pleased that they did.

Can you talk about the planning and executing of the IPO?

I was very involved in that. We really began pursuing this idea when I was elected Chairman in 2003. We'd started the process in 1999, but that had kind of gone by the wayside due to litigation. The Chicago Mercantile Exchange had become the first United States exchange to become a publicly traded company, and we were watching the results. It became more and more apparent that we had to follow in the CME's footsteps.

A number of things happened within that time frame: We simultaneously changed our clearing provider to the Chicago Mercantile

Exchange and went with Liffe Connect for our electronic trading system. The CBOT also successfully faced down a challenge for our Treasury complex when Eurex started a U.S. futures exchange. And finally, in 2003, we spent some time settling the litigation with the minority membership regarding what the amount of stock distributed to each of the various classes of CBOT memberships would be once the exchange became a for-profit company.

After that, we had to have a vote to demutualize. We had to get all the members to agree on the package. That was not easy, because they all had their concerns and wanted protections. It was a painstaking process, but we did it and I think the members were pleased with what we provided them. You're always walking in the land of the unknown, having to deal with the fear of change; but the vote to demutualize passed and the litigation was settled, and then we voted to go public in May of 2005. In October of 2005 we actually rang the bell at the New York Stock Exchange.

What was that day like?

It was so exciting. They do a great job at the New York Stock Exchange welcoming in new companies and making you feel at home. The day was a very special event and I was fortunate enough to take my whole family there. Our Board of Directors attended, as well as a few other members of the exchange. David Brennan, who was chairman of the CBOT when the whole process started, was there. I remember years ago discussing the topic of being a public company with him when it was first broached in the boardroom and I was one of the first "no" votes. I had said to David, "No, we can't do that. That's never going to work." But he convinced me otherwise, and now we are listed publicly. I think CBOT shares were trading around $190 this morning.

That's unbelievable. Where did the stock open?

The IPO price was $54, but the morning that we rang the bell at the New York Stock Exchange the opening range was around $80 and they traded up to $85 a share that day. So it was an exciting time. It was fun to stand on that floor. The New York Stock Exchange is a very different business than ours, but they actually had a crowd and it was similar to standing in one of the grain pits. They were all excited about opening the market and filling their customers' orders. In fact, they had a delayed opening. They couldn't open it for some time because the buy orders were too big. It was just an emotional high to be part of this historical marker in the long, rich tradition of the Chicago Board of Trade.

Who got to be with you to ring the bell?

I brought my uncle, Bernard P. Carey, who was chairman in the 1960s. I gave him the honor of ringing the opening bell. He was the chairman who preceded me in the family. CBOT President Bernie Dan was on the balcony, along with board members like C.C. Odom, Mark Cermak, and Bob Corvino.

How have things changed for the Chicago Board of Trade since it was converted to a for-profit corporation?

I think the decision-making process changes. You deal with governance issues. You have to have transparent reporting. It's no longer a members' club. It's a very different entity to run, and you have very strict rules on how to run it. Having watched the migration, it was a little bit of a cultural change for the Board of Trade. The members have done a tremendous job of adapting.

From the early days in exchange governance, when it was a member association, run for the members and by the members, to now being a publicly traded company, you have corporate governance issues, and you have to abide by the rules, whether it's the New York Stock Exchange or the SEC. We have a very strict set of rules that we have to comply with. So that's a big change for us culturally. But I think most people would say it is well worth it.

What were your goals when you became chairman of the Board of Trade, and how many of them have been met?

I think the first interview I did as chairman of the Board, I told people that I wanted to complete the restructuring process. It had been a work in progress for three years and it had taken many turns. Settling the litigation with the minority shareholders was part of that job. That allowed us to go ahead and take a vote.

We voted on the demutualization and the membership approved that overwhelmingly. Then we became a publicly traded company in October of 2005. We traded on the New York Stock Exchange, and my first goal was not the proposed merger, but in 2006 we performed our duty and looked at all the strategic alternatives and came up with a merger plan that I think created more value and caught the attention of the entire world when we did it.

Tell me what you see is the future of the Board of Trade?

I think the Board of Trade has a great future. I think there is a need for these markets to continue to grow. I think that commodity trading, the agricultural complex, will continue to grow because of the changes in demand for renewable fuel. I think that the Treasury complex is a valuable complex, and I think that the technology that we've put in place and the clearing agreements have been a "value add" to the customer. I'm very optimistic about the future. I think that the world is going to trade, and I think the world is going to be using the Chicago Board of Trade and all of its products.

Can you talk about what the CBOT means to the city of Chicago and what Chicago means to the Board of Trade?

The fact of the matter is that 150,000 jobs directly or indirectly are tied up with the exchanges here in Chicago—not just the Chicago Board of Trade, but all of the exchanges. Ours is a rich history. It makes sense that a Board of Trade would develop in Chicago due to the city's central location, which is close to the waterways and railways, allowing for easy shipment of agricultural products to the East. In today's world, with electronic trading, the tie is not so great. But a lot of us feel very loyal to the Chicago community and we would like to see the Board of Trade stay here.

Just for the public record, can you give us some of today's prices so that we have a historical record of where the market was at on April 5, 2007?

Prices are up quite a bit from last year. May corn closed at $3.59. Soybeans in the May contract closed at $7.60. December corn was $3.81. The wheat market closed at about $4.90. Soybean oil is at $32.95, and meal prices are $213 in the nearby. Gold is about $670 an ounce, and the 30-year bond closed at $111.09. Probably more important to understand is the interest rate. The interest rate has been trading around 5 percent or less for most of the year.

Any predictions for the near future?

There will be very busy agricultural markets for the summer and there's hope for a good growing season; otherwise the farmers will be complaining. We are going to have continued volatility in the grain sector, because the demand is just tremendous.

Last question: What would you like your legacy to be to the Chicago Board of Trade?

When I took office, a Board of Trade seat was trading for $300,000. There was no exercise right that had been separated. It was a bundle and my job was to unlock the value. And my legacy to the exchange is to be a part of a process that finished something that we started in 1999. We finished the process of demutualization. We became a publicly traded company. I think we've restored our image as a global player, and I want to see that continue.

It's a marvelous legacy.

Sometimes you get lucky.

CHAPTER 5

Traditions Passed Down

Thomas J. Cashman

Even before he graduated from Fenwick High School, Thomas J. Cashman knew quite a bit about the Chicago Board of Trade. Three of his uncles, George, Ed, and Gene Cashman, were well-known, well-liked, and well-respected members of the CBOT. The Cashman family was renowned for their excellent trading skills and for their generosity.

Tom Cashman attended Loras College in Dubuque, Iowa, where he served as junior class president and then in his senior year as the Student Senate president. After graduating in 1960 with a degree in chemistry, he went on to Northwestern University, where he earned his master of science in chemistry. While attending college and for a few years afterward, he served his country as a member of the U.S. Army Reserves, becoming a radio school honor graduate.

In 1962, Tom became a member of the Chicago Board of Trade and started working as a self-employed grain broker, a position he still holds today. From 1980 to 1992, Tom worked for the Cashman Oil Company as its vice president. He also worked for Victor Grain in the same capacity.

Tom has volunteered his extra time in service to the CBOT. He has given countless hours to improving the exchange. In 1973, he became a lifelong member of the American Soybean Association. He joined the National Feed and Grain Association in 1976, and has continued with that membership to this day. In 1979, he became a member of the CBOT Floor Governors Committee, and by 1981 he was its chairman. From 1982 to 1984, he was a director of the Chicago Board of Trade.

Mr. Cashman has been a respected member of several other Board of Trade committees, including the Chicago Board of Trade Clearing Corporation Nominating Committee for two years (he became chairman in 1990). He also served on the CBOT Nominating Committee, the Special Committee on Compensation Policy, and the CBOT Task Force for the Mansfield Room Reconstruction. He served as chairman of the CBOT Auction Markets Political Action Committee (AMPAC) and the CBOT Committee on Ethics and Integrity. He was also chairman of the CBOT Committee on Appeals.

From 1992 to 1996, Tom worked on the Mid-America Commodity Exchange Committee and also served on the Chicago Mercantile Exchange/Chicago Board of Trade Members Advisory Committee, working on the Joint Strategic Initiative Committee.

Although he was always busy serving his exchange community, Tom also found time to support many outside endeavors. Those included the American Cancer Society and the Village of Kenilworth Village House Youth Board. He has been a director of the American Ireland Fund since 1991. He has also been active in the Cedar Park Association, the Williams Bay Lions Club, the Williams Bay Planning Commission, the Geneva Lake Association, and its associated Environmental Educational Foundation.

Tom has been a trustee of numerous organizations; among them are the Woodlands Academy Board, the Mundelein College Board, and the Fenwick High School Board. He has also been a director of the Irish Fellowship Club, and from 2002 to the present he has been its vice president. He has served as a director for the Irish Georgian Society since 1994. He also assists the Friends of Kishwauketoe Nature Conservatory and works closely with the Hundred Club of Cook County serving as both a director and vice president. He has also been a very active member of Old St. Patrick's Church, working on the Board of Trustees, the Patrician Society Leadership Council, and the Sesquicentennial

Committee. His family was honored at the Old St. Patrick's Emerald Ball.

Tom has also devoted many hours to serving his alma mater, Loras College, on the Board of Regents, the Regents Emeriti, the Capital Gift Campaign, the National Alumni Board, and the Mathias Loras Society.

Mr. Cashman has acquired many deserved honors. He was a member of the Fenwick High School National Honor Society and was inducted many years later into the school's hall of fame. He was cited in *Who's Who in American College Students* and was inducted into the Delta Epsilon Sigma National Honor Fraternity and the Alpha Chi Sigma Chemical Honor Fraternity.

Among his many awards are the Lakeland Hospital Margret Schloemer Humanitarian Award, the Loras Club of Chicago, Francis X. Parker Volunteer Service Award, and the doctor of letters, *honoris causus*, from Loras College.

Currently, Tom holds memberships at the Union League Club in Chicago and in Wisconsin, and he is active at the Lake Geneva Country Club and the Lake Geneva Yacht Club.

He has been married to his wife Jacquie for 42 years. They have five children and three grandchildren. Two of his sons, Tom and Brendan, are shareholders of the CBOT.

****

Let's talk about your life at the Chicago Board of Trade. How did you first hear about the exchange?

Basically, I heard about it from my Uncle George, my godfather, who was the first member of the family to be involved with the exchange.

How did he come to the Board of Trade?

When he was in high school, he actually used to ditch school and come down to the Board of Trade. He'd hitchhike down Madison Street to work in the afternoon as a settlements clerk for Stratton Grain. My dad, being the oldest one in the family, would take off after him and try to get his brother to come back home.

Did that work?

Not really. I'm sure Uncle George finished high school, but after that he was stuck on working at the Board of Trade.

Why did you want to go into the business?

Well, the business itself is very fascinating, besides having a family interest. It's quick, and there is a lot of mathematics involved. I was always interested in mathematics. It's very challenging, and it's very romantic, if you can use such a word for a business.

I can see how it would be termed romantic and seductive. Let's talk about your family history with the Chicago Board of Trade.

My Uncle George was the first to become a member, and then he bought a membership for my Uncle Gene, and then one for my Uncle Ed. Uncle Gene and Uncle Ed were both policemen. They actually traded in the morning, from 9:30 A.M. when the bell was rung to the close at 1:15 P.M. Then they left and worked the shift at the police department from 4:00 P.M.. to midnight.

They worked like that for several years, splitting their days between the Board of Trade and the police department. They had very few hours when they weren't working at one or the other. Eventually my Uncle Gene and my Uncle Ed actually did well enough at the exchange that they retired from the police department. They both remained very supportive and loyal to the police department throughout their lives.

Tell me about some other members of your family.

After that, my cousin Bill Sullivan got a membership. His mom was a Cashman. Then I was fortunate enough to get a membership after I finished my graduate degree in chemistry at Northwestern University. There were many more cousins and second cousins who came down to the exchange. Through the years, we have probably had a total of 20 to 25 people who have been at the CBOT in one capacity or another.

The Cashman name is very well known and, more important, well respected. How do you think that happened?

My uncles were guys of very, very high character. They never would do anything that would imperil the quality of the kind of trade we had, and the integrity and the honesty of the business. They would never cut corners. They always had way too much respect for the Chicago Board of Trade and for the customers that used the CBOT. Deep down they were very good, hardworking, honest guys. That sense of honesty and integrity has filtered down to all their nephews and nieces.

It wasn't always easy. They both had young families at the time, and they would ride a police car from 4:00 P.M. to 12:00 midnight. Then they would get home at 12:30 A.M., jump into bed, and be up again by 7:30 A.M. Then they raced down to the Board of Trade to have breakfast and see what was on the morning wire and what the lines were and what was going on. They thought about things like, "Is rye going to be higher today? Is wheat going to be lower?"

At that time they were basically both brokers in the rye pit. The exchange does not trade rye anymore. Rye is an interesting story. At one time we grew 29 million bushels of rye a year in the United States. There were some days when we traded 50,000 contracts in the pit. It was a very interesting period of the exchange.

How did someone who was working as a policeman find out about the Board of Trade?

They found out about it from their older brother. Being at the Board of Trade was a completely different life from anything anyone in my family had done before my Uncle George became a member. It was very captivating. You don't come down here normally and stand around and just let time go by. If you're a member, and a broker especially, you come down and you learn. You find out what the important things are that drive markets, and you start trading. It's just a wonderful, wonderful way to make a living.

Why do you think the Board of Trade has so many trader families?

Number one, I think it is because a lot of us have been successful. I also think there is a lot to be said for the tradition of passing down a business within families. You read in the paper every day when a policeman dies and they say, "Well, his father was a sergeant in the police department." You'll read about firemen who die in the line of duty, and this just happened two weeks ago with a gentleman named Grant who was killed; his father was a fireman. And so I think it's a very natural thing for the city of Chicago and people who came from very modest means to emulate their parents and the leaders in the family. And if they're successful and they do what they really respect, it seems quite natural to follow them in their line of work.

You talk about the city of Chicago. What do you think it means to the Board of Trade, and what does the CBOT mean to the city?

I know the city means a lot to the Board of Trade, and I know the Board of Trade is an integral part of the city. We supply so many jobs. We supply so much income, and are one of the economic engines of the city. At one time there was a rumor that the CBOT was going to move to a little town outside of Elgin because of the threat of a transaction tax.

The first Mayor Daley, Richard J., killed that tax notion pretty quickly, because he knew that Chicago and the Board of Trade were synonymous. Remember the proper name is not the Board of Trade; it's the *Board of Trade of the City of Chicago.*

That's a very good point. Tell me how you got your membership.

I went to graduate school at Northwestern University. I had just taken my orals and earned a master's degree in chemistry. That next fall, my sister got married, and my uncles, George and Gene, were at the house afterwards. We were all enjoying the exuberance of the day. And they said, "What are you going to do with yourself now that you're out of graduate school?" I said, "I'm going to Monsanto in St. Louis to interview for a job this week. They're going to give me a job in sales. I don't really like chemistry, so I think I'll just go out and sell products for them." Well, my uncles listened, and then they had another beer and started talking to each other. The next thing I knew, and it was a Saturday, my Uncle Gene said to me, "Come on down Monday about 8:00 A.M. We want to talk to you."

So at 8:00 A.M. that Monday I went down to the Board of Trade and they said, "We're going over to the Continental Bank." And I said, "How's that?" They said, "We have to open a bank account for you. We want you to buy a membership." So we went to the Continental Bank and my uncles funded an account with a check for $10,000. I lived alone with my mother. My mother and I did not have a bank account. All the bills were paid at a currency exchange. So they put $10,000 in the bank in January of 1962, and I bought a membership for $6,600, $6,000 for the membership and a $600 transfer fee.

How long did it take you to pay that back?

My uncles would never allow me to pay back a penny of that. It was an investment in me. They were beneficent, great, wonderful people, and I'd be willing to say that if they had the money in 1962 and that membership was $50,000, they would never have expected me to pay back a penny of that, either. Every membership that they bought in the family, there was never a repayment for any of it.

It was bought as a gift. In my case it was a special gift, because my father had passed away very suddenly during my senior year in high school. And because of that, my Uncle George and Uncle Gene acted as surrogate fathers to me, and they always took care of me.

Tell me about Gene Cashman.

My Uncle Gene was a very unusual person. There are many legends and stories about him. People talk about the policeman who came to the CBOT and made millions. He was very successful as a speculator. This was especially true in 1973 when we had this huge meal shortage and we had crop problems and soybeans traded at an all-time record high futures price at $12.90.

However, Gene is really better known for how good he was to people down here. There are several different instances I could cite where he would take care of people he didn't know or he'd never heard of. I would say that my uncle never met a person he wouldn't help. For example, in the middle of a big market, somebody told Gene that there was a phone person named John who worked for Bache and Company, who had a sudden heart attack and had to have open heart surgery. This was back in the 1970s when open heart surgery was an extremely dangerous operation, and the cost of it was $10,000 and the guy didn't have any health insurance. My uncle didn't know him, but paid for the operation and paid for his hospital stay. I'm not so sure he ever even met the guy.

That's amazing. I have heard many wonderful stories about him.

He was just a very giving guy.

How about your Uncle George?

My Uncle George was my godfather. He was the first in the family. He actually passed away in 1968, before we got into the big markets. He never was able to enjoy a lot of the fruits of the big markets and the money that was made, especially in the early 1970s. But he was a wonderful pit trader.

He and Gene both loved horses. In their leisure time, once or twice a week, especially when the tracks were open here, they'd go home by way of Hawthorne Park or Maywood Park and watch the races. They ended up owning horses. In 1976, after my Uncle George died, my Uncle Gene owned a horse called Elocutionist, who ran third in the Kentucky Derby. It was a real thrill for the family. Uncle Gene loaded up about 90 family members and hauled us all off to Louisville for the Derby.

Elocutionist then won the Preakness, but was injured soon after and was never able to race again. And that year, the third leg of the Triple Crown, the Belmont Stakes, was won by Bold Forbes in the worst time in the history of the Belmont Stakes. Elocutionist was the only horse that was bred for distance in that whole field. Unfortunately, he was hurt, but had he been able to run in that race, he would have won two legs of the Triple Crown. It ended up that he was syndicated for $10 million, but his offspring never did anything.

It must have been wonderful growing up in a family like that.

Family parties were quite the deal. There were lots of celebrations.

How about Dan Rice?

Dan Rice is another legend of the exchange. I have kind of a close relationship with Dan Rice even though we never actually met. I did see him on the elevator a few times. There was a horse, Lucky Debonair, who won the Kentucky Derby the day my wife Jacquie and I were married, May 1, 1965. My wife still loves to tell the story. We were taking all these pictures when all of a sudden picture taking was over. Everybody had to go to the bar to watch the Derby. Ada L. Rice, Dan's wife, owned Lucky Debonair, and it won the Kentucky Derby that day. We always thought it boded good things for our marriage and our family.

Anyhow, Dan Rice was a marvelous trader and a big speculator. There were hand signals in the old days about who was doing what. And there was a particular hand signal, taking your hand and putting it to your mouth, called a "Rice," which indicated that Mr. Rice was buying wheat. Or Mr. Rice was selling beans.

Tell me about Eddie Mansfield.

Eddie Mansfield was absolutely the heart and soul of the exchange. Although he was never a member, he was the consummate guard of the front door of the exchange. He not only knew if you were a member, but he knew your wife, he knew your kids, and he always made it a point to ask you how they were doing, ask you how they were. He was one of the finest gentlemen I ever met in my life. Everybody was Ed's friend.

How did they honor him?

They honored him by naming the new grain room, which was opened in 1982, the Mansfield room. I think that's very significant about how wholesome, how caring, how wonderful the Chicago Board of Trade is: that they named a room after a person who was never a member of the exchange.

How about Vince Fagan?

Vince Fagan was a wonderful trader back in the very late 1940s and early 1950s. He was a crippled gentleman, and he used to stand next to a phone, and he'd trade by flashing orders in to the pit. Actually, the only ones that really did that on the floor were Merrill Lynch and Vince Fagan. He was a very big trader. He had a fellow named Joe Nugent who was his broker. Joe Nugent used to wear all these big, colorful jackets. Today everybody wears different jackets, but in those days almost everybody wore tan drab jackets. But not Vince's man Joe. He had a coat of many colors that he wore. He always was heavily perfumed, so you not only could see Joe coming, you could smell him coming. He would go in all the different pits and make the trades for Vince Fagan.

Vince was a very storied Board of Trade member. His moves in the market were watched and followed. He was a highly respected man. I never knew what happened to him, because in those days I was going back and forth to school. But one summer I came back and he was just gone. I don't know whether he retired or whether he passed on. He was certainly a wonderful gentleman.

Let's talk about another legend, Paul McGuire.

Paul McGuire was one of the cornerstones of our exchange. Paul ended up being chairman later on in life, after he had worked so hard for the exchange in so many different ways. He had served on many different committees. He worked on the CBOE, and was a trader there from day one to try to develop it. Paul was writing a history of the exchange when he passed away, and I heard it was half done. I don't know what happened to it. I know Jay Homan was going to try to get hold of it, but I don't think anything ever happened with it.

Paul was very studious, very bright. In those days you used to be able to smoke in the pit. Paul would walk in the pit and he'd be puffing on his pipe. And while he was doing it, he was trading small lots of beans or small lots of another commodity. He never traded big, but he would come in five times a day and 30 times a week, and he'd be making those small trades, and they added up to almost limit positions. He was a brilliant man, and very well respected.

With all these people smoking on the floor and the paper all over, was there ever a fire?

I guess once in a while a piece of paper caught on fire, especially if you threw the cigarette on the floor. I know that I had slacks that I wore to work that always had a hole in them. Jordy Glassman used to swing his arms, and I'd be standing next to him, and he'd hit me in the leg with his cigarette.

So it was a good idea to ban smoking on the floor.

That was one of the things that we were able to do during the few years I was on the exchange board of directors. Richard Stark, Roger Griffin, and I made a move to have all the smoking moved upstairs. Many people were upset with us, but it was the right thing to do. Today, we're all going smokeless, because we know smoking kills.

How about Eddie Byers?

Eddie Byers is a unique gentleman. He was a partner of J.T. McKerr, and he used to always have the limit position in soybeans. In my opinion, Eddie Byers is responsible for the greatest single trade in the history of soybeans. In 1973, the year soybeans traded at $12.90, Eddie Byers sold a million cash beans to a commercial firm for $13 a bushel. That is the highest price that has ever been seen in soybeans. But I still dream that one of these days I'm going to change the name of my wooden boat to *Beans in the Teens* and we will take out that high.

There is one more thing about Eddie Byers. One time he had some friends in from Texas and they were all sitting downstairs in this big round table enjoying lunch, and they were all bragging about what they owned. One guy said, "I've got 10,000 acres out in northwest Texas," and another guy said, "I've got 12,000 acres." They went all the way around the table bragging, and Eddie was not saying anything. One of the men finally turned to him and asked, "Ed, you don't say a thing. What do you own in Texas?" Eddie said, "I have 10 acres." And they said, "Ten acres?" They all looked at him like "So what?" and then he said, "Yeah, it's downtown Dallas."

That's a great example of one of the legends about the CBOT members. Speaking of legends, can you talk about Henry Shatkin?

Henry Shatkin was the consummate spread scalper. I know that's a lot to say in one mouthful, but Hank was a guy who would scalp a spread in and out all day long. He was very quick and a terrific pit trader. I don't think there's ever been a better one. He stopped trading relatively early in life, so I've never quite forgiven him for that. Why couldn't he stay down there and get old like the rest of us?

And how about Lee Stern?

Lee is a very, very bright guy. He is one of the best traders that ever came down here. Every once in a while he might get into a little scuffle or disagreement. Lee's famous story, which he loves to tell about himself, is about how he always would be fighting for quotes on the close, like "Well, I traded there; how come I can't get my quote?" One day he says, "You know what happened to me, Tom? One day the pit chairman had to leave, and I was on the committee. So the market's closing, and I'm the pit chairman. We had this big fight on the close and I had to throw out my own quote." Of course, he had to disallow his own quote.

The integrity of you and your family is certainly legendary. As a Cashman, what was it like the first day you came down on the floor as a member?

Well, the first day I came down as a member I was a little nervous. The first thing my Uncle Gene said to me was, "We want you to do the spread. We want you to go over in the oat pit, and we want you to buy 15 March oats and sell 15 December oats." And he said, "You gotta leg it. You gotta buy the March and sell the December. You just can't do it as a spread." So it took me about a half hour to do it. Of course, at that time, the oat pit was only trading about one trade every 15 or 20 minutes. There was virtually no trade at all.

I guess I'll never forget it. They were so wise to send me to the oat pit for two reasons: number one, because it was very quiet, and number two, because all the brokers in the oat pit were 60 to 85 years old. Gene knew that no one was going to hurt me and no one was going to let me get into trouble. It was a great place to go in and try to develop my confidence. It certainly isn't easy to be confident on the first day as an exchange member. But that trade forced me to execute a trade where I couldn't get too badly hurt; if I had gone into the middle of the bean pit, I would have been eaten alive.

Many of the pits had a volatile nature. Tell me some of the battles that you have seen.

There have been some shoving matches and battles and fights over quotes through the years. Surprisingly enough, they all pretty well get ironed out. Every once in a while, there have been a few swings at people. It's sometimes a rough place when you are working in an open auction market that's very physical. People are yelling and spitting. The brokers are trying to do the best they can for their customers at all times, and the locals are trying not to be disadvantaged. With all that action and tension happening at once, most of the members still perform magnificently.

How is it at the end of the day, after many of these people were swinging at each other, they could have dinner together?

They don't all go out and have dinner. There are a few grudges, but in general, people do get along. People do explain to each other after the battle that "Yeah, I know I was off the market, I guess, but I didn't see the other guy." And, "Did you see him?" And, "How come I got shoved and I didn't get that trade?" Things have a way of ironing themselves out, and then there are some things that don't. There are some intense grudges that do exist on the floor. I think it's just human nature.

Some people think trading depends a lot on the brawn of the individual. You have a master's degree in chemistry and are very well-spoken. Can you speak of the intelligence of the CBOT membership?

Well, there's a lot of ways to skin a cat. There are guys who do the crush in beans. There are guys who do the spread; they do butterfly spreads. And depending on the guy you're talking to, some guys have a really high form of intelligence, or at least in their own little niche.

Regarding the physicality you were talking about, we used a lot more hand signals to trade across the pit. We didn't have quite the innovative communications technology that we have today. That's the reason for the athletic part of the trading game. You're running around doing the best you can for your customer. You want to spot the best places to position yourself. So it isn't just something selfish, or something you're trying to do for yourself. You're also trying to do it for the customer and the exchange.

That type of thinking speaks to the integrity of the members.

I think integrity is the key ingredient to our business. You never want a customer to get a worse fill than he's entitled to. For us to be a bona fide institution that provides the service that it does, that defines risk, discovers price, and transfers risk, we have to have the customer get the best price that he can. If that doesn't exist, then the exchange couldn't have lasted as long as it has. For every customer who has been disappointed because he thought he should have got a better deal, hopefully there are two or three who said, "Thank God I put that order in at the Board of Trade, and thank God I got a better price than I could have if I'd done it someplace else." We do everything with a sense of integrity and pride in our business practices.

How about the role of tradition?

Well, again, tradition exists among families for sure. It exists an awful lot in people who are my age who want to pass down our experiences to younger people. I feel this way especially with my sons. I want them to live up to the traditions of the exchange, where the best buyer meets the best seller. Everybody gets the best deal that they can get by using our facilities and our marketplace.

Tell me about the first lesson that you learned.

I guess one of the big lessons I learned is, first of all, be loud. You have to be very dynamic about how you fill an order, how you buy it from someone, how you sell it to someone. Don't let there be any doubt of who you're trading with, and make sure you get the quote out, because if those things don't happen, a lot of times the customer is going to be disadvantaged. I guess the lessons that I learned were from watching my uncles and how they operated when I was working as a clerk and a messenger in my high school days. I watched very carefully how they did things. I observed their integrity and honesty. Again, all of that goes back to tradition.

How meaningful is the expression 'My word is my bond'?

In our business, "My word is my bond" is paramount. If a person makes a trade with someone, he lives up to it. He doesn't run from it. Now, there have been instances in the past, very, very few, where guys did run out on trades. If it happens too often, no one will trade with them and they are gone from the exchange. But when you make a trade, you're good for that trade, and you have a house that backs you financially or you wouldn't be down there trading. You lose all credibility as soon as you say, "Oh, no, I didn't do that with you." It would be the end of you, as far as anybody believing in you being a trader is concerned.

Explain the expression, "Don't give anything away."

Well, again that happens when markets get very busy and it's hard to determine what is the best bid or the best offer. "Don't give it away" is an expression about a fill that you have done that isn't as good as you would have liked it to be. Every once in a while you'll fill an order, and afterwards you'll say, "Gee, I had to fill that and it was terrible. I feel like I had to give it away." It's a phrase that says that you're just not happy. I know that you can't be happy all the time. Every once in a while, you just won't fill the order the best that you thought you could have. Sometimes you're being supercritical of yourself. Sometimes you feel you could have done a better job. Either way, there are days you just feel bad about the way things turned out.

How important is it for you to service your customers?

Oh, it's important. It was far more important years ago than it is now with the electronic age. Today, people are much more concerned with the speed of execution and the price than they are about how well you manage the order and how long it takes you to work it. Sometimes it's an all-day thing or an all-week thing. A friend of mine, Keith Bronstein, used to get orders where he would work them for two or three days, and they were huge orders from New York. Those kinds of things just don't happen anymore, but it still boils down to being responsible to your customer.

In those days you would take your customers out to lunch once in a while. You would take the time to talk to them and find out their needs. You'd say, "What can I do to better serve you?" Today you don't even know who you're filling orders for. Everything is just consolidated to a point where human nature is not quite part of the game it used to be.

How important is the role of self-regulation at the CBOT?

One of the keys to our industry is self-regulation. We do that to make sure that our business stays honest and has a high degree of integrity.

We keep a really strong leash on our members to make sure that they're performing to the best of their ability and they're not breaking any of the rules.

What committees have you served on?

I worked on the Membership Committee. I was chairman of the Floor Governors Committee. When a person's been around as long as I have, obviously you are going to find yourself on committees. With the short hours that we have, people who have any kind of love and care for the institution are going to want to give some hours back in the afternoon and want to do the best they can to keep the place operating the way it should.

What were some of the things that you were able to accomplish being on these committees?

While serving on the Floor Governors Committee, we established some decent conduct rules that probably weren't there before. We did a lot of search-and-destroy type of missions. We were trying to remodel the Mansfield room, and the total cost was going to be somewhere between $20 million and $30 million. Luckily for the Board of Trade, David Fisher nixed the whole project, because he said we didn't have the money. Three or four years later it was a moot point, because we never needed to expand because of the electronic trading. So it was fortunate we never did it.

What other committees did you serve on?

I served on the Appeals Committee, and that was very interesting. I'm not sure we even have a committee on appeals anymore. I think that appeals are handled by arbitration or something else. The Appeals Committee was called on when there was a judgment made in one of the other committees and there were some questions about the ruling. They could come to the Appeals Committee to ask for relief of some sort. It was our job to listen to the grievance and then report back to the board of directors.

It has been mentioned that one of the most important things that the Chicago Board of Trade does is serve as a role model for a worldwide price discovery mechanism. In what instances do you find this to be true?

In all instances. We open the market and the best buyer meets the best seller from 9:30 A.M.. to 1:15 P.M. in the pit. Now we have screen trading side by side with the pit trading, so there are two mechanisms that allow for price discovery. Again, it's the best buyer meets the best seller and it is all under scrutiny, with people doing the best they can. Our exchange provides an open auction market trade for three hours and 45 minutes every day; and there are longer electronic hours.

One example of the CBOT's role in worldwide price discovery was the Russian purchase in 1973. Can you tell me about it?

At that time I was one of the three brokers who had orders from Cook Grain to buy a certain amount of beans. As far as I recall, the amount we bought was probably 30 million beans. It took us all day to do it. Bill Fritz, Tom Brown and I were the three brokers who bought the stuff. Cook Grain gave us a five-cent level to start with. For example, say the market had closed at 340 and the market was supposed to open lower. They'd say, "Well, go to $3.45 and buy all the beans you can."

Now, I didn't know what to do with something like that. I'd never had an order like that. So I bought about a million beans, and I walked back there. I said, "I've got a million beans here." And Karl Estes, the floor manager for Cook Grain, said, "Just keep going." I said, "Keep going what?" He said, "Take another nickel, and buy all the beans you can."

So this went on until we had—actually, I think the number that sticks in my mind was a total of 26 million. In today's volumes, that would be nothing. And interestingly enough, after we bought all these beans, and again it was the story of the year, the market actually set back seven or eight cents, and didn't start rallying until about 10 days later. And then it went up all the way to, eventually, $12.90 a bushel.

How do you think the farmers, the managers, and others around the world benefit from what goes on at the CBOT?

They benefit because we do the best job of discovering price and because we are the price that everybody refers to. When you have a basis quote for soybeans, soybeans are 20 under; that means they're 20 under the Board of Trade price. They use our closing price. If they're 10 over, they're 10 over the Board. We are still the reference point of establishing price in the world.

Outside world events can affect trading at the CBOT. How about the Chernobyl incident?

When that reactor blew in Chernobyl, it was really an interesting situation. At the time, I was at a Board of Trustees meeting in Dubuque. It was on a Friday and I was short corn and beans, not very brilliant. And the officials didn't announce it until Monday. On Monday, the market opened 20 higher and closed up the limit. Then it traded sharply higher again Tuesday, and that was it. Then it turned around and started back down. But we were all stuck short. We had huge supplies of both corn and beans at the time.

Needless to say, it was a very interesting period. It created very erratic markets because no one had ever experienced this type of thing before and we had no idea how it would affect the crops over there or if it would affect us here. And they still say there are effects from Chernobyl that go on in Russia today.

How about the China purchase in 2003?

That's one for the books. The Chinese bought all our beans, booked all our beans, ran the market up, got out, and then canceled all the contracts. That's one of the worst things that ever happened in the history of the grain business, the way our commercial firms lost a fortune. Our market went from $10.64 back down to seven something after they did that. The Chinese sure must have made a lot of money in that market. Now the contracts for those kinds of purchases have been rewritten.

The CBOT continues to be in the forefront of affecting global markets. Where do you see its competition coming from?

There is competition coming our way from other exchanges in the United States and from new exchanges opening around the world. Things are rapidly changing in the marketplace with the advent of electronic trading. Now trading is not hampered by time zones. It will be a huge challenge for us.

Electronic trading is just one of the latest innovations for the exchange. What has been the role of innovation in this industry?

The biggest innovation on the floor has obviously come through the screen trading, and also the headsets we use and the electronic order entry vehicle we use. They have all improved the speed of the order entry, the speed of execution, and the speed of reporting. For us to be competitive, we have to be constantly aware of different innovations that can satisfy the customers. It's what the customer wants. It is what the customer demands.

How easy was it for you to adapt to every change that came along?

It has not been easy, but I'm doing my best.

What was the first change that you can remember that sort of upset your way of life?

The electronic price boards. I didn't want them to put them in. I was so worried that the 20 to 25 guys who were marking the chalkboards were going to lose their jobs. I fought against it. Looking back, it was one of the stupidest things I've done. By the way, that was one of Ed

O'Connor's deals. It turned out to be a wonderful thing to do.

It seems like a Cashman "thing to do" to worry about the guys marking the chalkboard.

It was because they were everyday guys who were going to lose their jobs. We had a marker for every commodity. In wheat, the guy would put all the chalk marks up, and there was a guy to take his place so he could go on breaks. There were two people who worked on every board. There were probably 25 guys on the floor who would be up on the catwalk marking all these boards. Unfortunately, they were out of work overnight. I felt terrible.

It is very true that innovation often takes a human toll. There have been other times of crisis at the exchange. How about when beans were viewed as a universal hedge?

At one time we couldn't trade gold as a commodity at all. It was unlawful as a United States citizen. Beans were kind of a universal hedge when we didn't trade currencies. This is going back to the 1960s and 1970s. So if there was a financial crisis, people would buy or sell soybeans. If there was a drought in Brazil, people would buy or sell soybeans. And, of course, they grow beans in Brazil, but even before they grew them there, beans were the universal hedge.

I am not going to downplay the fact that the volumes were nowhere near what they are today, basically because we've globalized and because there are so many more people trading. There are so many more people who want to accumulate assets involving commodities and hard assets and soybeans and corn. These are significant things that weren't important to people 10 or 15 years ago.

Before we got into the hedge fund end of the business, which is what dominates now, we only traded beans for beans. We didn't trade them for anything else. Now we trade them as an asset class, we trade them as fundamentals, and we trade them as technicals. So again, the futures market's usage expanded. What had contracted, by developing other futures contracts such as gold, silver, the dollar, and so on, has now again expanded.

What do you think will happen to that agriculture market in the future?

I think we've probably seen the lowest prices in farm commodities that we'll see in a long, long time. I think that more people will not only want to accumulate assets as far as grain and oil seeds are concerned, but they will want to trade them. The users and the consumption keep going up every year. Our supply, if it's not stagnant, goes up at a lesser rate. Now that we've brought another seven million acres into production this year, I can't for the life of me feel that those are going to be really quality acres, since they were out of production.

I think that there's a lot of things going for higher prices. Years ago, beans were an inflation hedge. We got away from them being an inflation hedge, because we oversupplied and the government paid people to grow grain. Once again when they're an inflation hedge, they're going to act like gold and silver—maybe not to the same extent.

Do you feel there's some government influence in the markets?

Well, I think there always is, yes. And the more the government participates in the grain business, the more difficult it is to have higher prices. This is because the government pays people to grow grain, and it pays supports. The farmer has gotten very good at selling his crop during the growing season, and then waiting to get his loan deficiency payment (LDP) in the fall.

Last year the farmer got a little fooled because the markets took off on him. And I'm not so sure those days might not be over. I believe we need some changes in legislation. But again, it is because of the pork barrel interests of the Congress and keeping their constituents happy, which are more important to them than worrying about the price of grain and how much money it's costing the taxpayers to fund the farmers to grow our grain and make a lot of money.

Would you like to talk about some of that legislation you'd like to see happen?

I don't know what they'd do. How do you cut out programs? I really think a change has happened in the past few years, with the advent of the LDP payments being so prominent in the low-priced markets. Years ago when the government would give you the crop estimate, the farmer would underestimate his crop because he wanted higher prices. Now, because he sold his crop during the growing season, he wants the LDP. He overestimates his crop because he actually wants the market to go down so he gets the LDP. He still has his cash crop, and he's hedged his crop at a higher price. So, I think it's a totally different phenomenon going on now in the country.

Can you address the impact of the CBOE?

I don't know a lot about the impact of the CBOE, but I do know that it has been a tremendous success. The O'Connor boys were significantly active in starting it. I know that Paul McGuire and Ralph Peters were very active in trading in the options markets. Personally, I was very uneducated about what options were and how they would contribute to the markets the way they have.

We have a cliché that we use in our business: "the wave of the future." The CBOE was truly "the wave of the future" when it started and continues to be successful today. Electronic trading falls into that category of "the wave of the future," too, although the future is here today.

Do you have any thoughts on the subject of consolidation?

The new waves that are coming are the consolidation of exchanges, and what's going to happen when that happens.

It's a good time to be near the end of my career, as far as our stock is concerned. I hope I don't live to regret that statement, but I think exchanges have to consolidate, because of costs. I think that the exchange is going to be bought by somebody. It's going to be a good deal for the current member/stockholders. What happens after that is anybody's guess.

How did you deal with the idea of going from being a member to being a shareholder?

It was difficult to live with, especially when, at our earnings, a lot of us didn't have the confidence that we would have the successful stock experiences we have had. I think we were really hesitant to go along with it. And yet it's been a wonderful thing.

A lot of members resist change. Why do you think that is?

It is the fear of the unknown. You're afraid of what's going to be coming around the corner. Obviously, now with the advent of electronic trading, some of us are worried that we will go the way of those people writing on the chalkboards. The open outcry markets aren't as active as they were, and they're not as liquid as they used to be, because so many orders are done on the screen. People say they can't make the money they used to make. It isn't as easy to make a living trading in the pit as it was at one time. So that's part of the fear.

Do you think there's still a place for pit trading?

Yes. I think that if we get into a big market, we're going to need all the different ways to trade. And I think we're going to need the headsets and the Electronic Clerks. I think we'll need pit trading and electronic trading, because you can see the volumes today compared to what they were 10 or 20 years ago, and they're extraordinarily higher. And what happens if we go up one more octave, as it were? I think that there's going to be a place, a real need, for floor trading. I also think the commercial firms, as a whole, prefer pit trading. I may be living in a dream world, but I hope that floor trading will remain.

Let's talk about some of the historical events that happened when you were on the floor, like the assassination of JFK.

I was in the pit. It happened around noon. There was a fellow in the bean pit named Bill Kentnich who was a big, heavyset guy. I would hate to even hazard a guess at Bill's weight. He always had a towel around his neck after about 11:00 A.M. because he was sweating so much. I remember that he was up on the top step of beans. All of sudden he took a step down and started selling beans and selling beans, and no one knew what was going on. He was a broker for Bache. It wasn't Pru Bache (Prudential Bache) at the time; it was just J.S. Bache and Company, I believe.

Anyhow, all of a sudden it's 12:15 P.M., and the word's getting out. "Did you hear the deal?" "What's the deal?" "Kennedy was shot in Dallas, but he's okay." And then the market sorted itself out. But I'll never forget the image of this huge man, 300-plus, wading down into the middle of the bean pit and just selling beans, and to everybody he could. Of course, afterwards, we get downstairs and the newspapers are out. Kennedy is dead.

We all stayed downtown and went to the Gateway, the little bar near here. We just sat there and watched the news. We were all so shaken by it; just dumbfounded. Just so shattered. It was one of the worst experiences of my life. I always was a John F. Kennedy fan. I loved him.

That was a terrible time for the country. Can you tell me about the time when there was a fire in the CBOT building?

There was a fire in somebody's office, and the exchange shut down the elevators. I specifically remember this, because the fire was on the 36th floor and our office was on the 40th floor. And I, thinking I was in shape, went up to get our jackets, because everybody had to have their jackets to leave. I walked up the stairs from the first floor all the way to the 40th and came down with the jackets for everybody. There were five or six of us in our little office. Eight years later I ended up with a heart attack. I'm lucky I didn't have it that day.

If a young man came to you and said, "Gee, I think I'd like to start my career at the Chicago Board of Trade," would you encourage him to do so?

Depending on what he wanted to do, yes, I would. I would not encourage him to walk into the pit and be a pit trader right now, because I think the future there is a little muddled.

How about being a screen trader?

I would encourage that, for sure. I'd encourage being involved with different investment managements and teams and things like that, too.

Can you make any predictions about where the exchange will be in five years?

In five years, I think that most trading will have migrated to the screen. There's some chance that it won't, but mostly I think that is what is going to happen. I think that a lot of us senior members will be sitting in an office trading and using a screen. And I think the Board of Trade will be making a lot of money with this system, and, hopefully, it still will be providing the service that it has provided for all these years and that has allowed me to have a very successful business life.

You said that the Board of Trade has allowed you to have a successful business life. What do you think you've given to the Board of Trade?

I don't know. I certainly haven't given enough. I served one term as governor. I served on a number of committees. I did some things, but I don't think I'll ever be able to pay back the Board of Trade for what the it has allowed me to accomplish in my 45 years as a member.

Tommy, you've done everything you could to bring pride to the Cashman name and to the Chicago Board of Trade!

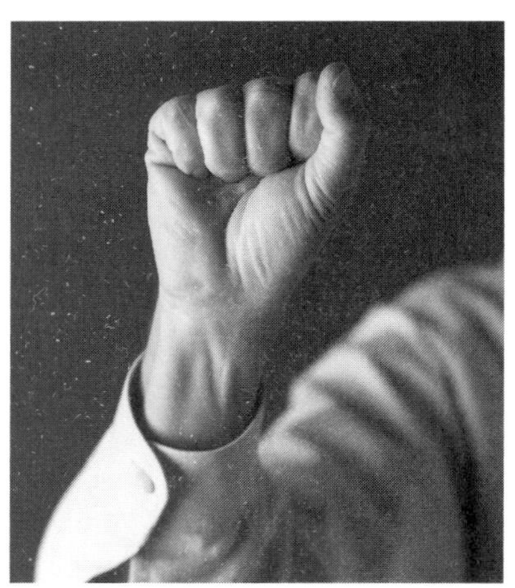

CHAPTER 6

Architect Of Change

Bernard W. Dan

Bernard W. Dan began his career in the financial industry in June 1983 after graduating from St. John's University in Collegetown, Minnesota, with a bachelor of science in accounting. His first job was with the National Futures Association and the law firm of Schultz and Chez, LLP. In 1985, he joined Cargill Investor Services, Inc. (CIS), serving in various operational positions. In 1986, he was assigned to the CIS division in London as an administrative manager responsible for all operational activities. In 1989, he was moved to the CIS New York regional office, where he served as an administrative manager and subsequently was named CIS assistant vice president in 1991. By June of 1991, he held the title of vice president.

Continuing his career with that company, Bernie Dan was named director of Cargill Investor Services (Singapore) Pty. Ltd. He served in that position until April 1997, when he returned to Chicago to become vice president, Global Head of Execution. In 1999, he was named president of Cargill Investor Services, Inc. and he was elected to a three-year term as a governor of the Board of Trade Clearing Corporation (BOTCC). He served as the BOTCC First Vice Chairman.

After serving as the president and CEO of Cargill Investor Services, a wholly owned subsidiary of Cargill, Inc., Mr. Dan joined the Chicago Board of Trade in July of 2001. He served as the CBOT Executive Vice President and was responsible for the CBOT's open auction and screen-based business units, as well as the exchange's product development and marketing initiatives. On November 5, 2002, he was appointed president and chief executive officer of the CBOT.

Under his direction, the CBOT went from a membership-based operation to a demutualized organization. He was at the helm for the creation of an initial public offering (IPO) on the New York Stock Exchange and was instrumental in the merger between the CBOT and the Chicago Mercantile Exchange, which resulted in the CME Group Inc., the world's largest and most diverse futures exchange.

Bernie is currently a board member for the National Futures Association and OneChicago. He is a member of the Board of Trustees for Fenwick High School and serves as a member of the Board of Regents for his alma mater, St. John's University.

He holds memberships at the Executives Club of Chicago, the Commercial Club of Chicago, and Operation Hope Incorporated, where he is on the regional board of directors.

Bernie's primary residence is in Glen Ellyn, Illinois, and he also has homes in Montana and Florida, where he is an avid golfer. He is married and has four children.

****

Can you tell me the first time that you ever heard about the Chicago Board of Trade?

The first time was probably in 1983, when I had my first job with the National Futures Association, which is a self-regulatory body in this industry. The CBOT, at the time and still today, was viewed as the leading exchange in the world.

What did you do before you came here?

Before I came to the Board of Trade, I was president and CEO of Cargill Investor Services, Inc., which was one of the largest global futures commission merchants within this industry. It had a very strong presence on the CBOT grain floor and a long history in the Board of Trade's financial complex, as well as about 50 other marketplaces around the world at the time. So I had great exposure to the global futures industry, as well as the CBOT.

What was your job with Cargill?

My job as president and CEO was to strategically position Cargill Investor Services as a leading futures commission merchant. It included customer contact, service, product capabilities, and things of that nature to grow our business. It included direct dialogue with the CBOT leadership at the time, and a direct involvement as a member of the Board of Trade representing Cargill.

What enticed you to come to the Chicago Board of Trade?

I was very involved in the CBOT as a member, participating on a host of committees. I was actually on the first restructuring committee; I served on technology committees; and I was actually asked to participate at the time for the CEO search. During all of my participation, I got a clear understanding of the strengths of the Board of Trade, its brand name, the diversity of its membership, and its successful track record over 150-plus years; and I became very intrigued about what a great global market model it was. Through that involvement, I got very excited about potentially, one day, becoming part of the Board of Trade. I wanted to be part of the effort to continue that long legacy of success.

What was your first position at the CBOT?

I joined the Board of Trade as an executive vice president, and I was responsible for the business development activities, electronic trading, as well as the open auction trading. I had a very unique job. It allowed me to directly interact with the members and with the customers, and to leverage some of my longtime experience in the futures industry to try to reposition the CBOT as a global market leader.

How has your job changed over the years?

It has changed dramatically. When I joined the Board of Trade, I viewed it as a corporate turnaround challenge. It was a time when membership values were probably at recent lows. There wasn't much strength within the balance sheet. There was a lot of tension between the membership and the management. And there was a lot of external pressure and competition. So it was that environment that enticed me to become part of the CBOT. It was my hope to try to restore the Chicago Board of Trade as the leading global marketplace in the world.

We had to rebuild our market structure; we had to reposition the CBOT as the leader in terms of supporting its global brand, as well as really adopt and embrace electronic trading, which was fueling significant growth not only in the industry, but at the Chicago Board of Trade as well.

So I'd say today, when I look back over my years at the CBOT, we really moved a very strong, membership-driven organization through a period of demutualization, and then we successfully had an IPO and created some liquidity for the longtime members who are now shareholders. I'm very proud of the fact I was a part of it, and frankly, without the support of the board of directors, as well as staff, it would have been very, very difficult. So it's been a true team effort.

When you came down to the Board of Trade, did you ever want to trade?

No, I was never much of a trader. My background is more in administration, accounting and operations finance. Because I got very close with the users, I understand how the markets operate. I worked and lived in London, New York, and Singapore, as well as Chicago, so my global work experience has contributed to some of my success. I always recognized that there are significant roles that you can play without being a trader, and that I could use those strong skills as a complement to those of the CBOT membership.

You said you came in at a time when there was a lull. How were you able, with your skills, to make that turnaround happen?

Well, I think there are three things I focused on. First, it was very important to have open and objective communication with the CBOT member leadership, as well as with the broader membership. Knowing this, I was able to effectively communicate with the members and they were comfortable expressing their thoughts to me. From that communication, I was able to assess how we could better position the Board of Trade.

Second, using some of my historic experience, we took a very detailed look at the CBOT market model as it existed in 2001, analyzing what were its strengths and weaknesses. We reviewed some of the growth trends within our industry, and we determined, through strong analysis and strategic review, how to best position our market model for future growth. The board of directors embraced that plan, and that's what we've been driving the past five or six years. We had a very detailed strategic plan.

Finally, I was very focused on how well we executed, and ensured that we hit milestones. Then we communicated successes internally, so that the staff gained support and excitement for the progress we were making. We communicated externally, so that our competitors and users around the world knew of the progress the CBOT was making. And frankly, they embraced our model very, very well.

I've been told by a number of people that you were able to accomplish the impossible, and they say that because you have personal skills that enabled you to bring people together from different factions. What do you say about that?

I'd say one of the advantages has been my Cargill experience: being able to live and work in different cultures and different countries. It created an opportunity for me to listen more and learn about other people and what drives them. I've been able to translate that to different constituents, whether it is employees or members or the board of directors. Equally important is that I'm not afraid to be wrong and I am open to learning new things.

Some might say I accomplished the impossible, but if I did so, it was with a very, very strong team at the Board of Trade, a very strong staff, and with really strong support from the board of directors. I'd say it was a combination of many things. I saw opportunities for the CBOT and was able to project what those opportunities were, and then employees, staff, and members embraced those opportunities.

What do you think is the hardest part of your job?

The hardest part of my job is dealing with the 3,000 members and all the great ideas they bring to us each day. It has been about figuring out how to sift through those ideas and how to respond to those members, because there's so much passion with being part of the Board of Trade. Everybody has very strong convictions about what's the best way to move the market model forward. So each day, over the past six years, I had to decide how to really channel some of those ideas into what became our successes, while also dealing with those that, while very strong, were really not part of our long-term model.

It's really the people who have made the Board of Trade strong. It's been the smart, dedicated, successful people in and around this marketplace who really valued the CBOT franchise for almost 160 years, and have wanted to see it last for at least another 160. And so dealing with and addressing those great emotions and passions have often been challenging, but it's been rewarding and fun at the same time.

You just mentioned the CBOT being around for 160 years; how does the CBOT's integrity play into its longevity?

Integrity is very important in our industry, and it's a hallmark of the CBOT. For 160 years, integrity has served as one of its value propositions and one of the most significant features of the Board of Trade. All the original members and all of those who have followed them have played a role in maintaining integrity.

What separates the Board of Trade from any other exchange in the world is that focus on integrity. It's the way we govern all of our technology decisions; it's the way we govern all of our oversight; it's the way we communicate internally to come up with great ideas and challenge each other. And it enters into every facet of our organization, and it will continue to allow the Board of Trade to separate itself from its peers.

How does self-regulation play a key role at the Board of Trade?

Self-regulation works in tandem with integrity and all the rules and regulations to create the confidence for market users to come to this marketplace each day. Every order that comes to the Board of Trade, regardless of whether it's open auction or electronic trading, deserves the privilege of market makers competing for that order in an open and transparent manner.

Users know when they have to make a trade or use our markets to hedge, and they can do so with confidence because of our rules and our regulations, our structure, and the integrity our people demonstrate each day. Our rules and regulations allow for strong regulation and oversight, which create integrity and confidence, which are tested each day as world or macroeconomic events bring people to the Board of Trade because they have the confidence in our market model. And that's something we work hard to maintain each day.

With that confidence, how do you see the role of the Chicago Board of Trade in today's economy?

Today, the CBOT plays a tremendous role in the global economy. Recently, we've been tested in many ways, whether it's the conflicts or questions about interest rate directions or anything to do with China. Each day the CBOT gets tested, and each day our staff and employees come to work expecting the unexpected, because that's how world events are played out in the marketplace. That's our job to ensure that we're well positioned to deal with peak times and volatile times. It's a significant role, a role that the Board of Trade, in any type of corporate structure in the future, will continue to play.

Where do you see the CBOT going in the worldwide markets?

I'd say that the financial services industry is converging quickly. We're seeing consolidation on an international level. We're seeing convergence in terms of products; we're seeing cash products, futures products, and over-the-counter (OTC) products all being traded on the same platform. The CBOT clearly recognizes those trends, and we've built systems and processes to capitalize on them. As we look forward, we're going to try to get deeper into the financial services industry, offering a broader product and service suite. We will capitalize on some of our strengths and focus more on global growth and participation.

Do you think that as the CBOT changes as an industry, you'll lose something in terms of service?

No. That has been one of the things I've been very clear about in communication with employees. I usually have quarterly meetings. In the early days, I had monthly meetings with all the employees; and I focused on the fact that even in a world of technology, the one key way we can differentiate ourselves is through our service levels. I've always stressed that we want to be the best in customer service. This is an area we can control ourselves, and really sets us apart from our competitors.

I don't think that theme will be lost; the employees really embrace it because they've seen the benefit of focusing on serving the end user. As technology becomes potentially very generic, and capability becomes almost the same, the CBOT has instilled in our workforce that the way we can differentiate ourselves from other marketplaces is by providing strong customer service.

I know you said you served on technology committees and you have some technology background. How did that help you?

The key was really focusing on how to create the best architecture that anticipated the growth trends we were seeing. My technology background allowed me to really focus on three things: Scale was very important, speed to market was very important, and strong project management was very important. Those three components have allowed the Board of Trade to take full advantage of its technology platform, to partner better with other technology companies, and to leverage the user base by creating greater capability and functionality to enhance trading opportunities.

We've been fortunate to recognize early trends and build our market model accordingly to take advantage of them. We have a document I'm very proud of, that not only assessed the market in the year 2001, but also predicted what the next three to five years would be like in this industry. It's that blueprint we've been working with as a management team to better position the Board of Trade. Most of the assumptions and projections that we made in 2001 have proved to be true.

Let me ask you, then, about your blueprint going forward.

The future for the next three to five years is all about product convergence, better use of technology, and global participation. All of those themes are going to drive better network management, better partnering around the world, and product innovation, which is a hallmark of the CBOT, as well as really understanding what customers and market users value about the marketplace and how we can help with their changing risk management needs. The emphasis is on understanding the customers and the users, so that we can create products and services that meet those needs. And that's something that, absent technology, we can do ourselves and we can do with the right number of resources that are well-educated, are well-positioned, and understand those goals.

Let's talk about your role as an architect of the planning and the executing of the IPO.

I think the IPO was one of the most exhilarating accomplishments for this institution. It was a long process in the context of demutualization, gaining the support from the members at the time, and then addressing on a global scale the broader value that the CBOT offered the investing public. That was a very interesting, educational process. It was demanding in terms of time.

The "road show" was really fun. We learned a lot about our colleagues who were a part of that show, and about the investor community. We had a great story to tell, which started back in 1848, and we built on it, talking about all the progress that this institution has made in almost 160 years. It was really important to show investors that the CBOT was here to stay and that it was built on a strong foundation and was positioned to be very, very successful in the future. The road show was fun, because we had so many strengths to build upon.

Was it harder to convince the CBOT members or the people outside of the Board of Trade that this was a good thing?

Initially, it was hard to convince the members, because the long history of the Board of Trade and its strength were about the diversity of the individual members and their contributions to the CBOT's success. One key change of an IPO is that you're introducing a different constituent. This initially created some concern among the membership, but as they saw how financial services were changed, they embraced it, and they overwhelmingly supported the vote to move it forward. Given our current performance in the equity markets today, I think they're very pleased.

What was it like to stand up there and ring the bell?

It was a great experience for me personally. I mean, it had been five-plus years of hard work, teaming with the board of directors and the staff to fully realize and fulfill all of our dreams. We were emotionally tired; we were physically exhausted; but it was still fun. It was great to make the first trade with Charlie Carey. Charlie and I have been joined at the hip, so to speak, for the past five years. We have been the driving force behind the Board of Trade's success. So it was rewarding to have Charlie and me ring that bell together.

Also, Charlie did a very amazing thing that day. He invited his Uncle Bernie Carey, a former chairman of the Board of Trade, to ring the bell, which was a way to recognize all the members who went before us and their contributions to the success of that IPO. That was a very important thing for the CBOT to recognize Bernie Carey, and he did a great job in representing all the members who went before him.

How did your job change once this happened?

Post the IPO, my job has been focused in a couple of different areas. One is dealing more with outside investors, with analysts, with the different demands that the constituencies might bring. I've had to explain not only our historical performance, but each quarter. Investors and analysts want to know how the Board of Trade will position ourselves for future growth, and how we're addressing some of the emerging trends. So I'd say I've gotten more externally focused. We have a very strong management team and staff, but historically their involvement has been more internal. I've been very comfortable to direct my attention in other areas, and can do it because of the confidence I have in the strong team backing me.

How about the innovations? How have they affected the CBOT?

The CBOT's history has been biased toward product innovation. But it's not only about new products; it's about maintaining some of the existing old products. When people think about corn or soybeans or wheat, our core products for many, many years, they don't realize that the product designs have changed significantly over the years to meet the economic needs of users. Clearly, the Board of Trade has a bias for product success; look at how much volume we do by product. It's a key driver. And so our economists on staff spend a lot of time and energy in trying to partner with firms that bring new product ideas to the CBOT.

One of the key challenges for the CBOT and every other marketplace in the world is to continue the innovation associated with product development and ensure that the products that we put forward, whether new or existing, meet the economic needs of the natural buyers and sellers. That's an ongoing challenge that the CBOT will have to continue to focus on. Given the long history of innovation in this area, I'm very confident that the CBOT will continue in that rich tradition.

Can you share with us any new products on the horizon?

I can't share new product ideas. All I will say is the CBOT clearly understands the emerging trends within the broader global commodity world and where the production shifts are changing. We have to track these trends, and we have to then interpret them in terms of what they mean to our product, and how we can better position the CBOT product mix to take advantage of that.

There are a couple of examples where we've been a little bit early with products, but we think, in the long term, they are going to be successful. One is in our South American bean effort, which specifically recognizes Brazil's production of soybeans. And the second is ethanol, capitalizing on the emerging trend within the United States to use ethanol and other alternative fuels as a means for energy. Those directly impact the CBOT marketplace, and we've introduced products to try to reflect those growing trends.

Tell me about the benefits of the global derivatives market and how that provides good things for the shareholders.

The global derivatives market means one thing: more participants around the world. The benefit to investors is the more people we can connect to our network, the more people we can have actively trading CBOT products globally. This will drive greater volume and will translate into greater earnings and revenue growth for the CBOT investors.

Can you tell me about the farmers, the fund managers, and others around the world who rely on the CBOT markets?

Market users, whether they're a farmer, hedge fund, managed futures fund, or bank, are going to benefit from the centralized liquidity that the CBOT offers the marketplace. The centralized liquidity is a diverse group of risk takers. Diversity is one of the key things at the CBOT, particularly for a liquid pool of capital. That helps us smooth out what I would call kind of macro-disruptions in the marketplace, where people come to the CBOT for the integrity. They can do so because we have a diverse pool of liquidity.

And so users, farmers, banks, hedge funds, and managed futures funds benefit from that centralized pool of liquidity as well as the diversity, because we don't want any sort of concentration in any one group. That doesn't make a strong market. We want strong participation from a multitude of groups and/or people, so users benefit. In turn, they benefit because the spreads and the markets and the prices that they get are the tightest and the deepest in the world.

Do you think the CBOT has a global impact on the markets?

Yes. The CBOT brand is strong all over the world. Asian farmers, farmers in South America and elsewhere in the southern hemisphere, they all look at CBOT pricing, and they use it as a benchmark to bring their local crops to their central market to get a price to sell them. There are stories about this all over the press. For example, the *New York Times* had a great article about a farmer in India. Each day he goes to the CBOT web site to get the closing price for soybeans, and that's the pricing information that he and his family will use when they bring their crops to the central market in this little village. And that's the impact of technology, the globalization of our industry, and, frankly, the importance of the CBOT marketplace worldwide.

In the future, are there any Chicago Board of Trade traditions that will be preserved?

The CBOT has at least three traditions that I think will be preserved in the future. One is the focus on product innovation. The CBOT has been a leader in this area since its beginning in 1848 and will continue. Another is the value of transparency that users of any profile—farmers, banks, hedge funds, managed futures funds, commercial bank users—will get as a result of the benefit of market makers competing for their orders. Those users know they'll get the best price at the time they enter the market, and transparency is key. Then third, the service levels of the Board of Trade, across all of our products, will be maintained in the future, because that's what other marketplaces around the world have used as their benchmark, because all other exchanges in the world are, in a way, derivatives of the CBOT market model.

When you look back on your personal tenure with the Board of Trade, can you give me some high points?

When we made the decision in 2002 that the CBOT wanted to have an autonomous market model and that we were going to compete in a very aggressive manner with the rest of the world, that required us to make significant decisions with respect to our longtime clearing partner, it required us to make decisions with the new electronic trading platform, and it required us to revise a host of rules. But that fundamental decision, to be a global market participant in a consolidating financial services industry, was the high point. That decision created a lot of work, a lot of energy, and a lot of pressure, but that fundamental decision was the high point.

I'd say the second high point was the IPO. I mean, that is something that, from a personal perspective, was a great accomplishment. It was a thrill to be in the New York Stock Exchange ringing the bell and participating in the first trade. It was the culmination of a five-year period of a lot of hard work and effort.

You've said you don't keep your eyes glued to the stock price, but considering the interview you are giving today may be read 25 to 50 years from now, could you give us a recap of the stock from its open to where it closed yesterday?

Let me give you just a profile from when I joined the Board of Trade in 2001 and how the Board of Trade was valued at that time versus how it's valued today. When I joined the Board of Trade, the full membership of the Board of Trade had a value of $240,000. And that was in a membership organization where there were three key components of a full seat bundled together: the members' equity, the CBOT trading right, as well as the exercise right associated with the CBOE.

So if we fast-forward to the IPO, at that time we had demutualized, and the share component of that full member seat alone had a value of 27,338 shares times $54. And that was our IPO offering price. Our first trade occurred at $80.75, which I made, along with Charlie. And yesterday, which was April 3, 2007, we closed at $186.56. You can see the dramatic value creation associated with just one component of that full membership, which is 27,338 times $186.56. And so that total package is probably worth, from the share value, over $5 million. That does not count the CBOT trading right, and off the top of my head I think that has a value of about $400,000 today, if not more. And clearly there is a market value for the CBOE exercise right, which right now, I think, has a market range of about $150,000.

So I'd say that the CBOT member, if we date back to 2001 when I started, has reaped the benefit of a lot of hard work and a lot of really good strategic positioning of this market model, and it's been reflected in the way outside investors and other interested parties have valued the now three components of that historic membership value.

That's quite impressive. Let's talk about the third thing that you accomplished.

The third thing that I think was an accomplishment for me personally, as it was one of the goals I had when I joined the Board of Trade, was to restore the CBOT as a globally successful franchise. I contributed to that, as did all other CBOT employees and the board of directors, and I'm proud of the role I played in that.

Can you discuss any low points?

I didn't often view things as experiencing a low point. I would focus more on the greater challenges. You know, my time at the Board of Trade has been exhilarating, fun, and challenging. I suppose one could say we had low points, but whenever these setbacks came, we tried to find a positive resolution or to just learn something from the experience. Sometimes we just went back and evaluated why the idea wasn't accepted, and we analyzed the way we thought about it, the way we presented it, and what we could learn. I am goal-orientated, so I just viewed these instances as a challenge. I didn't view them as a low point. And I'd say that that's kind of point one.

Point two is that going into our challenge with Eurex, we had a lot of concerns about whether all the decisions and market positioning ideas we implemented were going to be successful. We were highly confident, but we didn't know. And so I'd say there was probably a little bit of a low point related to uncertainty, because we felt we did everything we could do but we just wouldn't know unless the market embraced it.

So I wouldn't call it a low point; I'd call it a point of uncertainty that involved devoting a couple of years of hard work to position the model and just wondering whether it was going to be successful. We knew we did the right things, but the judge was not us; the judge was the market participants.

Being goal-oriented, tell me how those goals fed into the idea of merger development.

When the board of directors and I, as a representative of the management team, looked at the long-term prospects of the Board of Trade, we evaluated lots of options about the strategic future of the Board of Trade. We looked at the financial services industry, global consolidation, trends in the marketplace, the New York Stock Exchange and Euronext merger, as well as other exchanges going public. From these discussions we evaluated our ability to stand alone and compete. We weighed the benefits of partnering with another exchange.

Those were the ongoing strategic assessments that we did. It was the same process we used before we decided to do the IPO, after we did the IPO, and leading up to the proposed merger announcement with the CME. We felt that the long-term future of the Board of Trade and its shareholders was better placed with the CME. That was the decision the board of directors reached in the early part of October of 2006, and it is the one that to date we still believe in.

When we look at the future, it's about global participation and whether or not we have sufficient operational, financial, and tactical resources to compete on a global scale, across a diverse product suite of cash, futures, and OTC products. And it's that sort of trend line that we've been monitoring to determine the long-term future of the CBOT.

In terms of future competition, do you think it'll be more from the over-the-counter (OTC) segment or from other exchanges?

Future competition will come from two areas: One is in the over-the-counter world, across all product categories, whether it's our U.S. Treasury and agricultural complexes, our emerging alternative fuel complex, or our equity index complex. The OTC products are competitors today; they'll be greater competitors in the future.

We're also going to see, because of technology and new exchanges emerging in parts of the world like India and China, new competitors in our own asset class. That's why it's very important to have a global business where people can easily access your product. So those are our historic competitors, and will continue to be very aggressive competitors in the future.

Can you make a prediction about where you see the Board of Trade five years from now?

In five years, I think the CBOT products will continue to be benchmark products around the world. The agricultural sector will continue to develop and mature even more than most people realize, because of globalization of the agricultural sector and the impact of energy. I think that the CBOT products and the brand associated with CBOT products will live forever.

What do you think the Chicago Board of Trade has done for the city of Chicago and vice versa?

The CBOT, along with the other marketplaces in Chicago, like the Chicago Stock Exchange, Chicago Board Options Exchange, and CME, has contributed a significant number of jobs in the banking industry and many other sectors all across the city of Chicago. Because of all these exchanges, with the CBOT having played a big part, Chicago is the Derivatives Capital of the World. No other city in the world can claim that title.

The concentration of professionals in this industry in Chicago has been the principal reason driving innovation and success in our city. It is very important to maintain this distinction in the future. It's a huge advantage when we are competing with New York, the Equity Capital of the World, and San Francisco, the Venture Capital of the World. To have Chicago be one of the leading cities in America, with the tag name of the Derivatives Capital of the World, is a form of recognition that no other city can claim. There is no doubt that the CBOT has played a significant part in creating that success.

You have talked about the legacy of the Board of Trade. What do you think your personal legacy will be to this institution?

I hope that when people look back on this time period when I was the CEO and president of the Board of Trade, I would like them to recognize me for my hard work, for being focused on goals, and for having demonstrated a track record of success.

CHAPTER 7

Straight Talk

Burt Gutterman

Burt Gutterman graduated from the University of Wisconsin–Madison in 1970 and began his career at the Chicago Board of Trade. In 1971, he purchased a full membership at the CBOT and started developing floor and back-office skills while employed by Rosenthal & Company. He became a limited partner at Rosenthal in 1972, assisting in administration and floor execution. He began proprietary trading at Rosenthal and continued such trading throughout his career. In 1974, Mr. Gutterman along with Barry Goodman and Ron Manaster, started Goodman Manaster & Company.

Mr. Gutterman was elected to the board of directors of the CBOT in 1986. He served for six years on a variety of committees. Burt was a cosponsor of Project A, the CBOT's electronic trading system, and played a significant role in the exchange's $185 million trading addition. In 1995, he was elected as Governor to the Board of Trade Clearing Corporation, the clearing entity of the CBOT, a position he held until March 1997. He joined Sangamon Trading Inc., a commodity trading adviser, in April 1997 as chief executive officer, and co-founded Endurance Asset Management, a fund of funds manager, in October 2003.

Mr. Gutterman is married and has three daughters.

****

Before we start our interview, you've brought in a passage from a book that you'd like to read.

I've been thinking about this interview and how to capture some of the color, the flavor of the Board of Trade. It's something that is difficult to describe. Perhaps it's best stated by Frank Norris, who wrote a novel in 1903 called *The Pit*. I dug up a copy of the book and went through it. It is a love story that really doesn't pertain to the Board of Trade, but to augment the love story, Mr. Norris put in the economics of grain trading at the turn of the century. I think it really captures the color and flavor of our trading floor. I would like to share just one little paragraph.

> "Then suddenly, cutting squarely athwart the vague crescendo of the floor came the single incisive stroke of the great gong. Instantly a tumult was unchained. Arms were flung upward in strenuous gestures and from above the crowding heads in the wheat pit, a multitude of hands, eager, the fingers extended, leaped into the air. All articulate expression was lost in the single explosion of sound as the traders surged downwards to the center of the pit, grabbing each other, struggling towards each other, tramping, stamping, charging through with might and main. Promptly the hand of the great dial above the clock stirred and trembled and as though driven by a tempest breath of the pit, moved upward through the degrees of its circle. It paused, wavered, stopped at length and on the instant, the hundreds of telegraph keys scattered throughout the building began clicking off the news to the whole country from the Atlantic to the Pacific, from Mackinac to Mexico, that the Chicago market had made a slight advance in the May wheat which had closed the day before at 93⅜, had opened that morning at 94½."

How does that affect you?

It brings forth the emotion that I felt as a trader on the floor and captures the explosion of sound and the excitement and aggression that occurred in that split second when a market opened.

Do you remember your first day on the floor?

Yes—absolutely! I remember coming down here with my father, and we had a close friend here whose name was Hank Bartelstein. I had wanted to become a member and was showing my father the trading floor with Hank as our guide. And I remember as we left the floor my father said, "Are you sure you really look at this as a career? I've been here 10 minutes and I have a terrible headache." But I really enjoyed the experience and was confident it was the job for me. That was a day that I'll always remember, because even though my father was in the automobile business, he, too, was involved in the auction market, in buying and selling cars. But it was in no way preparation for what occurred on the trading floor.

Why did you want to be part of the industry?

It's interesting. I really didn't know a lot about the Board of Trade prior to becoming a runner. I had originally wanted a summer job from college being a runner at the Midwest Stock Exchange, because I think everyone has some familiarity with equities. They're names that you handle on a day-to-day basis. But unless you're in the agricultural community, you're really not familiar with how the staples end up on your table, whether it be a meat or a grain.

I remember searching around and attempting to find a way of getting on the stock exchange floor, but I couldn't. The best I could come up with was the Chicago Board of Trade. So I became a runner for Hayden Stone for two summers. And I certainly earned my spurs being on the tail end of the abuse from the brokers. You had to watch out if you gave them the wrong order or if you weren't polite or shoved it in their face the wrong way. So it was an interesting time and kindled my interest in trading agricultural commodities.

How did your dad feel about that business?

Well, he was surprisingly supportive. I guess anything to get me out of the house! I was actually thinking about the Board of Trade and going to law school. And I went to DePaul Law School at night for about a month. I quickly realized that I couldn't do both. I made my decision and stayed with the Board of Trade.

How did you buy your membership?

I got a loan from my father that I repaid, and it was all of $32,500. It was one of my better trades.

Tell me about some of the CBOT legends that you heard about or knew.

They were more contemporary than some of the huge legends that were known with their names on doors, because their days had passed and they were off the floor. Whether it be Julius Frankel, who might be sitting on the side of the pit, or Dan Rice, the occasional legends that I saw were Eddie Wilson and Red Rose.

There's a good story about Red Rose. He came into the beans in the early 1970s, during a big bean market. There were a lot of what were classified as "young Turks", people who had purchased their memberships within the past five years as the grain market started exploding and really had a feeling they understood the market completely, yet their experience was rather limited. Red had had a great deal of experience and suffered through both the ups and downs of a variety of different markets. He came in as a savvy veteran, and a local started bidding up the market.

Red came into the soybean pit, and it was the lead month and I remember him, all of a sudden, saying "sold" to this local who was bidding for a large quantity. Well, then began this ritual of one person bidding and then the other person saying "sold." And the quantities kept growing.

Finally, Red came over and I happened to be standing near the local who was bidding up the market. And Red said, "Son, I have five more to sell than you want to buy. So what is your number?" And it was just like silence. You know, it was like your mouth drops open because it's the ultimate challenge to say, "Okay, let's just call your bet and you can raise however much you want to raise, but I have five more than you want to do." It just demonstrated to me some of the history of the exchange and the savvy veterans who were on the trading floor.

How about Hank Shatkin?

Hank was just a fantastic trader. He was fast. He was intuitive. He could smell blood in the water better than anybody. You really didn't know what he was doing. He was quick when he executed his trades. He was accurate and was extremely well liked. He was a legend because of his ability as a spreader, which was something that I tried to emulate, but I would always fall far short.

Who was one of your mentors?

I guess Les Rosenthal was probably the best mentor, but it was probably in a way that you wouldn't expect. When I came to the CBOT in the early 1970s, you had to have a membership to answer the telephone. You couldn't even pick up the phone without being a member. It's kind of the whole evolution of the exchange of opening up to the outside, and they were very protective of the marketplace. They wanted to make sure that it remained relatively closed and structured. So all phones had to be answered by members, which was naturally a governor on growth.

I went to Rosenthal & Company, because I did not have any of the background of a trader and I didn't want to go right into the pit. I wanted to develop some skills other than trading. I went for the interview with Les, and I remember sitting down and the first thing he said to me was, "I want to tell you two things. First, don't expect me to give you any brokerage, and second, don't expect me to teach you how to trade, because you're going to have to learn on your own."

Now, that was very wise advice. As you look at my career and the careers of many others who succeeded and failed, anybody who tried to trade differently than what their personality was, their core, who tried to be something other than what they were, they became out of place and vulnerable to failure. The people who remained within their discipline, who remained within what they understood as their limits, within their propensity to take risk, they were the ones who succeeded.

Did you learn that by observing the behavior of members on the floor?

You observe people, and I guess perhaps you decide what you like and what you don't like. There were certain people you observed, whether it be Hank Shatkin or Barry Goodman, who was a very gifted scalper in the corn pit, or Bobby Goldberg, who was a wonderfully talented broker in the corn pit. There was Don Herr, a great spreader, and Jordy Glassman, who was a great spread broker. By watching those greats, you picked up the values, the trading styles, and the execution styles of all these people.

Then you would ask yourself, "How do I refine my ability? How do I take advantage of what the market opportunity is? How do I maintain myself as an honorable person within the society that exists on the trading floor?" All of those were anecdotal examples that would occur on a day-to-day basis rather than somebody mentoring you and putting their arm around you and counseling you on how to do something.

You talk about honor on the floor. How about the word 'integrity'?

Integrity existed on the floor because of the high intensity of trading. Unless you had an honorable marketplace where people could be trusted at their word, you'd have huge amounts of discrepancies and losses, and the market wouldn't be able to function. So people automatically expected that whatever you did, you stood by your honor and you stood by your trade. If you were confused as to what occurred, then you went to a third party who might have remembered better than you did. Then you would respect their judgment and, regardless of the financial consequences, you'd make the decision of settling the discrepancy and moving on.

How did you settle up at the end of the day?

I was a runner in 1968 and 1969. I was a witness to the first technological innovation on the trading floor, which was replacing the Teletype and chalkboard pit reporters with the electronic boards that recorded the prices. I didn't witness the reconciliation of trades that used to occur in the lobby of the Board of Trade. That was another innovation that occurred at the Board of Trade Clearing Corporation (BOTCC) in the 1960s. I think that happened with the introduction of mainframe computers matching the trades as opposed to yelling and screaming in the lobby to reconcile differences.

At the end of a day when I was trading in the 1971 era, you simply turned in your cards. They were keypunched on IBM 80-column keypunch cards and then turned in on a batch basis to the BOTCC. Then they were read, because they all had little punches in them and then they were processed that way. There were two reconciliations, one in the afternoon and then one the following morning. And by the time it came to the following morning, over 99.9 percent of the trades were consummated.

How about the role of tradition down at the Board of Trade? What would it mean?

Tradition could be viewed two ways. One, it was important in terms of values, like honoring a transaction and making sure that you followed the rules. But tradition also could be a legacy of what could be called provincial, which is not being willing to experiment with new ways of transacting business. You had to balance the tradition with the innovation. The exchange was a melting pot of ideas and of traditions. Through dialogue and through entrepreneurial spirit, a lot of those ideas were able to blossom.

How about the idea that there was a fixed membership?

Well, a fixed membership was 1,402 full seats. You could say the first innovation had to do with expanding the trading floor to allow for there to be phone clerks without holding memberships. That freed up those badges for members who wanted to trade. It allowed us to utilize all 1,402 seats to be brokers or to be locals in the pits. That put a whole new category of people on the floor that were phone clerks. They had rules that they had to follow in terms of registration and of conflict of interest and so forth. That was the first attempt to address the boom that was occurring in commodities by adding more memberships to the trading population, but it was insufficient.

The next step was Les Rosenthal and his idea when he was chairman to create a variety of categories to trade the new instruments that were created under his stewardship. Those were the financial products, first with Ginnie Maes and then with Treasury bonds. As the volume grew in those products, people realized that we needed new traders to trade them. And that's where the innovation came for a variety of classes of membership.

Now there was a lot of conflict, because there were people who believed in tradition and they didn't want to expand the membership base, because potentially it was diluting the value of their seats. Fortunately, the majority ruled and Les's vision was put into practice. It allowed for the dramatic growth in financial instruments that far overshadowed the grain volume in the 1980s.

With all these new products and innovations, an important aspect of the business is the rule of self-regulation. How does that apply?

In terms of a judicial process, whether it be a minor infraction on the trading floor or a major infraction involving a position limit or a financial discrepancy of a clearing member, you want to be judged by your peers. They understand the rules. They understand the common practice. So there's a balance there where you have to enforce the rules, but you also have to understand custom and usage.

Having a regulator that's never been in the trading floor and that's never suffered the heat of battle, well, it really is not the best solution. Self-regulation allowed for flexibility in modification of our rules to adapt to changing environments. And throughout the 1980s and 1990s as the markets changed, if we had just had a regulator that was viewing the rules in a rather inflexible posture, we wouldn't have grown as dramatically as we did grow; but we had a board of directors and judicial system that took into consideration changing practices.

Tell me what you did in terms of committee work to support this self-regulation?

I served on the Business Conduct Committee prior to being on the board of directors. We faced a variety of challenges in terms of both pit conduct and firm conduct. Then those issues were sometimes brought up to the Board level, where you would have to consider rule changes. If we'd had to go to Washington for all these rule changes instead of just to the Board level, we would have found that we would have continually been behind in terms of keeping up with a changing, dynamic market.

The Chicago Board of Trade has been said to be a worldwide price discovery mechanism. Would you say that's an apt description?

It absolutely is. I think that we pride ourselves on the transparency of the marketplace. It doesn't matter whether it occurs in the pit or on the screen. We have a price discovery mechanism that allows for multiple participants to be involved and to allow for a price to be determined by as many people as possible.

What that does is it provides the best price to the end user. It also allows for a timely price reporting worldwide. And it also provides for complete transparency, so that everyone can see what the marketplace is doing. Right now we're coming to grips with that as a business model. It is between those people who believe in an auction market, whether it be electronic or in the pit, and those people who believe in an off-exchange derivative market where you don't have the same attributes that you have in an auction market.

How do those two compete?

Some of our competitors are, in fact, users of our market. The challenges that the exchange faces are basically to make sure that our end users direct their orders to a transparent marketplace for price discovery, as opposed to taking and internalizing an order flow and allowing for a price discovery mechanism that's fragmented. That might serve to widen the margins and the profitability for those firms, but in the end it does a disservice to the end user and the liquidity of the market.

The word 'service' is a very important word in your industry. Can you tell me how it works today and how it might work in the markets of tomorrow?

It is incumbent upon the exchange to provide for innovation, and that's really the key to service. It is our job to make sure that the market is transparent and that rules are enforced. This will help guarantee that all users are treated fairly. It has been a challenge since the inception of the exchange in the mid-nineteenth century.

I'm reading a book called *Nature's Metropolis* by William Cronon (W.W. Norton, 1992) that covers the period when the Board of Trade began in 1848, but it was not the CBOT as we know it now. It was really an organization where it was trading on the cash market, which was on the docks of the Chicago River. The grain came from a variety of locations either by barge or by ship to Chicago. Our founding fathers introduced standardization, which enabled the innovation of grain elevators and also enabled grain shipments to grow in size. Originally, they were in these sacks that made it very difficult to move grain.

All of a sudden with the advent of standardization of grain grading and elevators, you had an explosion in the grain trade in Chicago. Eventually, it became known as "Change," where they started trading without the actual receipts of the grain. It became the beginning of the futures contracts. I think that began in the 1860s, maybe 1870s. That really was the beginning of the Board of Trade as we know it today.

How did that guarantee service?

Service has always been a byword of the Board of Trade in developing ways of meeting the need for farmers and commercials to gather and exchange their goods.

Do you think that agricultural products are going to be booming, or do you think that they're being phased out because of other markets?

I think we're entering a new era here where agricultural commodities are viewed not only as a feed grain and a food for human consumption, but also for a source of energy. I'm sure that was never envisioned, but here we are today with ethanol. I'm sure there will be some other biofuels that will be coming down the pipeline. Grains are going to be nature's bounty that blesses this country. Hopefully, through a transparent marketplace, we'll be able to accommodate the needs of our consumers not only in terms of food, but also in terms of energy.

You've been really invested in innovation at the Chicago Board of Trade. Sometimes that involved butting heads with other members to get them to see the wisdom of the changes. Please take us from the chalkboard and the Teletype and move us down through Aurora and Project A.

I was elected to the Board the first time by, I think, two votes. There were five candidates elected and I was the fifth candidate who made it.

Bobby Goldberg was chairman, and he nicknamed me "Landslide." So, I was always viewed as somebody who was willing to be outspoken and willing to take the bull by the horns. As a consequence, I was appointed to a committee that had to do with electronic order routing. Really, that was probably the first step that the exchange took in terms of introducing technology that would eventually lead to its use in the pit.

As we worked on the order routing system, it became obvious that a printer couldn't print an order in the pit. We were looking for ways to increase exchange productivity, and a printer just became a device that was too cumbersome to use in the very hectic and challenging environment as a trading pit. I was meeting with Delores Paneck, who was part of the technology group at the Board of Trade, and I said, "I think we can take a broker's deck and replicate it on a laptop computer." To do this, I took what I had learned during my first year on the floor as a broker and translated it into the functionality that would work on a screen.

From there we were able to have the first innovation that allowed for electronic order delivery. It took some time to get it to where members would accept it. In fact, it was probably pretty well close to eight or nine years and a number of iterations before people thought it useful. To this day, it was a great first step. It certainly was a productivity gain. But it opened people's eyes as to allowing them to understand how technology could further the growth of volume on the exchange floor.

Today the pits are highly electronic and the broker workstations are in every pit, but it's very difficult to say they equate to the productivity that occurs on a screen. It was useful then and it's useful today on the trading floor, but it wasn't the end result of technological innovation.

As far as electronic trading was concerned, that really came out of the Chicago Mercantile Exchange's development of PMT, which stood for "Post Market Trade", and the CME's joint venture with Reuters. It eventually became Globex, and I'm sure Leo Melamed had no small role in coming up with that name. Today it's a household name, like Kleenex or some other household good you rely on every day and use for business, whether it be for blowing your nose or determining a price. Our response was to come up with an electronic trading system, and it was called Aurora. It got its name from the goddess of the dawn in Roman mythology. We felt it symbolized the dawning of a new era.

Tell me about that.

Aurora was a five-member committee, and our job was to try to replicate electronically what occurred in the pit. And our chairman,

Jack Kinsella, and the committee members took that assignment very seriously. Globex was a pure alphanumeric trading system. It was basically a screen with line-by-line bids and offers of all the products that the CME listed. We attempted to replicate the membership privileges that occurred on the trading floor and put them on a screen. We had virtual pits where members could enter, and they couldn't be in more than one pit at a time. It became a very big challenge to incorporate the technology requirements of such a venture.

In those days it was on an Apple computer and it was very graphic intensive. The system required a lot of communications bandwidth to transmit all this information on a global basis. The technology wasn't there at the time. The thickest telephone line that you had for computers was what was called 19.2, which is a third of what it is today on dial-up. Imagine how everyone is impatient with dialing into a computer today on a modem, and take one-third of that and attempt to put that on a trading system. I guess no matter how you try to slice it and dice it, you wouldn't be able to have split-second response time that would work on a global basis.

The idea, while it had merit, would work only on what was called a local area network. That meant it could be used only within the city of Chicago, within the downtown area where you could have high bandwidth. That did not meet our business requirements, so we ended up migrating and joining together with the CME on Globex.

As Globex evolved with the CME, we had to meld our different business practices. It was something we were able to do, but then all of a sudden we came into the same technological problem that Aurora faced. Our technology provider was questionable as to whether they, Reuters, were going to deliver their product on time.

As a consequence of that, I went to the chairman of the Board of Trade, Billy O'Connor, who was another big innovator at this exchange. I mean the legacy that he left this exchange with his brother Eddie is amazing. He and Eddie were the creators of the CBOE. Billy had an incredible trading ability. Together with Eddie, they founded O'Connor Partnership, which was eventually a highly computerized and innovative trading firm that was bought out by Swiss Bank, which is now UBS, Union Bank of Switzerland. The O'Connor brothers led all the dramatic innovation on a firm level that is in effect to this day.

So I went to Billy and said, "Look, we need to create an electronic system as a hedge against Reuters not delivering, and I can do this in less than a year." He asked for a budget, and I developed a budget of $2 million. We delivered it on time and on budget. But now this was a local area network system. I worked with one technology person and then a small committee, as we went from concept to actually programming it and putting it into effect. It was launched with the first instruments being barge freight. I remember Billy trading the first contract on the system.

Pretty quickly, we had to refine the system. We reached a point where the CME and the Board of Trade split. The CME stayed on Globex, and the Board of Trade was forced to go its own way. We were not only able to utilize Project A as a trading system that was on a local area network, but we were able to expand it to a wide area network that was really state-of-the-art.

Tell me the story behind Project A.

Project A is an interesting story. We came up with Project A basically using the Aurora model. I was on the Executive Committee at the time, and Billy was not a man to mince words. There were several Executive Committee members and staff members who had gotten together a list of names to call the system. Our in-house counsel was at the meeting as well. We were expecting to have a protracted meeting to come up with a name. Choosing the name for the system was the first item on the agenda.

Billy said, "Well, let's see. Let's take the first letter in the alphabet, Project A. That's the system. All right, what's next?" So what was expected to be probably several hours of discussion ended up being done in 15 seconds, and the name stuck and it worked. And the system worked and I'm proud that I was able to contribute to it. It pointed the way for further advances in electronic trading at the exchange.

What happened next?

We reached a point with Project A where we were able to successfully combat Cantor Fitzgerald's attempt to challenge our marketplace and financial instruments. We did this by trading our instruments on a screen. Project A proved successful in meeting that challenge.

Now the question came: What do we do? We own a system. Do we make that system more robust and end up being in the technology business? Or do we outsource? That really was the decision that the Board faced, and the alternative at the time was Eurex. Eurex was an innovation created by Andersen Consulting, which became known as Accenture, which had been sold to the Swiss Exchange, which in turn was sold to the German exchange and became known as DTB and then eventually Eurex.

Eurex, at the time we were making our decision, had just successfully taken the German bund, a 10-year German government debt instrument, back from London, where it was traded in a pit. All of a sudden you had the first challenge to open outcry. It occurred in Europe with an electronic exchange taking the market from an open outcry exchange.

At that time, the London International Financial Futures Exchange (Liffe) took its system, which was called APT, and developed it into a more robust system that became known as Liffe Connect. It became the state of the art at the time, far superior to the functionality and usability of Eurex. Liffe had already lost the bund to Germany, to Eurex. They were able to resurrect their exchange on a variety of instruments. They became the success they are today because they developed their own system and were able to respond quickly to the needs of their members.

The Board of Trade, in contrast, chose to outsource, and we went with Eurex. And although we viewed them as a partner, they had another view of the Board of Trade as potentially somebody they could utilize and exercise hegemony over. It became clear that the functionality that they wanted for their markets, which was necessary, was not the same functionality we needed for our markets. Eventually, it reached a point where we had to decide whether to stay with Eurex and its platform or to go somewhere else. The decision was made to license with Liffe Connect, and it was a wise decision to make.

But didn't the CBOT have the ability to be a clearing provider?

The CBOT outsourced the clearing of trades to the Board of Trade Clearing Corporation. Had we become a clearing provider, we would have found ourselves with a valuation today far in excess of what the market is valuing us.

When I hear my fellow members complaining about the market value of our shares, all I can think about is the decisions we made as members voting for joining Eurex as opposed to developing our own platform. Also, we voted against Common Clearing, which would have provided us with one-third ownership with the CME in a Common Clearing entity in Chicago. The impact to our valuation would have been dramatic. It would have translated into billions of dollars.

Were those things suggested to the membership?

Oh, absolutely. There was a healthy debate. But the membership rejected the idea. Maybe it was because of tradition, or the fear of the unknown. You talk about expanding into areas you don't know, like clearing, because the CBOT had its trades cleared by the BOTCC, which was a separate entity from the exchange. The origins of the Board of Trade and the BOTCC were kind of out of the same embryo. They were on the same city block and there was a common ownership and leadership in the two entities.

As our markets became more global, though, the participants of the two boards of directors became different. And all of a sudden, the priorities of those boards started diverging. In the past, people might have viewed what was good for the Board of Trade as being what was good for the BOTCC, but that no longer held true. The BOTCC served a valid purpose for the Chicago Board of Trade in guaranteeing its trades, but that purpose was better served, I believed, by the Board of Trade controlling the clearing process.

It became a very heady and divisive debate, and in the end, the membership voted to continue with the Board of Trade Clearing Corporation and turned down Common Clearing. So for those members who may question why we're valued at what we're valued, they need only look in the mirror. They should think back on their votes to realize that, at a minimum, the Board of Trade would have been worth several billion dollars more than it is today if we had become a clearing provider.

Why do you think people have such a hard time with change?

Well, you know, change is just different. Sometimes it's an inch at a time and sometimes it's by leaps and bounds. Change can occur in a variety of different ways. It can occur because of rule changes: rule changes at the exchange level in terms of financial requirements, rule changes in terms of how business is conducted, or rule changes in terms of accommodating how business occurs in the pit. The origins of electronic order routing, the origins of having a telephone (headsets) in the pit, and the origins of having flashing—all these changes had the members thinking, "Wait. How is this going to affect me? I don't understand it. What I don't understand might affect me adversely, and therefore I'm going to be opposed."

I think that it's incumbent upon the leadership to lead the way. They need to describe the pluses and minuses of every change. I can remember Billy O'Connor doing that very clearly when we realized that Aurora was not going to be a viable alternative as an electronic trading platform and we agreed to join together with the CME on Globex. One of Reuters' demands was that they wanted in the contract that we would, if the time came, list grains during the daytime on Globex.

I remember Billy O'Connor conducting floor meetings. Rather than hide the issue in the fine print at the bottom, he just addressed it head-on, and told the members the bad news right up front. He said, "While our Board believes in open outcry and we would be opposed to listing grains electronically, we want you to know that the potential exists and it's in the contract."

Sometimes it takes those kinds of leaders, whether it's a Billy O'Connor or a Les Rosenthal, to lay it on the line, to show the pluses and minuses and provide the leadership for the direction of the exchange.

You were certainly one of the leaders to encourage change. Let's talk about the new trading floor and how it came about.

I was on the committee and I was on the board of directors. I felt strongly about the inadequacy of the existing 1930s grain room. As I look back on it, clearly what dominated were the inefficiencies of allowing our volume to grow and the need to address the backlog of people and firms that wanted to participate in our financial products. What was more important, and what's perhaps overlooked in this decision, was the life safety issue of our old trading floor.

The financial instruments were traded in the old grain room that was built in the 1930s. I can remember the running of new telephone lines to a booth. It required our technology department to put on helmets with little headlights like coal miners would use and go down underneath the wood floors and crawl around to try to run a telephone line. I can remember incidents occurring when we were renovating a trading pit and trying to add additional booths.

For example, we closed the visitors' gallery to add more booths to provide access for our firms. During this renovation, I remember meeting with a man from Illinois Bell with the head of the Technology Committee, the head of the Communications Committee, and our electricians. We were looking at this huge bundle of telephone wires and we were assured by Illinois Bell that these wires were all dead and they could be cut and we would be able to reroute these wires. Then we could reutilize some of them for new service to these booths. We waited until the market closed and then cut the lines to start rerouting the wires. Lo and behold, half the floor lost their phone service.

So our trading floor was a little bit long in the tooth, and we needed to address the technology issues, the accessibility issues, and then, as I mentioned, the life safety issues. I'm sure that while Chicago looked fondly on the Board of Trade as being an engine of employment for the city, we also were aware that they kind of looked the other way in terms of some of the life safety issues that we faced on our trading floor.

There was a plaque that was on the entrance to the trading floor that certified capacity at, I believe, 1,200 people. In the 1980s, there were probably 3,500 people on our trading floor. So you could only imagine what would have happened had there been some of kind of tragic event. How many people would have lost their lives? As a Board member, I certainly wouldn't want that on my conscience. That became a very, very strong point for me to instill in our members as the major reason why we needed a new trading floor.

When you moved to this new trading floor, what happened to the business? Did anything change?

Not really. We had some pretty heated discussions at the Board level in terms of whether we should have a new trading floor, not so much because of the dawn of electronic trading; what was more important to some of the Board members was the value of tradition. So you talk about this friction between tradition and innovation. It had to do with the tiering of the booths outside the pit, so that all of the phone men could have a view of the pit to flash orders or to view exactly what was going on in the marketplace. On the grain floor, we weren't able to tier the booths up because of ceiling restrictions.

Some people looked at that as proprietary information as opposed to the transparency that the exchange believes in, in terms of price discovery. When we had the idea to build a new trading floor, we wanted to provide for our members a marketplace that was as transparent as possible. Some people value tradition over transparency, so discussions became rather heated. There was some compromise made, but I was proud that the booths were tiered very steeply and provided for member firms to be able to see into the pit and transact business as efficiently as possible.

Tell me about the CBOE creation.

The CBOE was really an innovation that was partly out of the gleam in the O'Connors' eyes of providing a transparent price discovery mechanism for what was then an off-exchange instrument: options on equities. Those were listed over-the-counter by firms in New York. If you bought an option from a firm in New York, you had to exit that position with the same firm. That presented problems for large positions and for what the price would be, and as a consequence, for the transaction costs. The spreads between the bids and offers were large.

So the Board of Trade embraced the idea of creating a Chicago Board Options Exchange. The exchange would publicly, in a specialist outcry environment, be a transparent price discovery mechanism, which would allow for an explosion of instruments to be transacted and transmitted around the world. It became a huge success. What began in the coffee shop of the Board of Trade grew to the point where we had to double-decker the floors of our old grain room and provide for expansion space for the CBOE before it eventually moved across the street to its own building.

The success of the CBOE was one of the reasons I knew that I could buy my CBOT seat. I felt that it was a great idea to provide a transparent price discovery mechanism for equity options. At the time I thought, "I'm paying $32,500 for a seat and that is a lot of money, but if I'm wrong, I know the CBOE will work and I know my investment will be protected."

How about interest rate futures? How critical were they?

Richard Sandor and Les Rosenthal and a couple of other innovative members who were on our Board were able to come up with this idea of listing what was viewed as a very challenging instrument to put into a futures contract. Thanks to the intelligence of Richard Sandor and the innovative spirit of our Board and the guidance and leadership of Les Rosenthal, we were able to get those products introduced. They just caused a whole new growth in volume at the exchange, to the point where they are the leading instruments in our exchange. If it wasn't for those instruments, we wouldn't be valued at even a fifth of what we are today.

How about the MMI contract?

That was interesting. The Board of Trade, I believe, turned its head when Standard & Poor's came and offered us a futures contract based on the S&P 500. Everyone has their cross to bear, and I guess that's one of the mistakes that we made as an exchange. We attempted to rectify that with having a Major Market Index, which emulated the Dow Jones Index, which at the time the CBOT could not license to trade, and with having a NASDAQ contract.

Unfortunately, we were never able to get either off the ground. We've now reintroduced a Dow instrument, and I think because of an electronic medium we were able to take it and make it a successful product. It's continuing to grow today.

Tell me about the flood of 1992. Can you discuss it in terms of the incident, and can you also discuss it in terms of being closed for a couple days?

When we heard about the flood, we didn't think that it was going to impact our exchange, even though we were built in the 1930s when coal was a fuel that powered the heating plant at the exchange. No one really understood what the impact was going to be, until all of a sudden we got a phone call from our maintenance people saying that water was flooding into the utility room from near the ceiling.

I remember going with the exchange President Tom Donovan. We went down to the utility room and there was a huge number of staff there with mops. We could see this access door that was up near the ceiling, and you could just see that the water was flooding in. Those poor guys were trying to mop up the water, but they were not able to stem the tide. I felt like I was in a boiler room in the *Titanic*. These guys were trying to turn on the pumps, but to no avail. We knew that we had a major problem.

So we started sandbagging at the various levels up from the utility room and we were fortunate in that the water came to within one step of the telecommunications level. If the water had flooded the communications level, all the phone lines would have been soaked. We would have been out of business probably for months, not just days.

It was a tough situation, but on the other side of the coin stood the leadership of the exchange. We had a very extensive insurance contract and we had a very understanding insurance provider, Chubb. They immediately realized the nature of the problem and basically told the Board of Trade to do what we had to do to get back to business. With that mind-set, we were able to locate portable generator units and cooling units, so that within a weekend, we were able to reestablish cooling to the exchange. After only one day of a rather ugly, overheated trading floor, we were able to restore business as usual.

My hat goes off to the staff and the exchange leadership for taking the bull by the horns. They had the foresight to have an insurance contract and an insurance provider that didn't look over every check being written and just gave us carte blanche to get back up and running.

Did the flood have an effect on the economy?

Certainly the downtown area suffered dramatically in terms of loss of business, but not the Board of Trade. We were disrupted, I think, for only a partial trading day and then one full trading day.

How about the soybean scandal? Can you comment on that?

Let's go back to 1989. I was on the Business Conduct Committee listening to the staff explain how Central Soya, a business that was wholly owned by the Ferruzzi Group, an Italian conglomerate, was accumulating a large soybean position. We brought them in and asked about their intentions and what their economic needs were, because as a commercial, they did not have a speculative limit on the number of contracts they could hold, whereas an individual did. So we wanted to make sure in terms of the integrity of the marketplace that, as the spot month neared and the futures price converged with the cash, it was going to accurately reflect what the cash market was in Chicago, or what it was in St. Louis or Toledo based on a differential.

Central Soya was a large long in soybeans. The first time around we warned them that their position, even though they called it anticipatory hedging for their commercial needs, was viewed by the exchange in another way. And they did not heed the indication that we were going to view a rule enforcement in a harsh manner. Instead of reducing their position in whatever expiration month it was, the position continued into the following month.

At that point, they came forward to the committee and we had to recommend a liquidation of their position. Then, that had to go to the board of directors for ratification. So the committee voted to order liquidation of Central Soya's position. It became a rather adversarial relationship with some of the commercials. One of the commercials sought to level the "perceived injustice" that was committed by condoning an FBI undercover agent to operate as an employee of the commercial firm. In that commercial's mind, that led to settling the score, because it exposed members of the floor to legal consequences. It was a very dramatic time for the exchange.

I was trading in the soybean pit at the time. In fact, I actually traded with the undercover agent. Fortunately, he stood behind me, because sometimes even though you believe what you're doing is honest and straightforward and you are following the rules of the exchange, somebody who might be from an outside regulator or a court system, who does not understand custom and usage, might view your actions differently. So I was fortunate in that the trades that I made with the undercover agent were beyond reproach.

Some of my fellow members suffered because of either unethical activity or activity that was technically incorrect in terms of a court of law, but it was accepted in custom and usage. And it was unfortunate.

A number of our members were indicted. A number of them went to jail, some for as little as $50 or $100, and it was unfortunate because of the way it was done. It exposed the exchange for its inability to respond and modify its rules, which had been made to keep the integrity of the marketplace paramount. We never had that opportunity prior to the investigation. We were never alerted to the improprieties that occurred in the pit. Some of them, as I said, were custom and usage. Some of them were far worse, though, but they were a minority of the members and the overall marketplace nevertheless was painted with a broad brushstroke.

In fact, I went to a Commodity Futures Trading Commission (CFTC) hearing for an individual involved to try to testify on his behalf, because what he did was no different than what any other member did in those days in terms of reconciling an outtrade. Had the rules been structured in a different way, I guarantee he would not have not violated them. So it became a wake-up call that the exchange, once again, was answering to a larger audience.

In some ways, it was the same challenges that faced the Board of Trade in 1848. The founders had to come up with a way of uniform grading to permit the farmers to deliver their goods to market. They had to provide a uniform way of distributing the grain, and provide regulations for the elevator operators and the Board of Trade inspectors to ensure that the grading was done in an honest and open manner. All of these challenges continually faced the exchange over its history, and this is just one more example of coming to grips with a larger audience in attempting to keep the integrity of the exchange at the top.

How did things change after this sting?

The soybean scandal was a catalyst for a number of real changes, as well as for attempting to embrace new technologies to improve our audit trail and demonstrate the integrity of our market. The directors responded aggressively. We changed our rules.

One of those attempts at innovation was an electronic trading card. We put a lot of money into improving our audit trail for open outcry, and we tried to come up with an innovation called a handheld terminal, which was really the first attempt to have what today is known as a personal organizer—a Palm Pilot or a Treo or a BlackBerry. It was our attempt to have an interactive communicating device that would allow a trader to record his trades and have them immediately time-stamped and have a perfect audit trail. It was a daunting task.

Our members certainly spent many hours coming up with ideas on how to do it, and the exchange spent a lot of money trying to do that as well. We did it together with the CME, and in the end we launched our device. The CME was skeptical, and they were still in a training mode. We launched the device on the floor and I actually used it. It was a challenge. It had a lot of functionality, but you could look at it as analogous to the technology that was used for the first landing on the moon with Neil Armstrong and Buzz Aldrin.

If you looked closely at the computers they used to land on the moon, they had as much horsepower as a calculator that's given away free at a bank today, and that's what we were faced with in terms of incorporating technology into a device that a local could hold in his hand and use to turn scribbled orders into alphanumeric characters, or could be clicking on a key and translating that into digital information and then transmitting it to the BOTCC to match.

Needless to say, it was a major leap forward, but it wasn't practical and it wasn't cost efficient. I think electronic trading has proven to be the perfect audit trail. There are some downsides to electronic trading, just as there are downsides to everything. But open outcry has seen a migration to the screen and we'll continue to see it happen. What it has done is it has leveled the playing field and opened our markets to a variety of users who were reluctant to participate because an order was delayed in terms of its execution.

Open outcry trading sometimes raised question marks in some people's minds about whether their trades were executed or whether their orders were handled properly. Today, they can execute their own orders. Electronic trading has expanded our grain volume dramatically, as it expanded our financial futures volume. So I look to the exchange to always be pushing the envelope, whether it be on our own or with the CME. We will continue to provide our futures markets with innovation.

What is your take on the restructuring? Do you think it is going to move the Chicago Board of Trade forward in a new direction? Or do you think the CBOT is going to continue to maintain the old traditions, just in a new place?

The CBOT has gone through a variety of iterations over the 160 years of its existence. I have no doubt that it will continue to take shapes and adopt technologies that I can't even anticipate. But I think that what we're seeing are economies of scale in terms of the global marketplace, and as soon as we introduced a huge productivity gain like electronic trading, which enables a trader to participate in a variety of markets simultaneously, in contrast to the past when in order to trade other contracts he had to physically get out of one pit and walk to another pit, and then add the fact that firms are able to reduce their personnel and minimize errors, these are all dramatic achievements. And I am sure change is going to accelerate.

I look to future generations of members to introduce new ideas on how to trade electronically. Whatever forms they take, whether it be a virtual pit or a new functionality that exists on the screen, it will enable our markets to be faster and more transparent and more efficient in terms of execution cost. That will be terrific because everybody benefits, not just a select few.

What would you say is your personal legacy to the Chicago Board of Trade?

My personal legacy to the Board of Trade is that I never hesitated to speak my mind. Sometimes it wasn't very popular with the members, but as Billy O'Connor and Les Rosenthal demonstrated, sometimes the members need to hear the good and the bad. They need to hear it straight, and I prefer that to operating in the dead of night and surprising members with rule changes or policy changes. My experience is that if there is to be a change and the members haven't had it fully explained to them, they naturally view it negatively. My job was to tell it like it is.

CHAPTER 8

A Twist of Fate

Daniel C. Henning

Dan Henning was born in Oak Park, Illinois, on December 8, 1944. He graduated from Fenwick High School and went on to earn a bachelor of arts in business administration from Western Michigan University. From 1962 to 1967, Dan served in the United States Marine Corps Reserve. During that time, he went into the management trainee program for the Central Soya Company and became familiar with the Chicago Board of Trade. From there, he spent a year as a commodity account executive for Merrill Lynch. In 1971 Dan became a floor manager for Bache and Company.

In 1972, he paid $39,500 for a CBOT membership. Early in his career he was a floor trader and broker. Later, he became a sole proprietor–clearing member at D.C. Trading Company. He stayed in that position until 1987, when he formed his own group, Henning-Krajewski Trading Company. In 1993, Dan partnered with Charles P. Carey to form Henning and Carey Trading. They have been together ever since.

He is married and has five children; three of them carry on his legacy as CBOT members.

****

How did you first hear about this business?

My mother's friend had an employment agency in Oak Park, and right out of college she recommended I go see her. I went to see her and they had three different opportunities. Central Soya was one of them, and being of the old school, she said, "Go with the food company. People have to eat." So, I took her advice and was hired by them to head a crushing and research facility on the West Side of Chicago. In April of 1968, I started in a management training program.

Actually, I ended up at the Board of Trade by accident, because any personnel promotions at the company I was working for were made on a "time spent" basis, and there was one fellow who had been working longer than me. He was being transferred to the Board of Trade, but at the last second he decided to go back into the insurance business. At that time, I was supposed to go to Dubois, Indiana, and be an egg manager, which I guess is where you sit and watch 60 women count eggs. When the other man left, I was offered the CBOT spot. So, really I got it by default. I'll never forget the first day I showed up on the floor. I looked in the pits and I said, "I'll be here forever." I just knew it. I felt it.

What about the business felt so good to you?

Well, I played a lot of sports, and I think I immediately identified what was going on there with what I had done in athletics. Actually, I had hoped to be a baseball player. I'd had some pro offers and a college scholarship, but then I got hurt in college. At that point I was a little despondent about my future. All of a sudden it struck me, what am I going to do now? Nothing seemed quite right until I saw the CBOT, and as soon as I saw it I just knew it was where I was supposed to be. You know, it was like love at first sight.

Tell me how you bought your membership.

I bought my membership with 110 percent financing. I was a young guy who really had no connections and no family money. One day when I had an opportunity to get in the pits, I talked to about 10 different individuals on the floor and told them I wanted to go to work in the pits. Just on a handshake, I got $45,000 from 10 guys. I just told them, "Look, I'd sign any document you want." But back in those days they just said,

"Hey, your word is your bond." And I said, "If I have to work in a gas station at night the rest of my life, I'll pay you guys back," and I meant it.

How long did it take you to do that?

About six weeks. I got involved in a broiler market and it took off, and I was on the right side of it. It was unbelievable.

Word has it that you met your wife down on the floor.

I did. Debbie was a floor manager for H.S. Kipnis and Company, and I was, at that time, a wheat broker, and we were very busy then. It was during the Russian wheat purchases. I had seen her on the floor and thought she was a beautiful woman. By the way, she still is. One morning, she came into the pit to talk to me about a price fill. At that moment, I had lots of people talking to me at one time and she was kind of being very aggressive. So, I basically gave her some lip and she just walked away and said, "Okay, stupid," or something like that.

Well, that afternoon I happened to run into her at one of the local establishments and I offered to buy her a drink, to apologize for my bad behavior. We started talking, and right away I knew that I was going to marry her. So, I guess my whole life has revolved around those kinds of decisions.

How about the decision to have children?

I wanted to have 10 kids, but I got started a little late so, we had only five: three boys and two girls, which included a set of twins. Three of them work at the CBOT. My attitude toward the business was I wanted to expose all the kids to the industry, but I didn't want to influence them for or against it. I wanted them to make up their own minds. The girls said, "No way. This is too crazy." The boys were the opposite; just as soon as they were exposed, they grabbed onto it and embraced it, and now all three are on the trading floor. One is in the wheat pit and two are in the corn pit.

How often do you discuss markets?

My wife says about 10 times a day. It's a business you live, breathe, eat, and sleep. This is not a part-time deal.

Did you want to teach your kids about the integrity of the Board of Trade? What does integrity mean in this business?

Well, it's the most important thing that there is. It started with me buying my membership and the bond, the word, the trust, the promise of doing what I said I was going to do. I always felt that someday maybe my kids would follow in my footsteps, and I shudder to even think about bringing them into an atmosphere where I wasn't respected. So I am sure that influenced me to always try to do the right kinds of things. I always tried to be upright, honest, and forthright, and that's really what makes this place so unique and special.

Tell me about some of the people who were legends in their time and what they represented.

There were so many legends down here. I couldn't count them all, but I guess the first one that comes to my mind is Gene Cashman, who was just a wonderful man. Everybody looked up to him. He had a heart of gold. He had tremendous confidence in himself, and it just radiated to everybody around him. He built a large entourage of people who followed him and believed in him, and he was the kind of guy that, whether it was a runner on the floor or one of his many friends and family members, they could equally approach him. He would take all the time anyone needed to explain what he thought the market was going to do.

In the early 1970s, he was on the right side during those huge soybean markets. And, you know, it was almost like God was on his side. Gene was kind of leading the whole charge. Here's a good example of what kind of man he was. One day, we were limit up when an order came in through one of the commercial desks out of Europe to sell 10 contracts. The clerk who brought it up had written it as 1,000 contracts. It broke the market off the limit and Gene was the one who bought them.

At first, Gene thought they were trying to squeeze him out, trying to put some pressure on him. Then the word got back to him that it was a mistake. They really wanted to sell 10. Most people would have just taken advantage of that, but Gene went completely the other way. He went over and talked to the clerk and found it was a legitimate mistake. He busted the trade and that let the clerk off the hook completely. That could have been a very expensive error, but because of Gene's benevolence and the true, kind man he was, it all worked out.

How about Ralph Peters?

Ralph was kind of a peculiar guy; he seemed a little aloof, a little hard to get to know. In my early days at the CBOT, when I was with Central Soya, I walked into the old lunchroom, which is where the CBOE started. I got a cup of coffee and a doughnut or something. I looked around and there was really no place to sit. Ralph Peters was sitting by himself at a table. I figured what the heck, I'm going to go over there and introduce myself, and it turned out he was very kind and nice. So I got up the nerve and said, "Ralph, you're one of the legends down here. Do you mind if I ask you what your secret is?" He went, "Oh, no problem."

He took a salt shaker and a pepper shaker and put one in each hand. He said, "This is not that hard. Markets go down here and they go up here. You've just got to find out what your timing is going to be. My timing might be a year or two. Yours might be two seconds, but use those parameters and really stay disciplined. Just stay with it, and it'll work for you." Then he continued, "The problem with people is they keep switching their parameters. If you try different things, you have to have the consistency of a program for it to work."

Did you follow that advice?

I did, or at least I think I did. I remember the story so clearly from almost 40 years ago. I decided I was going to be a spreader and found my risk/reward parameters. Unfortunately, nobody is perfect, so there are times you violate those parameters; but most of the time, I try to live by those words.

Speaking of legends, I heard you admired Dick Frymire.

Dick was my favorite. He was the most brilliant trader I ever knew personally. He had the natural background for our business, because he grew up on a farm in Iowa. Then he went to the University of Iowa. When he graduated, he worked in the grain elevators, the fields, and everything. He actually bought a lot of farmland and he then became the floor manager for Staley and Company, and that's when I first noticed him. Their desk was right behind Central Soya's desk.

I'll tell you a story that illustrates how respected Dick was in those days. The Brokers Inn was across the street from the CBOT. When things on the floor were slow, we'd go over there and get a drink; and Dick was in there a lot. Everybody would be talking markets, of course. But when Dick would start talking about the soybean market, whether it was bullish or bearish, everyone seemed to tune in. In those days we didn't have cell phones, so you would notice guys drift off into the hallway and pick up a phone, and everyone knew what they were doing. Everybody wanted to know what Dick was doing, and many tried to copy him.

What I learned from him was that you have to be your own man, because you can't really follow anybody, because good traders change their minds constantly. And he traded so many different markets: the long one, the short one, switching back and forth; different options, different months. So, he taught me that you've got to be your own person.

Did you have a mentor, or did you learn to trade from experience?

I think you learn from experience. It's kind of like riding a bike; you just get on it and do it. You can't really get the knack from books on trading. It's something you have to learn by being there and watching and then doing. Trading is an art. It'll never be a science. You just never know until somebody gets in there how they'll react.

Tell me about some of the traditions down at the floor.

I guess the first thing that pops into my mind is just getting my membership and how proud I felt that day. It was a dream come true. I remember going out that night celebrating. I was just so happy that I found something I wanted to do and I felt I'd be good at it, because I loved it so much. I still feel that today. The feeling of camaraderie you develop with the other traders is very special.

How about the tradition of wearing trading jackets?

Well, if you look at the old pictures of the Board of Trade, you know the old traders wore top hats and suits. We used to trade cash grain on the floor and they'd be throwing corn all over the floor. As time went by and as the pits got bigger and more active, it wasn't very functional to have suits and top hats on. So they started wearing trading jackets on the floor. At first they were all the same color, but then someone came up with the idea to have their jackets be a different color, so they would stand out in the crowd. Others soon followed suit.

Many of the trading jackets had a story behind them. Companies chose different colors and symbols. I'll tell you one really funny story. I was trading in the wheat pit at the time and we were the closest pit to the visitors' balcony. I had just met my wife, and at that time I had on a striped trading jacket. It almost looked like a referee's jacket.

My wife had some customers in town, and she had them up in the balcony showing them around and overhead this man explaining what was happening on the floor. He said, "You see, that's the wheat pit. You see the guy in the middle with the striped coat? He's the referee." Debbie didn't bother to correct him!

Many times they could have used a referee in the pits! Tell me about the first lesson that you learned.

I was trading through Goldberg Brothers and I started in the iced broiler pit. It wasn't too long before I felt quite successful, and then I became a little overconfident. One day, I walked in; I had a 100-lot position in iced broilers, which during those days was a very, very large position. That day, they called the market sharply higher.

So, I saw Dave Goldberg walking over to the pit and I think he's gonna tell me, "You're a genius! Way to go!" and pat me on the back. But he comes in and pulls me aside, in only the way Dave could do it, and he gave me a little scowl and said, "Are you crazy? You get out of that stuff right now!" I'm thinking to myself, "What the heck?" Well, you know, I respected him, so I did what he said. Within 10 minutes the market was limit down. I would have been a big loser. It showed me that overconfidence could be a killer down here.

Did you teach that to your sons?

I've tried, and they pretty well followed, but sometimes you just have to learn things on your own.

Give me an example of the fertilizer market. What happened with that?

Well, I thought it was going to be a huge success. Every farmer uses it. It was anhydrous ammonia and diammonium phosphate. And I was hoping to be a leader in some new agricultural contract at the Board of Trade. So, when they started it, I volunteered to be a market maker and I actually had a dual function; I was a broker and a market maker.

The open interest in the contract started building, and we seemed to have success. But during that period there was a tremendous consolidation in the business. From 20 or 30 major producers it went down to three or four. What usually happens in those sorts of situations is people really aren't interested in sharing information and price discovery. So the markets weren't working anymore. What really ended it for me was when I was trading in anhydrous ammonia and I started buying the March, and selling to the nearby, looking for it to go to "full carry."

A hurricane hit the New Orleans area, which was the main producing area for anhydrous ammonia at the time. It took me two weeks to get out of the spread, because there was a very small open interest. It cost me about $250,000, and I said to myself, "Well, there's my investment in the Board of Trade. Oh, God, I'm done." The fertilizer market never made it, and I think it was mostly due to that consolidation and that people in the cash market didn't really seem to want it.

Did anybody ever challenge you on the floor?

Oh, every day, multiple times a day. There's definitely an ongoing ego struggle. It's a macho business, and every once in a while you have to stick your nose into something. I was once in the wheat pit and I was probably one of the bigger traders in there. One time, shortly after a new trader had started, and you know how we've talked about ethics and reputation? Well, this guy in my opinion was a snake. I didn't like him from day one. He had this nasty little habit. He'd be bidding for something or offering something and I'd yell "sold" to him and he'd pretend like he didn't hear me. He was worried that if I did the trade, it must be no good for him.

So, he did this to me two or three times and I talked to him. He said, "Oh, I didn't really see you." I said, "Come on! That's a bunch of BS. You saw me!" So, I let it go for two, three, four times. Then, one day, I was up in the top of the pit and he was standing in the center of the pit bidding for something, and I made a move so he'd see me. I yelled, "Sold!" and I know he heard me because he looked startled. I yelled, "You heard me, sold!" He tried to put his hands down and I yelled, "Hey!" and he looked up at me and gave me the bird signal.

To tell you the truth, I don't even remember what happened after that. Generally, I don't have much of a temper, but this just absolutely infuriated me and evidently I flew down to the bottom of the pit and did the old baseball umpire belly bump and he hit the ground. A man named Pat Morris, who's a big strong guy, grabbed me and stopped me, and he was laughing about it afterwards. He said, "I was standing there, kind of on the side. Then you came flying by and I thought a locomotive came through here. That's what kind of collision it looked like." And then they got me off the floor to prevent any further physical confrontation.

Evidently after I left, the guy called in the floor guards and he was telling them what happened. But he was such a bad apple that the other guys in the pit just shrugged their shoulders. They said, "It's a physical business. Sometimes people fall down." The guards couldn't find one witness. This is the kind of business where you can't hide. I mean, everybody knows what's going on, and if you build a negative kind of reputation, you'll soon alienate and isolate yourself.

You know, we hear a lot of stories about being in the pits, but it seems like even though you're competing for business, sometimes you guys walk off the floor with such long and fast friendships. How does that happen?

Well again, my first experiences of life were centered around sports and I think anybody who's played sports at a high level understands the camaraderie and the competition athletes are involved in. To give you an example, like a heavyweight fight, you'll see two guys out trying to kill each other for 15 rounds and in most cases when it's over they're hugging each other because they respect the job the other is doing. They know what you're going through. And that's kind of like trading. We all go in there and are very competitive. But when it's over, most of us are pretty good friends because we respect each other.

That understanding and respect make it possible for the members to legislate for themselves. That leads me to ask about the role of self-regulation.

I feel it's the best. I think if customers knew how much the traders really care about the outside customers, they'd be shocked. I used to do a lot of traveling around the country, and you could always sense that air of mistrust for the floor members. I think it was almost that there seemed to be a farm attitude versus the city members. But I can unequivocally say that 99 percent of the guys on the floor really care about their customers and bend over backwards to provide a service because they realize they're our lifeblood. And I really don't think the customers understand it. I think they see some of the success of some of the traders and there's some jealousy, but I can assure you that most people really try to do the right thing for their customers.

Did you serve on any committees?

I was on a whole bunch of committees. I served on fertilizer, membership, the floor governors, and new markets, and I was on the board of directors from 1990 to 1992. Being on the board was another dream come true. It was the epitome of happiness to me. I'm an old sports guy, so to me it was equivalent to making the all-star team and it was special. It gave me a chance to do something significant for the industry that I love. And I hope I did.

When I started on the board of directors, I felt we had to make some positive changes that were important for the growth of this business. Around 1990, the controversial area was commodity hedge funds. Paul McGuire, who had been chairman for years, was very old-school. He was anti-agricultural options trading and he was anti-growth of the commodity funds. He and his cronies did not want things to change. At the time, I was chairman of the committee that made the decision on what we were going to recommend for the position limit size of funds.

So, I saw the interest and I saw the markets expanding, and I made a decision to allow a larger increase in position size than he felt was justified. It was tough for a young guy like me to stand up and make these major decisions, especially with the old guard, who were well-schooled and around for a long time, telling me that I'm crazy. However, I just stuck with what I really felt in my gut, which has got me where I'm at today; and obviously that was the right decision.

What were some of the achievements that happened under your tenure?

Well, I think that would be the major one: the fact that our business without the funds would not have had the degree of the success that we did. If you can get one thing done, I think that's a lot. I think a lot of people go through this business just to wave to people and shake hands and hug. I wanted to make at least one major change, and I think under my direction that happened and I'm very proud of it.

And then, when it was time for your retirement, tell me about the speech that you made.

It is customary when your tenure on the board of directors is over to say a few words at a dinner for the outgoing and incoming directors. To tell you the truth, I can't remember exactly what I said, but I remember that it was at the Art Institute and it was for the members and their wives. And I got up and felt very emotional looking back at being given the chance to serve the CBOT and to reach all my goals. I just wanted the new directors to know how special and how honored they should feel to have this privilege. I wanted to encourage them to set their sights on goals that would give them an opportunity to make a difference. I wanted to inspire them to carry on and not stand still; to keep improving. And I walked off and my wife said, "You could hear a pin drop in the room." It was pretty special.

Quite a proud moment. You feel pride in a business that attracts all kinds of people. Can you tell me about the diversity?

You've got college professors, high school dropouts, and everything in between. Today we have computer traders, too. There's a huge mix that make up the trading population, and I think that's one of the things that makes it work. There's not a whole lot of redundancy. If everybody in the marketplace was trying to do the same thing, I don't think it would work. You need people to approach the market in different ways and from different styles, and that's really what makes a marketplace. The CBOT has historically been the marketplace for all types of people.

What would you tell someone who wanted to go into this business today?

The CBOT is a unique opportunity for anyone, because this business never stops changing. I really believe today you almost have to recreate yourself every year or two to remain successful. The people who try to stay with the old ways of doing business, the old ways of trading, they're out the back door. You know, you can't ever stop improving. You can never rest. I think it is a great business for new, young traders, and is still a great business for seasoned traders like me.

The Chicago Board of Trade is the model for worldwide price discovery. What does that mean to you?

Early in my career, I did a lot of traveling in the farm belt and I'd go to these small coffee shops in a little town in Illinois. I would have an opportunity to talk with farmers. The one thing that the farmers all had in common was that they all knew the prices at the CBOT. Whether from their local radio stations or some other form of communication, it just seemed like wherever I'd go, whether they liked the CBOT or hated it, they were tuned in to the exchange. We always seemed to be at the forefront of a lot of people's interest.

Why were you meeting with the farmers?

As a young man in about 1970, I was hired by Merrill Lynch as a commodity account executive, and, at that time, they had an interesting new concept where they wanted to hire people from the commodities business to go to specific areas to educate the farmers, processors, grain handlers—everybody in the agriculture business. They wanted to encourage them to become more active in futures. So, after being trained in New York, I was sent to Tulsa, Oklahoma, to try this out.

Why Tulsa?

In that area of the country there were a lot of broiler producers. Back in those days, people were very suspicious of futures. I think there were a lot of people who didn't trust the system at all.

One of my first encounters with this feeling was with Tyson Foods in a small town in Arkansas. I got an appointment with them and I showed up in my Merrill Lynch gray suit with my perfect white shirt and my tie. My meeting was with a guy who made all Tyson's hedging decisions. I go in, and he is sitting there wearing bibbed overalls and he has on cowboy boots, with his feet up on the desk. I started giving him my Merrill Lynch spiel about why he should use futures more. He just looked at me and said, "Boy, I kind of like you for some reason, so I'm going to tell you, you got to stop this New York crap out here." He said, "Talk Arkansas. Just tell me, what do these Merrill Lynch people want to do with these broilers?" So I took my coat and tie off and I said, "You're right. This isn't me, anyway." And I actually opened the account the first day and we did a lot of business with them.

Another time, I had to go out to Lubbock, Texas, which is in the middle of nowhere, out in the panhandle of Texas. Mostly there's lots of cattle, with just a couple of people. I gave a seminar to some local cattle raisers and it was kind of the same situation. I still had my Merrill Lynch suit on, because the company expected me to do that. In the meeting, there were probably 20 cattle people. I started going through my regular spiel again, and some of the guys weren't paying any attention.

So, I paused in my speech and said, "Does anybody have any questions, or are there other things that you want to talk about?" And one of the guys raises his hand and he goes, "Hey, kid. How many cattle do you own?" I said, "Sir, I don't own any cattle." He says, "Well, how in the hell can you tell us how to hedge 'em?" And I said, "You're right. Let's go over to the bar." And I added, "I'm buying."

So, we all went over to the local saloon and just started talking. The guy says to me that this is what they really wanted: more common talk. They don't want the New York attitude. After that, I did a lot of business out there, but I did that job for only nine months, because I realized how much I missed the Board of Trade. As soon as the opportunity presented itself, I came back here. I could have kissed the ground. It was like coming back from the war or something. I really missed it. And I've been here ever since.

How does the Board of Trade really serve the farm community?

It provides a hedging and price mechanism that was never available before. It provides a real structure for the farmers. In the old days, the farmers would raise their corn and bring it to Chicago on their wagons, and if you happened to be the guy on the third day, you might end up dumping it in the river, because it was first come, first served, and if you didn't get it sold, you had a problem.

There had to be a solution to this type of waste. Futures markets actually started on a street corner, and people started locking in prices. They came up with the concept that farmers didn't have to bring in their crops immediately. They could bring them to Chicago later in the year. And it has evolved into what it is today.

What do you think is the future for the agriculture markets?

I think the sky is the limit. CBOT President Bernie Dan told an interesting story at the Futures Industry Association convention. He said that in the past year or two, if you go to China, they're having some seminars on futures trading. More recently, thousands of people attend the seminars. And with China being the emerging market, I see food and all soft products being so important. The Chinese really want to get involved. I think they're going to embrace these grain markets, because we're in a whole new era here and I think it's going to be led by the Far East and what they do.

What do you think of the impact of interest rate futures?

That probably was the biggest change in our business. You know, history speaks for itself. Look at the depth of the market there versus trading the soft commodities. You've got only so much grain to trade, whereas the financial markets are so much deeper, and the futures fed off that and created this gigantic trading volume that none of us could conceive of 10 or 15 years before.

Can you talk about when the CBOT was involved in the FBI sting? Tell me what it was like to be on the floor during that time.

The word that comes to mind would be shocking. I was watching TV and all of a sudden it flashed across the screen that there had just been a big bust at the Board of Trade. It was in the headlines of all the papers in town. Everyone at that time was freaking out because they didn't know what was going on. I think no matter what business you're talking about, if I walked into your business tomorrow and said, "You know what, we've had two undercover agents working in your office for the past two years," anybody is going to stop and think, what did I say? What didn't I say? The level of scrutiny was so intense that it was scary to even the most honest person.

So there was a lot of fear and a lot of uncertainty, and people obviously were very, very concerned. And I've always felt the government sometimes is a little unfair and what they try to accomplish and what actually gets accomplished are two different things. I'm all for getting the bad guys, believe me, but not the way they went about it.

For instance, most of the guilty pleas were on trading after the close, which should have been legal and today is legal. There's no fraud involved in that. At the time it was a law in the books and they enforced it. But you had lives being ruined and people going to jail for making a trade after the close or just trying to even up their position or fill an order for a customer.

I had one of the undercover agents walk into my office. Of course, at the time I didn't realize he was an undercover agent. One of the guys from the bean pit introduced me to him. Supposedly, he was a new trader in beans. And he said, "Uh, I see you got this fast-growing operation here. I'm interested in maybe trading through you. What can you do for me?" So I gave him our speech about how we provide services in a comfortable environment and we do a lot of risk management work. He said, "Well, you must do a little something extra. I mean, look at the way you're growing." And I remember thinking that was kind of a peculiar question to ask. And that ended it. Of course, he didn't trade through us and the next time I saw him was on TV.

It was a terrible time. The government spent a lot of money on this investigation, and once they put their money behind something, they want some bodies.

How about some of the outside things that happened in the world that affected the floor, like Chernobyl?

Well, actually I was at a funeral the day Chernobyl hit the market. I had heard some of our traders were in trouble. There was a huge amount of money lost that day and there was uncertainty of what this was going to mean. Was this the beginning of the end of the world? What about the grain? Are we ever going to be able to use it again, or are they going to have to recall everything? So, it caused a tremendous amount of market volatility, and basically the people, as I recall, had kind of a bull market going at the time. The floor just dropped out. It didn't give anyone a chance to get out. It was a very bad situation.

Do you want to comment on the grain embargo?

Yeah, it was the dumbest thing I've ever heard of. It accomplished nothing. It set us back in the world competitive picture for a long time. And, you know, that's how the South Americans really got involved. We were cutting off exports, and then we went over and President Carter said, "Let's teach them how to grow this stuff," and here we are today fighting with the Brazilians trying to remain as a leader.

How about the role of innovation at the Board of Trade?

Well, I think we've pretty much been at the forefront of innovation. I mean we have to be or we're not going to exist. This is the kind of business where you cannot stand still. In the Board of Trade's long history, we've always made critical decisions to make changes and innovations when needed. There aren't a lot of other businesses that have survived for almost 160 years.

Are there any other products that you thought were new and interesting?

Yes, iced broilers. You know that was where I got my start and that market originally flourished. There was a lot of interest in iced broilers when we first opened that market. It was originally traded in the old soybean pit on the edge and it grew in volume and attracted enough traders where we actually had to establish its own pit. It really looked like that market had made it and then the same thing happened: That business really consolidated. It went from many, many producers to very, very few; and it seems to me whenever that happens, they like less and less price dissemination.

What would you say was the biggest industry change?

Oh, no question: the technology and the funds participation. I'm a risk manager for Henning and Carey, and I look at some of the positions and the size and numbers these fellows are able to move around in the pit and it's just mind-boggling. I remember when I first started trading, some of the older guys would look at me and go, "You're crazy. You're trading numbers we've never seen before." And I didn't even realize it. I just was reacting to what I thought were opportunities in the marketplace. But those guys were still living in the past, and it wasn't happening when they were doing it. Now I'm kind of going though the same thing. I see people trading numbers that seemed impossible years ago.

Fortunately, the history of the Board of Trade is that no matter what happens we always seem to be able to accommodate the volume. When the funds came in, people were very concerned because of their size and their momentum. But people develop the strategies, and now we're able to handle that and accommodate their business.

Do you do any computer trading?

I'm real old-school. My kids laugh at me every day because I've actually never turned one on. Now, I've got a lot of people who work for me who are very good at it and it's kind of an old joke there, too. At home or in the office, they say, "Come on, we can teach you." And I say, "Guys, you can't teach the old dog new tricks. I just don't want to do it." When I was in college at Western Michigan in 1967, there was not one computer class there. All that stuff pretty much started right after that and I just never got involved. Then, by the time it really evolved, there was so much catch-up that I didn't really feel like doing the work. I was lucky, because I always surrounded myself with people who could. That's how I was able to survive.

Can you just tell me how you formed Henning and Carey?

I'd had experience in the clearing business. I actually started in 1978 at D.C. Trading Company, where I was the sole proprietor, the trader. Eventually that became the Henning-Krajewski Trading Company. We took on customers and it evolved into a pretty good-size company, but it broke up. It actually got too big, too quick. That was one of the problems. There was some infighting with the partners, and I'd actually made up my mind when that ended that I didn't want to do that anymore.

I actually signed a note, a noncompete, for an 18-month period. And during that period, five or 10 traders came up to me and said, "Aren't you going to get something new going? I really enjoyed working with you." So, I was thinking, well, maybe I should do it on a small scale. So I started looking around and that was about the same time Charlie Carey was evolving in the business. He had some customers he wanted to bring along, and he asked me if we could do something together. I already had established Henning Trading Company and then brought him in and we changed the name to Henning and Carey. We've been in the business together about 14 years and it's a very nice business.

Has your business changed in that 14-year period?

Well, again, the biggest changes are in the past six to nine months with the electronic trading. We have a good mix of business. We have financials, grains, and metals. We've always felt that we had to diversify. You know you can't put all your eggs in one basket, and I think that's a good lesson in this business. And now as the business evolves, we're trying to do a little better mix of business. We're doing some fund business. We're doing some commercial business. We just built a strictly electronic room for people who are more comfortable in that environment. We've got a lot of things going.

One of the big changes at the Board of Trade was the CBOE. Can you tell me about that lunchroom beginning?

I can remember when the CBOE was in the old lunchroom, which they converted into a trading room. The O'Connors were really the moving force behind the CBOE, because conceptually, these are stock options. Why wouldn't New York do it? It was the stock capital of the world.

I think we had a lot of doubters here in Chicago, but the O'Connors had so much vision, it was incredible. Everybody told them it wouldn't work. I remember Eddie O'Connor and Billy O'Connor walking about the floor trying to draft people to buy these new memberships. They were $10,000 and you could buy as many as you wanted. I bought one, just because I believed in the O'Connors. You would follow them anywhere, like following Patton into battle; they're just brilliant people. One of the ideas behind it was diversification. If commodities go stale, we've got stock options. I don't think New York ever believed we had a chance, so they kind of ignored us, and all of a sudden they couldn't ignore us any longer.

Tell me about the IPO.

The IPO opening was in New York in October 2005. It was unbelievably exciting. I was asked to participate in it, which I think was a very high honor. It was a day I'll never forget. The excitement was just incredible. My wife and I and about 50 other members of the CBOT were picked up that morning by a bus and taken from our hotel on Park Avenue over to the New York Stock Exchange. I don't know if you've ever been there, but it's one of the most impressive buildings you'll ever walk into. And in front of the building was this huge banner, "Welcome CBOT, Newest Members of the New York Stock Exchange."

John Thain, who was the president of the New York Stock Exchange at the time, hosted a breakfast, and he got up and said, "You don't realize how exciting a day this is for us. This is one of the best IPOs in a long time. You guys are special. We're excited that you're with us." And then we were all asked after the breakfast to go to the floor, and Charlie Carey and a few others were invited to go up on the podium and we went on the floor right below them. When he rang that bell, my heart was beating so fast. It was unbelievable. Truly, it's a day I'll never forget.

What do you think is the impact of that IPO?

Well, obviously it was well received and then our prices tripled, then quadrupled from the original pricing. And I think it's good for the customers and good for Chicago. It's good for the members; it's something we needed in this environment to remain competitive. We need the capital. It's just been a wonderful thing.

What's your take on the merger?

Well, I'm happy to see it. I believe that it's in the best interest of Chicago, and the exchange will be served well by a merger between us and the CME. We have the natural synergies, the history, the products, the technology, the clearing arrangement and on and on and on. As an individual, that's obviously the way I'd like to see it go.

What do you think will happen to the Board of Trade in the future?

Well, of course, everybody has their opinion, and mine is probably in the minority, because of my old-school background and experience. Let me tell you a story. In 1968, I was first hired by Central Soya on the floor. Just a few months after I was hired, we hired our first computer person, a woman, and, to tell you the truth, I didn't even know exactly what they were doing. She was heavily technically oriented and a very nice lady.

One day I was talking to her and she said, "Dan, what do you hope to do down here?" I just pointed at the pit and said, "Well, that's where

I'm going to be." And she said, "Don't you understand that these are going to be gone two years from now? It's all going to be on a computer." That was in 1968! And all along the way there's been electronic trading and we've embraced it, which is good. I always equate it to Grandma's apple pie. There are certain old things that are still pretty damn good, even if they seem old-fashioned.

One of the reasons I'm really for the CME merger is once the CME moves over here it would set up a natural arena for more arbitrage business between the cattle and the corn and the meal and hogs. And the proximity of that would really, really enhance the trading value.

On a personal level, what would your legacy to the CBOT be?

I did everything I wanted to do. I have no regrets. I wouldn't change anything. I feel very fortunate. I got a little lucky, but I capitalized on opportunity and I couldn't be happier.

CHAPTER 9

Four Generations at Work

Jordan A. Hollander

In September of 1940, Jordan Hollander was at the University of Illinois, majoring in agriculture. He was well aware of the Chicago Board of Trade, because his father, Oscar, was a member of the exchange. During his college years, the CBOT asked the sophomore to travel around and give lectures to farmers and other interested groups on the purpose of the Chicago Board of Trade. Although his knowledge at the time was superficial at best, he took this opportunity to learn more about his father's business and to hone his skills as a public speaker. He quickly became an important educational ambassador for the industry.

By 1942, Jordan Hollander was serving his country as an enlisted member of the Air Force Reserve. In 1943, he was called to active duty and served in the Army Air Force. When he was honorably discharged from service in 1946, he chose to begin working for his father's company, Hollander & Feuerhaken. A year later, he was able to buy a membership in the CBOT for $5,000.

Jordan worked very hard learning about the exchange and how he could best serve the interests of the industry. In 1950, he became a partner in his father's company. Although helping to run the company was very time-consuming, he still found time to volunteer on many committees. He served on the CBOT Transportation Committee, was chairman of the Cash Grain Committee, and was the president of the CBOT Cash Grain Association. From 1976 to 1978, Mr. Hollander was a director of the Chicago Board of Trade.

Jordan's greatest pride doesn't come from his own years of service to the exchange. It comes from watching the third generation of his family working at the Chicago Board of Trade through his company: son Glenn Hollander (married to Sandra) and Avi Fromm (married to Wendy). He is looking forward to seeing the potential leadership of David Hollander (married to Alila) and Matt Fromm (married to Sara). It is his fervent wish that the fourth generation of Hollanders, Brenden and Nicolas, and Benjamin Fromm will keep the tradition going.

****

Tell me how you first heard about the Chicago Board of Trade.

I think I first heard about the exchange when my mother took the bottle out my mouth. It's very true. My father, Oscar, was a member of the Chicago Board of Trade trading in the corn pit. From the time I was a small boy, I remember he used to bring me down on Saturdays when the CBOT traded until noon. My dad would put me up in his office with a pencil and a trading card to scribble on. And then somebody brought me down to the trading floor, just as the market was closing. I can still see my dad's head bobbing in the corn pit trading. If I was a good boy, he would reward me with a delicious surprise of a corned beef sandwich and a chocolate phosphate. Being with my dad was always a treat.

I remember another story about the early days I spent with my dad and the CBOT. Whenever we would enter the Board of Trade building, Dad would point to a brick on LaSalle Street and say, "Jordan, that's my brick, and someday it's going to be your brick." I think that maybe I did the same thing to my son Glenn when he became a member. I don't know which brick it was, but I kind of just motioned in that direction.

That sounds like a nice tradition to pass on. Can you think of some stories that your father told you about the Board of Trade during his early days?

Dad started out when he was 11 years old working for a firm, which was a partnership. That business ultimately became our firm. It started in 1906, and as one partner retired, somebody else bought him out. To my recollection, the names changed until a company called McKenna Rogers was bought out by Strausser and it became McKenna Strausser. When Mr. McKenna passed away, Mr. Strausser turned the company over to my father. My father then took a partner, Ray Feuerhaken, in 1942 when the company started. I joined the company in 1946 after I came out of the service.

What made you want to be part of this industry?

My major was agriculture in college. During my sophomore year, the market was very quiet and there was virtually no trading. The Board of Trade was trying to get the rural areas to understand the technical reasons why the exchange existed. We are a federally licensed auction market, and there has to be a good economic reason for our existence. One of the reasons is to help price the grain that is raised by farmers and then sold by farmers in country elevators. There was a need for a hedging market.

At that time, the Board of Trade had nobody in the education department to explain the basics of hedging. They knew what hedging was for the big commercials, but there was very little hedging done by country elevators and farmers. Dad called me up and said the CBOT wanted somebody to give them a basic explanation of how this process worked at the Board of Trade.

Here I was a college student with no real experience at the CBOT. I knew nothing about farming, and I was just learning what agriculture was all about; but because I was interested, I went. This was before the war. So I did a couple of talks at the Board of Trade and some rural communities. Being there, in an educated position, got me interested.

Then the war came, and I was in the service for a few years. As soon as I got out, I just naturally came to the CBOT. At the time, jobs were very hard to find. I got discharged on a Thursday, was offered a job, and started here on a Monday; I've been here ever since.

With your speaking background, I'll bet you can explain what ceiling prices were.

All grain was priced by the government at certain levels, whether it was St. Louis or Davenport, Iowa, or Des Moines, Iowa, or many other points. What we had to know was the freight rates. You could actually price grain from any market if you knew what the freight rates were to the destination. So the ceiling price eliminated the need for price determination, because the government said corn was worth X dollars at St. Louis, or X dollars at Des Moines, Iowa. And all you had to do was take the freight off from each one and see which gave you a better price to go to its destination.

Sadly, at that time there appeared to be actually no economic reason for trading to continue. There was absolutely a minimum of trading, if any at all, and the price of a membership went down to nothing more than the transfer fee. If I remember correctly, when I started in 1946, you could buy a membership for $50. I kept saying to my dad, "Don't you think we ought to buy a membership?" And my dad said, "No, you've got to pay dues." And I said, "Okay." And the next trade I said, "Don't you think we ought to buy a membership?" And my dad said, "No, you have to pay dues."

By the end of 1946, he said to me, "You know, I think we ought to buy a membership." And I said, "Are you going to pay the dues?" But by that time memberships were $5,000. I had a note with me that I signed for my father for $4,500 as an advance for my membership, which we ended up buying in 1947.

How did you pay it back?

I paid it back with $25 government bonds. I bought bonds every year, every month, for $18.75. When I accumulated all those bonds, I said to my dad, "Dad, I have money for you, but at maturity level." He said, "I'll take it," and I was thrilled, because now it was my membership. One day he said to me, "You know, I think we ought to give those bonds to your sister." I said, "Thanks a lot, Dad." But that's how I got the membership.

Can you remember being on the floor as a child?

Dad was not a cash trader in those times. He was a small trader in the corn pit. I don't know if they allowed young ones on the floor at that time, except for one day during the holiday season. They would bring all the kids down and they'd have a clown on the floor. I clearly remember being there.

My recollection of the original floor is exactly as it was until the new floor opened up. There was a corn pit, soybean pit, oat pit, and soybean oil and meal pits. There were support telephone systems all the way around. On the LaSalle Street side, there were tables where the cash grain samples were delivered. That's what we did. Every boxcar that came into Chicago was sampled and the paper bags were put on our tables to sell. We would display those bags to the different buyers and get their bid prices and then determine which was the best price.

Can you describe the trading floor in your early days at the Chicago Board of Trade?

There was no market during World War II. There were traders around, but I can't remember any volume. I just knew that when I started in 1946, we had just begun talking to small commercials that we dealt with about hedging in the market. We were one of the first firms that offered this service and tried to stimulate this sort of business.

I remember that the price of a membership had fallen to just the $50 transfer fee. I believe that only started to escalate in 1946. If there was any trading at that time, it was minimal.

How were the members dressed?

In those days, almost everybody wore a suit jacket, and many of the members wore hats. Smoking was allowed, and lots of members smoked pipes and cigars. Dad was a big cigar smoker. I remember a couple of top hats. I think that was the big thing prior to my coming here. There were only one or two left once I started my career at the exchange. After that time, all hats disappeared within a year.

We all wore jackets and ties. Later we got these barber jackets in different colors. The personality of each company or trader emerged through the color or pattern of your trading jacket. It was really a great idea, because people who traded in the pit wanted orders to reach them as soon as possible. The jackets made it easier to distinguish the traders from each another. Over time, their jackets became louder and brighter.

The first way to communicate prices on the floor was with chalkboards. How did that work?

Western Union was the big communications company at the time. They would send a price from the trading pit to the clerk in the booth, who would then submit it to the chalkboard level. The chalkboards were high above the trading floor on the east wall. There was a platform that ran the length of the chalkboards. Men and women walked along the platform with chalk in their hands to mark up on the chalkboards where the grain prices were currently trading.

We completely relied on those prices. The prices might be 30 seconds late, maybe even a minute late; but those were the market prices that we all went by. And those were the prices that the traders in the pits used to take their positions and determine whether they were buying and selling. The grain we sold was predicated on those prices and the basis differential that existed above or below that current price.

I heard you know a great story about the women who worked on the chalkboards.

It happened in the Buffalo market and in those days they hired women to be chalkboard markers. Some of ladies wore very revealing skirts, and the men would stand under the level looking up supposedly at the prices. But, believe me, they saw more than the prices.

Tell me about the first lesson you learned down at the Board of Trade.

When I became a member in 1947, my father-in-law, within the first week, gave me $5,000, and said, "Trade for me." Now, prior to that my dad had always warned me to never take personal trades from a customer, a friend, and/or the family. Okay. But I didn't listen to him, and I took the money and I went in the market and bought $5,000 worth of oats. I went up to the office and then came down about an hour later. I looked at the market and I yelled, "Help, Dad!" We got out of the trade and I lost $5,000 in one swoop. That was the best lesson I learned. God bless having a wonderful father-in-law. He said to me, "That's a great lesson. From now on, listen to your father. Don't ever trade for a friend, a customer, or a relative on a speculative trade." That's still the lesson we follow today.

Let's talk about your commercial customers. How does your business operate?

We were one of the first commodity firms to bring hedging to the country elevator and the farmer. Prior to that, they relied strictly on the prices that the country elevator gave them. The hedging was done by the big commercials.

Somewhere in the mid-1940s, we began to approach the elevators and the farmers with lessons in how to hedge their grain. This is the basis of our business today. Basically, our business today is to speak with farmers and country elevators. We give them advice and help them determine where to sell the futures or where to sell the cash and how to maneuver their positions to best protect their sale and a carrying charge.

Do you think that the business has changed over the years?

No, the same fundamentals of speculating and price determination still apply in the marketplace. The method of doing it might have changed a little bit. Options came onto the trading floor, and people are using the option markets to facilitate their hedging at times. It takes the next generation to understand them better than I do.

What role does the Chicago Board of Trade play in the worldwide price discovery mechanism?

Well, the Chicago Board of Trade is the world marketplace for price determination. For grain and soybean producers, there are other markets in the world, but nothing to compare with the Chicago Board of Trade. Orders that go into the trading pits come from all the big importing countries and exporting countries in the world.

The price discovery process at the CBOT involves not only buying and selling from the Chicago market and from the United States market. It's also buying and selling from Russia and China and certainly Brazil and all the other agriculture producing and importing countries for food. Although the Chicago Board of Trade certainly has a global reach, our company deals only in domestic business. We've never gotten into the international business.

Do you see more competition now than in your earlier days?

I don't see it in our end of the business, but I would assume there is. Fewer small competitors produce more direct buying volume versus yearly yields.

Does the advent of a new agricultural product like ethanol play into your business?

Ethanol is a big factor, because ethanol production is taking part of our corn production. In Mexico, they've already had a few riots because the price of tortillas has gone up because of increased corn prices. The ethanol people get the grain first, because their ethanol production plants are so close to where the corn is growing. The other markets must overbid the ethanol producers to get grain. What that does is limit the amount of free grain that comes in from the market, because the ethanol producers are taking it all. This is certainly affecting Iowa, which is the biggest producer of corn in the world and certainly in the United States. Today, there are some counties that must bring corn into the country to satisfy local needs and ethanol usage.

All of this is a very important component in considering the price structure, and we've seen it in the market this year. When I left to go for my winter vacation, corn was about $2.25. When it hit $4.00, I didn't believe it. Now it's trading even higher, so the ethanol situation certainly is a factor in the price determination at the Chicago Board of Trade, which is the marketplace for price determination.

Any predictions as to where it will go?

No. I think there is a fine balance between production and usage.

How important is the word 'integrity' with this business?

If you don't have integrity, you don't belong in the business. The integrity of the exchange's membership is what keeps the marketplace honest. A large percentage, the great percentage, 99 percent of all trades, buying and selling, balance out. Those that don't generally are worked out by the following morning before the market opens. You have to be able to trust the people you're trading with, and if you don't have that faith in each other, there's no integrity in the marketplace. Without integrity, the Chicago Board of Trade could not exist.

Many say the motto of the CBOT is 'My word is my bond.' How do you feel about that?

In the marketplace, your word is your trading price; and those balance out. The reason 99-plus percent of these trades balance out is because someone has given their word about the selling price or the buying price. You give your word. It is your bond. We buy grain, as an example, from farmers and country elevators. We don't pass contracts for a day or two and it could be 10 days before we get it back. So, the contracts are our bond. Occasionally there are arguments and disagreements, and we handle them in a certain way.

Give me an example of this.

Generally speaking, if we make a trade with a customer and he says it's not his trade or the price is wrong, whichever it is, the first time they're right. There's no argument even though we might think they're not right. The second time they're probably right, and the vast majority of time, even though we know we're right, we go along with their interpretation. Comes the third time from the same customer, we really have to consider that we don't want to trade with a customer like that. If we're really wrong, they shouldn't be trading with us. So three times is a cutoff point for us. By the way, that's happened to us only once.

Really? That's incredible. You were discussing farmers and country elevators selling cash grain and how it affects futures and your business. Can you tell me more about that?

The other end of our business is cash business. We buy grain from farmers. When we buy grain, we generally are developing a position into the futures market. By the same token, when the farmers sell us the grain, they might be short—the futures against the cash position. They buy their futures back, and that's the balancing of the market, and that's the price determination depending on more buyers or more sellers. That's what determines a price level.

So you provide a great service.

We provide a very definite economic service in the market. Our service is not basically speculative in the futures end of our market. I think without service to customers, whether it is our customers or the big commercials or the foreign marketplace, there would be no Board of Trade. There would be no need for traders to take positions for or against, long or short, with regard to the orders coming into the pit. And that's the economic purpose of the CBOT.

Has that purpose changed since the time you joined the CBOT?

I don't believe so. There are more factors in the market today. Commodity funds are very large and use a variety of techniques to determine whether they want to be in the market. Their entrance and exit from positions can affect the market strongly. Sooner or later it is the value of the grain that will determine the price.

The same thing happens with the speculation. When a grain contract becomes current for delivery, if it is economically sound to deliver grain, then a short will deliver. If a long needs grain and the CBOT market is the most efficient source of supply, then he will stand for delivery. Otherwise both parties roll out of their positions and move on.

Do you think the business practices have changed?

I've been trading since 1946 and I don't see much of a difference, except the technical way in which we are presenting our orders. We used to write orders on an order pad and send them in to the brokers in the pit by paper. Now we send them electronically to the broker. We're even sending orders electronically into an electronic market. So, the method is different, but it is probably more efficient. However, the basic purpose of what we did and what we're doing is identically the same.

How hard or easy was it to accept these technological changes?

The technological changes were easy, but how to perform them, personally for me, is very difficult. I don't have a computer. I don't want a computer. If I want to talk to you I don't want to do it by e-mail. I want to hear your lovely voice. So, for me it's hard because I don't even know how to turn the computer on and I don't want to know how.

Do you think your son thinks about the business in a different way than you do?

I don't believe so. I think the basic nature of our business is the same. My son is more willing to look at market spreads and trade the market spreads than I am. I'm much more conservative than he is, and I would assume his son will be more active than he is, and then we'll go on to the next generation after that.

How does it feel to have so many generations down here?

Proudest day of my life. I'm 84 and all my friends wonder why I'm still working. I'm working because the beauty and the integrity of the marketplace still really excite me. It excites me to come down each morning and see my son and son-in-law, my daughter, and two grandsons in the office. I love that I'm still part of an active family tradition.

How about your recollection of going from the old trading floor to the new trading floor?

I was in Florida when we made the move, so it was easy for me. I left on the old trading floor and certainly it was very nostalgic for me; and when I came back we were set up in the new trading floor and all of a sudden I had to ask, "Now, where's soybeans? Where's corn?" My son Glenn was there, and he made it very easy for me. He did not make me feel like an old man. He never has. It was a vast room in comparison to what we had before. The old floor wasn't big enough to handle the volume that was coming. Certainly, once we got into options, it was way too small.

In many ways you've served the industries wearing many different hats. Tell me some of the committees you've served on.

I served on the Cash Grain Committee, but that was when grain moved differently. I also served on the Finance Committee and the National Grain and Feed committees. They were all related to the actual movement of grain, not to the futures side of the grain. I was president of the Chicago Cash Grain Association and a Director of the Board of Trade for a few years.

Why did you volunteer to serve on these committees?

I think it's an obligation of all of us to participate and to keep the market running smoothly. It's not a question of money or prestige. It's a question of the market. It must be protected. Anybody who had the opportunity of participating at the exchange had the obligation to the marketplace to participate to the best of their ability.

Part of being on these committees dealt with the self-regulation. Please tell me about this.

When I first started, the biggest part of our business was the cash end. Now that's maybe a third of our business. Today futures are the most. The integrity of our orders is based on the integrity of the Board of Trade. It's based on the integrity of the people we trade with and the integrity of the brokers we use. If we question the procedure and integrity of an order fill, it's our obligation to protect that order, and if it means changing brokers, we have to change brokers.

For the same reason, if our customers feel that we're not giving their orders the prime attention they deserve, it's their obligation to change traders. Fortunately, we've been blessed and that hasn't happened very often.

In terms of self-regulation, it is my firm hope, my great wish, that the integrity of the exchanges never changes. I sincerely hope that the government does not interfere with regulations to hinder the free marketplace that we have. There are times when funds are allowed to overposition and take positions that lead to the market going astray, or a large speculator can move the marketplace one way or another. But the marketplace, because it's free, always comes back to an equitable solution.

If the government gets involved in rules and regulations and tries to police us too stringently, I believe that the freedom of the marketplace will disappear and we'll be back to where we were in the Second World War, when the price of grain was predetermined by ceiling prices. At that time, there was no freedom of the marketplace to determine the prices and therefore the marketplace didn't exist.

So, I only hope that we don't have too much government interference. I believe in the rules that the government has to set up for the protection of customers, but other than that, I don't believe they belong as a party policing our own markets.

Can you think of some stories about when the Board of Trade self-regulated itself?

Two things happened that I can remember. In 1987, the stock market crashed. If I remember correctly, the Board of Trade had a small market in stock futures that stayed open and traded when everything else had closed down. A few Board of Trade members came in and bought the next morning, and that stabilized part of the stock market break.

Another time, which was very significant, there was a soybean oil scandal. I think American Express had the soybean plant where soybean oil was collected and was used for delivery against the soybean oil contract. They discovered some tanks with water in them, and the market became devastated, of course. The next morning, our members came in and stabilized the market by buying soybean oil futures.

Were there any other historical events that affected the market?

Just the emotional days. When President Kennedy was killed, there was a lot of crying. Even the Republicans, who are in the majority on the trading floor, were very sad. I don't really remember how the market went. I'm assuming the market broke and then it would have recovered shortly thereafter. But I remember the profound sadness. The market closed to protect the marketplace. That has happened two or three times when presidents passed away. When JFK's brother, Bobby Kennedy, was killed, we had another emotional day. How, in our country, could something like this happen? We were all devastated, regardless of whether we were pro- or anti-Kennedys.

After tragic events such as these, the markets soon recover. Whether it was the same day or the next day, the markets readjusted themselves and came back. That's the nature of a price-determining market. I believe in the 1970s, because of the Russian embargo, our soybean market went up the limit day after day after day. Sooner or later it reached the point where supply and demand came in. That's when we decided to expand limits so that grain could always trade. But limits are necessary to protect the banks and help the clearing corporation collect the money that they need to protect the marketplace.

Tell me about the role of a clearing organization.

The Chicago Board of Trade's clearing organization is necessary because it protects the integrity of the futures trading. If something goes astray, it's up to the clearing organization to make sure it balances out the first thing in the morning. We used to have the trades clear through the Board of Trade Clearing Corporation, but currently the Chicago Mercantile Exchange is contracted to provide that service. But no matter whether it is the Chicago Board of Trade or the Chicago Mercantile Exchange, the clearing process is an absolute necessity to ensure that all trades are matched and balanced at the start of the new trading day.

How important is a market maker today?

The market maker is the other half of price determination. The speculator is a market maker, because he's willing to speculate on the price—the short or the long side. If it was nothing more than speculators on the long and short sides, you'd have a casino. The movement of hedging by grain users and producers gives liquidity to the market and gives the market the integrity to continue. The speculator is a necessity to this sort of market, but he's only part of price determination.

Can you tell me some of the product innovations that you saw happening over time?

We tried chickens, but the chicken market didn't work here. But I think it was still active at the Chicago Mercantile Exchange. We were in the cotton market, and we were in the stock market. We were in the fertilizer markets. However, all of these markets couldn't sustain a legitimate commercial basis here, and therefore the speculators weren't around to trade. They couldn't help to develop a price-determining factor and they disappeared. Silver, gold—the Board of Trade is trying to make markets with these metals.

I've witnessed the innovation of options trading. When I was a director, I knew nothing about options and I wanted to vote against trading them. My recollection is that we voted for options because the Commodity Futures Trading Commission (CFTC) wanted another means of price determination and price protection. So, we voted for options to trade at the CBOT. I remember coming upstairs and saying to my nephew, who was active in the Chicago Board Options Exchange, "Well, what does that mean to us?" He said, "I'll tell you in a few years, Unc." What I found out years later was options are an integral part of price determination. The CBOE has a significant purpose and has done a good economic job. I am glad that we helped develop it.

Certainly, our basic commodity is still the grains. I'm sure that before I pass away, we'll be looking at a half dozen or a dozen more products, each one predicated on a commercial necessity for that type of market. It takes both the commercial interest and the speculative interest to make a price-determining market. You need both to make a new product succeed.

How do you feel about the idea of trading air?

I'm a firm believer that somebody who's a polluter shouldn't have the right to trade and buy the right to make more pollution from somebody who used less than their quota. Pollution is pollution. If we want to protect our shorelines and our children and grandchildren in the future, I firmly believe we've got to curtail pollution. Therefore, I can't see it as an individual. It might be a successful market, but I absolutely think it's a bad market idea. It would be like trading cigarette smoke.

Do you think the merger of the Board of Trade with the CME is a good thing?

I think that all the markets are now going toward the computer and electronics. Certainly a big electronic market has the capacity to handle a lot more than its individual market. Unfortunately, it's like the mom-and-pop grocery stores. The big chains put them out of business.

I think that merging with the CME will be good, individually, for each exchange. The Chicago Board of Trade will be losing its identity, but the economic pricing facilities will still be there. So, if it's economically better, and then I say, "Go for it." Just don't eliminate the competition in doing it. Competition is what's made our market strong.

Where do you see yourself, as an individual and as a company, in the new marketplace?

As a company, the partners at Hollander & Feuerhaken now are in their mid-50s and older. We will proceed and somehow find our niche. We will, hopefully, be doing the same thing we've done since 1942. We may be doing it a little differently, but we'll still be servicing agriculture in buying farmers' grain, selling their grain, and doing their hedging.

Personally, I'm just going to enjoy watching what the partners are doing. How much more time I have left I don't know. But I told the boys that I plan to be 100 and they'd better be in good shape to run a big party, because they're paying the bills.

What would you say would be your legacy to the Board of Trade?

I think the legacy of Hollander & Feuerhaken would be our name. I think it would be the reputation we've developed. The business was started in 1906 and we took it over in 1942 and changed the name. I think that we add a quality of honesty and integrity to the cash markets that we service.

I think our company has great respect for the buyers. The commercials who buy with us respect that we will produce the grain when we are supposed to, because they depend on suppliers like us to make their product. We never were in the sugar market, yet today corn produces sugar for Coca-Cola and Pepsi-Cola. These are new innovations of the product, but the basics are still there, the basics that we help supply.

So, I only hope that the future will allow the current partners, who are smarter than my father was and certainly smarter than I am and better qualified, to do what they're doing today to continue our firm. And I only hope that my two grandsons will push their fathers out. I hope that the fifth generation, which I'm holding in my arms as babies, will be in the marketplace, too. It's a source of pride to be part of this business, particularly in our aspect of the business, where we see both the speculative side and the commercial side. I know that we're an integral part of the moving and marketing and pricing of grain.

CHAPTER 10

The Experience of a Lifetime

Mary Ann Jablonski

Mary Ann Jablonski was born and raised in Chicago. After graduating from Kelly High School, she went to work for H. Hentz and Company as an assistant to commodity and stock traders. She received market comments by telephone and delivered that information to the company's brokers. In 1973, she briefly worked at Hayden Stone as a secretary, where she learned more and more about the industry. From there she went to work as an executive secretary to the office manager at Howard, Weil, Labouisse, Friedrichs, Inc. After that, she performed a similar job for Clayton Brokerage.

In 1975, Mary Ann found a home at Anderson Clayton Commodity Corporation, where her duties as an office manager allowed her to organize accounting and procurement systems. She remained in that job until 1982, when she went to work for Cargill, Inc., as an administrative assistant to the department head. There she streamlined trading floor procedures and she learned about options trading. She also provided customer service for many of Cargill's options customers and became options manager.

In 1985, Mary Ann saw a dream come true as she became a member of the Chicago Board of Trade. During the day she continued to work for Cargill, but her job was constantly evolving. Working with Cargill's futures and options department, she became a specialist in the soybean complex. She worked hard as a backup trader for crush spreads and futures. Mary Ann also began writing market commentary and analysis, which were very well received. She was an excellent customer service representative and served as the main resource for guiding visitors touring the floor and visitors' gallery. It was also her responsibility to research and prepare annual budgets and to hire staff.

While wearing so many hats, Mary Ann still found the time to serve on several committees, including Member Services, Market Efficiency, Options Settlement Task Force, and Flex Options. Her enthusiasm for the Chicago Board of Trade made her a highly prized member of every committee she served on.

In 2003, she returned to college to get a bachelor of science in business administration, followed by a certificate in executive leadership in 2006 from Lewis University.

Today Mary Ann works as a consultant for JPMorgan Chase. She has been married to her husband Gary M. Jablonski for over 30 years and they have a son, Christopher.

****

How did you first hear about the Board of Trade?

I was working at the bank across the street and I had a friend who was a recruiter in a personnel agency. He decided I wasn't making enough money. He thought I could be making more money working for a company in the Chicago Board of Trade, so he got me a job interview. I got the job and started to learn about stocks and commodities.

What made you want to be part of this industry?

In the 1970s, there were mergers going on throughout the industry. My boss at the time said to me, "Okay, you have a choice. Do you want to follow up in the stocks or do you want to learn more about commodities?" So I thought, "Well, I like to eat and I like to garden and I like to grow things," so I chose commodities and started to learn more and more about that. I took classes at the CBOT, CME, and Joliet Junior

College, which culminated in an associate degree in agriculture.

Do you remember your first time on the floor?

I worked for a broker who stood in the soybean pit. And one day he called and said, "Mary Ann, we're really busy. Come down here." I must have had a clerical badge of some sort, because I was allowed on the floor and I started answering phones and taking orders. I was just flabbergasted by everything that was going on and excited, and just wanted to keep doing it. I loved the business, I loved the pace, and I loved the feelings of exhilaration and excitement.

When did you get your first membership badge?

I got my first badge in 1985. It was a commodity options badge. Commodity options were just making a reappearance, and I volunteered to learn more about them. That was my first membership. And then in 1996, I got a full membership at the Chicago Board of Trade.

What was the acronym on your badge?

My first badge was OPT for the options trading market. The acronym I really wanted was MAD, a combination of my maiden name, but it wasn't available. Somebody in the bond room had MAD and I had to wait for them to give it up. I just kept checking every month, and soon enough, the man gave it up and I was able to take MAD.

Do you know any stories about how the Chicago Board of Trade came to the LaSalle canyon?

In the early days, the Board of Trade actually rented space from various buildings in the downtown business district. At the time, the business district was very small. It was only a few blocks. It was bound on the north and the west by the Chicago River, on the south by Randolph, and on the east by Dearborn. After a few years, the Board of Trade helped to build a Chamber of Commerce building on LaSalle and Washington, and they were looked upon as mavericks, because nobody in the business district went that far south.

Then the Chicago fire happened, and just about everything burned down. While the Board of Trade was operating out of a temporary facility that they named the Wigwam, they started looking for a building site. Everything south of Washington was not held in high regard, because it was not part of the prime business district, and so land values were fairly inexpensive. Sometime during that time period, a CBOT committee chose the site at LaSalle and Jackson. That block was already there, and in fact, there was a building on the back part of it that had a 99-year lease on the land. The training yard was also in back, off of Van Buren, so there was a precedent for that site already being part of the canyon. The CBOT Building Committee was very smart in choosing that location. When the first building went up in 1885, it was the tallest structure at the time because of a 300-foot tower they had on it, and it was also the first commercial building that had electricity in the city of Chicago.

What is on the top of the building?

On the top of the current building, built in 1930 at the same location as the 1885 building, is Ceres, the Roman goddess of grain. What's interesting is that when the sculptor created the statue, he did not give it any facial features because he thought there would never be any building tall enough to look down on her. That was true for a while, because from 1930 to 1965 the Board of Trade was the tallest building in Chicago.

Many of the iconic symbols that represent the Board of Trade are female, while most of the people working on the trading floors, particularly in the agricultural markets, are men. Do you think that means anything?

That is interesting. From my own experience on the agricultural side, the entire time that I have worked on the trading floor, I never thought about the fact I was working with a group of men. They were just always my associates; maybe that's what helped me survive and flourish.

There is a line of thought that many women are not exposed to the agricultural part of the futures business at the college level.

Perhaps part of the problem is with universities and schools; they focused on financial markets, so, unless you happened to know about agricultural markets it was not something that was talked about. Even when I was taking an economics class, the professors talked about speculating and hedging using examples in the financial markets, not the agricultural markets. I am happy to say that today this is changing. Even high schools are noticing the opportunities in agriculture, because of the high-profile biofuels debate.

Who would you say was your mentor?

My mentor was Peter von Eschen, a former boss of mine. He had a steel-trap mind. He was a Marine, very diplomatic and very sympathetic, with a very logical mind. He was an excellent mentor who certainly taught me, as well as others, all he knew.

Do you see many people mentoring each other on the floor?

Yes, I do. There are brokers who will take someone under their wing as an assistant. The broker will go ahead and show them not only how the pit runs, but how they do their business. That person learns what goes on in the pit, the courtesies that are required, and the importance of integrity and pit presence.

What's the first lesson that you learned?

The first lesson was "Know your customer, check everything, and don't assume anything."

Would you say that those lessons still apply?

Maybe even more so today, because the pace has increased so much.

What products have you traded?

I have always been in the soybean complex. I trade soybeans, soybean meal, soybean oil, and their respective options. I do it not so much as a trader, but as a broker for the company where I currently work.

Did you serve on any committees?

I served on several. I've served on the Member Services Committee. I've served on Flex Options. I've served on the Market Efficiency Committee and on an Options Settlement Task Force.

Which one did you enjoy the most?

Oh, I enjoyed them all, because whenever an effort is put into something, you certainly get something out of it. It is a good feeling to be part of making the rules of the Board of Trade and working for the betterment of the entire trading community.

Is it something you get paid for?

The committee service is strictly volunteer work.

How does the word 'discipline' apply to the business?

If you don't have discipline trading, you're not going to last very long. All of the large traders may look like they willy-nilly trade by gut feeling, but they're really disciplined. They have a plan, and they check their positions throughout their day. If they don't, their risk managers do and call them constantly.

Who were some of the legendary figures you knew or heard about?

Some of the people who come to mind are Julius Frankel, Richard Dennis, and Tom Baldwin. Julius was a very good trader. I heard that in his later years, he had some problems with mobility; he could not stand or walk for a long period of time. A chair was placed outside the trading pits so he could sit when he got tired and then walk back in as he needed. He was very generous. His wife died from cancer and he contributed heavily to the University of Chicago and Northwestern Hospital. He also was generous in helping some clerks with their education expenses.

Richard Dennis was a very large speculator, and he traded by using a method of following trends. He started a fellowship of students whom he taught to trade in the same manner. Somebody called them "The Turtles" and the name stuck. Mr. Dennis made a huge amount of money with this group.

Another legend that comes to mind is Tom Baldwin, who was a successful financial floor trader. I heard that he started out as a very small five- and 10-lot trader and progressed to be the largest speculator in the financial pit. At some point, he paid cash for the Rookery Building down LaSalle Street and he supposedly had that building restored.

Who are some of the legends you knew personally?

Usually when people talk about legends on the trading floor, one thinks about how much money somebody made or lost. But the two legends I have in mind are legends because of their integrity and high values. They are Peter von Eschen and Tom Cashman. People seek them out for their opinions, and they are truly the epitome of what integrity is all about at the Chicago Board of Trade.

What does that word 'integrity' mean in terms of the CBOT?

Integrity means a lot of things in terms of the Board of Trade. One example I can give regarding how integrity works at the CBOT relates to an order that was given to us by a client to buy a deferred futures contract, seven or eight months out. The liquidity in the deferreds was not that great at the time and, on top of that, it just wasn't busy. The client had put in a market order. The broker came running over to the desk and said, "Look, the offer is nine dollars away. I really don't think that you should pay this."

To me, that shows great integrity, because as it was a market order, the broker could have just filled it and pocketed the commission and just said, "Well, it was a market order. What was I supposed to do?" But he felt that it was important to come back to the client and say, "This isn't right. You should not be paying this much." At the very least, he saved the customer about $900 per contract. The intangible savings were priceless.

Are there other stories that speak to the character of the CBOT?

Absolutely. In 1982, the Chicago Board of Trade built a new agricultural trading floor and the Annex. When it came time to choose a name for the floor, they didn't name it after a politician or a former CBOT director. Instead, they chose to name it after a gentleman who had worked for the Chicago Board of Trade for 60 years, Eddie Mansfield. He was the security guard at the entrance to the trading floor. Eddie was always there to greet us on the fourth floor. He was kind and very knowledgeable about the CBOT and would be happy to help you in any way that he could. So they named it the Mansfield Agricultural Room.

What a great story. How about some examples of traditions at the Board of Trade?

There are many wonderful traditions at the Board of Trade. One of the traditions that comes to mind is how traders talk about deferred trading months. When we talk about red months and green months, it is a throwback to chalked price board days. For example, if we were to talk about November this year, in the old days it would have been written on the chalkboard in white chalk, and next year's November would have been coded in red chalk. And then the following year would have been written in green chalk. To this day, we ask for red November or green November or just November.

Another tradition would be the trading jackets. Trading jackets on the trading floor evolved from when people first wore suits on the trading floor. Well, suits were very heavy and cumbersome and they made the traders very warm and uncomfortable. As more and more activity came to the trading floor, traders wanted something lighter weight that still looked very businesslike.

The jackets evolved even further with color coding. The Board of Trade supplied the members with blue coats and phone clerks with red jackets, and the runners pretty much wore gold jackets, and I think staff wore brown jackets. Later it went even a step further with each trader, each group, each company gradually picking their own colors and their own styles.

Another tradition is observed when somebody who has been in the pit for a while, perhaps as an assistant or as a clerk, finally gets their own membership. When they come to make their first trade on the trading floor, in that pit there's usually a round of applause, and that's very, very nice.

How about the equipment that was being used on the floor in the early days?

It's very funny, because this was in the 1970s and not ancient history, yet some of the equipment being used amazed me. I was surprised that the machinery was actually still being used. For example, in the 1970s, I actually learned how to operate a plug-in switchboard. Also, in the 1970s, when I was working as a secretary, for a copy machine what we actually used was something called a mimeograph machine. It used a heavy type of carbon paper that was clipped to a drum and you had to spin the handle to run off your copies.

There was also some kind of a pre-fax machine. I cannot remember the name of it, but you would spin the handle and somehow words would be magically transmitted over to another location. Computers were not really widely used on the trading floor until sometime in the 1990s.

Can you talk about how the communication technology on the trading floor evolved at the Board of Trade?

Communication happens in a variety of ways. We speak certainly by voice and by eyes, by lips, but also by hand signals and by telephone. Now we have the option of communicating by headsets and also by the use of electronic order routing.

What's that?

This system, called the Comet Order System, was initiated by the Chicago Board of Trade as a way to make open outcry more efficient. In the old days, what we used to do was write up an order on paper and give it to a runner, who would take it in to the pit broker. That broker would hold on to the order until it was executed. Once the order was executed, the broker would toss it over his shoulder onto the floor. The runner then would hopefully find it on the floor and bring it back to the desk. A clerk would then call back the customer. Clerks would re-endorse the order so that it could be keypunched and then get repunched to go to the clearinghouse. As long as I have been talking about this process, that's how long it took. Steps were repeated, and that allowed room for error.

Around 1995, the Chicago Board of Trade asked me to test a prototype that they were coming out with; it was a system that would replicate an order form using a machine. The very first prototype was actually an old computer. I would take the written order, type the information into the computer, and it would be transmitted to a printer at the edge of the soybean pit. A blue light would go off. The brokers had their backs to the printer, so they couldn't see when an order was coming in. Sometimes I would type the order and send it and then run over there and tell them the order was on the machine before they picked it up.

Well, things got better as we worked the bugs out of the system and it has evolved into the sophisticated technology we use today, called Comet. Today's system actually replicates the look of an actual trading order on a computer screen, so there's a buy side and a sell side. It has a point-and-click technology as well as handwriting recognition. All relevant information that would have been written on a paper order can be reentered into Comet. This includes an account number, who entered the order, whether it was to buy or sell, the price, special instructions, and which broker the order should go to.

Once it gets to the broker's device at the pit, he simply looks at the order on the screen, makes the trade, and puts the fill information into the order routing device. From there the order can go directly to the desk, but it also loops around into the clearinghouse. Additionally, if the company chooses, it can be routed to a company's web site, where a customer can pick it up.

We have practically eliminated all the room for error, and the system is continuously upgraded. We are always trying to do it better. That is one of the goals of the Market Efficiency Committee that I work on. I am very proud of that.

That's amazing use of technology. Do you think that it helps with the transparency of the market?

The transparency of a marketplace has to do with knowing what kind of traders are participating in that marketplace: whether it's speculators or whether it's commission houses or commercials. So, do I think the electronic order routing system really helps with market transparency? Yes and no. I mean the same information was out there before. I don't think anything changed that much. However, if anything, there was a little bit less transparency, because it wasn't necessary to give the names of houses traded with unless asked.

When you talk about speculators, who does that describe?

A market maker is a speculator who is putting his money on the line. This type of speculator provides liquidity to the marketplace and also provides stability. The speculator will continue to provide a bid and an offer regardless of market conditions, even in the adverse situations. He will be there and continue when everyone and anyone is selling. And regardless of which direction the market is going, the market maker will provide a market.

Do you think the Board of Trade is a role model in price discovery for the worldwide markets?

The liquidity of the Board of Trade marketplace is one of the most important features of the exchange. The liquidity is so deep that when events occur around the world, people look to the Board of Trade to find out what the real market reaction is.

What role has innovation played in open outcry?

I think the innovation of the marketplace has a lot to do with some of the things that we've discussed. The electronic order routing, the Electronic Clerk in the pit, the headsets that people use, and bringing computers onto the trading floor so people can check their positions during the day—all of this helps to make a quicker marketplace and fewer outtrades.

What's the biggest change you've seen in trading?

Probably the use of the electronic equipment on and off the trading floor has been the largest change that I have seen. It certainly has quickened the pace. There used to be a line of people standing behind brokers with paper orders, literally, five, six, ten deep, and now you do not see that anymore.

Do you see any difference with the outtrades?

Oh, yes. We're getting closer and closer to real-time clearing. With the Comet or an Electronic Clerk, the trade clears automatically. It's a done deal, so that cuts down outtrades considerably.

What do you see is the significance of the commodity and derivative options trading?

The commodity and options derivative markets serve to provide a wider venue for producers, processors, speculators, and investors. It gives them what amounts to an insurance type product, where they can choose their price floor or price ceiling, and even after that, take advantage of a further rally in the market or a further break in the market.

The derivatives markets have personalized it even more, because users are able to choose very specific strike prices or expiration dates, or focus on a need of a particular customer. In any case, most of them were hedged eventually on the Chicago Board of Trade, which has regulated commodities.

There were a lot of historical events that have happened that have influenced things on the floor. Let's talk about a few of those.

I remember during the crisis in Chernobyl the trading floor being very, very busy for a week or two. The fear was that the radiation would get into the ground and Russia's crops would be destroyed and that would affect the supply of raw commodities throughout the world. The greater fear was that the radiation cloud would spread to other countries and deteriorate that supply even further.

Winds blowing radiation and affecting markets? That leads me to

ask about how weather affects markets.

Weather markets are the craziest of all. It is possible for limit up and limit down days to happen on the same day because of a change in the forecast or a little spring shower that has come up all of a sudden. It is very strange, because one day somebody can say, "Well, we're rallying because there's too much rain." And the next day it's "We're breaking because there's too much rain." And so it's very much a matter of perception on the part of the customers.

Tell me about the Russian grain embargo.

The grain embargo of 1980 had to do with the Soviet Union invading Afghanistan. As a result of that, the United States decided to place an embargo on grain exported to the Soviet Union. The farmers were not happy about the embargo, and they were not happy that the Chicago Board of Trade temporarily suspended trading. So, they came with a convoy of tractors and surrounded the Chicago Board of Trade. I remember that there was only one entrance that we were allowed to come in and out of, because the CBOT leaders were concerned something might happen, but nothing ever did.

The most important thing about the embargo was it probably escalated the rate of international commodity trading by other countries, and especially by Russia, by about 10 years, because the Soviet Union had to find other sources for its necessities; and at the same time, other countries such as those in South America realized that there was money to be made by exporting goods to countries outside of their borders.

You were on the floor at the time of the Crash of 1987. Tell me what that was like.

The Crash of 1987 was very interesting. Most of us on the trading floor had never been through anything like that before. I remember being over at the options desk and keeping an eye on the stock market going down 500 points. People were selling commodities at that time because they were in sync with the stock market, and also people were selling commodities to raise funds to pay for their margin calls on the stocks that they owned. Peter von Eschen came over and gave me some reassurance about the financial stability of the U.S. markets. Hearing it from him made me feel more confident.

How about the flood of 1992? Were you involved in that at all?

The flood of 1992 caused the Chicago Board of Trade to shut down for a few days. At that time, a lot of the electrical equipment was kept down in the basement, so we had no telephones; a lot of the communication was gone. We were allowed to go on the trading floor, although I remember it was dark. I actually had a flashlight. I remember walking around with it. And, typical of the traders at the CBOT, there was a bid and an offer on a fish out of the basement. I don't believe a trade was ever executed, but there was most certainly a bid and an offer.

How about the war in Iraq?

The war in Iraq has probably brought more focus on outside markets than we ever had before. We look every day at gold and silver. We look at crude oil and natural gas. We do this because all of these markets are affected by the war in Iraq and political problems elsewhere.

You've talked about the CBOT's involvement in world events. Now, what do you think of the Board of Trade's effect on the world economy?

People from the other countries still look to see what is happening in the United States and the Board of Trade. It's funny, though; sometimes as the markets progress on a day-to-day basis, other countries will say, "Well, Chicago was down yesterday or Chicago was up yesterday. That's why we're up or down." But by the same token, when we arrive in the morning we take a look at what the other exchanges have done overnight, and often give that as an explanation on why we're higher or lower.

If you had to describe your job, what would you say is the best thing about it?

The people. Most certainly meeting the people and talking to the customers on the trading floor. There are many different types of people. In fact, the best thing about my job is the different people we work with. We have doctors and lawyers on the trading floor. We have people who have never finished high school. We have women who are single mothers. We have people who have worked in different careers and have come to the CBOT and seen something, felt something, and decided that this is the career path that they wanted to take.

Why would you tell somebody to make their career at the CBOT?

First, because it's an experience of a lifetime just to see it. You can see how economic events that happen in the outside world do make their mark on the trading floor and how people react to them. Also, if you are the kind of person who likes high adrenaline and a sense of excitement and works well under pressure, it is certainly a job that is much different from sitting behind a desk anywhere. I love my job and would encourage people to give it a try. It is a wonderful place to work.

CHAPTER 11

Service Provided in High Style

Paul R.T. Johnson

Born and raised in the city of Chicago, Paul R.T. Johnson came to the Chicago Board of Trade after attending college at Louisiana State University in Baton Rouge. Choosing his alma mater as his acronym, he began his career at the exchange. He formed an execution trading group that filled customer orders, and in 1985 sold that business to the ING Group. He worked with them as co-head of institutional sales until that company was bought out by ABN-Amro. In 2001, he became the CEO of Boston Cabot, which trades futures, as well as arranges billion-dollar loans for hedge funds with ABN-Amro and other firms.

Mr. Johnson is a principal of Boston Cabot with Series 7, 24, 53, 55, and 63 licenses. At one time or another, he has held memberships at the Chicago Board of Trade, the Chicago Board Options Exchange, and the Chicago Mercantile Exchange.

A large part of his 20-year career at the CBOT has been spent in volunteer services, having devoted considerable time and effort for the good of the exchange. To this end, he has served on the board of directors of the CBOT, and was chairman of the Floors Committee and of the Market and Product Development Committee. In this role, Paul forged alliances with other exchanges and companies, for example with Dow Jones & Company to create the Dow Jones futures products. He also rewrote the Treasury complex contracts and helped launch the Fed Funds futures contract.

Married in 1988 to Renee Martin, Paul joined a family steeped in Board of Trade tradition. Renee's grandfather, George Martin, was a prominent member of the exchange. Her parents, Robert and Rita Martin, are both members. Her Uncle Larry was a member until his death a few years ago. Renee's brothers, Bob and Ryan, were both members of the CBOT, as is her sister, Rose Schneider.

Although she started as a schoolteacher, Renee became an active member of the CBOT and traded on the floor. She holds memberships on the Chicago Board of Trade and the Chicago Mercantile Exchange. Currently she is with the CME, clearing her customer business through Cantor Fitzgerald in euro options.

This family connection continues with Paul's brothers. Richard works quoting Treasuries over the Internet to hundreds of customers, and Clifford trades bonds and notes.

Paul Johnson is a highly visible member of the CBOT. Known for his immaculate and highly styled attire, he has represented the exchange with foreign heads of state, trade missions, U.S. senators, state representatives, and governors. He has had many meetings with the presidents and governors of the Federal Reserve.

Often sought after as an expert in his field, Paul Johnson has appeared hundreds of times in the media. He is often quoted by international, national, and local television, radio, and print media. These include CNBC, ABC, CBS, NBC, CNN, the *New York Times*, the *Chicago Tribune*, the *Financial Times*, and the *Chicago Sun-Times*. *Cigar Aficionado* magazine featured him in an article called "Stress and the Big Dogs." The book *The Mind of a Trader*, by Alpesh Patel (Financial Times/Prentice Hall, 1997), devotes a chapter to Paul R.T. Johnson and his trading styles.

Paul lives in Bridgeport Village, Illinois, and serves on the local parks advisory council and also on Old St. Mary's school council. He and his wife Renee have three sons, Trey, James, and Thomas.

****

We're going to talk about your career at the Chicago Board of Trade. Can you tell me how you first heard about the exchange?

I was eight years old at the time and my mother thought it would be a good idea to bring her children to the Board of Trade. She thought it would be fun for us to watch these crazy people, waving their arms and shouting. I clearly remember being fascinated by it. She read me all the placards in the visitors' gallery and introduced me to the agricultural markets. That was in the 1960s, and I was hooked.

Then she bought me a subscription to the *Wall Street Journal* that I actually read for a few months, but soon comics became more interesting than markets or even sports. So my attention waned some, but the interest was always there. That was my first taste of the CBOT. It was a decade and a half or so later that I wound up in the business. From that first experience with my mother, I was always fascinated with the markets. I really like the economics of it, and the trading part of the business seemed like fun. It seemed like a good place to be, and it has been.

When you went to college, did you study finance?

I studied drinking a lot. Oh, and finance? Yes, I did that, too. There were some economics classes I recall and some creative writing classes. Speaking of classes, today I know that studying economics and finance makes you more aware of what is happening in the world. It's becoming much more important. In the earlier days, it was more how you were able to perceive what was going to happen.

Actually, going to college was how I got the initials on my badge. LSU is what I've worn for years. I wanted to have my own initials, but every combination of PJ or PRTJ—I happen to have two middle names—was taken. I saw some guy with SMU for Southern Methodist University, and I said, "Hey, that's an idea." So LSU has been my acronym for a few decades.

Why did you choose Louisiana State University?

My father is from Alabama, and some of his family moved to Baton Rouge many, many years ago. We went to visit them when I was in high school. I had some older cousins tell me great stories about LSU. They said they would love to have me come to school there. They told me how much I would enjoy having some family in the town. They said, "You could do your wash here, and we'd be here just in case you got short on money." I was pretty sure that would happen. And then *Playboy* magazine happened to rank LSU as the most partying school in the nation two years in a row. That did it for me. I thought it would be a great place to learn, and I liked the idea of having family there. So it all seemed to come together.

I'll bet. Why did you want to be part of this industry?

I think my interest was twofold. One, I knew that there was money involved in it, and money helps you with a lot of things. Money is certainly not everything, but it helps quite a bit. The second reason was the excitement of it. People who were at the CBOT seemed to enjoy it. Not that growing up I knew that many people in the business. In fact, to get my first job here, I actually went knocking door-to-door. I didn't have somebody who said, "Okay, come on." I had to find somebody who would give me a chance.

That chance came from a man named Gary Houseman. He said to me, "Okay. Come on in, kid, and stop wearing those suits." I always wore business suits. He said, "You know, you're going to ruin those things." So I took his advice and I slowly dressed down. Over the decades I have slowly dressed back up. But it was the love of money, and the chance to make money in a business that was exciting, that made me want to be at the Chicago Board of Trade. I suppose that's what anybody really looks for: to enjoy their work.

Do you still feel that way today?

On most days, yes, I do. I still like doing it, even though the business has changed. It's funny. The business that I'm in now is strictly electronic trading. It's more on the commission side. I miss some of the flows and the camaraderie of the people on the floor. I saw that you interviewed Rick Santelli. He and I used to see each other on the floor. The floor was a place where you had the same people next to you every day. Today you see them every now and then, and you catch up a little bit. But it's not the same.

It was fun in the beginning to be on the floor and hear all these stories. It was always interesting to see things happening and be surrounded by people energized by their trading. Now it's just my brother and a few other people in an office. You have to make phone calls to find people. In the early days of my career, you could hear and feel a lot more. You felt a lot of things that you definitely don't feel today.

But there are good things that keep the business interesting today. There's a lot more information at our fingertips. We have more than we really ever had. I know so much more, so much faster, than when I was just standing near or in the pit. Sure, there were certain advantages to life in the pit, but there were disadvantages, too. Even though today I am just sitting at a desk, things still change at any given moment.

How did you buy your membership?

At that time I had two partners, Avi Goldfeder and Norm Black, and we had just left Shatkin Arbor, which had become LIT. Some of our customers weren't crazy about that. Les Rosenthal was looking for some people to help augment his floor operations for a new company that was funded by ING. We happened to have a profitable business. We got together with Les and his partner, Bob Collins, and we started Quantum. Les and Bob suggested that we stop leasing seats and buy them.

Bob Collins financed our first seats. We thought, "Here we go!" Then I bought an AM (Associate Membership). I had been leasing COMs (Commodity Options Memberships) and AMs in the past. Since that time, I've bought and sold others and still have seats. If I had been really smart, I would have listened to Brian Monison 20-plus years ago. He had said, "If you're really ready to buy a seat, come by." And, of course, I said, "Doesn't he know I make only $25,000 a year? I can't afford the $40,000 for a seat." I didn't realize he was going to finance it for me. We would have wound up making more money. But, such is life.

How about your first opportunity on the floor? What was the business like at that time?

I didn't spend a lot of time in the pits. I was more of a desk jockey. My customers were various hedge funds and banks that I would talk to. We did have some large private traders; but typically we serviced the hedge fund or bank. I would flash into the pit when somebody would want me to do something. My job was to execute trades and analyze information. I had to garner information and find things and come up with strategies and trades. I would watch things that people wanted. There were a few times that I'd go into the pit to fill something, but it was very rare. I did it a couple times in the options.

There was one time in the fed funds pit when there weren't enough people. Our desk was actually right up against the railing. There was only one broker in the pit at the time and I gave him a headset. I told him about the order. He said, "Well, we'll sell those," and I'm like, "There's nobody to do it." So, I had to go do it myself, but quickly, before someone else came in and hit the bid.

Instead of going around to the ladder to get in, I decided to jump over the railing and I kind of missed partway. So, now my customers knew that I literally busted my balls for them! The important thing was that we did fill the order and everybody seemed happy.

So, you certainly were in the service industry.

Ah, yes, very much so. And truly at the CBOT, service is everything. You've got locals who take the other side of trades; their job is to get along with other people around them and provide liquidity. But, as a broker, you've got to let people know what's going on and let them know why somebody did something. It's your job to let them know who's doing something and what's about to happen, if at all possible.

If we didn't provide that service, I don't think our industry would be around. Of course, the markets have changed. The whole business has changed. The services provided by some people are a little different today. Nonetheless, we continue to provide great service.

How about your family being involved in this business?

My family wasn't really involved, except my mother, for pushing me here when I was young. However, my in-laws have actually been in the business for generations. My wife's grandfather, George Martin, was a member down here. For a long time he was a cop. He started trading in the afternoons until he made enough money to be down here full-time. Then his sons, Bob and Larry Martin, were here for years. My mother-in-law, Rita Martin, also became a member. She was a schoolteacher. Her husband told her, "You're off in the summers and our markets are busiest in the summers. You need to come down here and trade." So, she came down and began working on the floor. She's still a member.

My sister-in-law, Rose, is a member; Bob is a member; Ryan used to be a member. My wife, Renee, is a member of the exchange; although physically she is at the Chicago Mercantile Exchange these days, she is still very involved with the Board of Trade. So in some ways, it's in the blood. As a matter of fact, that's how I was elected to the board of directors. I got the family vote and then one other, and I was pretty much good to go.

Let's talk about some of the legends from the floor.

There are probably a lot of other guys who spent their days in the pits who could tell you a lot better stories than I can. But I remember one that is interesting. It's about a man by the name of Charlie DiFrancesca, "Charlie D." Charlie was just one of those really nice guys. He was very bright and very successful.

Charlie D. was one of those guys who would take the time to talk with you. From the biggest trader to a runner, you could ask him anything and he would stop and give you the answer. If you asked him why certain things happened, he'd stop and explain it to you. You didn't necessarily find that with some of the people. If you were a member, you were a member. If you weren't, you weren't. With Charlie everyone was equal. He was a very kind man who really loved the business.

I'll tell you another story about Charlie's goodness. His brother was diagnosed with a type of bone marrow cancer. I am not sure of the whole story, but I know that Charlie went in to have a test to see if he was eligible to donate some of his marrow. It turned out that he had it worse than his brother. The cancer was more progressed. He had some surgeries that tried to correct it and he spent a lot of time in the hospital. I know they removed his ribs.

Charlie loved the business so much that even as sick as he was, he couldn't stay away. He would come in, protected with a flak jacket, straight from the hospital, sick as he was, because he loved trading so much. The guys who stood around him in the pit would prop him up, because it's a very physical business being in the pit. It was so physical that people were falling out of the pit, breaking arms and legs. There were guys who would hire football players to hold their spots. Those same tough guys would make sure that Charlie didn't get hurt. He would have a limousine take him from the hospital to the exchange and back, every day, for as many hours as he could do it. He literally did that until the day he passed away. He was successful financially and successful in life, too, because he gave back to so many people.

How about Tom Baldwin?

Tom's is a great success story down here. He started with $25,000, which is not an insignificant amount of money. To start his business, he needed to get the capital and have somebody believe in him. He turned that initial investment into tens of millions of dollars. He is still quite a successful trader. He trades from his house in upper Upper Michigan. He's making great money by anybody's standards, but less money than he'd typically made in the past.

Tom was a guy with a lot of insight into the marketplace. He understood what was going on. He had seen all sides of trading, because he went from being the smallest trader to being the largest trader. Of course, there are some stories about him. I'm sure you could find some people to tell you about a fight he had with George Seals. I think Tom actually stabbed George with his pencil. He told the investigating committee that he did not mean to do it. That it was an accident. And his defense was "I didn't mean to stab him with my pencil. I was trying to punch him in the head." I'm not sure what the fine was, but it all got worked out.

Those are the sorts of stories that you'd hear, because it was a physical world down in the pits. You had guys pushing you. As a matter of fact, we had to build the new room because of the tightness. It got to a point where the clerks would be on the top step around the ring and looking out at guys like me who would flash them orders. They would stand belly button to back. If one guy turned to do something, he would push four guys that way, three guys behind him.

We eventually put in rails and spacers to stop guys from falling out of the pit. There were guys getting hurt on a daily basis. It was quite a physical job down there.

There were some clerks who were light enough that if they turned or leaped up to do something and the crowd moved in on them, they didn't come back down on the floor. There were times when our clerk would yell, "Hey, guys, I'm not touching the floor!" He'd literally be off the floor for five minutes. He would still be able to do his job, because he could turn and what have you, but he'd be off the floor.

So, it was quite a physical job inside the pits. This was especially true in the bond pit. We had to build the new floor because we were missing out on so much business because there wasn't enough room on the floor. I wish we'd done it 10 years earlier. Of course, hindsight is always 20/20. I could think of a lot of other things we should have done, too. But the expansion allowed us to trade a lot more.

Tell me about that new floor.

We had talked about it for years before doing it. We finally opened it up in 1997. Of course, there were a lot of arguments, even on the design of the floor. As it turned out, it was the mirror image of the old floor, just a lot bigger. There were times when guys like Tom Baldwin, Rich Stanfel, or Steve Anichini were trying to fill orders and they couldn't get to the guys who had a bid, if they needed to hit it, or lift an offer. Literally, they couldn't move their arms or get to somebody. Tom, like some of the other large locals, couldn't get his arms up, so he didn't make trades.

We were crowded at the desk. I had 11 guys at one point in a very small space. Luckily for us, we were on the end, so we could work around the corner. But on busy number days when the government issued financial reports, the financial floor was where things were happening. I would have to lean in, grab a phone, and lean back. Everybody knew they had to get out the other way. People were holding their orders down so they could write them. Then they had to get them in, because you had to have them time-stamped to make sure everything was done properly.

The new floor afforded us an opportunity to work more efficiently. Before, we'd miss calls because we couldn't get to the phone and we couldn't always give the best service to some of our customers. Once we were on the new floor, people could trade more because there was more room. We could get more orders and then volume started to grow.

With all those people pushing and shoving, you still maintained a business based on integrity.

Yes, that's very true. If you didn't have the integrity of the trader, you wouldn't have an exchange. It would mean that people would walk away from losing trades, because all you have is the word of the two people who were involved. In an instance, maybe 5, 10, 15, 100, maybe thousands of trades take place. If there wasn't integrity behind those transactions, people could easily walk away and say, "Oh well, yeah, I forget. I didn't trade with Lisa or Bill or whoever." Or they might suggest, "Let's split that." Then what would happen is you'd have a breakdown. In truth, there are times when people don't remember things and you do work it out. But even those outtrades are handled with integrity.

The exchange is a place where you knew if you did an order, it got filled properly. If somebody called me and said to do something and I said, "You were done," that was it. If there was any question after that fill, I had to eat that error to give that customer the price that they were promised or what was valued.

Everybody along the line had their place where the risk was passed onto. And, if they accepted that risk, it didn't matter if it was a winner or a loser; they always stood up to it. I said, "I did this," and that's what has made it work for almost 160 years that we've been an exchange. At the Chicago Board of Trade, people make a trade and they live up to it. It's something you don't see in a lot of other businesses.

Can you talk about some of the traditions related to the CBOT?

One is of course what we just discussed: the integrity of the exchange. That in itself is a great tradition and that's what keeps us going. That integrity allows us to pass on a world of transparency for the outside world.

Another tradition is the colorfulness of our trading floors. We have a tradition on the floors of wearing trading jackets. We do this for a couple of reasons. One is to protect your clothing. The trading jackets are a little lighter in weight than a suit jacket. The trading jackets were also used to identify the different groups in the pit or different companies. It made it easier for the runners and others to spot the people they needed to bring the orders to. This was especially true in the grain room.

This tradition of wearing jackets was important so that you stood out and were easily identified. I remember we actually wore one of the first sort of ugly jackets, and then we tried to get more colorful as the years went on. Les Rosenthal had originated the idea with Quantum. Quantum was financed by ING, which is a company based in the Netherlands. The Dutch flag is red, white, and blue like the American flag. What a great idea to have red, white, and blue jackets. Well, it turned out to look more like a Domino's delivery man jacket. But we did stand out!

We went with it and it seemed to be the first foray, at least to the Treasury room, of ugly jackets. Then there were more colorful jackets like hunter orange. Today you've got 8,000 fabrics, and people are wearing everything and anything they can. You know, you've got to wear something that distinguishes your company. The good news is that they wear out, so you get to change them. This is especially good if you have an unlucky color; you get to change that. It really is part of our tradition of being colorful. We try to have fun with it.

How about the different categories of people who work at the CBOT?

There are different groups in the sense of who makes up the marketplace. There are the locals who trade their own money. Some trade for just five bid at six and they're five bid at six the whole time. They sell six five times and scratch the sixes and move on. Then there are other people that will position themselves a little more to try to buy those same fives and then sell them to someone else at 10 or whatever level. Sometimes it is days later or sometimes seconds later. It just depends.

You have people who are creating liquidity for a company like, say, General Motors that wants to build a plant somewhere in the Chicago area, and they need to lock in some financing. So they call J.P. Morgan or Chase Manhattan, whoever. Of course, now they're one in the same.

They will try to lock in that funding using interest rate products. They'll come in buying or selling, depending on their need. Then they will come to the pits and provide liquidity, hoping someone is on the other side. That's where the locals come in.

Or, you have guys like me; they're talking to various hedge fund clients who say, "So and so is trying to price a deal. They want to fund this or that project for 30 years." Then everyone is involved in trying to position themselves in a way to provide the liquidity for this commercial buyer/seller.

Sometimes there are people who just want to buy a house and lock in their mortgage rate. There are many clever ways to do this and many creative financing ideas. The existence of our liquid markets has facilitated the American dream of owning a home.

I haven't even mentioned the options players, who are trading for different reasons that provide liquidity. They all come into that collective pool that allows the Board of Trade to have great liquidity and price transparency that you don't find anywhere else.

How did you feel going from being a member to being a shareholder with the IPO?

You know, it's funny. I wasn't initially warm to the idea. I didn't quite understand how, in the mid-1990s, we could unlock the value. I needed to have this explained to me in a very simple way so I could understand it and explain it to others. This was my job as a member of the board of directors. Once that happened, I realized it was something that we obviously had to do.

At the time, the exchange was going through a sort of restructuring. We had always been a member organization and we operated like a member organization. For example, if there were three guys who thought a certain way and they were real loud about that opinion, then we would do what they were talking about, and then by the afternoon they would realize they were wrong and they'd say to go the other way. This of course usually happened after we had already told the staff to get 50 guys and send them out there across the country. It was often the case of too many chiefs.

I also realized that if you had a strong, accountable corporate governance you would then become more efficient and run better. Top it off with unlocking the wealth that was in the seat. I never had any idea it would be as much as we've had it become.

That was just one of the many times that my opinion was challenged. Sometimes it was when I was trying to figure out what I was doing on the trading floor or arguing with some TV interviewer or sometimes arguing with my wife; but we usually didn't do that on the trading floor. We'd save that until we got home.

How about the discussion of electronic trading? Where did you stand on that issue?

Electronic trading was always okay by me. I was involved with the Aurora project. The Aurora project was sort of another take on the Chicago Mercantile Exchange's electronic trading system called Globex, which of course is still around. But Aurora was a trading screen with all of these little icons. There would be LSU, and BT, and LAW: all the trading names of the members. So, if I'm going to trade with someone, I click on the icon and sell 10 and you'd see how many he wanted to buy or sell. It tried to mimic the trading pit. Well, it never really got off the ground.

At around the same time, the CME was building Globex with Reuters; and I had just been elected to the board of directors at the Chicago Board of Trade. Reuters and the CME wanted to have us involved. I was looking over the documents, and actually it was a lucky thing for the CME, I think, that we were involved, because the contract said that after 10 years Reuters would own it all. The CME was just going to be a customer. Reuters had it all. So the question became how many billions would Reuters have now that the CME wouldn't, if they had stayed with the original contract?

So in order for the CBOT to participate in Globex, we said they had to change the deal to where we would own our products, and they would own theirs. That's the only way I would do it, and I said, "This is the deal breaker. How can you vote for this?" And, of course, they changed it, and Reuters was more than happy to do it.

In the end Reuters wound up getting out. I believe the number I heard it cost them was upwards of a hundred million dollars. They walked and got little to show for it. Of course, the CME has a lot to show for it. They built Globex into a successful trading platform and were able to go to the marketplace before we were. We know they built themselves into a much stronger entity and got lucky with the CBOT yet again.

If we look at CBOT history, we were actually in the electronic era before the CME. We were interested in becoming a public company before them, but we had our membership problems just as they had theirs. Because they had stronger leaders who were able to say, "Move forward now," they went ahead. As an institution, the CME was fortunate to have gone public first. As members, the CBOT traders have been greatly enriched.

Let's talk about some of the times that the CBOT was able to "move forward."

Our CBOT innovators, led by Doc Sandor, came up with this Treasury bond contract with an 8 percent coupon. That was a great idea. They also had Ginnie Maes, which were initially traded in the old South Room. It was a very small room where guys were practically hanging from the rafters to trade these products. The room was not well ventilated and it was tough to work in there, but people worked very hard to create this new market.

In the early days it was tough, but we were getting ourselves into a marketplace where we could trade Treasury bonds in 32nds. That meant that basically for a security with a $100,000 face value, each tick was worth $31.25. While we offered this transparent marketplace with tight bid/offer spreads, the banks had been trading these instruments with a $1,000 price spread between bids and offers.

So, the banks had it real good. The banks really didn't want us to do too well because they loved what they had. "You wanted to buy a bond; oh, we'll sell it to you up here. Oh, you want to sell the bond; we'll buy it down here." You know, they wouldn't do nearly as many trades as they could do, but they didn't have to do as many. When you can make $1,000 many times over without doing anything other than just showing up, it was great.

Then the CBOT changed everything. We said, "We'll come in and we'll tighten the markets." That tightening of the markets was looked at as both good and bad. It created opportunities for guys who were willing to get in and out quickly, but it also meant that it became a more and more efficient market. Even with the efficiencies there are still things that move. The Treasury world is growing by leaps and bounds, especially with trading the products electronically.

How about some of the other things that you were involved in helping to create?

For years I was on the Market and Product Development Committee, and eventually I became the chairman. When we talk about creating products, there was actually a point in time when we were launching anything. Somebody had an idea, and we would throw it up against the wall. If it stuck, then we'd say, "Let's launch it." But people got tired of trading our little products, because there were so many and as a salesperson you can sell only so many things. You have to have a real economic interest, a reason to do something.

It was a hard time for all the various firms' information technology departments. Every time we came up with something, they'd have to write new code, and it was a lot of work. It would cost a lot of money and they couldn't be sure they'd ever make it back. Sometimes there were firms that wouldn't even write the code, so we wouldn't clear them.

Some of the hard work that had to be done was stopping the rush to find new products. My job as chairman was to set up criteria for starting new markets. You would have to at least pass a "red face test" to prove a reason to do it. It's why we don't trade lettuce on the floor. Fresh-cut flowers sounded nice, but then we realized the markets weren't quite there.

We always were in the market to find ways to stimulate volume. One of the things I wanted to have was a stock index. Of course, we wanted the Dow, but I never thought we could get that. But it turned out that Pat Catania, who was the senior vice president at the time, did a lot of work with the boys like John Presbo and Dave Moran at Dow Jones. We wound up getting a license to trade the Dow Jones product. It was something I wanted to have, but never thought we could get it.

Members made money initially. The exchange didn't as much, but then our business model was different. It was more member opportunities as opposed to the shareholder value that we are today. But it has grown into something quite good. For me, I can take pride in being the chairman responsible for the complex's start, as well as the chairman of the Floors Committee responsible for building the space.

Tell me about your involvement in the fed funds contract.

I have really enjoyed being involved in creating innovations for the exchange. In the 1980s, there was a fed funds contract. My customers had wanted it, so I fought very hard to try to get that going. Actually, the fed funds contract is one of the exchange's well-kept secrets. It always plugs along and does quite a bit, and it has created many millionaires out of that small pool of traders.

We rewrote the Treasury contract, and changed the coupon in the late 1990s. That was something I was a little afraid to do, because you need to be cautious about tampering with success. We were always looking for new products as well as validating our current products. The Treasury complex is the exchange's baby, but something wasn't quite right with the product. However, I thought, you mess with that and you may screw everything up. I feared that I would be remembered as the idiot who ruined the contract. What was happening with the contract was that the pool of bonds was getting smaller and smaller because of the 8 percent coupon, and we needed to make slight alterations to a few things. I thought maybe we could let it go for two years. Then we started to realize it could kill us. To do nothing would be to not do my job.

Pat Hillegass, a grain trader, had said, "Paul, if this were any other product, we'd structure this differently. At the very least, you need to hold some meetings and talk to the major market participants to see if we should do something." He was right. As chairman of the committee, I took Joe Nicoforo, Andy Wallace, and options trader Steve Johnson to New York and other places and we talked to people who were deeply involved in our market. We formed a consensus around the changes in the contract that needed to be made. What actually sold people, was that they understood that without a change in the contract specs, it would be possible to manipulate the contract. With that in mind, they agreed to the change.

Cantor Fitzgerald was a new exchange. It saw a chance to offer changes that I wanted to do, but we had political resistance from people who didn't want me to have credit for the improvements. That thought was part of the problem of our corporate structure. As it turned out, Cantor made it easier, because the first day they launched their Treasury contract, they had specs that were similar to what we wanted to do to our contract. All of a sudden, the politics were gone and it was time to "do the right thing." Often there are worries about the monies involved and what's the right thing for the exchange. In the end, people end up doing what's best for the exchange.

One of the right things for the CBOT is the ability to self-regulate. How does that play into all of this?

You need to self-regulate and everybody needs to be a participant in that. If you don't participate, things break down. This is especially true with an open outcry system where people could cheat if they didn't have the integrity that we have to have to be on this exchange. It is an essential part of being a member of the Board of Trade.

Self-regulations mean that you have people who are in pit committees that monitor what happens every day. We also have an exchange staff that watches people. Of course, electronically it's much easier to time-stamp things. On the floor or if you're at a desk, you time-stamp it when you get the order, you time-stamp it when you put it in, you time-stamp it when you get it back.

So, regardless of where you are placing the trades, on the floor or electronically, people need to feel secure that the exchange is watching each transaction and providing for complete transparency. Our job is to make sure not only that the farmer in Iowa is getting the right price, but that the banker in New York or in London knows that he could come to the CBOT where he is going to get a fair price. And with self-regulation we can provide that.

Let's talk about some of the firsts at the CBOT. Tell me about the first night of trading.

The first night of trading, we had everybody there. Everybody was really excited about it. As a matter of fact, Avi Goldfeder and I spent an hour on the *Len Walter Show* talking about it. Wow, this night trading was going to be a great thing, because this is the late 1980s and we're going into the 1990s and Japan is the powerhouse. Of course, if I had been reading the right history books, I would realize that the 1980s were going to end. We'd know what would happen in the next 16 or so years. We'd have understood the theory of economic cycles, but we didn't read the books.

So we started night trading and it was a crazy night. It was fun to see the volume. At the time, we all thought that this was going to be a wonderful thing—and it was. Many people were trading. You just started to get tired when you came in at 7:20 A.M. and it was eight or nine o'clock at night.

It got to be a long day and we realized we couldn't do it. We had to rotate shifts and then we didn't want to rotate. A lot of firms shut down their desks, so we did business for other firms. We were actually profitable, but only because we were doing everybody else's business since they couldn't be profitable at it. As it turned out, night trading was a nice idea whose time had come and gone. By then, electronic trading systems were just coming into their own.

It's interesting because today we hear that people trade all night long at home or in their offices.

That's true. It's the beauty of electronics. You can trade the hours that you want to trade, and you trade where you want to trade. We used to do some studies on how to reach people, especially in parts of Europe. Computers make markets so much more accessible all over the world.

Electronics make that possible in an instant. Everybody has access to us with a phone call. Everybody knows that it's so easy to call a brokerage firm, open an account, and have some screen that they can trade on. It has made our job a lot easier, as an exchange and as brokers. It's so much easier for the clearing firms to go after that business.

We talked about the new financial floor. Do you remember the first day of trading in the Dow pit?

The first day of trading in the Dow pit, I was trying to allocate all the Dow spaces to help build the volume for the complex. What worried me was here were a few spaces that were more attractive than others. People were trying to do some sort of arbitrage between the cash and the futures or the Standard & Poor's and the Dow products. This caused some ridiculous fights, but that's what we did on the floor. There were fights when somebody thought something was important that wasn't.

The first day of the Dow was really quite exciting. We were all ready to go and hoped things would happen. Personally, we were backing some option traders and a few others to try to provide market liquidity, and it worked out for a while. Unfortunately, the volume waned. The S&P was the real product.

Dow Jones & Company basically dictated the Dow 30. The plans were to make the contract a smaller size, which our research showed some market players wanted. I'd like to take some credit for it, but really they told us what they wanted and I said, "This is what we're going to do." They replied, "Your opinion is wise." And it grew from there.

The S&P mini-contract was developed by the CME to compete against our Dow contract and created a cash cow. They made a ton of money. If we hadn't won the Dow, they might not have created the minis.

Tell me about being on the floor during the Crash of 1987.

That was an interesting time. Actually, I spent most of my time over at the CME during the crash, because bonds were limit up. The only thing that was trading was bond options. My partner could handle that pretty easily without me, and since I got my start at the CME, I went over there to help. Those guys were going crazy. There were no limits and the markets were moving everywhere.

Of course, I was a little sad because I was buying 20-lot bond calls every day and I was going to have to pay up a tick and I didn't want to do that at the close. So I missed $60,000. It was especially a lot of money because I didn't want to pay 11 instead of 10. I didn't know if I was going to be selling pencils the next day. The Dow was down 500 points, which today is no big deal, but that day we didn't know what was going to happen. I had my friends calling me asking what was going on, and the market was wild and the bid/offer spreads were insane. People were quoting euro spreads 40 bid at 50. They'd normally be 41 at 42, but they were quoting them 10, 20 ticks wide and I'm looking at the pit.

I had some friends over there who had a negative net worth then and by the end of the day they were worth millions. The TED (Treasury bill/Eurodollar) spreads went crazy and other things like that. You really had to be careful filling orders. You didn't want to do anything at the market, because you didn't know where it was going to be.

It was a crazy time, with lots and lots of opportunity for anybody who was ready to take it. I sat there because I wasn't really allowed to trade. I was a member of the Board of Trade and I came over as a clerk to help, so it would have been breaking rules, so I didn't trade. It was a tough thing to not do. But at the same time, I probably wouldn't have done it anyway. It was scary to know that if you missed, you lost so much money; that it could have cost you everything. A lot of money was lost. But a lot of the smart guys got a great break that day. Even though it didn't look so good at the beginning of the day, they came out doing well. Many have gone on to do good things since then.

Where do you see agriculture going at the Board of Trade?

I think if certain things happen this summer, they could have Treasury-like volumes. I think this is the time when the agricultural markets can break loose, especially with electronic trading of grain during daytime hours alongside the open auction market.

The thing about electronic trading is that many of my customers have big egos, and taking a loss in front of me is difficult. Once the grains went electronic, their trades are, "Click. Click. Paul doesn't know I'm losing money but—" and they trade so much more. And it's so easy. As a matter of fact, it's faster than they could do it with me. So, that's what's happening with agricultural products.

Now, let's combine that with the demand for ethanol, which is continuously growing. If we get a drought or something crazy happens, then the agricultural markets, especially this year, could see their volume triple just during the summer. Maybe it will happen; maybe it won't. If it doesn't happen this summer, it's still going to continue to happen over the years. You're bringing more people into the agricultural markets and there's more and more of a reason to be there. So, it'll continue to grow. I have a feeling that this may be a breakout year, which just means that in the years down the road things will be just that much bigger.

You seem to think that the electronic era has been a boon to your business. Why was the CBOT so slow to embrace this technology?

The electronic age at the CBOT was something we were involved in early on, but didn't quite follow through. We had Aurora that we really didn't use at the Board of Trade and we had our deals with Eurex and Globex. But it's funny. Technology scared people here. You know, telephones scared people. They didn't like the idea of people calling down to the floor to put an order in. They thought it was going to kill the business. "Flashing your order into the pit—are you nuts? That's gonna kill the brokers." "The guys in New York are going to take advantage of those new trendy traders and trade."

Phones weren't so bad. Flashing wasn't so bad. Then, of course, we tried to put phones in the pits. Members protested, "Are you nuts?" I was chairman of the Floors Committee and I'd have to calm people down and say, "Relax. It's okay. You should just call from the desk so they don't have to run over there." They protested, "No, they'll have too much advantage. They'll be talking. It's like seeing it in the pit. You can't do that." Of course, eventually we let people call in.

We had to spend months putting in place all the technological advances that we needed. Today all of this is common practice. Even electronic trading is common practice, because it's so much faster. We spent a lot of time resisting this innovation. We used to joke about how you couldn't get things done and the trader systems would break down in some of the earlier incarnations. Today the systems work really well. They keep going and they keep allowing more people to trade.

I've backed many screen traders. It's not as risky as it might seem. The decision to back someone with $25,000, $50,000, $100,000—whatever it is you're putting on the line—is not so risky anymore. I can have that trader sit at a desk and I can watch every trade that's made on a screen. If he is sitting five feet away or 5,000 miles away, it doesn't matter. I can know what the trader is doing instantly and I can shut him off at a moment's notice. So, with that type of system in place it is much easier to back a bunch of people; and there is a lot that's going on.

So, electronic trading has brought us a long way and I think will continue to do so. Almost everybody has a cell phone in the pit, and that was unheard-of years ago. And now, almost everybody has access to the Internet that's as fast as anything else these days. So, technology keeps going. It almost makes me laugh thinking about when we were designing the Treasury trading floor. Only a decade ago, people argued that it was going be too steeply tiered. People would hire clerks to stand next to Tom Baldwin and watch what he did all day and report on it. But they couldn't figure that out when they stood right next to him. That was their only job, to watch one guy, and it didn't work.

Nevertheless, we didn't steeply tier it as I would have liked, but it's all sort of a joke now because electronics are making this place so much better than it ever was with its great history.

Give me your prediction about what will happen when the Board of Trade merges with another exchange.

My heart is with the CME. I know all those guys, and I know them well. I was on the Market and Product Development Committee in the 1990s, and one of our charges was to work on alliances with other businesses or exchanges; the CME happened to be one of them. And I know I thought it would be great to have us merge at some point.

Just think of the economies of scale; there are so many things we could do together. I know Scott Gordon, who used to be the vice chairman at the time and I was just a member of the board of directors. He and I had been friends and we talked about it and we tried to get groups of people together. We actually had a lot of dinners over the years, which was nice because there was always a steak and wine and cigars involved. There were certain bonds that were formed. Usually it was Charlie Carey and I, and Scott Gordon and Jimmy Oliff, and Terry Duffy. There were a lot of groups. We'd rotate people in over the years to try to build that positive feeling about a merger.

But Leo Melamed said, "You'll never do it until we're public companies," and it turned out he was right. I mean we even had cross margins set up because of these meetings. Nobody used them, but we had them. We couldn't get anybody there at the time, but now maybe it will happen with the merger. I am confident that the merger of the CBOT and the CME will be great. I have supported that notion since the 1990s.

Do you think the world is watching to see what happens with these exchanges?

The media has played a large part in our success today. Through coverage by sources like CNBC with Rick Santelli, the world is aware of what is happening in the markets on a minute-to-minute basis. Rick is a perfect example of someone who talks about the markets from a position of experience and knowledge. He was a member of the CBOT and basically did what I did for many years. He talked to customers and discussed the markets. One of the things I think has helped our industry, besides the great membership we have and the salespeople that are out there, is the media bringing us to the world and the world to us.

The media has certainly played an important role in highlighting the changes to our industry. In the early 1990s, television started coming down on the floor and taping market opinions. They would film on a Thursday but not air the tape until Monday. They might tape two different clips, each with a different market outcome, and they would air the correct view after the market on Monday.

Of course, today all of that has changed. Now we get minute-to-minute updates, right from the floor and in real time. The media have brought the world to us. They know about our colorful jackets that I talked about earlier. They know we will provide them with accurate prices. The media showed our exchange to everybody and made it exciting. The world wants to come and hear our perspectives.

Your personal legacy to the Board of Trade, what would that be?

I don't think I have a personal legacy. I hope I added a little liquidity over the years, and they allowed me to have a lot of fun. It's funny; you try to give something back by serving on the committees or serving on the board of directors. Although we did get great dinners out of it, except for the few that were rubber chicken dinners, we never got paid. It was all volunteer work.

I hope my legacy was that I added something during the time I was here. I brought in some new products. I helped new trading groups develop, as chair of the Floors Committee, especially on the old floor when things were so tight. There were times when if you moved one guy, you'd have to move 12 others to accommodate that one person. I hope I helped others in some way. If I helped somebody get a little bit lower mortgage somewhere on the South Side of Chicago because of what I did sometime in the 1980s, 1990s, or this century, then I feel my time here was worthwhile.

CHAPTER 12

Creative Partnership of Brothers

Edmund J. O'Connor

Edmund O'Connor has been a member of the Chicago Board of Trade for more than 50 years. As a young Chicago boy, he attended St. Ignatius High School; he went on to graduate from DePaul University and the DePaul University Law School. He joined the U.S. Marine Corps in 1943 and was sent to the South Pacific where he served his country from the backseat of a dive-bomber. He was honorably discharged in January of 1946.

Although Mr. O'Connor had a law degree, it was very difficult to find a position in a law firm after the war. His first real job was as an insurance adjuster. To earn extra money, he worked after the close and some evenings at the Chicago Board of Trade. In 1952, he wanted to buy a membership at the exchange. For this he used some of the money he had made while he was in the service and borrowed some from his parents. The rest he borrowed from his sister. All the loans were paid back with interest.

When Eddie's brother, Bill, returned from his service in Korea, he too bought a membership, using the family's kind offer of a loan. The O'Connor brothers quickly learned how to trade and how to make the most of markets. In 1959, they formed O'Connor Grain, so they could clear their own trades. That evolved into a customer business, clearing for locals. The company remained in that position until the name was changed to O'Connor and Company in 1970. At that time, it began clearing more than just grain trades.

Besides running his own company, Eddie was a very active member of the Chicago Board of Trade. He volunteered his service to numerous committees and was a sought-after member of many important groups. He was on the committee that put up the first electronic price boards. In the beginning, many members at the exchange found the success of these boards questionable, and the innovation became known as O'Connor's Folly. Although Eddie recognized the need to have a bigger mainframe computer for the price boards to service the needs of the exchange, he had a budget and couldn't go to the big IBM units. Only years later, after he left, did the CBOT put in better computers to operate the price boards.

Eddie O'Connor served as the chairman of the Rules Committee for many years. He was part of the group that wrote the regulations for the exchange to be self-policing. He also wrote regulations to prohibit certain actions on the part of the members. Much of this work was then taken over by the Commodity Futures Trading Commission. The CFTC used Eddie's guidelines while determining goals and, in fact, didn't touch the wording he had provided.

Eddie served on the board of directors at a time when the leaders of the exchange pursued more diverse and innovative products to trade. Among them were Ginnie Maes and then later the Treasury futures complex. These were highly successful markets and led the exchange to move away from just an agricultural base.

While these new contracts were worthy accomplishments, Eddie and his brother Bill are best known for their hand in creating the Chicago Board Options Exchange (CBOE). The O'Connor brothers had observed the stock options market over the years and thought it would be a perfect fit for the Board of Trade. The CBOT members, however, initially thought it was another example of an O'Connor's Folly. Together, the brothers opened First Options to clear trades for member firms. They eventually sold First Options to the New York Stock Exchange's

Spear, Leeds, a specialist firm, and later it was sold again to Goldman Sachs, which owns it today.

In 1978, Eddie started O'Connor and Associates at the CBOE. It was one of the first purely derivatives trading firms. They did no business with the public. He sold that company in 1995 to the Swiss Bank Corporation.

Mr. O'Connor is active as a charitable donor to Northwestern Memorial Hospital. He is a member of Bob-o-Link Country Club in Highland Park, Illinois, and La Quinta in Palm Springs, California.

He was married for 50 years, and has two daughters, three sons, and 10 grandchildren.

****

Let's begin by talking about your history with the Chicago Board of Trade. How did you first hear about the exchange?

My brother Billy became interested in it. We talked about the exchange and thought it sounded like a good business. At the time, I was in law school. Then Bill was drafted and went to serve in Korea. I knocked around for a couple of years after law school and then joined the Board of Trade. This all happened when Bill was still in Korea.

I had a cousin at the exchange named Pat Shay and I talked to him about the business. He introduced me to a few other people at the CBOT and I determined this would be a good place to work. I didn't like what I was doing, and I was looking for a chance to go somewhere else.

Why didn't you become a lawyer?

It was really because there were no opportunities for lawyers in 1950. The only opportunity I had was as an insurance adjuster. I did that for two years. Frankly, I didn't find that very interesting. I knew I didn't want to stay in that job. The Board of Trade looked like a good place to work. As soon as Bill returned from service, we became partners. We set up the firm in 1959 and we were partners until the day he died.

What was he like?

Bill was a fun guy. He liked to have what I would call "innovative fun." He tried to ride a motorcycle, but that ended with disastrous results. He liked to fly airplanes. In fact, he tried to build his own airplane, but he never finished. We had a building on Hubbard Street and he built the plane inside it. He never got to the point where he had to solve the problem of getting it out of the building.

After that adventure, I am sure the Board of Trade looked like a tamer idea. Tell me about the business in the early days of your career.

My brother was the type of guy who was very forward-thinking. He could see possibilities before anyone else. He really liked the Chicago Board of Trade, and his enthusiasm was catching.

What about the business did you find exciting?

It was a business where you could express yourself. It was a business where you could work hard and see the results, and I enjoyed that. In fact, I enjoyed every day I went to work.

Where did you start?

I bought my membership in 1952 and I started trading oats. At that time, oats was a very, very slow market. It was a good place to start, because I was very frightened. I couldn't open my mouth. You don't start off as a supreme trader on the first day you walk into the pit. Within six months, I caught on and graduated from the oat pit, and I went to trade in the corn pit. I stayed there another six months and went on to the bean pit. That became a very active market.

Who was your mentor?

My mentor was a man by the name of Max Witts. He taught me by example. Witts told me there was a lot more to learn about trading than just standing in the pits. So I went and researched markets from years past. It was a very rewarding experience. I learned that studying market history and theory was a good companion to actually trading in the pits.

In those days, to research markets, you didn't have computers. All the work had to be done by hand. The Board of Trade had a small library of past markets from every year, going back 25 or 30 years. I studied those.

Did you find a trend? Did you see charts?

I looked at charts and graphs. I saw seasonal patterns in the market primarily. It was only a percentage thing, but it was a very high percentage thing.

Did your brother trade next to you in the pit?

No. We always did our own trading, but then we would work together on market strategies. It made it a lot easier. I'd research one thing and he'd research something else. Then we'd put the conclusions together and decide how to trade the markets. I think I was a little more aggressive in trading than he was, but our styles were basically the same.

When did you form your own company?

We started O'Connor Grain in 1959. We just cleared our own individual trades. No public trades. Shortly after that, we started clearing floor traders, because at the time we were spreaders. All the spreaders had to clear their own trades during the early period in the markets, because we were paying more in commissions than we were earning. We had fixed commissions in those days, so they couldn't be adjusted by negotiation. We had to clear our own trades. Look at Dave and Bobby Goldberg, Henry Shatkin, and Lee Stern; we all had to do it just to earn a living.

What was the commission on a trade at the time?

It was $1.50 a side.

How many trades do you think you did on an average day?

Those early markets were very, very tight. It's hard to remember exactly, but it's nowhere near the volumes that you see today. We were trading very, very low margins in very slow markets. Eventually, the markets picked up, especially the bean market.

There's a lesson that people say they learned from you. They said that if you have a bullish story on corn that means to go buy beans.

That's right. I always did think like that. Also, we always bought beans around my birthday and then around Billy's birthday we sold them. Over the years it's worked out beautifully.

According to some of the very best traders, they say if they had followed the Ed O'Connor rule in 2007, with corn and beans, people would have made a lot of money. Do you think that's true?

Yes, it's very definitely true this year. Of course, this year is an unusual year, but the same rules apply. There's a lot of money being made down there now on that particular formula. I still trade a little bit, and I'm still involved in the market: long, long beans, short corn, but a lot, because I don't trade that much.

I'd like to talk about some of the legends you remember.

Larry Ryan was definitely a legend. I saw him once or twice in my life. He was getting ready to retire from the market about the time I was going into it. One of the stories I heard had to do with a man named Gus Staley. He was the one who introduced soybeans into this country. Soybeans replaced the oat acreage that was diminishing because of mechanization. They didn't need the oats, because they didn't have the draft animals to feed the oats to anymore. But something had to go in, because the acreage was switched every year. So they brought soybeans in to replace the oats.

Old Gus Staley was the only one who knew what to do with those soybeans. He had a big sign on his place down in Decatur, Illinois, offering $1 a bushel for beans. Well, Larry Ryan and another CBOT legend, Dan Rice, were offered a chance to go through the Glidden soybean processing plant that was located here in Chicago. They were given a guided tour all the way through the place. At the end of the tour, the man who was guiding them took them into an open area and said, "This is where we keep our soybeans." But there were no soybeans in there.

So Larry and Dan looked at each other and came back to the Board of Trade, where the soybeans had just been put on the board, and they began buying soybeans. And their buying took soybeans up to above $2. They put a dollar a bushel on soybeans, and soybeans never went back to a dollar. Never!

What's the highest you've traded them at?

I probably traded them at $10. When they went to $13, I was not involved in the soybean market. At the time, we had just opened the CBOE and I was spending my time down there. So I really wasn't a feature in that market.

Any other legends whom you knew about?

There was a man named Crawford. The story goes that he was a dentist. He came from Washington shortly after President Roosevelt was elected. The Roosevelt administration was going to do something to encourage farmers to stay on their farms. At that time, this man Crawford started a big market in wheat and almost broke the CBOT.

He was selling puts, and he used the money from margin to buy wheat. So as the market went up, he was selling more and more puts and buying more and more wheat. Now when the market turned around and went down, he couldn't get out of the market. Actually, he was never able to get out of the market. It got very cheap and almost broke the Board of Trade.

Were there other instances when that type of market happened?

It never happened again, because there was a law passed against it. The trading in puts and calls actually was options trading. But these options were not cleared through the clearinghouse. They were cleared in the back offices of the firms, so the clearinghouse never saw those options. The clearinghouse could never evaluate them and could never see the risk, because they used many houses to do it.

Let's talk about a couple of other people who were influential at the CBOT.

Dick Uhlmann was a nice man, but he was never on the floor. At that time, we had Uhlmann Grain, which was an old-time grain firm, and they had country elevators. They had a string of them that they'd had for a couple of generations. I met Dick once or twice, but I never worked with him on the floor. I did work with his son Freddy. I was told that Dick was working on a study of the Board of Trade. I heard he put a lot of work into it, but I never saw it. I wonder if it ever got done.

How about Julius Frankel?

Another fine man. He was a character. He was from the old country in Germany. He had earned quite a good reputation in the grain world before I knew him. We became good friends and I enjoyed being on the floor with him. We had dinner together many, many times. I miss him.

He had a way of bringing people together for dinner that were market people. He'd have a broker, Billy Fritz, a processor from central Illinois and other interesting people. It was always a nice gathering. He'd have it maybe twice or three times a year in the old Pump Room.

How about the McKerrs?

They were two brothers, Jimmy and Charlie. They were both really nice guys. After the markets were closed, I used to play a little gin rummy with Charlie. Jimmy never played cards, but we would have a cocktail or two in later years. I spent a lot of time with them.

The McKerrs cleared for people like me. Charlie was a broker in corn. Jimmy was a fine spreader. That's how he began clearing his own trades. We broke away and cleared our own trades for the same reasons.

Jimmy retired at a very young age. He was only 55 years old. Charlie had been killed in a screwy accident, trying to get into his own house. He tried to go through a window and fell back onto a concrete slab, hit his head, and died. And after that, Jimmy wasn't happy with anything down there. With his brother gone, he didn't see any reason to stay. He retired and went down to Florida and stayed there until the day he died.

What can you tell me about Gene Cashman?

Gene was a fun guy and we did a lot of things together. In fact, when they went into the oil business, we drove to Grimes County, Texas. By the way, he was successful in that business, too.

Did you and Gene ever exchange market ideas?

No, we had two different approaches to the market. I don't know what his basic philosophy was as far as trading was concerned, but he did very well. He didn't know what mine was, and we did very well. We were all individuals.

Tell me about the trading day.

They rang the bell at 9:30 A.M. and they closed at 1:15 P.M. Most people just disbursed and went on their way after the close. Not me. On many days, I couldn't even go to lunch, because I needed to stay focused so I could study the markets.

What made you and Bill decide to form your own company?

Basically, it was to save money, and it worked very well. As we got bigger, we hired clerks and started clearing for other locals and then other commercial accounts. Our business kept growing every year.

You also are credited with being in the forefront of the creation of the Chicago Board Options Exchange.

The opening of the CBOE was a big thing for us. The concept for the exchange was very easy, because it fit right into the program: the trading and clearing of the Board of Trade. It was a highly controversial thing, obviously; otherwise the Board of Trade would still own it.

Why was it controversial?

The Board of Trade has a board of directors, but each member is entitled to their own opinion and very often it will be expressed. Then pressure was put on the board of directors because "this thing is never going to work, so why spend money on it?" As time went on, more and more people began to feel the same way. So the board of directors was pressured from outside to abandon the project, which they did.

How did you eventually sell the board of directors on the idea?

You have to realize that the Board of Trade at that time was in a diversification mode. For years it had been nothing but a grain exchange, and now the board of directors, at least that one year, had decided to diversify. It was diversifying into finding a trading opportunity that was not correlated to agriculture. The Board chose stock options and thus the creation of the CBOE.

At the time, I was a vice chairman of the CBOT. The chairman was Bill Mallers. He said to me, "Okay. You research this, and you go do it." That put me in the spot where I was now developing the CBOE. The next year I was supposed to be chairman of the CBOT, but I didn't see anyone who would run with the CBOE. So I took over the CBOE and left the board of directors of the CBOT.

What was your goal for the CBOE?

Well, nowadays it's not what it was originally supposed to be. I thought it would be just a market of a few stocks and especially the more active stocks. I didn't see the development into what it became. It was after the opening when I began to see it. We traded a thousand contracts the first day, which was beyond our wildest dreams.

I heard you and your brother did a road show to promote this idea. You went up to people and got them to buy CBOE memberships.

Every time somebody had a good day, either Billy, myself, Pat Hennessy, or a few other people went up to them and convinced them they should buy a membership. We had to sell 280 of them to open up our doors and pay off a loan that the Board of Trade had guaranteed at the Harris Bank. So the Board of Trade was out of it completely when we paid the bank off.

How much did you sell them for?

They sold for $10,000. I bought two. I still have one.

When I interviewed Dan Henning, he said that if you and your brother were selling memberships on the CBOE, he knew it was a good deal. Why do you think you were so respected?

I don't know. I worked with people and we helped each other and did a lot of nice things. Being at the CBOT was a royal life. We were a very nice, closed little unit and you got to know people very well. I've tried the best I could. We had some friends, but we had a lot of enemies, too. Our friends were always quiet, but our enemies were always vocal.

What happened next?

We got 75 members to put up $10,000 each. We needed 280. We hired a fellow named Gary Knight to sell memberships all over New York City. A lot of members had to buy memberships, just in case. Then we opened up First Options to clear for member firms. We had to have the wirehouse input.

Initially, firms didn't staff up in Chicago. It didn't take long for them to see the volume of business it was creating. Then they came quickly. We cleared for 25 firms and we were even helping Merrill Lynch, which had only one girl on the floor. Merrill then cleared its own trades.

Many major New York firms then sought and got access to the exchange. Initially, no one committed to clearing the locals' trades. Soon the Goldberg brothers and Harry Brandt opened up their firms to facilitate local trading.

Were all the members of the CBOT given a membership to the CBOE?

They were given the "privilege to trade" on that exchange. They had to qualify themselves. They had to take the tests. They had to become broker/dealers, like all of the traders on the CBOE had to become brokers also. They had to qualify and so forth. Some Board of Trade people did the things needed to qualify to trade.

At one point, we were stopped by the SEC (Securities Exchange Commission) from issuing memberships and putting stocks up, because they felt our development was just too fast. It had to lay back and get control of the markets. During that period, we needed traders in the worst way. So, all those memberships that we had sold to the Board of Trade members were put in use either by just granting them the use of them or by some people actually leasing them during that period. That began the concept of leasing memberships. It never had been done before. As many of the Board of Trade members retired, they would lease their memberships to the CBOE and have a good income.

Today, of course, we know there's a squabble about the issue. At the same time that we opened, Leo Melamed at the Chicago Mercantile Exchange had started the International Monetary Market (IMM). He gave every single member of the CME a free membership.

Now the Board of Trade's individual members thought that I should have done the same thing and given them the free memberships even though we were two different organizations now. But the Board of Trade was no longer a part of the CBOE. They washed their hands of us by guaranteeing that debt at the Harris Bank.

I know it might be a little bit on the elementary side, but what was the economic purpose that you felt was being unfilled that the options exchange would fill? And how did you engineer and design the options exchange to then capture that market?

We had to answer that question for the SEC too. We did so by saying that people who are stock owners could basically sell options to increase their income. If they sell an option and the price of the stock goes up, when it reaches the option price, they could buy the stock back or they could buy an option to offset that option. But in all cases, they are going to be able to increase their income. But now they could turn around and sell another higher option. It proved to the SEC that this could be done on the buy side.

On the sell side, if you were uncomfortable with a stock and you had to hold it for a certain period of time, for tax purposes as an example, you could buy a put. That put would protect you at a certain price, even if you were not able to have the full long-term capital gain on the stock.

Would you say creating the CBOE was a major accomplishment of your life?

Yes, I think so.

How do you feel about the current situation today? Are trading rights to the CBOE part of a CBOT membership?

I'd never thought we would ever sell or trade memberships for stock. It is beyond my wildest dreams. So actually what's happening is something I never expected to see happen. But, now that it is happening, I think the CBOE really has not handled this right. By admitting that there was value there, they opened up the issue.

In order to actually exercise your privilege you had to be a part of that exchange. You had to take the test and you had to become a broker/dealer. I never envisioned that something like this would happen. I think there's going to be equity given to the members as a result of it. I don't know what it's going to be. It will be a settlement of some sort.

When the CBOE first came out, the memberships cost $10,000. What do they cost today?

I think $2.5 million is the last quote I saw. It is well beyond anything I ever thought.

The expression "My word is my bond" is an important part of being a member of the Chicago Board of Trade. What does it mean to you?

It means that you honored your trades. Every day trades were written on a card and handed in to be cleared. And you expected the person that you made the trade with to honor his obligation. And I think that happened all the way through my life with the Board of Trade.

Here's one example, and there were many. One time, I was a spreader in the pits in a busy market. Because trading was so fast and furious, a lot of my trades didn't get written down. I couldn't read my own cards for those trades. But those trades all came in and they were checked.

Here's a better example. One day, Jimmy McKerr was so busy that he never wrote one name on a card. He just wrote numbers. He handed the cards in and they all checked. "My word is my bond" plays to the honesty and integrity of our business.

What are some of the traditions related to the CBOT?

People wanted to wear a jacket that was different so you'd be recognized easily. I remember that there were hats worn by some people at the Board, but eventually that stopped. I guess you could say that our trading pits were part of our tradition. They were there before I came and they were well designed. They had small pits for small trades and large pits for larger trades. They were good for trading, because it put you in a position where you could see the entire pit. And you could make cross pit trades that were very easy.

What is the importance of a clearing corporation?

We wouldn't be anywhere without a clearing corporation, because it put together the trades to the various clearinghouses. It matched those trades. There would be a list of outtrades the next day; either you might have a wrong price or you might have a wrong volume or something like that. But most of the time, those all got resolved on the floor before the market opened. Every once in a while one slips through the cracks, but it is a very, very good system.

Were you ever involved in a dispute?

Oh, sure. We settled it right down the middle. Honest disputes can occur very easily.

How about the first lesson that you learned?

Take your losses quickly. The quicker you take a loss, the better off you are. That still applies today in our business and in life in general. You need to think that way about everything.

Did anybody ever challenge you about anything?

Not too many times, but there was one incident I remember. There was this guy on the floor. He was with Continental Grain. He came up to me when the market was closed and he said, "You know, Ed, I thought I had an export order, but I didn't have it." This was in beans. And he said, "I bought 200 beans that I shouldn't have bought." So this was after the close. I took the beans. Then he went to Lee Stern and did the same thing. So Lee now had his beans and I had the beans.

Before the opening the next day they found out he was doing some finagling within Continental Grain. He had been doing it for quite some time, and he confessed to everything and confessed the fact that Lee and I had taken the beans from him after the close. Well, that was a no-no. You weren't supposed to trade after the close, but everybody did trade a little bit for evening-up purposes. Today they allow it. But back then they just turned their back on it.

I was on the board of directors at the time and I had to exclude myself from the deliberations, and the Board weighed strongly that we did a wrong thing. But I think it was like a six-month vacation. Well, the members of the Board of Trade convinced the Board that they should really rethink it. So they rethought it and they gave us 60 days or 30 days. But the next morning, I had a bunch of beans to dump and Lee had a bunch of beans to dump and everybody knew that we did. So we lost on that, too.

Would you tell me about some of the committees you served on?

I was on the Rules Committee and the Floor Governors Committee. I am sure there were more. People at the Board of Trade are known for doing service for their industry. They feel they can do some good.

Give me some examples of the good that you did.

The CBOE is certainly one example. We wrote rules for the regulation of certain practices to be involved in the Board of Trade. And by the way, when the CFTC (Commodity Futures Trading Commission) took over the job of regulating the Board of Trade, they took those rules that we wrote, word for word, and included them in the regulations.

That leads me to ask you about the CBOT being a self-regulatory agency. How important is that?

It's important, but I've always questioned the ability of someone, as an agency, to be self-regulating. I sometimes think there's too much brotherhood involved in something like that. We're all members of the same organization; we're all buddies. The ability to self-regulate sometimes becomes not so feasible within that type of structure.

Did you see evidence of that?

No, I don't think I saw any evidence of that, because the Board of Trade really and truly did a pretty good job of doing that. Other exchanges did not.

How did the creation of the CFTC or the NFA (National Futures Association) impact the CBOT?

I think that things are handled very, very nicely by the CFTC. I am not sure that the NFA does as effective a job.

Would you describe yourself as a trader or a speculator?

A trader. I bought and sold with an eye toward a profit. I mean that's all I did. I was basically a spreader. Some people did call us gamblers, but only those who were not familiar with what we do. It's a common opinion of a lot of uneducated people. It's a matter of risk. A gambler has no way to determine his risk. We use risk control along with those mediums that we work with. Personally, I take risks for me. I never had a public business. I had a commercial business.

And how about for the farmer?

Well, farmers have used the markets for many, many years. When the price is high and they're satisfied with the price, they'll hedge their crop. That's what they did this year in corn. They did a tremendous job. That's what the market is for. The farmers sell to the nearest country elevators, and the elevators then turn around and sell in our market. So that flow of orders from the country lands in Chicago.

Would you describe the CBOT as being a model for worldwide price discovery?

Yes, it is. The buyers and the sellers meet here.

And how important is the transparency that you provide?

The transparency is there so anyone outside our markets can see exactly what is going on. They can comfortably base their decisions upon our transparency. The more people who see it and get knowledgeable about it, the more business we get, and that's, I think, very important to us.

How is the Chicago Board of Trade different from over-the-counter (OTC) or other exchanges?

The Board of Trade has a clearing corporation, which guarantees every trade on the exchange. Other organizations that are providing a marketplace don't necessarily have that background. In places other than the CBOT, you have to trust the firm you're doing business with rather than trusting the clearinghouse. There's a tremendous risk there. The clearing mechanism of the Chicago Board of Trade makes us unique. The clearing organization does a fabulous job.

How about the role of innovation, things that you've seen change since you first got there?

We've been a grain exchange for years and years and years. We were innovative basically for only a short period of time. And in that short period of time we ended up with the bond markets and the CBOE.

Why do you say that innovation only lasted a short time?

Because people were not really interested in it. They weren't interested in finding new markets. They watched the CME basically put market after market up there and fail, but the ones they kept were winners. Just take a look at that market right now. The CME actually took the best bond market away from us: the Eurobond. I still don't understand why we didn't get that. Innovation just seemed to disappear.

How about the innovations that have occurred during your time at the Board of Trade, like going from a trading card to an electronic trading card to all the other new trading vehicles?

Well, they all were necessary in this electronic age. I had never traded on the floor with the electronic trading card. But it had to be done to take advantage of the true electronic benefit to the exchange and its members. I think it's a wonderful thing. But that makes the trade from the point of execution purely electronic. It goes right into the Board of Trade clearing firm, and from there the same impulse goes into the clearinghouse. It's just one straight-through thing. It is wonderful.

When they first brought up the idea of electronic trading, were you in favor of it?

Yes, I was. In fact, Billy and I talked about it, and I think we were seeing some of the things we thought would happen. Of course, we never expected that we would be a public stock, but we did expect the electronic world to expand.

Have you traded electronically?

Oh, yes. It's a straight-through process and you get your confirmation immediately. You don't have to wait, and it's a little less expensive.

Would you say that's the biggest change that's happened in your industry?

Yes, it is. I think the biggest thing that's happened is the development of electronic trading. If you look at the markets where electronic trading has started, it has dominated the markets. There's no question about it. I think our bond market is strictly an arbitrage between the floor and the electronic exchange.

Do you think there's a place for floor trading anymore?

I hope so, because I did most of my trading in the nonelectronic market. I feel it can still handle volume better. You have a trading crowd, and that crowd will produce more volume at a time than you can get on the electronic market. Now sometimes electronic markets are deeper than the floor market, but I still see the floor market as being deeper.

Do you think electronic trading will still give excellent service to the customers?

I think eventually the wirehouses' orders will all be electronic because of cost. And it doesn't make any difference; all they look at is the bottom line. Our service will always be excellent.

Tell me about the importance of interest rate futures and your remembrance of being there at the beginning.

Well, it evolved. The market did not open as a bond market as we know it today. We traded the Ginnie Mae contract, which was an agency contract of the government. Then the bond market division began, with the long-term bond market coming on first. It was so successful they opened up markets in the 10-year, 5-year, and 2-year, and it's been that way ever since. And it's still a big, big market volumewise.

Like anything, the younger members accepted it and the older members didn't. It was something that was different for them. As it turned out, these new markets were never developed by the existing members of the Board of Trade; they were developed by new members. We had sold new memberships to these people who were making these markets, and the Board of Trade members could participate if they wished. If they didn't want to, they didn't have to, and we found very little participation by the Board of Trade members in the new markets.

The CBOE was the same thing. There were a few people who came over, but not many. I'd say you could count them using both hands. I don't think I cleared for any CBOT member who went over.

Why do you think as a group, the Board of Trade has a hard time dealing with change?

Like most people, they're comfortable where they are and they're too old to learn new things. There was only one guy, and his name was Paul McGuire, who seemed to understand and like new market ideas. Paul was a wonderful guy. He took an interest in every one of these things, and he participated in the new markets. He was an academic, a professor I believe. He understood the need to change. Because he was always interested and supportive of new things, he remained a young man all his life.

What types of business ventures evolved from your activity at the CBOE?

We started First Options, and then sold it because we did not have the capital to successfully run it. We were way over our heads. The company was bought by the New York Stock Exchange's Spear, Leeds, a specialist firm that did very well with it and then sold it to Goldman Sachs, which still owns it today. We then started O'Connor and Associates in 1978 as purely a trading firm. We sold it in 1995 to the Swiss Bank Corporation, because we didn't have the capital to take advantage of it. But we did well with all the ventures.

Are new products being created for the agricultural markets?

I don't know. There aren't too many different things that agriculturally are grown that don't have a place to hedge. You have different vegetable oils, besides soybean oil. But the soybean oil market will handle the hedge on those products, and the same thing with meal. Maybe someday we will be trading in the ethanol market.

Let's talk about the significance of commodity and derivative options trading. How did it change the marketplace?

In the study I did on it, I determined that when the options market is used with the stock market, it should eliminate a lot of swings in the market. There is a tendency to keep the market more stable. I definitely found it to be true in stocks. Options seem to violate everything that I have thought about that market, but at the same time, maybe if options weren't there, the swings would be larger.

Everything is so dependent upon weather. Look what's happened this year. The wheat market just went along fine until we had a freeze. I think options are something that are used primarily by commercials today, rather than by the public. They hedge more with options than they do with the contracts.

What do you think will be the future of the options markets?

It's going to be a big future. Look at those options volumes; they're increasing more and more, and they should be. They're used as a medium for controlling risk, and that's what options should be used for. As I said before, memberships originally cost $10,000. Today memberships are valued at $2.5 million. It's well beyond anything I ever thought.

I want to talk about some of the historical world events that you can remember having an impact at the Chicago Board of Trade.

Monday morning of the same week that Kennedy was assassinated, some very ugly trades had to be liquidated. There was a man named Anthony De Angelis, who had been a world vegetable oil trader and he had lied to the industry. He had a big, huge position and no product to back it up. He was found out, and he had to be liquidated in the market on this one Monday morning.

Of course it had been rumored that he was in trouble for quite some time when the market was going down. But we finally got him. By Tuesday the market was very steady and we basically had no problems at all. Then, at the end of the week, after we had all unwound our positions, somewhere around one o'clock, the word came down about the Kennedy assassination, and that destroyed the markets again. So we had bought soybean oil and sold everything else on Monday, but on Friday everything else went down but soybean oil. It was a bad week.

Do you think that markets are affected by different presidents that you have seen in your lifetime?

No, only once when a president did something did it affect the market. That was in 1973 when Nixon embargoed soybeans. It had two effects. The short-term effect was to stop a market from going up. I think it probably was pretty much finished anyway. But it forced a market drop immediately.

A secondary effect was that our CBOT customers began to think of this as a nondependable supplier, and they went down and made big investments in Brazil to grow soybeans. We've suffered from that ever since. Of course, it probably would have happened anyway, because the world needs more soybeans.

Do you know where somebody has actually cornered the market?

I've read about it, but that happened back in the late 1880s or 1890s; somebody named Benjamin P. Hutchinson did actually do that in the wheat market. I read a book on it one time, and I guess you could say it happened because of the man's ego.

His nickname was Old Hutch. He lived in the Atlantic Hotel, which was right across the street from the Board of Trade in those days. Apparently, he fell down the stairs at one time and the word got out that he was severely injured, and the wheat market broke. And he got himself into a wheelchair and got wheeled out onto the floor of the Board of Trade and dictated the price where wheat was going to go immediately, and, in fact, it did. He took complete control of the wheat market. Personally, I have never seen anyone corner the market, but I have seen a lot of big egos.

What do you see as the CBOT's affect on world economies?

There's the hedging aspect. I think it provides a service to growers and users worldwide. They can hedge their crop if the price is right, and they could buy the crop if the hedge is right. It works two ways.

Do you think there will be exchanges opening up in places like China or India, and will they provide competition for the CBOT?

China already has an exchange. I don't know if India has one. The Chinese exchange provides service to their local farmers, just as we provide the service to our local farmers. That's more important to them, I think, than the Board of Trade. We sell so much to China that it has to be hedged in our market. It doesn't do them any good to hedge it in their market, because they don't provide the soybeans; we do.

Seeing worldwide participation, what do you predict will be the future of trading?

You're going to find traders develop forever. The electronic market is going to have to have traders. It has a combination of the two now, but the efficiency of the market is going to be much better when the trading is done purely electronically.

What is your reaction to the merger of the Chicago Board of Trade and the Chicago Mercantile Exchange?

It's a wonderful thing. The CME, as a financial institution, is a very strong exchange, and I think the combination of the two would work well. I think you will see that as the interest grows in our markets, the stock value will increase.

Where do you see your place in the new marketplace?

I'll be a stockholder, period. I'll keep most of it and with some of it I'd like to diversify a little bit.

How about your CBOE pieces?

I'll sell those.

Do you think that there will be a place for old traditions in the new marketplace? Do you think the integrity will still be the same?

It doesn't have to be, because you're sitting at a machine. You make a trade; you've made a trade. There's no more "My word is my bond," because you don't say anything. You make a trade. So the old world we lived in just disappears. But you can still trade.

Are you still active in the markets?

Yes, I still trade.

What do you trade now?

Anything that looks good to me.

Do you have any children who are traders?

I have two sons and one son-in-law who are traders.

Have you taught them everything you know?

I tried to, but, you know, that doesn't always follow through. They're all individuals. They have done a fine job of developing their own trading styles.

Is there a place in the new marketplace for the families to continue doing business together?

I think there is definitely a place for that. Sons seem to follow in their fathers' footsteps to a certain extent. You don't get all your children in there, but you get some of them. And yes, I think that we'll still grow. And this new market is going to need market makers.

When people talk about Eddie O'Connor in connection with the Chicago Board of Trade, what would you like them to say?

Well, since I enjoyed myself all the time I was on the floor and was part of the exchange, I just hope I gave something back to the exchange that provided so much for me. I never thought about a legacy. I lived my life as a trader, and I think it's been a wonderful life.

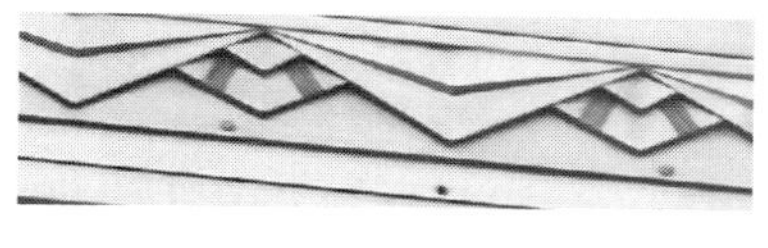

CHAPTER 13

Hard Work and Imagination

C.C. Odom

C.C. Odom came to Chicago from his home state of Texas, armed with a lot of knowledge and experience. Having started his undergraduate studies at Baylor University, he went on to get a bachelor of arts degree in economics from Texas Christian University (TCU). In 1967, Mr. Odom got his master of arts degree in finance from TCU. By 1968, he had formed his company, Odom Investments, which is still in operation today.

From 1971 to 1973, C.C. was an allied member of the New York Stock Exchange. In 1973, he became a member of the Chicago Board of Trade, and still holds that membership today. From 1974 to 1991, he held a membership with the Chicago Board Options Exchange, and from 1979 to 1984 he owned a membership on the New Orleans Commodity Exchange.

C.C. Odom's commitment to the well-being of the Chicago Board of Trade is legendary. He has served on many committees. Among those are Floor Governors, Membership, Member Relations, Metals,

Silver/Gold Pit, Special Committee on CBOT/CBOE Joint Access, Special Marketing, Special Floor Concepts, Membership Unification, Nominating, Audit, Transaction, and the Executive committees.

C.C. has been the vice chairman of the board of directors, the Board of Directors Executive Committee, the Metals Committee, and the Lessor Committee. He has served as chairman for the following committees: Membership, Member Services, Governance/Nominating, Public Relations, Ad Hoc Bracketing/Time Stamping, Lessor, Metals, Metals Options, as well as the Special Committee on Floor Access, the Silver/Gold Pit Committee, the Silver/Gold Copper Regularity Subcommittee, the Blue Ribbon Committee for Long Range Planning, and the CBOT AMPAC Steering Committee.

Mr. Odom has been involved in the development and implementation of a number of new products for the CBOT. Among those are the 1,000-oz. silver futures, one-kilogram gold futures, and 55,000-pound copper futures, as well as the reintroduction of 5,000-oz. silver futures and 100-oz. gold futures; he also served as an adviser for the implementation of electronic trading of 100-oz. gold and 5,000-oz. silver futures. For the CBOT, C.C. helped design, develop, and implement the 1,000-oz. silver options on futures, and for the New Orleans Commodity Exchange he was instrumental in bringing to the marketplace the rough rice, short staple cotton, and Gulf delivery soybean futures.

Beyond the Chicago Board of Trade, C.C. Odom is a man who has devoted his adult life to serving the entities that he has joined. To name just a few of the jobs he has held, he was chairman of the board of the New Orleans Commodity Exchange, a director of the International Precious Metals Institute, a managing director of the Virginia Trading Company, chairman of the advisory board for Money Week Financial Productions, and a trustee for the Traders Foundation.

Besides his memberships in the various exchanges, Mr. Odom is or has been affiliated with many other business entities: CCO Venture Capital, Argent Venture Capital, Precision Detailing, Inc., Mission Capital Funding, RBC Development Corporation, Alexander Billing and Consulting, Frontier Healthcare, Goldenberg, Hehmeyer and Company, COR Limousine Company, Virginia Trading Company, C.C.J. Inc., Walston and Company, and Rock'n C Ranch in Sisterdale, Texas. He is always busy working as many as three jobs at a time.

C.C. is a member of many professional organizations, including the National Economics Honor Society, the National Cattlemen's Beef

Association, the National Quarter Horse Association, and the Japanese Karate Association. He is a member of many social clubs: Dominion Country Club, Evanston Country Club, the Racquet Club of Chicago, the Union League Club, and Club Giraud and the Argyle Club in San Antonio, Texas.

C.C's charitable activities include serving on many boards to help other people. He has been a director of the Better Boys Foundation, the Chicago Landmarks Preservation Council, the Mission Road Developmental Center, the South Texas Community Foundation, and Mission Road Ministries.

Mr. Odom is a man who has worked hard all his life to develop and build the industries that have captured his imagination and business acumen. His resume is that of a man who has devoted his life to serving many organizations and people.

Finally, one partnership that he is particularly proud of is his 34-year marriage to his wife, Roxanne.

****

Before we start, I have to ask you: What does the "C.C." stand for?

Only the CIA knows that it stands for Chester Carlyle.

Thanks for sharing that! Okay, we are going to go back and talk about your life at the Chicago Board of Trade and get some insights from you. How did you first hear about the CBOT?

I had known about the Chicago Board of Trade most of my business and academic life. I became closely associated with the Board of Trade when I came to Chicago in 1971. I was a principal in a capital markets and commodity firm, Walston and Company, a large nationwide firm, and our Midwest headquarters were here. I was really good friends with a lot of traders at the Board of Trade. Shortly after I came to Chicago, our company became a candidate for a hostile takeover by Ross Perot, the former presidential candidate. This was the first time that the commodity industry had been associated to any degree with computers.

President Nixon asked Perot to please invest $60 million to computerize the back-office services of the large brokerage firms, because at that time, even though the securities volume was very light compared to the volume we're realizing in the equities, the firms were having to close down for at least a day, sometimes a day and half, each week to reconcile trades and security deliveries. So, to make a long story short, that did not work out. Mr. Perot had major investments in Walston and Company and in duPont Glore Forgan stock brokerage. Looking back, these investments were probably two of the very few business ventures that resulted in failure for Mr. Perot.

I had done quite well with the company as a principal. Most of my assets at the time were tied into the stock of that company. The stock was failing, and I decided it was time to move out of the corporate world and go into more of a free, entrepreneurial situation. I had always loved the Board of Trade and I had been trading for my own personal account for a while, so I decided to make the transition.

What made you want to be part of this industry?

There's a myriad of reasons. One is there is freedom. There's the entrepreneurial spirit: knowing that you can be whatever you want to be, depending on your capital, mind-set, discipline, and desires. There are very few restrictions. I liked the entrepreneurial spirit of the people here, and, as they used to say, traders were "the last of the American cowboys" who were on LaSalle Street. So it had a great appeal.

How did you buy your membership?

I financed it through a bank here. As I indicated before, the stock allotted to me from my company was worthless; but there was some that was held for a long time in trust until everything was settled out.

How long did it take you to pay it back?

It took me only six months. There was a great deal of good fortune and divine intervention. I was fortunate in doing that. You have to understand that the seats weren't trading for $2 million or $3 million at the time. They were relatively inexpensive. My seat was $46,000. That gives you an idea of where we were as a marketplace. The markets weren't quite ready to take off. It was just a few months before the grain markets really started to accelerate. This invigorated the commodities business at the CBOT.

What did you first trade?

I started out in soybeans, which was just beginning to gain major momentum with the Russian imports of U.S. soybeans. All of these things created a very wild market. It was not anyplace for a rookie to be out on the floor. I tried to learn as much as I could and still stay solvent.

After a few months I started trading oats. My desire was to ultimately wind up in silver. It was something I had traded almost exclusively before I became a member. And I wanted to go to the silver pit, but I wanted to get the proper experience before I went there.

What attracted you to work in this milieu?

I liked the independence and I liked the mixture of the different cultures that were trading on the floor. We had individuals who were MDs, PhDs, MBAs, policemen, and athletes. There was a mixture of everything. There was not one profile that constituted a good trader. There were traits, however, that one would have to possess to be a good trader. I liked the profile, the mix that was down there. It was very, very interesting and very collective.

Can you remember your first day down on the floor?

My first day on the floor was very intimidating. I was scared to death. It was frightening. I was terribly intimidated by the bravado, yelling and screaming of the people. I found out in a very short period of time that this was just part of the action that was inherent in the pits. These traders sometimes were mad, but most of the time they weren't. I thought everyone was mad all the time, but that was not the case.

Again, I was working with a small amount of capital at the time, but I wanted to get acclimated as quickly as possible and get that first trade in. I'll never forget the first gentleman who traded with me. It meant a lot, and his name was Tom Cashman. He's part of the Cashman family that's been here for generations. I think that I had to have someone come over to help me write the trade data on the card. I'd been practicing, but I really didn't take into consideration what would happen once that trade was made. It took some acclimating to find out who was serious and who wasn't.

Tell me about some of your mentors.

I was very fortunate to have three very fine mentors: Lawrence Blum, Irwin Eisen, and Julius Frankel. They came somewhat accidentally because of my wife, Roxanne. We got married about the same time that I bought my membership. She was an independent businesswoman herself, and she set up clearing operations for respective security firms. With the advent of the CBOE, she started numerous clearing operations for CBOE members.

I became very close to two gentlemen she was working with. They were floor traders at the time while also having a clearing operation. They helped tremendously as I went from pit to pit. They were people who would certainly help and give advice, and it was much appreciated.

I made a tremendous number of mistakes, like anyone would initially. You know, you fail miserably at times. If you were ever going to be successful on the floor, you needed to know proper protocol in a respective pit. You needed to learn what to do. So yes, I had some very good mentors.

How about naming some of the CBOT legends?

There are so many potential legends at the Board of Trade. Some of the ones who stand out in my mind in the earlier times were Dan Rice and Jesse Livermore. Rice and Livermore were both commodity traders. Livermore, however, was more active in the securities market. They took great chances. Ralph Root was another legend, and also one of my favorites is Joe Dimon. Now, Joe Dimon was very successful in a time when people usually didn't make the kind of money that he made. One year in the soybean market, which I believe was 1952, he made $12 million. He was very eccentric, and he would carry around with him a million dollars in a briefcase. And that's not just urban legend. That's been verified by the people who dealt with him and knew him.

There were a lot of people who probably deserve mentioning. Sometimes a legend is more acclaimed for the exploit-like nature of what they did, rather than what they actually did. I won't mention a name, so I can protect the gentleman's family, but a real legend is about one of the old-timers who had made some tremendous money in the rye market. And after a celebratory night of cocktails, he bought a Rolls-Royce the following morning. He decided to drive it home, but he drove it through the plate-glass windows of the dealership. So I would say he's a legend. Not only was he a good, good trader, but that incident was something he carried with him most of his entire life.

How about some of the people that you knew?

I've been fortunate to know some very, very fine traders and gentlemen, too. One of the finest was Gene Cashman. Gene sort of brought the Board of Trade into the current generation. This transpired from basically when the big grain markets started back in the early 1970s, and I think he was the biggest trader during that time. He had positions in most of the bean and bean complex products. He was a fine gentleman who made a tremendous amount of money.

He started out as a policeman whose beat was out in front of the Chicago Board of Trade for many, many years. He got to know the traders coming in. He liked the business, and then, one day, he found a sponsor and he bought a membership. Together with other members of his family, Gene was very instrumental in the growth of the CBOT. He sponsored nephews and then other people's children and so many people down there. He was truly a legend.

Another legend is Richard Dennis. He was one of the biggest traders in the history of the Board of Trade. He made a tremendous amount of money. He was excellent. In fact, he set up numerous programs, not just computer trading programs at the time, but some mathematical formulas that seemed to work very well for him.

Another legend was Rick Barnes, who was an unbelievably big trader and still is. He went through periods of time, like anyone who was successful, when there were lots of ups, and other times when there were just terrible, terrible downs, but he bounced back and became very successful. Ralph Peters was a very big grain trader. When the large silver market came along, he was a dominant factor in that market.

Two gentlemen who also have to be mentioned were Eddie and Billy O'Connor. They were very successful commodity traders. They were two of the gentlemen who founded the CBOE. The O'Connors were two of numerous individuals at the Board of Trade who sponsored many people and continuously helped them out. They also excelled in their outside business ventures and securities trading.

Do you think there's a key to being successful?

You know, success is pretty well what one makes of it. Like I said, this business affords individuals the opportunity if they have the capital, discipline, and mind-set to trade successfully. You can be as successful as you really want to be. No one is going to tell you at the beginning of a trading day that you can do this or you can't do that. Almost anything is possible as long as you follow the regulations of the association. You can be as conservative as you want. But the fact of the matter is, nobody is standing over your shoulder and saying, "No, you can only do this," and you're through for the day. You know, that's the wonderful thing about this business.

Is there a characteristic everybody has to have to be successful?

I think that the biggest characteristic that makes one successful is discipline. Discipline is the key word. People often ask what the most important thing in trading is, and the answer is discipline. Many, many traders think that if they were smart enough to put a position on, that position should be successful. What they don't realize is the market is the final arbiter. The market is never wrong. The traders might occasionally be wrong, but the market is never wrong. Discipline should never go away, even with electronic trading. It's the one staple that predicts whether someone is going to be successful.

How does integrity relate to the business at the CBOT?

Well, you know, integrity means many things to many people, but what it means to me is the corner post of what I call the "Four Pillars of the Chicago Board of Trade." They are: *integrity, price discovery, transparency, and liquidity*. Those four pieces all represent the Board of Trade and what the Board of Trade stands for. That's how it's been able to have the credibility it has had with the users of the market for almost 160 years.

If we talked about tradition with those pillars, what would you say?

I would say tradition falls in line with integrity. Tradition is something that is not just promoted but must be promoted continuously to perpetuate the four pillars. You can't have one without the other. And tradition is something that we need to continue and protect to have the users find their common goal where buyers and sellers come together.

Can you tell me the first lesson that you learned down at the CBOT?

I will go back to discipline again.

Do you think that you see discipline being passed down to the new traders in the computer age?

It's difficult to see. I think that these traders, new traders who are coming down now, whether they trade in open auction or they trade the electronic market, are much more risk takers, and they trade larger positions than we did in the past. They have different risk management controls now. That is particularly true with electronic trading, where they have alerts that go off if someone trades over what their positions should be as assigned by the clearing member. There are risk managers to monitor traders and their trades daily in open auction too.

Today it is easily done, because trades are put into the clearinghouse every few minutes, so that people can keep up with their positions. In the past, heads of clearing firms or their appointed employees would come around either at the end of the day or even at the end of the hour or maybe after the end of four hours, whatever necessity might dictate. It was hard to monitor.

Now you make a trade with someone and it is picked up immediately by the clearing operation, so the people who are in charge of risk management can control it better. But the people who are trading right now, the size that they trade is just incredible and it's just going to get bigger and bigger and bigger, which is a wonderful thing.

Absolutely. You have a personal tradition of keeping a plaque on your desk.

It's true. I look at it every day, and I think this goes back to what we spoke of earlier. It's about people supporting people and helping people who are in need of capital or market strategy. This is a great institution for that. The plaque says, "Never forget the person that gave you your first break." I think about it all the time. I never let Hunter Pearson forget it.

Let's talk about the role about self-regulation in the industry.

I think it's probably one of the most important things that has happened to the industry. In the year 2000, Congress legislated the Commodity Futures Modernization Act, and that was the beginning of many great improvements for all commodity derivatives exchanges. Before the Act, there was a very sluggish bureaucracy within the CFTC because of the number of people who were involved, and the slowness of getting something through a government agency was inhibiting. The Act vested the respective exchanges with the authority to address and change the situations. Contract approvals, regulation approvals, rule approvals—things of that nature were the beneficiaries of the Act.

Our Office of Internal Investigations and Audits works like a Swiss watch right now. It has the latitude and speed to keep everything in line, and the CFTC depends on that so much, plus the budget of the CFTC was cut by quite a bit by not requiring as much manpower. We're very cautious about what we want to protect as much as possible.

What type of lobbying efforts happen in Washington in terms of self-regulation?

That's an ongoing procedure. We have lobbyists in Washington. One, in particular, who has been with us for over 35 years, is a very fine gentleman named Tad Davis. We also have three young ladies, Julie Bauer, Anne Klein, and Alison Wolper, in our Washington office. They are there not only for lobbying efforts, but also to work on an educational basis with the Congress. This is an ongoing effort.

We have a political action committee here at the Board of Trade. I chair that and have for about the past five years. Our committee is titled AMPAC, which stands for Auction Markets Political Action Committee. Let me make it very clear that this is not something that we use to buy votes from the legislators. It's an educational process, because many of these people, depending on what committees they are on, important committees like the finance committees and the agricultural committees of both houses, need to know exactly what the issues are and understand how these issues affect our business.

We are bipartisan when it comes to that. In an election time, the same model is followed. We make donations. It's an ongoing process with Washington. It's a very, very important area. It goes back to the CFTC. Right now, we're working to ensure that the CFTC is reauthorized again. It has gone on about two years longer than normal. It becomes more of a back-burner subject for a lot of the members of Congress and not really a front issue. It is just a matter of getting our issues addressed.

What types of committees are available to support self-regulation?

We have basically the same committees that we had when we were a mutual organization. We have the Business Conduct Committee, probably the strongest committee as far as self-regulation is concerned. It's an arbiter of many things, whether they are position limits, trading situations or contract maladies. We have the Floor Governors Committee, which is very strong, and an Arbitration Committee, a Floor Conduct Committee, and respective product pit committees.

Tell me about some of the committees that you served on.

Basically, I have served on over 45 committees during my tenure and I've chaired 25 of those committees. And I've been very fortunate to do so. Now I am serving on my second go-around on the board of directors. I was a director back in the late 1970s and early 1980s and was vice chairman in 1981 and 1982. Currently, I serve on the Executive Committee and the Audit Committee and I chair the Governance and Nominating Committee and also the Transaction Committee now that we're doing so many negotiations with other entities.

Are these paid positions?

Some are. There are four authorized committees that fall under the regulations for publicly traded companies traded on the New York Stock Exchange. It is mandatory that they receive compensation. They are the Executive Committee, the Audit Committee, the Human Resources Committee, and the Governance and Nominating Committee. The board of directors is also required to get a monthly stipend in accordance with the New York Stock Exchange regulations. The board of directors and those four authorized committees do get paid. We also have special ad hoc committees such as the Special Committee and Transaction Committee that are in place right now for negotiations with the other entities. Those on these committees also get paid as they have meetings. So, there's latitude there for payment. Now members on the other committees I mentioned earlier, like the Business Conduct Committee and Floor Governors Committee, still do that on a gratis basis.

You've obviously done this so many times. Why?

It is really a passion. I love the institution. I love what it stands for. Again, to me it is one of the last bastions of free enterprise in the world. And I truly mean that in its truest sense. I have businesses on the side that have been successful and that I really like, but none of them even share one-tenth of the passion that I have for the Board of Trade.

Tell me about being down on the floor. Did you take that passion with you as a trader?

I was a trader and also a broker. I traded for my own account, and was basically a spread trader and I still am. I did not fill brokerage for normal retail customers that would come in through retail brokerage firms; but I did do brokerage for members who were trading on the floor in other pits who wanted to trade in the metals, primarily silver. I've traded for them and for different corporations during the big silver market. I also filled orders for the Hunt brothers during the silver crisis.

Can you tell me about that crisis?

It's a very detailed, complex story that probably gets more bad ink than it should. It was really a dislocation in the silver market at the time. In the early 1970s, silver was trading about $1.20 per ounce, just for the sake of a standard. Certain events transpired during this period. There wasn't the normal amount of silver stored in warehouses, either domestically or abroad. The lack of silver didn't meet the overall demand, complicating the situation. Silver users and traders realized this dislocation and started to accumulate large amounts of physical silver as well as silver futures.

The Hunt brothers and their many associates were the largest accumulators. Also exacerbating the silver price was the inflationary environment in the U.S. economy. Silver became considered a precious metal even though it was and still is an industrial metal. It is a poor man's gold that vacillates depending on economic swings, inflationary fears, and, again, dislocation.

In a brief two-and-a-half-year period, silver prices soared from $1.50 to over $54 per ounce. This increase represents the most significant percentage move in the history of regulated futures markets. However, the crisis began to subside somewhat in 1978 and 1979. Keep in mind many market participants were hurt financially in this meteoric upside move. Financial institutions, primarily banks, were on the verge of collapse.

Speculators were financing their futures trades via escalating margin requirements. Numerous individuals and institutions were financing actual physical trades. The situation became so severe that both the CBOT and the COMEX exchanges declared a liquidation-only mandate. New long positions could not be initiated. These mandates temporarily slowed the market; however, the factor that truly broke the silver market was the sales of personal silver items by moms and pops. They began to flood the market with silverware, silver services, silver jewelry, and the like.

Few days passed in which one didn't see in a periodical offers by vendors to buy the aforementioned silver. Shortly thereafter, the marketplace was flooded with enough product to get to the refiners and replace their depleted inventory. The silver crisis was a repetition of attempted market corners that have been tried since the advent of commodity trading. No person or cartel has been able to corner a market for any appreciable amount of time. The market is the final arbiter of price, and that price can be discovered by many circumstances, as I have explained in my examples.

We had heard that silver was stored here at the CBOT. Is that true?

That's correct. It wasn't always on a long-term basis. The exchange had a registrar here who checked the silver in and made sure that the integrity of the brand was good and that it met the specifications of the silver contracts, and the same was done with the gold. Then it would be shipped to one of the three depositories that we had in Chicago. Also during the crisis market, there were three depositories versus just one at this time: Continental Bank, Northern Trust, and First National Bank.

Were any of the silver or gold bars stored in the vault right here in the basement?

They were.

What else was in this basement?

By that time, they didn't keep too many of the grain samples down there for the testing or anything, but there were still some down there. Basically, it was just silver and a few bars of gold, again, before they went to the final depositories. And after the silver crisis, after all the silver basically went out of the Chicago depositories, it became a coatroom for the trading jackets for the members. There must have been at least 10 armored trucks that were in the front and on the sides of the CBOT building. These trucks were being loaded with a large portion of the Hunt brothers' physical silver. The trucks ultimately took the silver to O'Hare Airport and it was loaded onto planes to be flown to London, England, to be stored in respective warehouses.

There's a rumor that there were tunnels underneath the building.

That's not a rumor. There are definitely tunnels that are still there. Some have been filled in, but others haven't. For example, there are tunnels that went to the Continental Bank, to the Federal Reserve, to the Rookery building, to the Northern Trust, and to other entities that are still in existence. Some of them have fake walls up right now, but they're still there.

That's fascinating. So many things in the past affect the present. Let's talk about some of the historical events that happened in the world and affected trading, such as Chernobyl.

I remember Chernobyl well. The nuclear accident had a definite impact on our wheat market. The Russian crop was not the same as our wheat contract; however, the international markets' ripple effect certainly was reflected in our price basis. It had an impact for quite some time, but it eventually smoothed out. At the time, there was a lot of panic that would go from one market to the other just because of the Chernobyl situation. It was a very realistic panic at the time. It had a few more legs, as we say, than some of the other markets during comparable events.

Would you comment on the Major Market Index (MMI)?

It was a very nice little contract, but that's about all I can say about it. You understand that it's no longer traded. If it had been a good contract, it would have had sticking power; but some people think that it saved the day for the 1987 crash, and that's certainly not the case. The contract didn't have liquidity in the pit. It had some volatility, because there were very few resting orders, but the orders that were in the pit at the time were not that great that the brokers held. When the sell-off began, this market still didn't have the proper liquidity where institutions or individuals that wanted to use the market could really economically do so. It was okay, but that's about it. It was a nice little market when it was traded, but it had very little impact on anything nationally or internationally.

What do you think saved the day for the crash?

I would say common sense and value realization. Individuals and institutions that were in the market at the beginning of the sell-off were ignoring indicators, price-earnings (P/E) ratios, technical signals, and so on that forewarned an overbought status. The drop was so precipitous that it signaled value seekers about the presence of true investment trading opportunities. This type of decline might happen again; however, there have been stopgaps in the form of circuit breakers that have been implemented that temporarily halt markets on moves on the upside as well as the downside, so that orderly transactions can be realized and market users' orders can be more readily and advantageously executed. Circuit breakers are now in place at the New York Stock Exchange, NASDAQ, and American Stock Exchange, as well as other security and options exchanges.

Let's go back on the floor. Can you describe various trading styles that you saw?

Oh, yeah. There is a myriad of trading styles, and one catches on to what the others' trading styles are pretty quickly. For instance, traders can try to bluff if somebody wants to sell something you know they actually want to buy. They're trying to pressure the market one way or the other, and that is a trading style. You have other trading styles that are just people who are pure speculators buying or selling short contracts that buy or sell them for holding, or people who are scalpers who work for a minimum tick or transaction per trade. There are spreaders who trade different contract months. There are people who trade intra- as well as intermarket trades: arbitrageurs, hedgers, grain companies. There is a myriad of traders and trading styles.

And is the variety of trading styles growing?

I would say it's growing. It's staying pretty constant with open auction, but it's growing tremendously with the advent of informational and intellectual technology and communications technology. Market participants are continuously writing programs to stay ahead of the IT curve. They have black-box traders who are always competing with each other, and with people on the floor, so it's sort of a self-perpetuating situation.

Let's talk about the Chicago Board of Trade as a role model, as a worldwide price discovery mechanism. What can you tell me?

Well, definitely the Chicago Board of Trade provides worldwide price discovery in two categories. First is the price basis for grains traded at the CBOT on a worldwide basis. There's no question about that, and it's growing daily on a global basis. It is not only for domestic products, but also for export products that we have. And second, but equally important and even larger, are the Treasury contracts that are so important on a global basis.

As an example, the CBOT's 10-year U.S. Treasury note contract is the benchmark pricing for the world for that product. And as you well know, China and Japan have tremendous amounts of our open interest in the CBOT's Treasury products. But the U.S. 30-year bond was the benchmark for many, many years until the Treasury stopped issuing paper. The Treasury is issuing the 30-year bonds again and they still do a nice volume, but the fact of the matter is that the 10-year notes have now become the benchmark. And then we have the five-year Treasury notes, the two-year T-notes, and the fed funds futures that are used for price basing for international users.

Tell me what happens on a bank holiday.

This is something that I don't think New York ever did. They used to feel like we were sort of the tail wagging the dog. That's not really the case. The fact of the matter is that during bank holidays when the Board of Trade is closed, the cash dealers hardly do any business whatsoever. And because the Treasuries do have underlying cash trading versus the grains that have only a very small amount, these dealers have a very difficult time with their pricing mechanism and the volume just drops off to a very small amount.

The Board of Trade has moved away from being just an agricultural market. What are some of the new contracts?

We just had the 30th anniversary of the Ginnie Mae contract. In 1976, we brought out the Ginnie Mae contract and in 1978 the 30-year U.S. bond contract. Those were the first two nonagricultural products other than the metals that have been at the Board of Trade. They were the first interest rate contracts. They really were the harbingers of good things to come as far as the accelerated growth of the Chicago Board of Trade now is concerned. They weren't instant successes, though.

I will never forget these young members who would come down and sit around and sit around and sit around the pits during these sessions. Initially, the dealers did not want to allow the transparency that they would have to yield to having an open auction market where price discovery could be realized. They wanted to keep it behind closed doors, much like they do now in dealer-to-dealer trades. So in such situations you really don't have a true price discovery of the users of the market.

What happens is once one of these institutions says, "I think I'm going to try this market," another one says, "I don't want to be left behind." It is sort of like a train pulling out of a station. That is a terrible analogy, but it nevertheless is the case. And that's what happened. Just one after another after another, and then all of a sudden it was great for price discovery. The liquidity was there, and it was really the advent of the Board of Trade being a successful, global institution.

Where do you see competition coming from in the next five years?

I think the real competition is going to come from the major bankers, the investment bankers. I really do. They've made their stand now. In fact, there was an article in the paper about one major institution, Goldman Sachs, that's going to be building an office with six trading floors in New York City. They are interested in this. Only this is an interesting point: Only about 17 percent of all the trades of commodities and derivatives are done on futures exchanges. The other 83 percent is done in the over-the-counter market and it's done by dealers.

We are getting closer and getting more business all the time into these markets, because now the hedge funds see this is a viable alternative. Outside users and other institutions like the products we have, especially now with the advent of credit derivatives, which could be huge. It's in the trillions of dollars. That's the kind of thing that we have. Again, we have transparency, and that's what these individuals want. They don't want to have trading occurring behind the scenes in a "call around market," where dealers agree with each other on price and that's the only price the customer has available to them. People want to see prices, bids, and offers, appearing on a competitive trading screen.

Do you see competition coming from other exchanges?

Definitely! There currently is a tremendous amount of consolidation going on within the industry. This consolidation represents similar product competition, a desire for other exchanges' products, clearing privileges, capital infusion, global expansion, and so on. The capital that has to be allocated to intellectual and information technology (IT) is just staggering. It's hard to be a stand-alone entity, particularly with the amount of competition out there and also having to keep up with the upgrades and enhancements of IT systems.

Do you see new products that are going to emerge and generate more volume?

I mentioned a moment ago about the credit derivatives markets showing a tremendous potential. Along those lines, exchange-traded funds that zero in on respective products have a great future. They're popular in the securities industry right now and they are getting into the derivatives also. So I think that has tremendous potential. I think with agricultural products there might be a limit to what can be planted and traded, but there is potential for new markets in that area, too. With the ethanol contract and the biodiesel contract, that really falls under what we call our "wheelhouse" as far as doing things is concerned. I think we could potentially see terrific market opportunities.

We are now trading a South American soybean contract. It is hoped we will soon be trading a crude palm oil contract that will be very popular here in conjunction with our feed grain products. There are many more things like that. All of these have global appeal. We see this especially in the Asian markets. We spend a tremendous amount of time in China, Japan, and Singapore. We are in a joint venture at this time with the Singapore Exchange. We are currently trading a rubber contract.

How about swaps and mortgage-backed securities?

The potential is tremendous, if you look at the trillions of dollars that are trading in these markets now. To give you an idea, the Chicago Board of Trade and the Chicago Mercantile Exchange trade more in two days on a notional value than the New York Stock Exchange trades in a year. We trade pretty close to on a combined basis right now somewhere around $15 trillion a day. Notional value is the underlying value of the contract, not the margin value. For example, our Treasury complex contracts have a notional value of $100,000 per contract.

That's amazing. Where can it go from here?

With the electronic and computer-driven access to these markets now, you can't stay ahead of the curve, because they are perpetuating this kind of growth. And again, there are the creditability and integrity that go along with it in that people have the speed of access and the low cost of execution and things of that nature.

There is a term about new products called the "spaghetti approach." What does that mean?

Oh, that's something that we used to say in the old days because we brought out so many products and no one knew what was going to fail or what was going to succeed. You have to have the interest of all relevant parties. You have to have trading liquidity from the traders. You have to have committed interest from the users of the market. One never knows if it will be a commercial-based contract. Sometimes with a totally commercial base, you can't get other users in the market because the commercials can be so dominant.

We used to call it the spaghetti approach because we'd bring a contract or many contracts out and, like throwing spaghetti against the wall, we'd wait and see if it was cooked properly and would stick to the wall. Using this approach, we would start a market and see what stuck.

Speaking of a good idea that stuck, tell me about the advent of the CBOE and its effect on the city of Chicago.

It's been tremendous. The group of individuals I mentioned earlier started the CBOE as a hedge against cyclical or secular grain markets. We were just beginning to trade silver and gold, and everything else was agriculturally based. These products and commodities go through tremendous cyclical and secular changes, so that you could have tremendous markets for six months, a year, or two years, and then all of a sudden you could have a terrible market for five years.

What the CBOE did was give the members of the Board of Trade a chance to trade on an options exchange. It was the first fully integrated options exchange, and it's been wonderful for the CBOE and our CBOT members. Although I don't know the exact numbers, I know that there are many thousands of employees in the different tiers of jobs that are tied to the two exchanges. It has been tremendous for the Chicago Board of Trade and it's been tremendous for the city of Chicago.

What do you think is the biggest change that has happened in your industry?

Oh, it has to be electronic trading and computer programs. Like I said, the advent of intellectual technology is just staggering.

Give me a little background of how you came to electronic trading?

Well, it basically started in the back office versus on the floor for traders. The back office needed the computer technology to process the trades, because the volume was picking up rapidly on a daily basis. They needed that speed and matching ability to reconcile the trades and the monetary amounts. That was sort of the advent of it, but as it progressed, we were seeing a tremendous amount of electronic trading. For example, the Eurex exchange had its business model totally electronic. Eurex did not have open auction. It was totally electronic. And Eurex posed a real threat to open auction exchanges in wanting to list its contracts and become a competitor. That sort of planted the seed.

Then in the 1990s, particularly in the mid-1990s, we started developing our own system, and that was called Project A. It was very successful, but the administration and the board of directors during that time period were somewhat skeptical about the enhancement possibilities and the upgrade possibilities of Project A. This happened even though we had excellent user input and numerous outstanding consultants that said Project A was very good.

The users loved it and it did have all the enhancement and upgrade possibilities Eurex had, but the board of directors chose Eurex. There was a tremendous amount of capital outlay to meet the contract agreements that we had with Eurex, and the constant technology upkeep on the Eurex platform was a tremendous drain. Plus, at the same time that we were doing this, we were building the financial exchange floor, and quite honestly we were in a multi-multimillion-dollar debt situation at the turn of the century with very little working capital left.

In addition, when you're a mutual organization, you really don't have to answer to anybody except your members and there was a lot of spending that probably shouldn't have taken place. And again this financial trading building over there placed a tremendous debt on the Board of Trade at a time when the markets really weren't at their peak.

By 2001, we began to turn this around. It has been a real pleasure. We went from about a $245 million debt situation and 44 days of working capital to where we are right now, where we have approximately $550 million in cash. We have a stock price that's trading about $188 as we speak today, and we have suitors from around the world that want to have consolidation with us. So it has been a tremendous turnaround.

There's been great leadership and we've stayed focused. Our business model has proven it's excellent. It's the envy of many other exchanges. Our business plan is working well and will continue to do so.

How quickly did you adopt the new technology?

Admittedly, I came to it very slowly. And that was my protest against computers. But once I got into it, it was and has been very good. I still have not adapted as well as a lot of people. I've got businesses on the side, so I've got to concentrate on those, plus my Board of Trade involvement from the board of directors standpoint. I do trade electronically and I like it. However, I still miss the information flow that comes from the open auction and I miss the socialization. I feel that sitting behind a screen is sterile.

Now, I can see the young kids who have grown up with IT all of their lives; they transition well. But for people who have been traders for 30 or 40 years in an open auction arena, it's a difficult transition. You really have to want to do it, because there are a lot of people out there who write their own programs. They are as sharp as a tack. But there is little transparency compared with open auction going on in the pit. I might not always be right, but I can tell what's happening because of the information flow in there. And you can't do that with electronic trading. I think that the new group that has come in is much more adaptable.

As things change, do you think that the idea of service to people will change?

I don't think so. I think it will definitely increase. Faster executions, lower fees, and constant IT improvements and service will fuel the increase. The service will increase with the access that one has with technology. The services that are available both off and online have increased with the speed with which services can be offered. It cuts back tremendously on the manpower that's needed to service the various users of the market.

We have an absolutely outstanding web site for the Chicago Board of Trade, not just for the members, but also for the public to access. I've looked at every web site of every exchange and derivatives company in the world, from securities and commodities to derivatives, and by far, the CBOT's is the finest. It's constantly upgraded. You can get almost any information that you wish off of it. And I think that has enhanced the kind of service we can offer. When people don't know where to go for information, they can go online. And that is just going to increase as we move forward.

That sounds like a good thing. What about the significance of the commodity and derivative options markets?

Oh, I think the options market is in its infancy. It truly is a situation where in some instances the tail does wag the dog. Look at the ease of entrance and the easier risk control. And again, for hedging potential, it's fantastic. Also, these hedge funds love the options market. They can utilize their capital to a much greater degree in there. So, we're in a growth period right now and it will accelerate once the programs can be written properly for options. It's coming along very slowly.

Writing successful programs for options is in its infancy stage. The complexity of markets such as agricultural products that have old crop/new crop contracts as well as complex spread relationships, user demands, and a basic lack of cash markets provides examples of the difficulties. Similar problems resonate within other commodity and derivative contracts. It's primarily open auction at this time. But as programs are written and the satisfaction increases, that will change, too. It's explosive in this very nature.

And again, this is why we have price transparency. Options historically have been done on what they call a "call around market" basis, particularly in Europe. That's where all of this started, and it's done, as we speak now, in the United States, with a lot of these bankers that trade behind closed doors on a call around market basis. There's no transparency there whatsoever. You've got transparency here at the CBOT.

You've got the liquidity. The liquidity is incredible. Again, it goes back to the four pillars I talked about earlier: integrity, price discovery, transparency, and liquidity.

Those pillars have supported the CBOT moves into becoming a global presence. The world is constantly changing. How has the leadership of the Board of Trade responded to the changes of the external world?

Since 2000, and we use that as a landmark year, it's been unbelievable. We've had some tremendous leadership. We have it now from our management team. They've been extremely focused. They've all had industry experience. It is especially apparent in our IT department. CEO Bernie Dan, has done a tremendous job of keeping us on target. The board of directors has been focused under the leadership of our previous chairman, Nick Neubauer, and our current Chairman Charlie Carey. They're very aggressive. We've got a business model that it would take many hours just to explain. Today we're looking at world trading.

As to global trading, it's not just centered on our respective contracts. I've just gotten back from China, Japan, Singapore, and recently Australia. And we're really centering now, trying to focus on the Asian market. That's where the growth pattern is. It's just amazing to see what's happening in China. Once they get past their regulatory restriction, that's going to open up a whole new world. You can't quantify just exactly how much money is available, and they're so eager to trade our products, versus trading on their respective smaller exchanges. Up until now, they have been very insular within their country and heavily regulated as to what they can and can't do. The CBOT is going to have a big presence in the global markets.

One last question. You've obviously given a lot of time and effort to this institution. What do you think would be your legacy?

Well, I hope that the one legacy that I might have is that people will say that I had integrity, that I never hurt anyone intentionally, and that I was a good man. I don't really care if they felt I was a good trader or not. That would be a really small part of it. I think walking away with one's integrity, and that's reflected by the people you deal with, is the most important thing.

CHAPTER 14

In His Family's Footsteps

John L. Pietrzak

Preceded by his grandfather, Larry Pietrzak Sr., and his father, Larry Pietrzak Jr., John Pietrzak has added a strong link to the chain of family members who have been a part of the Chicago Board of Trade. Spending his childhood listening to stories about the exchange, Mr. Pietrzak understood the complexities and the opportunities that the industry could offer him.

After graduating from the University of Notre Dame in 1977 and then attending graduate school at De Paul University in real estate and international finance, John started his career in the financial industry by working on the professional staff of Price Waterhouse and Company in Chicago. It wasn't long before he decided to follow in his family's footsteps to the Chicago Board of Trade.

By 1979, John became a full member of the exchange. He immediately became an integral part of the industry, volunteering to serve on numerous committees such as Public Relations and Market Report. He held leadership positions on many of these groups. In 1987, he acquired a membership to the Chicago Board Options Exchange.

Continuing to be involved in the workings of the exchange and vested in its growth, John became a director of the Chicago Board of Trade and served on the Strategic Planning Committee. In 1997, he became a clearing member of the Board of Trade Clearing Corporation (BOTCC) and a clearing participant through Longwood Trading.

From 1997 to the present, John Pietrzak has been active as a general partner of the Sparta Group, a CBOE and CME member firm and proprietary trading group. From 1999 to 2001, he served as vice chairman and then chairman of the CBOT Nominating Committee. From 2001 to 2003, he served on the Board of Governors of the Board of Trade Clearing Corporation and was a member of both the Audit Committee and the Risk Committee of the BOTCC.

John took on the role of managing partner of Longwood Partners in 2002. This company is a private investing firm specializing in employee buyouts and private equity firm spin-offs. He continues to work in this capacity to this day. In 2006, he returned to the board of directors of the exchange and the CBOT Holdings Company. He also serves on the Audit Committee.

John has been married to his wife Rae, a physician in private practice, for 25 years. They have three children, Joseph, Caroline, and Alex.

****

How did you first hear about the Board of Trade?

We have a long family tradition at the Chicago Board of Trade. My grandfather, Larry Pietrzak Sr., started at the Board of Trade as a runner in 1913. He bought a membership in 1929 and worked for a broker by the name of Fred Lewis, who had his own clearing firm. In 1949, my father, Larry Pietrzak Jr., finished college and after spending some time at a bank, bought a membership.

I had worked at the Board of Trade doing various jobs as a clerk since I was in eighth grade. In 1979, after graduating from Notre Dame and spending time at the accounting firm Price Waterhouse, I came down to the exchange.

How did your grandfather come to the CBOT?

My grandfather was in eighth grade and cutting grass for a fellow named Tom Costello, who was a broker at the CBOT. One day he said, "You know, kid, your family could probably use the money. Why don't you come work for me?" So he came down here and worked for that gentleman for about four or five years, before hooking up with Fred Lewis. He and Mr. Lewis formed a very lucrative and long-term relationship.

Tell me some of the stories you heard about the exchange from your grandfather.

He told me about the price controls for World War II; how it got very, very quiet around here and seats changed hands for the transfer fee, which at the time was around $100. Back then people went out and drove buses and did other things, because the very lucrative market that was here during those dust bowl years came to a grinding halt because the government said, "Okay, corn is going to be 89 cents a bushel and that's all there is to it. No matter how much you grow or how much is consumed, that's it; that's the fixed price."

Did he tell you about some of the successful traders?

There were a lot of stories. There have been many very colorful figures here throughout the ages. For example, there was a guy who traded through the firm that my grandfather worked for by the name of Ralph Root. He was very eccentric. They call people with a lot of money "eccentric." They call people without a lot of money just "crazy."

One day Ralph Root called the office and said, "Look, I need a lot of cash." At the time, he might have been asking for $5,000 in cash. That was a large amount of money in the late 1940s. Ralph said my grandfather should bring it over to the Union League Club. So he gets the cash and goes over to the Union League Club and Ralph Root answers the door wearing a six-gun and a cowboy hat and not much else. There were a lot of guys like that.

Then there was a man everybody called "The Judge." I can't remember his real name or if, in fact, he was really a judge. He'd come here and trade when he wasn't in court. He had a very, very deep gravelly voice, so even if you couldn't see him, you could hear him coming.

More current characters were like Harvey Jaunich. He started out as a runner and he had a real feel for the markets. He worked for one firm and then actually had his own firm for a long time; he cut a fairly wide swath through this place with his antics. One time he bet the whole bar that he could pick up the table with one arm. So he went into the middle of the bar and then did it. There were other goofy things like that.

It was kind of a fraternal society.

For a long time, it had a club atmosphere. Then, as more money became involved with the advent of financial futures, it became more corporate. But there are still elements here that have that fraternal feeling. Most of it comes from being part of a family tradition of traders. There is our family, the Brennans, the Kerrigans, the Careys, the Hollanders, and many other families that have been at the CBOT for generations.

Why would people want to work with their families?

On those few days when my father and I would stand next to each other in the pit and we'd have a disagreement, I'd ask myself that exact question. Obviously, there's a lot involved in that decision. Theoretically, it's someone you can trust. It might be someone who raised you, but not necessarily a father-son relationship, but uncles and cousins and things like that. You should be able to trust them, and trust has always been a very large part of this business.

In this business, you make transactions worth literally millions of dollars with a wink and a nod and a flash of the hand and eye contact, and it has to be with people you can trust. If it's not someone you know from a family relationship, then you trade with other people based on your instinct.

It certainly helps if there's someone from the family there to help you develop your instinct. There are days when my father and I differ significantly. But it doesn't take long before I say, "I'm sorry. I didn't mean to yell."

When you get together outside of the Board of Trade, do you talk business?

Yes, we do. As a matter of fact, just before I came down here, I was on the phone with my dad and we were talking about some things for this interview. But before we knew it, he was asking about the market: "Was it limit down on Friday? Was it limit down on Monday? What's going on?" Nobody knows any better than someone who's been through this. So, yes, it always happens that way.

You have something in common to share.

Oh, yes, other than just Little League games and what their grandson is doing and things like that. There's a lot more. No matter how hard you try to explain to someone what goes on here, people who haven't experienced it firsthand don't really know.

I find solace in talking to someone who can totally understand what goes on here and what the tension and pressure are. I mean it's not like a doctor doing surgery, but there's a lot of financial tension and a lot of financial pressure. We work through that in different ways.

Can you remember the first time you saw the floor?

I started coming down here when I was probably four or five years old. What was really big for me was having met a lot of the traders when I was very young, like in kindergarten and first grade, and they were still in the pit when I got my membership. I can remember them as a young child, being only four feet tall and looking up to those guys. Then, all of a sudden, I'm standing across from them in the pit. I'm trying to profit and they are trying to profit. It was a really intense experience.

I think that this exchange is a spectacular place. I love doing business with the guys whom I've been calling "Mister So-and-So" for years and years. Those traders are just like family. And it might be an adversarial relationship at some point and it's a little tough to do, but I have great respect for most of the traders.

Why did you want to be part of this industry?

There's a very simple answer. I grew up around it and liked it. Then I went through college and I seemed to be very good at accounting. I thought I would go to work for one of the Big Eight accounting firms. I hoped I would be very successful and make partner and then retire when I was 55. It was a great career plan.

I graduated and went to work for Price Waterhouse. It was really a tough job. Some of the workweeks were 80 and 100 hours long. I took a serious look at the CBOT and saw that the workday was three hours and 45 minutes. That looked very, very appealing. From my family, I knew that at the CBOT, everybody's an independent business person. I liked that idea, too. The drawback was there is not the same security as receiving a weekly paycheck from an established accounting firm. But early in 1979, after getting a raise from, like, $13,500 to $15,500 a year, I decided to give the Board of Trade a shot. I've been here ever since.

How did you buy your membership?

The Continental Bank of Chicago was lending money not just to people who thought they had oil reserves down in Oklahoma, but lending money for seats, too. We went over to the bank, and they said, "You're 23 years old; you have no collateral. Why should we lend you any money?" And I said, "Because my family's been around for a long time."

Unfortunately, banks don't lend money because your family has been in the business a long time. My grandfather had sponsored Gene Cashman for a membership, and Gene had a better relationship with the bank than we did. So Gene called the bank and suggested that they lend me the money. When he asked, it happened.

I borrowed $200,000 from the bank and then borrowed some money from the family, and I paid $223,500 for a membership in February 1979. I was scared to death, because I probably had only $20,000 in the bank. I'd been scrimping and saving from my job at Price Waterhouse and everything else. I wasn't used to seeing things go down instead of up and paying the interest at about 21 percent at the time, which is when Paul Volcker started to hike interest rates. Somehow, we managed to get through that and make enough money to pay everything off.

That's great. Can you remember your first day as a trader?

Yes, I thought I knew a lot more than I did. I started trading and I got a losing position on. Then I tried to kind of buffalo the market. I tried to let everybody think there was something behind what I had done, but there really wasn't. I ended up losing money. I said to myself, "I don't think I'll do that again." So, I'd learned very quickly the market is going to do what it's going to do, whether you think you're right or not. That old adage about "buy low, sell high" or "sell high and buy low" works, but it also works in reverse. Here, if you buy high and then sell low, it costs you money and you try to avoid doing that too often.

Does it still hold?

Oh, absolutely. There are a lot of guys who are technical traders and guys who are fundamental traders. But if you're not in step with the market, no matter what tool you use, you won't be successful. It takes a certain amount of discipline, and all of that comes from 30 years of doing this to recognize when you're in step with the market and when you're not. So you learn new things every day, because the market changes.

What do you think has stayed the same since your grandfather was at the CBOT?

When guys scream and yell, they still spit in your face. When you're done trading, you have to scrub to clean up. At the end of a busy day, when you go to the dry cleaners or the grocery store and you have a conversation, people always ask if you have a sore throat. I always say, "No. This is what I sound like all the time." Then they ask, "Are you a coach or a teacher?" It's easier just to say, "Yes, that's it. I'm a coach."

You know, you can't explain to them that you stand around screaming and yelling all day for a living, because some people might think that's great, but most people just wouldn't understand it.

What's something new that you've learned?

We do a lot of screen-based training now along with open outcry. That's a learning experience every day. I am finding out what you can do and can't do, and how far you lead off. Do you trust the screen? Do you trust the guys in the pit? How deep are the markets? It's a very different experience. The marketplace is telling you, "This is the way we want to do business." Our job is to adapt to this new trading style.

Speaking of trading styles, can you tell me about Everett Klipp?

Everett Klipp was a friend of my father and grandfather for a long time. He had a clearing operation and he trained traders. His theory worked very well for many, many people who got very, very rich over a period of time. He told his traders that they had to "love to lose, love to lose, love to lose." He professed that if you got into the market and you established a position and it went against you, you should get out right away; and if you minimized your losses and learned how to let the winners run, you'd be very successful.

Everett made a lot of people very successful. Even though I took a different path, I was a broker and a trader which didn't fit Everett's model, I always tried to remember that. It's okay when the market goes against you. The important lesson is to get out. You can always reestablish your position, but "love to lose" was a great motto to remember.

How do you deal with stress on those losing days?

When I was single, and before having children, I used to go out and play golf in the afternoon or exercise or something like that. Today I have to go from work to soccer games and football games and fencing matches and swimming meets and things like that. You have to take a deep breath and say, "Okay, we start over again tomorrow." Hopefully, you learn from your experiences.

When somebody asks you what do you do for a living, how do answer that question?

My children have all been down on the floor. Two of my older children have spent a lot of time with me being my clerks during their spring and summer breaks. They have experienced the business firsthand, but when someone says, "What does your dad do?" they say, "Dad stands around with his arms folded and chews gum."

When people ask me what I do and I tell them I'm a trader, most of the time they presume you trade stocks. When you try to explain what commodities are, or how the open outcry system works, it's a little difficult for them to fathom.

Now that we're electronic, it's a little easier to tell them you do "point and click. It's just like e*Trade and Schwab." They go, "Okay. I get it." But if you try to explain further that we do it with corn and with gold and with Treasury futures and with stock options and things like that, then you lose them. After all my explaining, they still ask me to recommend a good stock. It is hard to explain to somebody on the outside.

In the late 1970s, and then again in the mid-1990s, when there were very lucrative commodity markets for corn and soybeans, you could always run into people at cocktail parties who would say, "Oh, yes, I've been long beans for a long time and I'm making a killing. You must just be knocking them dead." I would reply, "You know, I've been short as long as you've been long, so no, not really." Again, there are a few people who understand, but for the most part, people don't.

Why do so many people think of the Board of Trade as a place where everybody makes a lot of money?

It's because of the stories that go around about the really big successes like Tom Baldwin. There have been a number of people who have been through the grains and who have been fabulously successful. Then they go out and do other things like renovate the Rookery Building. Gene Cashman built a fabulous stable of racing horses. So you hear a lot about the success stories. What you don't hear is about the 80 guys who came down with their stake and then lost it.

Tell me about the CBOT as a self-regulatory agency.

That goes back to what I was talking about earlier: the importance of trust. There's the expression, "My word is my bond." If you make a trade with somebody, you have to understand that they're good for it. That goes to policing a lot of what might be perceived as not necessarily corrupt practices, but just not good trade practice. It's up to the members to make sure everything's on the up-and-up, because if people lose confidence in the marketplace, then they won't use the marketplace.

If you find somebody you make a trade with who doesn't honor that trade, then you don't trade with them again. We wouldn't want that to happen to our marketplace. Everybody respects the integrity of the marketplace and works to protect it. Overall, the paid staff does a very good job of policing everything that goes on, because the majority of our staff has a very good understanding of how things are supposed to work. They do a very good job of making sure it stays that way.

Have you served on any committees that deal with self-regulation?

I was on the board of directors earlier in my career, and I'm on the board of directors now. During my previous Board stint, I was on the Regulatory Compliance Committee. I've been the chairman of the Appeals Committee for a number of years. Being on those committees,

I was able to see the issue of self-regulation from both sides: from the inside, working with the staff, with Bryan Durkin and Dean Payton and the other people in charge of regulation, and then from the membership side as well. Most of my encounters with Office of Investigations and Audits (OIA) have been pleasant, because everybody respects everybody else.

I think self-regulation works very well here. I think the people in Washington understand how we operate, and that's important. They see it when they come to Chicago. We really like to get those people to come to the exchange, so we can show them how things work. Once they understand how we operate, for the most part they let us govern ourselves. That's why we are still a self-regulatory organization.

Tell me some of the things accomplished as a director.

That was in the early 1990s. At the time, we were talking about expanding to accommodate the huge trade in financial futures. It seemed like the electronic marketplace was still a ways off and we felt it necessary to construct the new building that houses the financial floor. Some might say that's not necessarily my accomplishment. Pat Arbor and David Brennan brought in a number of other people who worked very hard to accomplish that task. We needed that new space, so that when we were ready to go to an electronic marketplace, we had the market to deliver to that marketplace.

I'm not sure that I had any individual accomplishments. I always felt I was there to ask questions. I'm not smarter than anybody else and I don't have any great insight into the commodity futures market, but I try to ask common sense questions. If there's a problem area, then you try to be the conscience of the average guy. I think that was my role during my first tenure.

Around that time, there was diminished interest in the Board of Trade. How did the CBOT recover?

The Chicago Board of Trade is a fabulous old institution, and just like every other fabulous old institution, our fate doesn't just skyrocket all the time. We go through cycles, just as traders go through cycles and just as every business goes through cycles. You do everything you can to make sure you stay in the forefront of the financial institutions and the users of the marketplace, so when it's time for them to get back in, you're there and they know you're there to serve them.

It wasn't necessarily a big publicity campaign that brought back the interest; it was just making sure the users of our agricultural markets and our financial markets knew we were there when the time came for them to do their risk arbitrage again.

Were there new products that perked people's interest?

One of the things that helped was the ability of Board of Trade members to go over to the CBOE. Between the three markets—the equity markets, the financial markets, and the agricultural markets—somebody's going to be having a good time during one of those periods. It's been a great benefit for our members over the years, even if it was just to teach the members who were actually trading over in the CBOE.

How important is the service part of your business?

A large portion of what we did, up until the electronic marketplace, was customer service. Customers want to know what's going on. They want their information in a timely manner and that doesn't just include the execution, but what's going on down on the floor. We can accumulate the information that we get from the industry users, because those are the people that we talk to, but customers still want to know what is being said on the floor.

It is important for us to keep our customers in touch with what the professional traders are saying. They want to know who we have to trade with and who do we have to trade against. My grandfather did that, my father did that, and then everybody tried to kind of step it up a notch as the generations went on. We have been fairly successful with that kind of service for many years.

What do you see as the role of service in the computer era?

There's still the same demand for information. People want to know what the attitude is; they want to know what the professional traders are doing. It becomes a little more difficult to collect that information, because now the biggest bond trader might be in an office in Switzerland or the biggest agricultural trader might be in an office in Hawaii. All the trading no longer takes place on the floor. But those people still need to reach out to other people, so we try to make sure they have contact with the people who are still utilizing the marketplace.

Because the CBOT has gone global, how would you see the exchange as a worldwide price discovery mechanism?

The biggest thing we have to offer is transparency. We offer not just the liquidity, but the transparency. You know who's doing what and where, and you know what markets you can count on to get into and get out of. One of the big problems we've seen with fledgling markets is people wondering, "If I get in, where can I get out?" People who buy companies in private equity have exit strategies. So, if you trade, naturally you have to have an exit strategy. Well, the transparency of our market provides that.

If you buy it, we know that we can tell you where you can sell it. If you sell it, we know that we can tell you where you can buy it back. That's why we're here; that's why we have not just persevered, but have become the dominant market that we are in the things that we trade.

Where do you see the competition coming from in the future?

The subject of competition has been discussed since I was a little kid. I think it won't be a concern as long as the Board of Trade continues to listen to the people who use the market, as long as it provides the liquid marketplace, with the integrity that we have here, and people know that when they make a trade and they make money, they can take that money out.

I mean that this marketplace is better than going to the bank, because all that stuff gets settled up on a daily basis. The Board of Trade will continue to innovate and do things that are necessary. People talk about Google or eBay and things like that. I think, to a certain extent, those things will get molded into our market model. How that will happen exactly, I can't tell you. I'm not a futurist. But over the past 160 years, I know that we have continued to change and to remake ourselves so that we are not just relevant, but we're the leaders in what we do. I believe the institution will continue to do that.

On a day-to-day basis, tell me about your trading.

The electronic marketplace has had a big influence on how I trade. For example, the side-by-side trading in agricultural futures came into being in September 2006, and it's changed dramatically. Before, I'd put everything on a card, turn it in to my clerk and keep a count. Today, I'm trading on the screen, as well as in the pit, so I still give it to the clerk, but he's inputting things electronically, so that the electronic counts match. You watch the screen to try to get in step with that.

You begin to recognize patterns. I hate to use the word "tells", but the people in the pit always have their "tells." You can tell when someone's panicking, and you can tell when someone's confident and that they've got you. To a certain extent, it's the same thing on the screen. You see what those guys are doing; it's like well, guess what? They just sold it off two cents.

The trick is to be able to distinguish whether they are setting a pattern or stepping outside the pattern. You want to be able to determine if you're going to trade against them or you're going to trade with them. Are you going to be a doer or a joiner? To a certain extent, all of those things still happen; it's just a different venue.

It's exciting, but it's different. When they started to trade in the overnight session in 1996 or 1997, I signed up. I've been doing that Sunday night through Thursday night, every night since then. There is a routine to it. It's like when you come into the Board of Trade building and you put on your trading coat; it's putting the trappings on. It's the same thing with electronic trading. You go down and turn the computer on at six o'clock at night and it's the same routine. If you enjoy it, then it's not unpleasant. We do what we do, when we do it.

When do you sleep?

When there's not a whole lot going on, I try to get home before the kids get home from school, to take a little nap. If there are big markets going on and I have positions that I carry, when they start trading in the agricultures again at 6:30 P.M., sometimes I don't get a lot of sleep. They trade through until six in the morning. I usually want to track that and make sure that nothing goes against me significantly. If there's an opportunity, I want to make sure I'm there.

Is it ever possible to go on vacation?

I learned a very important lesson a long time ago when I went on my honeymoon. I made the mistake of taking positions. We were in Bermuda, and that didn't work out real well. Now when I want to vacation, I get flat or I have someone else watch my positions. I find someone I can trust. It might be a family member. Then I can really go on vacation. You just need to take a break. You can't just keep going.

Absolutely. What are some new products that interest you?

There are some new products that aren't necessarily new products. The Board of Trade has a portion of the metals market. The COMEX used to be the only place with a metals market, but we traded electronically here. When I first started working for the Board of Trade in 1970 or 1971, I used to mark the chalkboards for the silver market and the gold market in New York, so I felt I had a certain knack for that.

Now, being able to trade that market electronically through the CBOT, there's a tremendous opportunity for me, because I used to watch what the prices were doing and then try to predict what the next price would be. Even though I was just taking it off the ticker tape and putting it on the chalkboard, I learned what to watch. Being able to trade that market electronically offers traders a great opportunity.

I think the new commercial real estate contract that the Board of Trade is developing, with a whole line of new products, will provide tremendous opportunity. If you had something akin to that subprime mortgage market in a futures market at this point in time, it would be going gangbusters.

Are you ever afraid to go into a new market?

I am not necessarily afraid, because if you're afraid, usually you don't accomplish what you set out to do. You should put your toe in first, before you dive right in, just to make sure you understand the mechanics. Then, if you're confident, it's easy to ramp up pretty quick.

People feel these are opportunities.

It's not like the old days, where you used to have to step into a pit. Then you needed a physical presence and you needed to learn who the guys were and who you could trade with and who you weren't supposed to trade with. This is an electronic market. You put it up on a screen, watch it for a while, trade your one lots, and say, "Okay, this is what I thought it was." Then you're off and running.

Give me an example of the market today.

Okay. Today is Tuesday, April 3, 2007, and the corn for our delivery in December closed at $3.69½ cents—that's the settlement. We're on a big downturn after the crop report last Friday.

We were limit down Friday and limit down Monday, and it came off limit yesterday. Then we bounced, and then it was all over the place. I'm not sure where the stock market ended up or where the financial futures ended up; but now the world's concerned with the corn, because things like ethanol are going to save us from the vagaries of the oil market.

Any market predictions?

It's going to go down and then it's going to come back up. We look to other markets and world situations to see how our markets will react.

What do you think about the impact of the creation of the CBOE?

It was a tremendous opportunity for a lot of people: a lot of people at the Board of Trade, a lot of people who have never heard of the Board of Trade and the O'Connors, who put the CBOE together.

My grandfather, from the time I was very young, said if we had puts and calls on stocks we would be unbeatable. And then somebody actually did it, and I've actually been very active over there for about the past 10 years.

We have groups of proprietary traders, Sparta Group and Cassandra Group. They trade the indexes, various stocks, and equity options. It's been a tremendous opportunity, and continues to be, even with all the competition that they face.

With the Options Clearing Corporation (OCC) and fungibility, it's a much different market model than we have at the Board of Trade. The CBOE has been able to innovate and hang on to their index markets, and hopefully it will stay that way.

Do you see the CBOE proceeding in a different way?

They're going to try to do their IPO, and the world will have to decide what they want to do with that. Hopefully, there'll be some connection between the two exchanges in the future.

Speaking of IPOs, can you tell me about the IPO for the Chicago Board of Trade?

Preceding the IPO, we faced the competitive threat of the Eurex US exchange. I think once we got through that, it was clear that we were going to be around for a while. The marketplace had the confidence to buy stock in the Board of Trade.

The fact that the CME had done it before us had a lot to do with it. I think because we could meet the challenges in facing down Eurex US, it created a confidence to buy Board of Trade shares instead of buying Board of Trade memberships. The equity market's confidence in our shares tells you the marketplace has confidence in where we're going.

I'm not sure that the CBOT necessarily changed dramatically. People still had memberships. They came down, and they have trading rights and things like that. However, as the value of CBOT shares has grown, you are seeing some people saying to themselves, "I think maybe it's time to go do something else." People are considering that maybe they should retire or maybe they should start another business and be much less active. I think that's pretty much the effect the IPO has had.

What's your take on derivative options?

There's such a large over-the-counter market right now in commodity options. They call it a structured product. There's also a large over-the-counter market in equity options. There are a lot of things that the OTC traders can do that we can't do. For us, they have to be cut and paste; it has to be exactly the same thing, contract to contract. The OTC traders can customize things much more than we can.

It would be great if we could find a pattern to the over-the-counter product and do an exchange trade of products, so that they would have the benefit of clearing. Eliminating the counterparty risk is a big part of what we do. If you have a winning day, the money's going to be there, and if it's a losing day, you have to make good on it. That type of trading is mandatory in our business, whereas with the over-the-counter products, it might be six months before you have to settle on those things; so there is counterparty risk there.

Part of what we need to do going forward, and I think the CBOT and some of the other exchanges are also looking at this, is tell them that we're here, to insure their counterparty risk and to give them the transparency that they desire, especially in things that are kind of cookie-cutter, like swaps and other things. We're here and ready, so let us trade it.

Can you think of events outside of the CBOT that affected trading?

Yes, I remember the grain embargo very well because I still owed the bank a portion of my loan. At the time, the South American growing capacity wasn't very large, but they found a way to make it what it needed to be. The effect of the embargo was that our markets were very quiet for a period of time. I decided I was going to be in the agricultural markets. Because of the embargo, I thought maybe this wasn't what I had planned on, but shortly after that, we had a short crop and all of a sudden everything was fine again. The impact of that event gave the South Americans the impetus for developing a tremendous agricultural juggernaut. And it continues to grow every year.

How about the impact of the Crash of 1987?

My grandfather had passed away by then, but he'd been on the floor during the Crash of 1929. It happened during the dust bowl years, so this market wasn't necessarily affected to the same extent that the financial and equity markets were in New York. We were still very profitable at the Board of Trade because wheat and the other things being traded here were in demand because farmers couldn't grow anything.

When you look back at the stock market crash of 1987, nobody knew what to think. We knew that we opened, and especially with our link to the CBOE and many of the common firms, we knew there'd been a bloodbath over there. There were more questions than answers. When the federal government said everything was going to be okay, we asked, "What does that mean?" Who were they going to stand behind and who weren't they going to stand behind? Everybody had to settle up and everybody needed to meet certain capital requirements. Everything stayed intact here. It was a pretty nervous time for everyone.

Speaking of nervous times, tell me about September 11th?

I remember as I was pulling into the parking garage hearing on the radio what had happened to the first tower and I thought, "That's a horrific thing." At the time, I'm not sure anybody was even speculating that it was a terrorist attack.

Then I got on the trading floor and I asked someone, "Did you hear what happened in New York?" They had one of the major news services on the big-screen TV and so we actually watched the second plane hit. Then you knew it wasn't just a regular day anymore.

There was a lot of panic. There were rumors that there was a plane headed for Chicago and it was going to hit our building. People started saying, "Let's get out!" It was up to the board of directors to decide what course of action to take. They had to decide, "Do we need to be open for the integrity of the markets? Are there going to be problems in New York? Would member firms be able to service the market?" They did the right things. It was a very, very disquieting time. We were closed more than one day and not sure when we would open. Then we worried about what would happen with the marketplace.

Once we got home, it was so hard just understanding what was happening. I wanted to go get the kids out of school, because nobody really knew what was going on. It was only later in the day that I spoke to a friend who used to be in Navy intelligence. I called him and said that everyone in Chicago was very nervous. I told him we had heard that there was a plane headed for the Chicago Board of Trade. And he said, "I don't want to play this down and I don't want to make you feel bad, but you guys aren't even like in the top 100 of the target list." He continued to tell me that they'd go for the Sears Tower or someplace else like that first. Since that building is right down the block, it didn't make me feel a whole lot better. We were still pretty nervous. It was a terrible time for everyone.

We see how world events effect the CBOT, what do you see as the CBOT's effect on world economies?

We've made it much easier for all the people who buy our debt and use our debt, or use debt in their industry, to hedge that risk. And anybody who went through the interest rate spike in the early 1980s can tell you that there is risk. Interest rates don't stay at 5 percent all the time.

Certainly, other people around the world could tell you that. Australia just hiked its interest rates again. In the late 1990s and the early part of this century, people got used to very stable interest rates. But when there is volatility in those things, we are here to make it easier for people to lay that risk off and to use it as a tool in their financial planning.

We do this with more than just Treasury futures; we also do it with the equity index, with the Dow Jones, and with our agricultural futures, too. Everybody is using commodities as a component of their investment portfolios. They are using hedge funds and major pension funds and things like that. That is what we are here for.

Do you see any countries being CBOT's competitors in the future?

Now that it's an electronic marketplace, anybody with a big server room could be a competitor. Anybody with a better mousetrap could be a competitor. But as long as we continue to provide liquidity, transparency and a service that is special, as long as our mousetrap is better, we will not just survive, we will thrive.

We've touched a little bit on the technological changes that provide the ability to be more global. Can you talk briefly about the technological changes that you've seen during your CBOT career?

When I first started at the exchange, we used to have to get down here at 5:30 or 6:00 A.M. during busy market times to check the outtrades and to put the paper decks together and do all kinds of things.

Today, there is no paper anymore, so there is no deck to put together. The outtrades are much simpler, because there is continuous updating of trade matching and things like that taking place throughout the day. This is made possible through the electronic trading and the electronic trading cards that we use for open outcry. There has almost been a total transformation that will continue to evolve.

We are much more sophisticated than when I started in 1979, and it's all for the better. I mean the card and the pencil are still here, but we use them better. We are much more effective than we used to be.

Without a doubt, change is good. If you don't embrace change, you're doomed to failure. Knowing how to capitalize on change is what we do around here. As the world changes, we give the world the opportunity to hedge its risk, and that's what we're here for. And we do a very good job of it.

How do you view the CBOT's future with this electronic change?

Today, life at the exchange is like a big video game. The kids who train on video games and have tremendous reaction times and who recognize patterns are going to be able to apply those same talents to commodity trading, financial futures trading, and other types of trading. It's a new world.

What do you hope will be the mark that you leave on the Board of Trade? What would be your legacy?

That I did a good job here, not just in the day-to-day trading, but also in the leadership positions that people have elected me to. It's not that I'm smarter than the next guy; I just try to ask the right questions. That is what I'm here for, to ask the right questions.

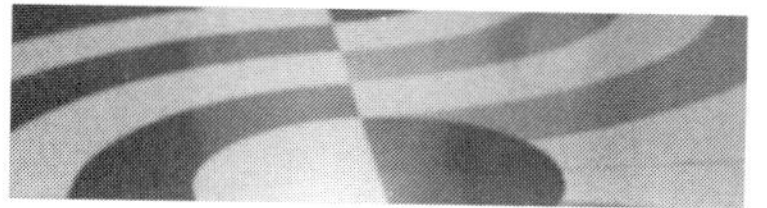

CHAPTER 15

Giving Back

Pamela R. Rogers

Born and raised on the South Side of Chicago, Pamela R. Rogers has brought to the Chicago Board of Trade a combination of intelligence, energy, loyalty and pride during her long tenure there. She attended Dixon, a public grammar school, then went on to Mercy Catholic High School, where she graduated with honors. She was given a scholarship to Loyola University and was on the dean's list.

In the summer of 1976, Mrs. Rogers came to the Chicago Board of Trade as a runner. Although her college major was premed, she soon found that her passions were for the financial markets. She learned more about the business by being a phone clerk and by 1978 had become the first female African-American to hold a full membership at the exchange.

While at the CBOT, Pamela has worked as a commodity trader and market analyst, oilseed desk manager, and crush specialist. Today, she works for Headway Inc. as a consultant to JPMorgan Chase. Before joining JPMorgan Chase, Pamela spent nearly 30 years with Cargill, Inc.

Pamela has served the industry in many ways. She has been on numerous committees, including the Arbitration, Executive, Education and Marketing, and Regulatory Compliance. She is currently the chairperson of the Membership Committee.

Her area of expertise lies in agricultural commodities. She is very well known for her technical and fundamental analysis of the markets. She has had more than 30 years of exposure to cash-related markets and is a respected crush specialist.

Pamela has been a full member of the Chicago Board of Trade for 30 years. She has dedicated her life to serving this institution. She devotes a good deal of her spare time to encouraging minorities to make the exchange their place of business. She lectures in schools and mentors students on the floor. She is open, accessible and honest about the Chicago Board of Trade being more than just a place to make a living. It is a place that offers great opportunities to make a special life.

Mrs. Rogers has been married for 27 years.

****

How did you first hear about the Chicago Board of Trade?

In 1976, I was a student in college. A girlfriend of mine was working at the CBOT and decided to go back to school out of state. I thought I might go down and see whether I could do it just for the summer. When I came down and got a glimpse of what was going on, my first impression was that it was very overwhelming. My second reaction was that it was fascinating; and third, it seemed very intimidating. But I took the job with a commercial firm known for educating their people well. They had a lot people working on the floor, and I found myself in a situation where I could gain a great deal of experience.

I was in college during those days, pursuing a degree in medicine because I thought I wanted to be a doctor. Curiosity led me down a different path and I did a complete reversal from premed to business. Up to that point, the only business-related course I had taken was Econ 101.

With only Econ 101, how did you learn the business?

I started off as a runner; running orders in and out of the pit. I had a desire to do more and to be a part of the exchange. Certainly, one of the things that I noticed during those early days was that there weren't a lot of women in the business. I think in that regard, I felt even more committed as a woman to try to make a difference.

I embarked with a goal to learn more about the mechanics of the exchange itself. The most striking thing for me was that no two days on the trading floor were alike. It was a situation where you had to resolve all business by the end of the day, because the next day the factors that affected the market could very well be different. As I became more interested in what was going on in this high-energy and extremely stressful environment and examined the opportunities a little bit more closely, I could see that this place held a future for me.

Luckily, as I was making this decision to change my focus away from medicine, I had a wonderful mentor, Peter von Eschen. He was my boss at the time. One of the many positive things I can say about him is that he always was willing to answer my questions, which I was relentlessly asking. I wanted to know things like what caused prices to fluctuate. Peter always gave me good, detailed answers.

When I came into the business, back in the 1970s, the commercials were very dominant factors in the market, as far as the grain business was concerned. In fact, grain sold to countries like China or Russia was hedged mostly through commercial firms at the CBOT. It gave me a better perspective of world markets.

I had an intense appetite to know about what was going on, so I became a phone clerk and began getting more exposure to the world. I was talking to people all over the world. I found out that this industry was much, much bigger than I could ever imagine. And one of the ironies for me is that I'm a city girl, while my mom and my grandmother grew up on a farm.

If luck is a residue of desire, then I was at the right place and time when several key people left to pursue other interests. The position for trader and crush specialist became available. I was an experienced phone clerk by that time, and my boss had a great deal of confidence in my abilities.

When he told me to get an application for membership, I nearly fell out of my chair. It was a little intimidating because there is an intense screening process and financial background check. But I knew I had a clean record and would make a viable member of integrity and of high moral and ethical standing.

Tell me what you remember about your early days on the floor.

The first person to approach me after becoming a member was Carol Ovitz Hancock. She became the first female member of the exchange in 1969. This was 1978, and there still were only a handful of woman members. So, for her to approach me and congratulate me on what was happening was a milestone and something I'll never forget. She was a person with whom I could share my viewpoint on issues as I saw them as a female in the business.

Unfortunately, even today, when people come to the exchange, they talk about not seeing very many women. What I find interesting is when you approach the CBOT building, there are two statues; one is the goddess of agriculture, and the other is the goddess of industry; and looking down LaSalle canyon, you can see Ceres, the goddess of grain, atop the CBOT building. So on an intuitive level, women have always been a part of the exchange.

There are several women who deserve honorable mentions. They were active traders and early pioneers in the soybean pit, dating back to the 1970s. Among those who have made a difference in my life are Abigail Fisher (deceased) and Debbie Groover. Alexis Genin was also a very special role model. She died a few years ago, but she was so well admired that there is a plaque dedicated to her memory at the entrance of the agricultural trading floor. These women are well known and respected for their contributions to the industry.

I think it's important to mention that the reason why I think this is a great place for women is because the futures markets provide women with an opportunity to have jobs with the flexibility to also have the career of being a mom. Because of the trading hours, you can be at home with your children before they go off to school, then come to work at this crazy place and do this exotic dance for about five hours, and then be back when the kids get home. For a number of women, this has been a great place that affords them the opportunity to juggle two careers. Actually, there are quite a few women involved in this industry. They might not be in the pits, but their presence is there.

Tell me about your family. Were they happy with your decision to come down to the Board of Trade?

My parents, Ben and Georgia Davis, knew very little, if anything, about commodity markets. My mother spent her career working at a local hospital and certainly would have been proud to have a doctor in the family. My father as a young man dreamed of becoming an airline pilot. That wasn't a realistic career option for any minorities back in the 1950s. I would say it was with mixed emotions that they applauded my decision to try to create new inroads for minorities in this business.

Tell me what you did with this mission to educate people.

Before I came into the business in 1976, I didn't even know that this building existed. I also noticed that people outside of the business had no idea what the people did in our industry. They would confuse commodities with stocks. Many didn't understand the concept of going short or selling something that you don't own. I felt a need to try to make people understand a little bit more about what goes on and what futures are and teach them about the business itself.

Was one of your goals to educate minorities about this business?

Yes. Over the years I have been involved with the Agricultural High School on the South Side of Chicago. I have mentored kids from there. I was active in the CBOT's 4-H program and the Commodity Challenge, through its Education and Marketing Committee. We also hosted a yearly crop judging contest for college students.

I have friends who are teachers, and they like to talk to their students about what I do. I visit their classrooms to give them the exposure to the business. I also have sponsored kids who come to visit the exchange. I have talked to numerous groups, including farmers. I have also done many trading simulations. I want all the visitors to the exchange to see the place and to get an understanding of what's going on. Hopefully, they might want to pursue careers in this business.

Do you think you can encourage more minorities to become involved?

I already have. I've been approached by young people who were amazed, first of all, to know that there's someone just like them in the business. They certainly have been eager to understand how I became successful. I was the first African-American female on the floor. I try to steer people I work with on the floor in the right direction, and hope that someday they might want to become members of the exchange.

So, you would certainly understand the idea of being a mentor to somebody.

I think I have been a mentor to many people. There are a few minorities on the floor who have worked for me who have become members of the exchange. So I feel I have achieved that goal.

Tell me about your mentors.

First and foremost, I owe much of my success to my parents. They were my role models growing up. They had a strong work ethic and made sacrifices so that I would have a better education to achieve any goals I set for myself. I'm fortunate that they are still alive today to see what I have accomplished.

My mentor at work was my boss, Peter Von Eschen. He opened the door for me with no regard to race or color. Being an ex-Marine, he taught me about discipline and inspired all of his people to excel further than he did within the company. I eventually was promoted to his position after he retired. To this day, we maintain a close relationship.

Can you give me a word picture of the floor of the Board of Trade when you started compared to now?

Actually, it's not much different in terms of the people. There is no in-between in this business. Either you can operate in high-stress situations or you can't. So, the caliber of people is pretty much the same. What has really changed is the business. We've electrified the execution process. But as far as the people are concerned, you have the same type of individuals. You have people who can deal with pressure in a very high-stress situation and a very high-energy environment. To be successful here, people have to be disciplined, quick thinkers. If you have those types of characteristics, then you can do well.

How about the fact that you've often said that you left your gender at the door?

In all the years I've been around this industry, it has been perceived as kind of a men's club. Well, this business can seem very intimidating. Seeing all those men in their colored jackets yelling at each other could be overwhelming at first. However, for me it was never a problem; I just saw people. My goal was to be perceived as an equal, and hoped that they would recognize that I was doing the same thing that they were doing every day. The men were never an obstacle, and it was never a barrier, because any negatives toward me were just words.

Do you think you wore a unique hat in any way?

No, not at all. I just felt I was given an opportunity to do something that not many people could do. I was going to make the best of that opportunity in the company of people with very diverse backgrounds. They were all people who were putting everything on the line every day, personally and financially.

Tell me about being a crush specialist.

The crush is kind of a unique spread relationship. It's the relationship between soybeans and the by-products of soybean meal and soybean oil. Commercial processors buy beans from the farmer, process those beans at special facilities where they extract the soybean meal and soybean oil, and then sell those by-products. They convert the costs to process those beans into a margin referred to as the gross processing margin. The same relationship exists in futures, called the Board crush. As a crush specialist I hedge their cash positions in futures.

Do you spend time analyzing the markets?

Actually, I wear a number of hats in that regard. A typical day for me is to come to work in the morning, read the tapes, and then make a few phone calls to traders I respect in the business. I get their opinions about what's going on in the market that particular day; then I formulate my own ideas about the market and I put out a market wire to offer customers an opinion on price direction.

On what do you base that analysis?

Years of experience. It's not something that you learn overnight. The market has a number of factors that affect price. They could be fundamental inputs such as the supply/demand. They could be technical factors, which deal with chart patterns, or in some instances, emotional or gut feel. Maybe for me it is a little bit of woman's intuition. We tend to see a lot of that when we get into the weather markets. So, I rely on all those different things.

Did anybody ever challenge your woman's intuition or opinions?

When you talk about opinion, I think it is a good thing to have a difference of opinion. In fact, there are several people who work with me, and it's not unusual for us to have different viewpoints based on the same factors. My bias might be bullish and theirs bearish. I respect their opinions because they may see something that I'm missing. I don't look at it as a negative challenge.

Let's go back a bit and talk about some of the people that you know of who might be considered legends at the CBOT.

One of the legendary traders is Arthur Cutten. He was known as one of the greatest speculators of all time. I think he was a big wheat and cotton trader back in the old days. He lost a vast fortune during the Great Depression. An interesting story related to him is concerned with the statues of the goddesses of agriculture and industry from the original 1885 Board of Trade building. They were lost during the time the 1885 building was torn down and were found many years later on his estate. They were restored and returned to the exchange and now stand in the LaSalle Street plaza.

The other legendary figure, who I actually knew personally, was Gene Cashman. I remember one particularly active day when suddenly trading stopped and there was this huge burst of applause. I turned to a couple of guys and said, "What's going on? Who is this man?" And they said, "That's Gene Cashman. Gene Cashman is the reason why a number of us are here. He gave us our start. In some instances there are people who have had some problems and he was the person who got them back on their feet. So, he's a very well-respected member of this exchange." Over the years, I have become very close to a number of the Cashmans. I can honestly say that to this day they represent the finest example of integrity at this exchange.

The word 'integrity' is important in this business. Why?

Well, it represents who you are. When you're involved in a business where your word is your bond, and it's legally binding, it's important that you know that the person standing next to you, that you're making a trade with, is someone that you can trust. It has to be someone who is ethical and who's moral. So, your integrity is very, very important.

And how about tradition in the business? What does that word mean to you?

Tradition? I think about the fact that open outcry has been a tradition for nearly 160 years and we're in the midst of seeing a migration from open outcry to more screen-based trading. Open outcry is organized chaos. It has become a unique art form, and I would miss it if it totally disappeared.

Can you tell me why people fail at the Board of Trade?

Two reasons come to mind. First, failure can occur when you don't understand the risk that's involved; and second, often people come here undercapitalized. To me those are the two reasons people fail.

Why do they succeed?

It is because they become disciplined and they don't try to hit home runs. They really, truly take the time to learn about the business.

What was the first lesson that you learned?

I learned that no one person or entity is bigger than the market itself. One of the things Peter Von Eschen was very good at was training traders. When I first started, we had a small account that allowed us the opportunity to take on small positions. Peter thought this would teach us about risk management. The idea was you had to come up with reasons why you should have a position on, whether it was fundamental, technical, or just your gut feel. Then you would trade that position. And one particular time, I decided to put on a position for what I thought were all the right reasons.

It just so happened I was thinking about my position, which was going against me, when Peter and I were standing at the corner about to cross the street. And he just looked at me and asked me, "What are you going to do about that position?" And I said, "I don't know." He said, "You don't know?" Then, he said, "Well, let me just give you a few words of wisdom. We're about to cross the street and we have a green light, but if we get run over by a car, it doesn't matter that we had the right of way; we're dead anyway."

What he was trying to convey to me was that you can have a position for what appears to be all the right reasons and it can still go against you. You have to be ready to react to that. So, I immediately went back and took the position off, because it was the wrong position to have on at the time. What he taught me was when you put on a position, you should always have three pieces of information. One, you need to know at what price you want to put on your position. Two, you need to know at what point you want to get out. And three, if it goes against you, you need to know where you want to cut your losses.

That's a hard lesson.

No, it's not, because, like most people who have been around a long time, we have enough scars on our backs to know that you don't stay with a losing position very long.

People have an image of the Board of Trade as being a place where people make a lot of money and everybody is a winner.

It's interesting you would say that. That image is one of the things some of us are trying to change. The CBOT is a place where you have an opportunity to make a living. How well you do remains to be seen. Not all of us can say we share the same level of financial success. In fact, for me it's never been about the money. It's because I found the business interesting; it was challenging, and in this job boredom doesn't exist. The circumstances change every session. My primary goal is to provide value and quality service for the customer.

How important is providing good service?

It's the number one concern, because it reflects on the integrity of the exchange.

Describe the role of the CBOT as a self-regulatory organization.

Simply put, self-regulation has worked for almost 160 years because the people who make the decisions have an intimate knowledge and understanding of the processes of this business. The exchange does an excellent job monitoring trading activities. I think when you talk about the experience level, it's usually individuals who, like myself, get involved with working behind the scenes of the exchange.

How does self-regulation mesh with the government agencies like the CFTC?

Those agencies maintain close working relations with the exchange to ensure that rules, regulations, and contract specifications reflect market conditions. Rules are revised or modified as needed.

Speaking of some changes, do you remember moving into the current agricultural trading room?

I remember the transition from the original floor, but first, let's just back up a little bit. When I came to the exchange in 1976, we had electronic wallboards. These boards malfunctioned a couple of times and we'd be transported back to the old days. There used to be people on the platforms and they'd chalk the prices on blackboards. When that happened I suddenly realized I was experiencing a little history. This is the way they used to do it.

I also remember the day we got the notice that the Board of Trade was making arrangements to have a picture of all the members on the old floor. To this day, when I see that black-and-white picture in which I'm standing in the bean pit with all my colleagues, it looks like something from the 1800s. There is also a picture hanging in the visitors' center gallery of the opening of the current agricultural trading floor in 1982. It was taken on the first day of trading on that floor. Jane Byrne, who was mayor of Chicago at the time, was there, and I remember the photographers being in the gallery, taking the picture.

I remember the bell ringing and the market opening and this huge roar, because the acoustics weren't very good. Someone in the planning stage didn't realize what the noise level was going to be like when we all came onto the new floor, and they ended up having to build some sort of contraption on the ceiling to deal with the noise. It was really bizarre.

Look at what's happened today. The original 1930 trading floor is now an office for a privately owned options firm. So, again, you have change. Nothing stays the same, folks. This business represents constant change.

Tell me some of the places you've been behind the scenes. What committees have you worked on?

Right now I'm chairman of the Membership Committee, and we're involved with the screening process for prospective traders. I enjoy that experience for a number of reasons. Foremost, I feel that by being a part of the process that screens the individuals coming here I can help maintain and ensure that these people have an optimum level of integrity and moral and ethical standards. It is our job to determine if they are financially sound and competent.

How about your work on the Arbitration Executive Committee?

Arbitration is an interesting committee, because you see the kinds of situations that occur in the pit every day. When there are disputes between two members, say about price or quantity, they should be reconciled by the end of the day or at the latest by the opening of the next day. When traders can't agree or compromise, it goes to arbitration.

A panel is formed that represents a cross section of their peers in the business. We'll mediate both sides of the situation and reach a decision. Whatever decision is reached is binding. That means that they can't go to an outside court or appeal their case elsewhere. So we try to comprise the panel with people who are unbiased and hopefully have no conflict of interest with the individuals or firms that are involved in the dispute. I find it fascinating because you see some very interesting situations. The process has allowed me to garner some basic knowledge about law.

Can you talk about the changes in technology that you have seen?

I came in as a runner a little over 30 years ago. At that time, we communicated orders to the pit via a runner who would travel from the desk to the pit, to a broker. That took time and in some instances it could be costly. I'm sure the Board of Trade figured out that in order to stay innovative and grow, and provide high-quality service for its customers, it would have to become more efficient. To do that, the exchange decided to look at ways that would allow us to expedite the execution to get orders to the pit much quicker.

They decided to electrify the order flow to the pit via Electronic Clerk, or EC as it is known. The order would go to the broker in the pit, and within seconds the broker would execute the order and enter the fill on his screen. That information would then go simultaneously back to clearing and to the customer and accounting. It expedited the order routing process and eliminated the need for runners and also reduced the amount of paper being used. Fast-forward to today, and we now have more screen-based trading. We're coexisting side by side with the screen-based trading; but more volume is migrating to the screen.

Some may argue that this is not a good thing, but for me, having been in this business for 30 years and experiencing constant change every day, this is just the reality. We have to embrace change. It reminds me of a story my grandmother told me many years ago. She remembered the ice man showing up at her door and telling her that it was the end of the world for him. Refrigeration was coming and his life was over. He said, “What am I going to do?” And she said, “Well, you can learn how to make refrigerators or you can learn how to fix refrigerators.” This story’s moral applies to today’s trading world: Electronic trading will create new opportunities.

So, for those of us who have been on the trading floor in an environment of open outcry, we now have two platforms to choose from, depending on price and liquidity. Sometimes I wonder where I will fit in after there is a total migration off the floor, but I don’t worry about it. I plan on being around until the lights go out.

Change doesn’t scare you?

No. You should always plan on the unexpected.

Some people worry that there will be changes in the service part of the industry.

I don’t think that will happen. You have to know your customers. Some customers require quick execution, while others want to provide market information and use discretion to execute their orders. For still others, the issue is cost for the level of service. I think the changes we are making will be of benefit to our customers. It will represent extra value and even better service for them.

You spent a good part of your career serving the CBOT as a volunteer. Why did you do that?

Why did I give back? Well, I just think it’s my nature. I happen to be the type of individual that if you’re given an opportunity to do something, then there is a requirement that you give something back. And so it only seemed natural to get involved. Besides, it was a curiosity on my part to know what was going on behind the scenes and to learn more about the number of processes that take place. So, it wasn’t difficult for me to volunteer my time. I enjoy it. I continue to love being down there every day.

Describe a typical day.

When I first come on the trading floor in the morning, I walk in with a sense of calm. I listened to the news. I kind of have an idea, particularly if we’re in a weather market, of what might be going on or what might have happened.

As soon as I reach my desk I go from the sense of calm to turning it up about 20 notches. I start to formulate my ideas to put out our market comments. I talk to key customers about positions, their formulas, and their trading plans for the session. This all happens about one and a half hours before the opening bell at 9:30 A.M.

The difference between today and the past is that we now have the electronic market trading ahead of us, which sets the pace for the opening. Years ago, that wasn't the case. But now it's changed, because we have the overnight electronic market that we watch. And then we have to consider any new developments between the time they stop trading until we start, and that time frame can be pretty intense.

Sounds like a lot of responsibility.

As I mentioned before, I wear a lot of hats, and that's the other thing that's really tough, because in the morning I feel that I'm analytical. Then the bell rings, and I become a trader. And then the phone rings, and you become a doctor, because you might have a sick patient on the phone, someone who might be on the wrong side of the market and needs advice. Or you might have someone who wants to get involved and wants your opinion. They want to know what to do and what I think is going to happen.

So while you're trading, you're also trying to make sense of what is going on. It can be very overwhelming, very challenging. If you're not the kind of person that can deal with that type of pressure, being down here is not for you; not at all.

And when you leave for the day?

It's kind of hard to slow down, particularly on busy days. Slow days, it's okay. It kind of reminds me of that famous episode of *I Love Lucy*, the one with Lucy and Ethel working in a candy factory. There's this assembly line and things are going well, and the candy is moving along the conveyor belt, and then, within a few minutes, it speeds up and they're trying to put candy in their pockets, in their hats, down their shirts. Sometimes I feel like that's what's going on inside me. I try not to show it on the outside, because there's my crew, people who are depending on me to make some very difficult decisions. And I've got to keep it together. But I know how Lucy felt!

Why do you think you've been successful in keeping it together?

Why have I been successful? Discipline. Motivation. A sense of understanding what's going on and not taking anything for granted. I think those things have gotten me through 30 years; but discipline probably is the most important of them all. I'm a very disciplined person when it comes to trading.

You also seem to be a person with excellent people skills.

Well, it comes down to the type of character you have. My parents would always tell me, “If you’re going to do something, give it your best; otherwise it’s not worth doing.” So, I’ve always been the kind of person that if someone calls me, whether I’m working a five lot or hundred lot for them, they are entitled to the same level of service. You’re just as important to me.

I think people know that is how I operate, so they always want to call and talk about what I think. It gets a little tough on busy days, but I don’t make a distinction between customers. Whether you’re small or large, you’re the same to me. I’m there for you, whatever you need: information or guidance. I’m there to provide whatever level of service someone needs.

It sounds like it’s a combination of intelligence and heart.

Yes, you could say it’s a combination of intelligence and heart, but it’s also a strong belief in your ability. I can speak volumes about what this place means to me, and the opportunities that I’ve had. I don’t take any of it for granted. I never have and never will. Someone else may come in and say, “Hey, it’s just a place where I come to work, and it’s just a job.” But it represents a whole lot more to me, because of the fact that not a lot of women or minorities are doing this.

It’s important that I convey just how strongly I feel about having the opportunity to do what I do. I’m a member of the exchange. Whether I’m talking to another member, another runner, a phone clerk, or anyone else, I give them equal respect; it doesn’t matter who it is. That’s something else I was taught. Some people might want to put you on a pedestal because you’re a member of the exchange, but really in order to get respect, you have to give it to everybody, from the runner on up, because you depend on them to make the order flow process work.

So, if you don’t have their respect or you’re not at least committed to that, then it makes your job even tougher. I’m telling you that if the electronic order routing system were to go down tomorrow, I would be ready to walk onto the trading floor and run in an order. I’m not sure if many other members would do that, but I would. I’m going to be there to make the process work, to make sure the customer is happy, and whatever I have to do to make that happen, I’m going to do it.

Do you think that floor trading is coming to an end?

Eventually. One of these days we’re going to walk on the floor and they’re going to say, “This is it.” So right now it’s tough. I say that because not only am I a member of the exchange, but I’m a manager and

I have a crew of young people who work for me. I worry about their career paths in this business. All of them have gone back to school and gotten their degrees. I've insisted on it, just because I felt that if this goes away, that they will have some options and they'll be able to transition into some other areas of the business. I've certainly told them the story about the refrigerator and the ice man. So, I can say that we're prepared to venture out toward new horizons. We're going to be here and, hopefully, be a part of it as we figure out where we fit in the new process.

And what would you like your CBOT legacy to be?

When someday I leave this place, I will look back and know that I have had an incredible opportunity. I'll know that I did the best I could. I have been honored to give back, and I am proud of my accomplishments. I'll walk away with no regrets.

CHAPTER 16

Unequaled Leadership

Leslie Rosenthal

Since 1951, when he started as a runner on the Chicago Board of Trade trading floor, Leslie Rosenthal has been directly involved in virtually every aspect of the futures and options industry. After graduating from Roosevelt University in 1955 with a degree in history, he served two years in the U.S. Army. In 1958, he became a member of the CBOT. Mr. Rosenthal worked for many retail brokerage firms, including Harris Upham and Lamson Brothers, as a floor manager and market analyst. By 1963, he was a pit broker in the wheat pit filling orders for such firms as Bache and Hayden, Stone.

In 1970, Mr. Rosenthal formed Rosenthal & Company and became its managing partner. It was in 1972 and 1973 that he began his remarkable climb to the top leadership positions in the futures industry. No single individual has yet to equal his record, set in 1978, of being elected simultaneously as:

Member, Board of Directors—CBOT
Member, Board of Governors—Chicago Mercantile Exchange
Member, Board of Directors—Mid-America Stock Exchange
Chairman, Board of Directors—Board of Trade Clearing Corporation

Les was a founder of the National Futures Association (NFA), a futures industry self-regulatory body that administers licensing examinations and registration for futures and options brokers, trading advisers, and firms. It also provides arbitration services.

In 1981 and 1982, Les was elected to two one-year terms as chairman of the Chicago Board of Trade. During his terms of office, he created new classes of membership for the CBOT to allow trading opportunities to develop. He was also responsible for enabling the innovation and growth of financial futures.

In 1988, when J. Robert Collins merged his own firm with Rosenthal & Company, the firm name changed to Rosenthal Collins Group. According to the Futures Industry of America (FIA), "Of all the brokerage firms that have sought to move the Chicago exchanges, few have had the influence of the Rosenthal Collins Group. Everyone who trades Treasury futures today owes Les Rosenthal a debt of gratitude, because he provided the essential leadership necessary to win the members' approval to develop and launch the Ginnie Mae futures contract, the world's first contract based on interest rates."

At present Les Rosenthal acts in an advisory capacity to various industry committees and exchanges, while serving as a managing member of one of the largest clearing firms in the futures business.

Mr. Rosenthal has been married for 52 years and has three children and four grandchildren.

****

How did you first hear about the Board of Trade?

I first heard about it when I was in high school. Then I graduated from high school and I was looking around for a job. At the time, the economy was sort of on the downturn. There weren't many jobs around. One of the jobs that I heard about was as a runner on the Chicago Board of Trade. So I applied for a job as a runner and I worked from 9:00 in the morning until about 1:30 in the afternoon. Then I went to college at a local university. That was the only way I could fit in an education and keep a job as well.

Did you graduate?

I graduated from Roosevelt University with a degree in history.

What made you want to be part of the CBOT?

In the beginning, I just needed the job. Being a runner was the only job that I could find that would fit into any kind of a program that was available to me. I really didn't know anything about it. I just happened to pick it up from a friend of mine and I came down, applied, and that was it.

Did you find it exciting?

Yes. I found it very exciting. It was pretty much a people business. It was a very active floor and I was right in the midst of things. As a runner, I was right down on the floor, taking orders from the telephone station into the pits.

How long was it until you bought your membership?

What happened was I worked at the CBOT all the time that I was in school. Then when I got out of school, I got married, and then I got drafted. It wasn't until two years after I graduated from college and I came back from the Army that I was able to think about buying a membership. To do that, I borrowed $5,000 from my father-in-law.

How did that work out?

It worked out pretty well. I paid him back relatively quickly, although he kept insisting that I owed him a little bit more. This didn't necessarily translate into money, but in things to do like hiring relatives and things like that.

Did you appeal those requests?

No. When I started at the Board of Trade, it was one of the things that just went on down there. It was sort of a generational type of a thing. In other words, fathers brought their sons down and brought their nephews down, things like that. That's the way the Board of Trade ran at that time.

When you first began trading, were you successful right away?

Well, there were some good days and some bad days. It wasn't always easy, that's for sure. My wife Harriet didn't want to come right out and ask how my day was, so she used to ask whether we were going to have "hamburger or steak for dinner."

That was a gentle way of checking things out. Tell me about some of the legends that you encountered at the Board of Trade.

When I came down to the Board of Trade as a runner, it was a little bit different than when I bought my membership. The exchange was in the process of an evolution. We were going from the normal type of things that had gone on there for the 50 years before that. So there were some real characters down there. There were many different types of traders on the floor.

For example, there was a family down there named Griffin. Bill Griffin was a big trader. There was a fellow named Joe Dimon who was a real character. There was a man named Vince Fagan. There were a number of people on the way out at the time. One of the biggest traders was Dan Rice. He was still active, but not as active as he used to be. So, what we had down there was a conglomeration of different personalities, all of which made for a very interesting workplace.

How were they different?

These people were risk takers. In order to be a successful trader at the Board of Trade, you had to have a personality that allowed you to be a risk taker. And it was generally so for most of the legends that I named, although there was some inconsistency to them. It was usually boom or bust, and you never knew what portion of their history they were going through at the time. Nevertheless it was all very interesting.

How does someone like Jim McKerr fit into that description?

Jim McKerr and I went head-to-head in the wheat pit for a number of years. Jim was an active wheat trader and a member of the McKerr family. There were a number of the McKerrs down at the time. Jimmy and I used to go at it in the wheat pit. One day I came down and found out that the positions I had on weren't doing too well. And I talked to the people that I was trading with at the time, and they suggested that I go out and try to get some money from somewhere, to see if I could shore up some of the trading positions that I had on. And so I went around asking a few people. I had a very difficult time, until somebody suggested that I go talk to Jimmy McKerr. I said, "Are you crazy? Why should I talk to Jim McKerr? McKerr and I are always fighting after every trade in the wheat pit, and he'd be the last guy in the world that would help me out."

But the guy I was talking to kept pushing me in that direction. He said, "Why don't you go up and try?" So, having exhausted all of my other resources, I went up and I talked to Jim. I went into his office and I said, "Jimmy, you're not going to believe this, but I'm, you know, in a little bit of trouble over here. I'm looking around to finance myself for a little while until I get back on my feet."

He did not hesitate for one second. He reached into the middle drawer of his desk. He pulled out a checkbook. He said, "How much do you need?" And I said, "You know, Jim, this really surprises me." He said, "That's the way we do it around here. It doesn't matter what happens, what goes on the pit. Once one of our own gets into trouble, we're all there to help out."

Isn't that wonderful?

Yeah. It was terrific.

That leads me to a question about the word 'integrity' and how it relates to the CBOT.

Integrity is a very integral part of the system here at the CBOT. It's changed somewhat now that so much of the trading is happening on the screen. In the electronic marketplace, you don't see the people eye to eye and you don't know who you're making your trade with, but integrity is still very important. But in the days that we're talking about, integrity was very important, because you made a trade with a person across the pit, and sometimes it wasn't anything more than a gesture. You would nod your head or you'd flick your finger or you would do other acknowledging things. You'd have to make sure that the person that you were making that trade with showed up the next day, even when the trade might be against him, because if he didn't, then you would be out of luck. There were very few instances that I can recall of anybody not showing up. Once in a while it happened, but most of the time the man who made the trade was as good as his word.

Can you tell me about some of those signals that you would give in the pit?

Well, sure. Depending on what portion of the trading community you belonged to, whether you were a broker filling orders or a trader trading for your own account, they varied a little bit. Sometimes, depending on the nuances of what was going on, if there was somebody across the pit bidding and you wanted to sell to that person at whatever he was bidding, you might not want the rest of the pit to know exactly what you were doing. So instead of making an open outcry and yelling "sold," you might nod your head or you might point a finger at him. There was always a way that brokers announced it to the pit as to what it was that they were bidding, at what price, and what amounts they were bidding on. There were finger types of signals. There were all sorts of things that were part of the culture.

You changed the culture a little bit. Can you tell me about that?

We had a difficult time identifying people who would be executing orders for us in the pit, because everybody wore the same drab jackets.

I came up with the idea that the best thing to do would be to go out and make trading jackets out of colored cloth. For me, that color was purple. I did this so that when my phone men were writing down orders and they would give them to runners, they would also only have to say to them, "Here, take it to that guy in a purple jacket." It wasn't long after I adopted that type of trading jacket that many other companies did the same thing. All the multicolor jackets that you see on the floors came from that idea.

Tell me how your business evolved from when you started your business to where it's come to today.

I started off as a runner on the floor of the Board of Trade and then I went into the Army. When I came out from the service, I purchased a membership. In those days you had to have a membership in order to be able to sit down and write orders over a telephone, receiving orders, writing them on a notepad, and that's what I did as my first job on the floor of the Board of Trade. Other than a runner, I was a phone man for Lamson Brothers.

Then I went from being a phone man to being an assistant floor manager, wherein I was helping the floor manager of a firm run the business on the floor. Then I graduated from that job to becoming the floor manager for the firm. This involved writing a market letter. And from there, I went into the pit as a floor broker and started filling orders.

Once I was in the pit and filled orders, then I started trading for myself. And the evolution of my firm came about just as many others did. There came a time when I figured I could do it just as well as some of the people around me. I thought I could do it with my own firm and maybe make a little bit more money. So I formed a partnership with another trader, Hank Shatkin, and we went into the customer business. Our firm was called S&R.

Do you remember the first lesson you learned at the CBOT?

The first lesson that I learned down at the Board of Trade was to never give up. If you do, you're out the door and you don't have a chance at coming back. We had many, many examples of people who were going through difficult periods and who in the terminology of the trade "busted out" and then came back. Personally, I've been through some of that in my own life. Having had those experiences, I became a part of the culture at the Board of Trade that helped the people out who were going through hard times. It was almost an inheritance handed down, not from father to son, but from member to member.

Have you passed that lesson on to your family?

I think that I try to pass it on to whoever listens to me. Some people listen and some people don't.

How about the word 'discipline'? Does it apply?

Discipline obviously applies to trading. Anybody who is disciplined makes for a much better trader. There are some cases when discipline stands in your way, but you're around much longer if you're a disciplined trader than if you're not.

Can you give me an example of a time when discipline can stand in your way?

There are some instances when discipline makes you exit a trade too early.

How about the idea of tradition in the business?

At the CBOT there were many traditions. That's basically one of the sad things that is happening right now. The Board of Trade used to be loaded with tradition. You always used to look to certain people down there. You watched what they did. It was a mentor society, so that people took others under their wings. In my mind, that basically was the leading guideline or the leading tradition of the Board of Trade.

Now that you're starting to move everything to screen trading and everything is electronic, there still is some of that tradition down there, but because of the demise of the open outcry system, that tradition is starting to change.

Were there pit traditions?

Yes, there were. It was territorial. You had a pit that was configured for different months, and what happened was the floor brokers, the people who were filling orders or acting as agents for other companies, established their own territories. Generally speaking, they tried to do it so that they would be within sight of their principal business. What that means is that they would be standing on the top of the pit, so that the person on the telephone could see them and they'd be able to signal certain orders in to them or ask them for quotations or things like that.

It became very, very important that you establish a certain position in the pit and that you went to that position every day at the same time, so that people would be able to identify where you were and be able to make their decisions based on your position in the pit.

What happened if somebody stood in your position?

That became a very difficult thing, because generally speaking, there is no outright rule that dictates where people can stand in the pit.

If somebody wanted to come in and infringe on your territory, they would be allowed to do it. You'd have to work it out between yourself and the other trader. Sometimes it got kind of physical, and other times it was just based on whether you'd been there longer than anybody else.

When it became physical, how did everybody work that out? What were the rules down there?

At times, things got rather heated. Things occasionally did get physical and there was a lot of shoving and pushing. Every once in a while it came to a point where you knew a few punches might be exchanged. And usually what happened was that the people who were involved in the dispute would go to the group in charge of pit governance, which was called a pit committee. That was where they tried to work it out. The pit committee tried to get between people and somehow or other mitigate whatever it was that was going on.

In that same vein, can you describe the role of the Board of Trade and self-regulation?

Self-regulation is something that the exchanges handle themselves. While there is a government regulatory agency that has oversight, we always try to keep as much in the way of regulation at the exchange level. To accomplish this task, there are many committees. Many people serve on these committees as volunteers. Each of those committees appoints a chairman.

To find members for these committees, which are part of the governance of the Board of Trade, we would hand out questionnaires to see whether any of the members would be interested in serving on committees, and the ones who were interested in serving on committees usually got appointed. So we had many, many committees at the Board of Trade, sometimes too many. I say there were sometimes too many because it often became burdensome to operate.

Why does self-regulation work for this business?

Self-regulation works particularly well in this industry. Before we invented the new types of memberships, we had 1,402 members. Each one of those members was invested in doing something that would govern the Board of Trade well. All these members had a vote and a say in who became the leadership of the Board of Trade. All wanted to make sure we presented the proper face to the public and there wasn't any criticism attached to the exchange that would have cut down on the trading aspect of it. The people who knew the industry most intimately were responsible for governing its participants and its practices.

How about the role of the CFTC?

The Commodity Futures Trading Commission (CFTC) evolved from something called a Commodity Exchange Authority (CEA). At that time there was very little oversight on the part of the CEA, and there was a hue and cry on the part of Congress, as there is in many instances, for more regulation. That's why the CFTC was formed. The exchanges had pretty good input into it, because we lobbied down in Washington to do things in the proper way.

During my last term as chairman of the board of directors for the Chicago Board of Trade, we put together something called the National Futures Association (NFA), which was, in effect, a private sector regulatory agency. The role of the NFA was to administer licensing examinations and registration for futures and options brokers, trading advisers, and firms. It would also provide arbitration services.

What we managed to do was convince the regulators that the industry was basically too big for any one type of regulatory oversight committee to be watching. We tried to put together a process in which the government was responsible for certain regulations, the exchanges had certain regulations, and the NFA had certain regulations, so that regulation, in effect, was shared by these three entities.

What do the people in the industry know that somebody coming from the outside might not?

Well, that's just it. The people in the industry know the industry intimately and they know when a regulation would adversely affect anything to do with the business. It's a better business judgment on the part of the private sector than it is on the part of government, as it is in anything else. There are many in-house committees that are responsible for making this system effective.

Which committees did you serve on?

I kind of made my way up through many of the committees, but the ones that I was most interested in had something to do with new products. I thought that bringing in new products was a very important aspect of the business of the Board of Trade. We have to keep inventing products that would appeal to people, rather than just continue on with the historical products.

You had something to do with several innovations.

Yes, we did. We had something to do with the structure of the Board of Trade, as well, because in the old days the way that you would promote a new product would be you would get some people who were members, and you would say to them, "You know, why don't you go over there? There's a new product being traded. We need some volume." I really believe people are attracted to commodities only if they see some volume. Then we would go even further to ask for their involvement. We would say, "Why don't you do your patriotic number? Go over there and trade 100 contracts or stand over there for 15 minutes and trade."

While trying to launch innovations, we discovered it was getting difficult to get people away from their normal course of business to do something in the way of sponsoring new products. We came up with a plan that allowed what we would call "developmental membership."

What we did was figured out a way that we could sort of "rifle shoot" a membership at a product. To do this, we originated a certain membership that could only trade a certain new product. And when you can only trade a certain new product, you have nowhere else to go for the trading day, so you're kind of glued to that pit. It became a very successful way of putting together support for a new product.

Can you tell me some of the names of those new memberships?

Sure. We had AMs (Associate Memberships). We had COMs (Commodity Options Memberships). We had IDEMs (Index and Energy Markets). They were specifically designed to encourage certain markets. A COM, for instance, could only trade options. An AM would trade financial instruments. An IDEM was a catchall for future product development; the thought being that we add the multiple stock index and energy futures. We had a couple of other new products that we were talking about trading and the IDEM could only trade those.

The result was that these memberships appealed to the general public. We discovered that many people were coming in to buy these kinds of memberships, not just current exchange members. They were low-priced and attracted many people who were doing other jobs. So if you could spare a few hours, you could buy yourself one of these memberships. You could come down and you could get on-the-job training at the Chicago Board of Trade. It was wildly successful.

Do they still exist today?

Actually, all of these memberships still exist and allow for participating in some of the contracts trading today. Aside from that, what is going on is they are getting phased out because there is no longer any need for a floor membership–sponsored approach toward new products, with everything starting to go on the screen. What advantages these memberships give are what the membership rates should be.

When you started at the CBOT, what did you trade?

I started off trading in wheat. I went into the pit to trade for some firms and to fill orders for some firms, like Bache and Lamson. After a while, as my career progressed, I gave up the deck in the wheat pit and I branched out into trading a number of other items. I traded soybeans. I traded corn. I traded financial instruments when they first came out.

How would you define being a speculator?

A speculator basically boils down to a risk taker. The theory behind the Chicago Board of Trade is that it's a risk transference mechanism, whether you're transferring it from a farmer to a trader to a speculator. A speculator is just a definition of a certain type of trader.

How is he or she different from being a gambler?

A gambler creates his own risk. As a speculator in our business, you assume somebody else's risk. So there's a definite economic value to being a speculator, where there isn't necessarily a value for a gambler.

And whose risk do they assume?

They assume the risk of anyone that comes in on the opposite side of it. They don't necessarily identify the person or the company. They could be taking the opposite side of a commercial grain company's hedge. They could be taking the opposite side of a farmer who's making a forward sale. They could be taking the opposite side of even a foreign entity that's doing something in the way of trying to price a product it's going to be buying in the next several months in the marketplace.

Do you think the CBOT is a global price discovery mechanism?

I think the term "price discovery" is the basic tenet of the Chicago Board of Trade. It's basically the reason that we became successful with new products, because all the new products that we've invented have been for the purpose of price discovery.

Has your company evolved with that idea?

We've evolved from the different types of needs that we saw in the marketplace. In the beginning, we started off as a local type of an arrangement, whereby we were organized to help clear some of the local traders that were trading in the pits. And then what happened was we expanded from that into some customer business. We got other broker/dealer type firms to come and give us their clearing, so then we became a clearing company.

Right at the moment, I'd say if you're asking me what the current version is of the Rosenthal Collins Group, we're morphing into a technology company. The reason that we're morphing into a technology company is because that's where the business is headed. Unless you do something to change with the times, you become nonexistent.

One of the biggest changes was options trading. Please talk about that, and the history of how and why the CBOE came about?

The CBOE was an invention of a number of traders at the Chicago Board of Trade who also were forward-thinking people. They thought about the fact that options were a great vehicle and there wasn't much in the way of an options transaction in the securities business. In order to be able to trade securities, the Chicago Board of Trade had a securities license at one time. By the time we got around to talking about the Chicago Board Options Exchange, that license had lapsed.

In order to be able to trade options on securities, which is what the CBOE does, we had to form a new exchange and we had to apply for a securities license in order to be able to trade options on securities. It was basically a product mix. If it had been the type of thing that we could have done it within the Chicago Board of Trade, we probably would have done it within the Chicago Board of Trade. But we couldn't do it for regulatory purposes.

What do you think was the impact of options trading?

It was interesting. I was involved in the Board of Trade administration at the time when we brought options on. Even the most intelligent people at the Board of Trade, and by intelligent I mean those with an understanding of what trading means, basically fought against options because they thought that they were going to take away from the volume of the underlying futures market. We had to make the argument that, contrary to what everybody was talking about, they were going to add to it. And we had a real fight on our hands to bring them through, but as it turns out, that's exactly what happened.

What do you think is going to happen with the CBOE?

I think that's a very difficult question, because the price basically dictates what's going to happen at the Board of Trade, meaning the price of the exercise right that the Board of Trade members have. Somewhere along the line, whether it's a court decision or it's some type of compromise, there's going to have to be some type of agreement between the Board of Trade and the CBOE as to how they treat these trading rights.

The CBOE certainly provided a big change for the exchange, but what do you think is the biggest change that has come about since you've been at the CBOT?

Well, we've had a number of different changes, but obviously the most current happenings have been some of the biggest. It's no longer a Chicago market or a U.S. market, but it is now an international market. It is not only an international market on the level of exchanges, but it's an international market on the level of governments as well.

We've got international involvement in our marketplaces that we didn't have before. We also have the advent of things like hedge funds and all types of new trading vehicles and mechanisms that basically dwarf anything that we've had in the past.

People talk about the business being a global one. What do you think of the opportunities to come?

We're on the brink of starting something new. We're on the cutting edge of opening up our marketplaces to a much greater customer base than we've ever had in the past. In the old days, you used to talk about a certain segment of our business being a customer-based business and people used to identify things like there's probably about 500,000 customer accounts in the whole industry. Now with the advent of technology, you're talking about opening up this thing not just to 500,000 customer accounts, but to maybe 50 million customer accounts.

It is no longer just the United States, where you have a lot of cross-selling that's going on with people who are trading securities, but also worldwide you've got new economies coming on. You've got China coming on. You've got India. You've got the European community. They are all looking to the Chicago Board of Trade for many types of products.

So we're going to be challenged, because we're not only going to have to invent products that appeal to people, but we're going to have to find ways to execute them. We are coming into the technology age right now, and we have to recognize that.

What do you think will be the impact of this worldwide trading on the service component of the CBOT?

Servicing the customers will be the key. After service, you've got something that we call in business "value added." So what you're going to have to do is differentiate yourself from the next guy. You're going to have to be able to offer certain things that the norm doesn't offer.

At the Rosenthal Collins Group, we always strive to be the standard in the industry. While we recognize that there will always be the new thing that people will be coming up with, we always try to lead the pack in anything that's coming on. Our company's goal for the immediate future is to grow our customer base.

What did you hope to accomplish in your years as CBOT chairman?

I was elected twice. In those days, it was a one-year term. What I wanted to do was basically establish what we thought was going to be the future of the exchange and the industry in general. We were just starting to get adapted to what was a different set of circumstances for trading old products and for types of new products.

In the old days, when you were thinking about bringing up a new product, it was generally some type of an agricultural product that had some type of a format with a deliverable stage. That meant that the farmer harvests it, you send it to an elevator, you issue an elevator receipt, you put it to the Board of Trade, and the Board of Trade starts circulating that elevator receipt.

Now what we had to do was talk about new things that were coming on, and we were looking at the financial instruments. We started off with Ginnie Maes, which were a government-backed mortgage type of a contract. But we had a lot of resistance to that.

Why was there resistance?

The traditional debt dealers wanted to keep the game closed to themselves. They didn't want an open, transparent system that could have price discovery and many participants. The interesting thing is that once it established itself, the dealers who resisted these contracts became the contracts' largest users.

How did you proceed from there?

We went from Ginnie Maes to government debt. Government debt grows every year, just like a corn crop grows every year, because the government keeps issuing the debt. We picked the long part of the yield curve. What we basically started trading were long bonds (30-year bonds) and 10-year Treasury notes.

The Chicago Mercantile Exchange picked up the short end of the yield curve. We just didn't have the wherewithal to be able to do it all at the same time, but it worked out very well for us. It was a different kind of commodity. Who had ever thought about commoditizing government bonds? You just didn't do things like that. Now of course they commoditize anything that comes up. We're trading emissions over on the Chicago Climate Exchange. We're doing all sorts of things, and there are all kinds of new products that are going to be coming along.

What new products do you think are going to have some success?

What we have to do right now is develop some of the things that we've started working on. We have to get an acceptance. Emissions trading, for example, is going to be one of the things that we look forward to, because we think that every year there is more and more awareness of what we're doing to our climate. As a result of that, we're starting to get some political pressure behind doing things in a "green" way. It appears that the general public is getting closer to accepting that. In the near future, I think it won't be too exotic for them to view emissions as a trading mechanism. I'm certain that's going to be the next big success.

How do you think people will feel about trading air?

The more information the public is exposed to, whether that's in newspaper articles, whether it's in magazines, whether it's in some type of a special documentary like Al Gore is putting forward, the easier it will be to gain the public's approval. I think we're starting to get more and more people aware of it, and it's going to become accepted much quicker than we once thought.

Can you think of any other new products that are on the horizon?

I'm excited by what we're doing right at the moment. I think it's a wonderful part of our existence that we've got all these new things going on. We're erupting in different types of energy that we're trading. There is a different paradigm to why people trade things. It's becoming an asset class.

People who never thought about trading commodities for anything other than their agricultural applications are now looking to feed crops to do many other things. For example, there are hedge funds looking at trading our corn contract at the Chicago Board of Trade, not because of the demand it might have on an international basis for feed for animals, but basically because of what effect it has on ethanol. Ethanol, in turn, has something to do with how you view the energy picture. They're all starting to become intertwined and are much, much more exciting.

Going back to some of the exciting times and things that happened on the floor when you were there, do you remember being part of the Crash of 1987?

Yes, I do. We were definitely part of it. Part of the trouble that we had was that there were members' firms that had positions on different exchanges, and in those days you couldn't offset one against the other. We had trouble taking monies from one exchange where a member had a position and giving it to them so that they could pay off whatever position it was that they had at the other exchange. But we had very good government cooperation on the part of the Federal Reserve and on the part of the Congress. Everybody was behind us, and we were able to come through. I think that you can point back to that particular occasion as something that proves to the world that we're able to weather storms like that.

How about the role of the MMI contract?

The contract was able to absorb some of the shock, which is one of the reasons for the CBOT's existence. We're here for risk transference, and that's one of the things that proved to be a big success.

What do you see as the CBOT's affect on world economies?

Obviously, we're the pricing mechanism for the world in grains and soybeans. This is because we're the primary market for that at the Chicago Board of Trade. The CBOT also has a great deal to do with the pricing of the U.S. government debt. Once we do something like that, it obviously has ripple effects on everything else.

I think the CBOT bringing in these contracts, and here again we come back to price discovery, makes it possible that everybody is able to identify where the contracts are traded, not just on a futures level, but also in the cash markets. It really narrows the spread a lot. It makes for easier access on the part of both institutions and individuals to purchase some of these instruments.

You know the CBOT and CME intimately. What do you think about the merger of these two exchanges?

I think that it's something that probably should have happened 25 years ago. I think that we had all sorts of initiatives to try, but we never were able to put anything together. It needed a perfect storm in order to be able to do that. So I think that's basically what happened here in the past couple of years. We had a perfect storm. We had a change in the structure of the memberships, and they both became public rather than private organizations. They had less of a country club, "members only" aspect.

I think that while it was different 25 years ago, maybe it was a good thing that it was difficult and didn't happen then. I think the members and stockholders, if you want to call them that, probably are getting much more value for things now than they would have 25 years ago. But the merger of the CBOT and the CME is definitely the thing to do.

What do you think the future will be with that marriage?

The future with that marriage is going to be the thing that Chicago needs. It will be great for our city. I think it will benefit both exchanges and their needs, because of the competition. People often refer to it as "the Chicago competition" between the two exchanges. But even that is changing. What's happening is we're starting to get a worldwide recognition of the value of these types of markets, and therefore the competition for these markets is going to be coming from overseas, not necessarily domestically.

Who do you see as the greatest competition?

I think that we have an indication of what the European competition is, but I don't think we have any idea what the Pacific Rim competition is going to mean to us. So I think you've got two developing giants over in the Pacific Rim. You've got China and you've got India, and there's no telling where they're going to be going. Those two countries are just starting to recognize the value of exchanges and what trading means. In the next 10 years, that's where the challenge is going to come from.

Do you think there will be a challenge from the over-the-counter markets or from other exchanges?

I think that there is competition right now between the over-the-counter markets and futures markets. One of the criticisms for the merger of our Chicago exchanges comes from the over-the-counter community. They think that a merger between the Board of Trade and the Chicago Mercantile Exchange is going to be poaching in the pond of the over-the-counter market. But I think that's the American way and that should be encouraged, not discouraged.

You've been described as a legend at the CBOT. One of those people was George Seals. How do you respond to that accolade?

First of all, I don't think I'm a legend. You know, I think legends are momentary. As far as I'm concerned, that's a misnomer. But I love George Seals and appreciate his kind thoughts. George was one of the first black members of the Chicago Board of Trade. He basically was one of the men who broke the color barrier. George had a great weight on his shoulders because he was under a microscope. Everybody was looking to George to see how he conducted himself. George was a wonderful guy and he was a gentleman. He was a pleasure to work with.

Rather than giving any credit to me about George, Henry Shatkin is the guy who brought George Seals on board at the Chicago Board of Trade. He's the fellow who sponsored him. George traded through Henry. George and I became friends just because of our contact on the floor and the fact that Henry was a mutual, respected friend of ours.

I had a lot of comical run-ins with George on certain things that were going on, and we just laughed things off. I think George was the perfect man to be one of the few who broke the color barrier at the Board of Trade, because he had a sense of humor, he had great patience, and most of all he had a lot of confidence in himself. You couldn't bring George down.

I think that describes you, too. You have been described as a strong, intelligent, capable leader with a great sense of knowing how to get the job done. What do you think is your personal legacy to the Chicago Board of Trade?

What we did, because it wasn't just me, was we had a breakthrough in trading customs. We accepted that you could trade something other than the historically deliverable grains that we had at the Chicago Board of Trade. This innovative way of thinking wasn't my invention. The credit for this insightful thinking goes to Richard Sandor. I think the invention of government instruments is the greatest legacy to the CBOT, because they have been the engine driving the exchange for many, many years, and will continue to do so in the future.

CHAPTER 17

Market Maker
Richard L. Sandor

Richard Sandor came to the Chicago Board of Trade while on sabbatical from his position as a professor at the University of California, Berkeley, in the early 1970s. He held a bachelor of arts degree from the City University of New York, Brooklyn College and a PhD in economics from the University of Minnesota.

His first job at the CBOT was as vice president and chief economist. Although he arrived there with no intention of staying, Dr. Sandor found his calling as the architect of the interest rate futures market. He was a pivotal force in changing how people looked at markets and what markets could do to help change our world. He was warmly referred to as "DOC"—his trading acronym and his professorial title.

During his tenure at the Chicago Board of Trade, he served on many committees, including the Executive Committee, and chaired at various times the Financial Instruments, Options, Strategy, and Ceres committees. He developed relationships both within the exchange and on the national front that were instrumental in his ability to challenge the marketplace to grow outside of its agricultural roots. His academic background clearly helped him direct his vision for changing the face of the marketplace. Although Dr. Sandor never returned to Berkeley, he found time to teach at the Kellogg Graduate School of Management at Northwestern University, where he is a research professor and currently teaches a course in environmental finance.

Richard Sandor was honored by the city of Chicago and the Chicago Board of Trade for his contribution to the creation of financial futures.

In 1975, Dr. Sandor left the Chicago Board of Trade to start a career on Wall Street, and ultimately returned to Chicago to form the Chicago Climate Exchange (CCX). Calling on many of the skills he honed at the CBOT, he was able to create this unique exchange. As the chairman and CEO, he administers the self-regulatory exchange, which is the world's first and North America's only multinational and multi-sector marketplace for reducing and trading greenhouse gas emissions.

In August 2002, Dr. Sandor was chosen by *Time* magazine as one of its "Heroes for the Planet" for his work as the founder of the CCX. In November 2004, he was the recipient of an honorary doctor of science degree, *honoris causa*, from the Swiss Federal Institute of Technology (ETH) for his work in developing innovative and flexible market-based mechanisms to address environmental concerns. In May 2005, he was named by *Treasury and Risk Management* magazine as one of the "100 Most Influential People in Finance." In October 2007, *Time* magazine named him as one of its "Heroes of the Environment" for his work as the "father of carbon trading."

Richard Sandor serves on the boards of American Electric Power (NYSE: AEP) and the Intercontinental Exchange (NYSE: ICE). He has been involved in numerous civic and charitable activities. He has served as a member of the board of governors of the School of the Art Institute of Chicago and is a major benefactor of the Art Institute. He is currently a member of the board of directors of the International Center of Photography, New York. He is also a member of the International Advisory Council of the Guanghua School of Management at Peking University.

Richard and his wife Ellen, a world-renowned artist, have one of the largest and most influential private collections of art (with an emphasis on photography) in the world. They have two daughters and four grandchildren.

****

Let's go back in your history prior to joining the CBOT. In 1969 you were a professor at the University of California–Berkeley at the Institute of Business and Economic Research. Can you tell me about the funded research projects they thought were of some significance and interest to the academic and business communities? What were some of your ideas?

My ideas at that time were pretty radical. Many people thought that they were bordering on the insane. In 1969, the futures industry was small. I got started in the industry by getting a grant from the Bank of America to start a commodity research project, and that's what really spurred me into the business. The reason I got the grant was because I had traded commodities, and the people who gave the grant thought, "Well, he knows a little bit about commodity trading and he's also an academic and maybe this would be a good idea." The purpose was to develop a feasibility study for an exchange in San Francisco and to basically explore what the problems and challenges were for an exchange. We were looking at both its institutional arrangement and how we could compensate for the fact that there were no locals.

This was a very interesting study. It was funded and organized through the university and we came up with what was then a very radical idea. The exchange was designed to be a for-profit institution. This was nothing like anything anybody had ever seen. Exchanges were mutually owned and member dominated, and the fact that shareholders could play a role was unforeseen in the 1960s. The second bit of the study suggested that the markets of the future would be electronic. That was particularly bizarre at that time, because the personal computer had not even been invented. So we published a study on the feasibility of creating a for-profit exchange. There was, in fact, not enough of a budget and the technology was still a little early for the electronics, but that was the heart and soul of the research that we did.

At the time you predicted that computers would allow for trading volume to be about 144 million contracts.

It was way above the volume at that time and beyond where anybody thought this industry could ever be. Even by the mid-1970s, the total volume for the industry was 30 million. In the late 1960s, I am not sure what it was, but I think well under 30 million contracts. So I think that we foresaw what was coming. If you were an academic and you had been educated where I was educated at the University of Minnesota and observed that the supercomputer was part of the academic world, you could recognize that there was a sea change going on. It wasn't particularly hard to do. It was relatively easy. But the predictions on volume were very, very short of eventually what did happen.

Do you have any reflection on what the worldwide futures exchange volume was at the close of business in 2006?

The close last year was 12 billion contracts worldwide versus an actual close of 30 million in 1975, and the Board of Trade was 50 percent of that 30 million. But we now have 12 billion. We had 10 exchanges, a lot of small ones. We've got 75 worldwide now. The industry has created an incredible amount of wealth.

I was taking a look at some numbers recently and was struck by them. If we look at the market capitalization of exchanges today, including the Board of Trade, Chicago Mercantile Exchange (CME), New York Mercantile Exchange (NYMEX), Intercontinental Exchange (ICE), and so on, we get a market cap. We're not sure about Eurex and Liffe, because they're now subsidiaries. But if you take a look at it, it looks like about $75 billion total. And if you consider the market capitalization of brokerage firms like F.C. Stone, Man Financial, and many more to come, my guess is that you can probably add another $50 billion or $75 billion.

Just to put it in perspective, the automobile sector in the United States is $30 billion. If we added up the total capitalization of Boeing and Airbus, it's less than the derivatives industry and its subsidiary member firms. Who would have ever thought that all of these planes flying people all over the world would have the same, or smaller market value as derivatives trading?

That's an incredible statistic. What brought you to Chicago. Can you tell me about it?

In order to basically implement the research for the Pacific Commodities Exchange, it required that I actually get into the real guts of an exchange to see how it operated. I spent a number of days throughout the course of a year visiting the CBOT. We had to devise an electronic algorithm and see if it was feasible. I had to understand the mechanics of pit trading. You had to know how orders were distributed. If somebody would sell things, would they give it to this broker or that speculator, and how would they do it? If they were offering, how would they do that? The offering could be a Dutch auction descending price or an English auction ascending price.

There were a lot of technical issues that had to be resolved. I met a lot of different individuals on my trips to Chicago, and one of the first people that I met was Warren Lebeck. I had decided at that time to teach a course, which again was on the fringe, because in the 1960s there were no courses in futures markets taught in business schools. They were typically relegated to agricultural schools. This was very revolutionary in 1969.

I always had a love of the practical, so I thought I'd bring in a group of guest lecturers. I decided I'd give an academic section and a practical section, so the students could have some breadth of understanding of how markets theoretically worked and how one could practically implement them. And that was disjointed, because a lot of academic literature had nothing about the real world, and the real world wasn't very connected to the academic literature. So that was unique.

Warren Lebeck was one of the lecturers at the class and asked if I would ever participate in the real world. I think I said only if the job gave me the ability to implement some ideas I had. I said it had to be potent enough, like the chief economist of the New York Stock Exchange or the Chicago Board of Trade, and that's where the conversation began.

You were fairly young when he made you an offer you couldn't refuse.

I was actually only 29 years old when we began discussions. The Board of Trade at that time had no formal research organization. Henry Hall Wilson had been called in to become the president. Joe Sullivan was in the planning department, but wasn't an economist. Henry felt that the wave of the future would be to have an academic ratification of the exchange, its functions, and the designs of its contracts. So he set up a search committee for a chief economist and apparently my name was on the search committee list. Equally if not more important, Warren Lebeck had said, "Why are you spending all this money on the search committee? Why don't you have Richard Sandor come to town?"

What was the role of the chief economist?

The role of the chief economist was a blank board with nothing on it. Henry said it could reflect my vision of that position. The vision that I thought was rational at the time was to have somebody who could represent the exchange in the public policy discussions taking place in Washington where the economic opinion of the exchange was valuable. Also, very critically, as the world was changing, the role would look into the design and development of new contracts.

When did you buy your own membership?

I bought my own membership in 1975.

Did you ever trade in the pits?

Yes. I did trade in the pits. I used to actually work from the floor with customers in financial futures, and then I would go into the corn pit and scalp the back options to learn the trade.

And having spent so many years discussing the academic versus the real world, so to speak, what did you learn?

I learned that I really didn't know an awful lot. I'd constantly be getting my hand signals wrong. I was discombobulated and guys in the pit would scream, "Hey, Doc, what's the matter with you?" So everybody started calling me "Doctor." My original badge was RLS, and then I changed the badge to "DOC" because I was so off, anything had to be an improvement.

How about the word 'integrity'? What did you learn about that word as associated with the Board of Trade?

The integrity of the institution was one of the things that attracted me to the Chicago Board of Trade. It had a reputation that surpassed anything. It had great tradition, and honor was something that was critical. As an economist, I was particularly struck by the fact that millions and tens of millions and hundreds of millions of dollars could be traded without written contracts.

This is something that academics never talk about, although I subsequently had a conversation with Ronald Coase, who won the Nobel Prize in economics, about this subject. He is now 96 years old and was utterly amazed when I showed him the level of transactions and how private contracting dispute resolution could all take place outside of the governmental framework. So the institution itself, and the way that it conducted itself, was innovative and really didn't have any other parallels in the private sector.

So you explained to him the role of self-regulation with the CBOT?

I was explaining to Professor Coase pretty much about enforcement, contract integrity, and self-regulation as the critical drivers that make futures markets work. This took place in the early 1970s.

Can you describe that role of self-regulation?

Self-regulation is really the promulgation of ensuring the markets are not manipulated. It makes sure no acts of illegal activity take place and contracts are honored, and there is a process for dispute resolution. All of those issues are taken care of outside of the court system.

It's pretty remarkable when you think of what takes place. Think about having a three-year wait for a trial and the expenses of judicial systems, litigation costs that could run $1 million or more at a clip. And compare that to the fact that you could have this amount of commerce take place in as efficient a way as it did. It was a remarkable thing to me as an academic.

So then it speaks to the character of the Board of Trade?

I think it very much speaks to the character that integrity underlies the entire notion of an exchange and its self-regulatory role.

Can you talk about the impact of the creation of the CBOE?

I think the CBOE was a very critical development in the history of the exchange. It was, in effect, the beginning of equity derivatives. It was looked at with a great deal of skepticism. It seemed quite reasonable to me as a student of economics. But people thought that these kinds of instruments were tricky. They were odd. There was something wrong with them. Puts and calls were relegated to dealers. I think that it was a symbol of an innovative spirit present at the exchange.

Talking about innovative spirit, you've been called the father of interest rate futures. What were you involved with in terms of new product development?

The first new contract that I developed was the Ginnie Mae futures contract. And it was predicated on the fact that interest rates would become volatile. I was thrown out of almost every major investment bank in the United States and told it was a stupid idea. They said interest rates didn't fluctuate and therefore there would be no need to hedge. That was true for a very, very selected period in U.S. history. That was the 15 years post World War II, from 1945 to 1960. At that time, there was no real volatility in the market.

Being a professor at Berkeley in the 1960s, with students bringing their dogs to class and being stoned half the time, you didn't have to be a genius to figure out the world was changing. We were watching the emergence of blue-collar workers sending their children to college. We were watching the emergence of free love. We were watching the emergence of a society that was becoming unglued because of the Vietnam War. We were unleashing the power of students to affect society, and you didn't have to be a genius to figure out that it wasn't an isolated event. It became clear that the world's markets would be affected by an unpopular war and a big deficit. Sounds a little familiar and similar to today, actually.

Yes, it does. How were those new contracts accepted?

The new contracts were viewed with a great deal of skepticism by a lot of people. On the other hand, we had some fantastic support. It's very important to realize that I really had taken a sabbatical from the University of California at Berkeley and I was a young man. I did not intend to stay in Chicago. I planned to take only one year, but then took an extra year in 1973 after interest rates became volatile and the idea got some traction. I'd always thought I'd go back and teach and it would be a fun experience being at the Board of Trade.

It didn't take long to realize that I had become enthralled by Chicago, become enthralled by the institution, and decided that I wanted to work on this new product. I had a lot of really personal privileges to meet many members of the exchange. Pat Hennessey was vice chairman I think at the time, and was very instrumental in urging me to come to Chicago. There were other people like Lee Stern and Henry Shatkin who also were instrumental. People like Dave Goldberg, as well as Billy and Eddie O'Connor, were critical in supporting the new idea, and perhaps I saved the best for last, and that's Les Rosenthal.

We had formed a financial instruments committee in the early 1970s and it had never met. Les became a member of the board of directors and immediately saw the possibilities. I was naive, not really astute politically, and didn't know what it took to really launch a new contract. Les was a fantastic mentor and helped guide me through the process.

One of the critical things that we dealt with was who would trade this new product, the Ginnie Mae. And we came up with the idea of permits, which was basically the right to trade that carried no equity in the exchange. The idea was to populate the pits with people who could make markets. And with what sounds like a very sober and unfair assumption, it was thought that 80 percent of them would lose money, but 20 percent would go on to be able to make liquid markets in new contracts. That was one of the real parts of the success. The other really untold story here is there would be no financial futures if it were not for the Ginnie Mae. The reason for that is a Ginnie Mae, a mortgage-backed security, was a security. It wasn't a commodity and there was no regulatory home for this.

Fortunately, we had the marriage of a very peculiar set of events, which enabled these contracts that now constitute 80 percent of the trading worldwide to be born. Number one, the 1973 market gave rise to the fact that Chicago grain exchanges became part of the public view.

The rise in food prices ultimately set off the regulators, Congress, and the press blaming it all on speculators.

I remember particularly going to Washington, and I think Henry Hall Wilson's request was to try to talk to members of Congress and talk to the *Washington Post*, and I was very diligent. I was really prepared. I said, "Well, the 1973 market circumstance could easily be explained. The anchovies had stopped running off Peru. Spring had come late. Fall was early. Our growing season that year looked more like Russia's, with only 150 growing days. The Chinese crop failed and the Russian crop failed." Then I showed them the trader statistics, which demonstrated that speculators were net short during the entire rally. So if anything, they were having a stabilizing effect, helping to reduce pressures on prices. Then I walked out.

I called Henry, and he asked how I did and I said, "I think we killed them, Henry." I was so wrong, I can't tell you. The next day's *Washington Post* said, "Chicago speculators drive up food prices." I didn't get one message across, not one. Every fact I raised was totally dismissed. It became clear to me, at least as naive as I was, that there was no hope that this industry would not be regulated. Given that it was going to be regulated, we had to redefine the notion of what a commodity was from something that was tangible to something that was intangible and also to vest in the regulatory agency exclusive jurisdictional responsibility.

This is the untold story, but really it was the driver for why we have interest rate futures and stock index futures. It was basically this notion of redefining a commodity as an intangible product and the delegation of exclusive jurisdiction to the Commodity Futures Trading Commission (CFTC). At that time I developed a relationship with Herman Talmadge, who was a senator from Georgia. I was in Washington moderating a commodity conference, and the senator and I met several times on issues for that conference. I took my kids to his office. We became very close, and I'd like to think that played some small role in an industry going from kind of plain grain and metals to wanting to embrace the world.

It was the leadership of the exchange, in ultimately accepting the responsibility of self-regulation coupled with the CFTC, that encouraged innovation and new product developments. If we were going to have a regulator, we needed one with exclusive jurisdiction and one that wanted to expand the definition of a commodity. The punch line to the whole story is, after all of that was said and done, the day before the Ginnie Maes were about to be opened, the Securities and Exchange

Commission (SEC) brought an injunction against the exchange saying that the product was a security. But we had really done our homework.

Phil Johnson, the counsel to the CBOT, had made sure that the legislative history made reference to mortgages. He and I also had worked closely with John Rainbolt to ensure the exclusive jurisdiction section. We had enlisted the Federal Home Loan Bank Board. We'd enlisted the savings and loans, which were as important as the farmers. We had enormous public support. As soon as the SEC saw that we had done our homework, they withdrew.

And other products?

The other products that I was involved with were really pretty simple. The Ginnie Mae was the tough one, because we had to answer many new questions, like what was the size of the contract, what were the price increments, how did you develop liquidity for them, and so on. Those were really hard challenges.

The Ginnie Mae was really a template for everything that followed. I had the privilege of chairing the committee that drafted both the long bond and the 10-year T-note futures contract. Those contracts were essentially the same size, the same notion of cheapest to deliver, and so the long-term bond is essentially a remade Ginnie Mae contract, as is the 10-year note.

The options contract was a little different, because "privileges" had traded in Chicago and were ultimately banned by the government. "Privileges" is another way to say options. And so this was a rebirth of an industry.

You would have thought it was communism the way people reacted—how it sucked the liquidity dry, how dangerous it was, how bad it was. As chair of that committee, I learned to take a lot of abuse. And essentially there was a big competitor. Security options traded at the CBOE, and I had significant debates with people suggesting that options on futures would fail and options on an actual security would succeed. We designed the whole contract from top to bottom, and, of course, it became very, very successful.

We did launch many new products under Les's leadership. We felt that there would be a change going on that the institution basically was not ready for, so we started throwing out new contracts. We threw out the four-year. We threw out a two-year. We tried to get everything launched before Les retired as chairman.

In all fairness to the exchange, there was a digestion problem. There were a lot of people who were against change and there was a reaction to Les's chairmanship. He had tough votes. He won the vote issue, basically the AMs (Associate Memberships) and COMs (Commodity Options Memberships), by two votes. Les had to call Henry Shatkin's office and have them get one of Henry's traders off a plane so he could come and vote.

It was a very controversial environment, and so everything that's traded now was already up and running in terms of its design in the four-year and two-year. And I think we left a legacy with the market makers and a notion of a whole new definition of the word "commodity". We also did something that was very unusual. The first poster for Ginnie Mae was a woman winking, and this was very radical in the 1970s. Ginnie Mae was her name. Many at the Board of Trade didn't like these new approaches, and I think some people were offended.

What's very important to me is what I learned from the failures I had. I had really attempted to, first of all, redesign the wheat contract, and I attempted to get something called "gulf wheat" off the ground, because gulf wheat or hard red winter wheat is bread wheat. What we trade here in Chicago is soft red, which is cookie wheat. And I thought this was irrational. It didn't make any sense whatsoever. We were exporting the bread wheat. This was where the volume of production was, so I recommended that we trade the bread wheat. It failed like a lead balloon.

What I realized then was if you didn't market it, you had no chance. And two, if you set up side-by-side contracts you would never get a new product launch. You had to cut off the old and redo it as new. It had lots of implications, which maybe we'll touch on later.

The second big failure that I learned from was the gold contract. In working with a number of traders there, I learned everybody wanted a kilo contract. And that's because it created the perfect arbitrage. So you could buy gold in one market, sell it in Chicago, and have no risk. That depended on the fact that there was an idiot on one side of the trade, because why would you buy and sell at a higher price than you could in the alternative market? This reaffirmed that futures contracts had to be designed with what I'd call "English." There had to be a little twist in them to attract speculators within narrow boundaries to create liquidity, and this was very, very unusual.

I did have some successes. I helped redesign the bean and corn contracts and wrote the first multiple deliveries. And so I had a few successes, but the failures taught me an incredible amount and the lesson is: Study failure as much as success because it's more of a laboratory for new ideas.

Back when you were at Berkeley, you talked about electronic trading. You changed the face of this industry.

The issue of electronic trading to me was very simple and straightforward so that even in the 1960s it was clear. Once the personal computer had been invented in 1973, by Steven Jobs in a garage in Berkeley, it became more evident. As the 1980s developed and we began to see the potency of the machine, to me it was unambiguous. But it was still opposed by everybody else at that time. By the time the 1990s rolled around, it was beginning to be more widely accepted. The Germans had succeeded with the bund contract. They had ended up almost causing the demise of Liffe, and they really taught the Americans about the power of electronic trading. We were not so quick to embrace it.

Cantor Fitzgerald understood this and bought a patent that had been written by Susan Wagner who worked at the CFTC. As it turned out there were some significant similarities between Susan Wagner's patent and work I had done previously.

When I described the ideas from the patent, my wife Ellen asked me, "Didn't you talk about electronic trading back in the 1960s?" and I said, "Yes." She said, "Where's that study you did?" I said, "I have no clue." She said, "Is it in the basement? And didn't you bring all your Berkeley files and didn't we store them downstairs?" I said, "I'll take a look at it."

So I sent two of my employees to look through the basement, Rafael Marques and a summer intern, Jenise Norgaard. They spent about five or six hours going through cartons and cartons of books. I called, and I remembered it was about 3:00 P.M., because Ellen was saying, "Did they find it?" And I said, "No, they didn't find it." Then all of a sudden Rafael and Jenise determined they couldn't find it and the search should be ended. They decided to repack all of the boxes. In repacking the boxes, and what a sense of irony and fortuity, one of them broke open and there was the study.

So I got the study, and sure enough it looked very much like the Wagner patent. I had the same schematics, the same flows, the same ideas. Ultimately, I think it was that paper that stopped the enforcement of the patent, because it demonstrated that there was "prior art," but the Board of Trade and the CME did agree to license it. This was before the existence of my paper was known publicly, and the significant and wise thing for the exchange to do was to purchase the license. But its applicability stopped at the U.S. border, and I gave the name of the study and the study itself to Brian Williamson, chairman of Liffe, so it wouldn't be ambiguous in terms of whether my idea predated the Wagner patent.

Quite a story. And how about working to save Liffe? How were you involved with that?

I was involved in Liffe from its very inception and had become very close friends with a number of people there and have stayed friends since. I was a consultant to a gilt dealer named Ackroyd and Smithers, and they had retained me to help teach them futures. I became very close friends with the then chairman, David Lee Roy Lewis, and also got to meet a young upstart in the business by the name of Brian Williamson. Brian and I became very, very close friends. And the story continues over time.

I'll share something else with you. Brian held a very successful tenure as founder and an early chairman of Liffe, but by the time the Germans started competing, Liffe was teetering. It was in very bad shape and Brian gave me a call and said the Bank of England was asking him to come and be chairman. So we went out to dinner when I was in London. He said, "What do you think?" And I said, "Don't do it, because Liffe may fail if it continues open outcry. And it's not so bad if it fails; there's an OTC market. The city of London would still maintain its pre-eminence." And he replied, "I think it will fail as well."

We spoke a little while later and he got more pressure; he put me on a committee and we had a special meeting. I was talking to Brian about it recently, because I'm writing a book now, and he told me the meeting had been held under the auspices of the Bank of England. Pen Kent was there, the chairman and CEO of Lloyd's Bank, Brian, and myself. And we said, "Okay. Let's take a look at this." And Brian ultimately agreed to become chairman of the Bank of England, but only under the condition that if it was not possible to save Liffe, he would elegantly close it.

We got together and it had become very clear that the only way to save the institution was to close the floor and just bite the bullet and get rid of the politics. Brian ultimately set up a group of committees. They worked on it. They closed the floor and then they went on to basically develop the exchange.

One other thing was that I had been very dumb about the value of intellectual property. I first coined the term "derivatives". My wife Ellen reminds me about that term and of many other things. She always said to me, "There's this word 'derivatives' being used out there. Didn't you use it first?" And the interesting thing is that the word derivatives was not based on what most people think it was based on. I used it in the calculus sense—of a first derivative. You had an equation and then you modified it, and I used it in the mathematical sense, as opposed to "derived from" or whatnot. It was a mathematical term.

So next time around, I heard that there were going to be short-term interest rate contracts, similar to the Eurodollars, traded at the CME and that there would be equivalent contracts traded in London. And so I coined the term "Euribor" and registered it in the patent office of Europe and then subsequently gave it to Liffe as a complimentary gift and it became one of the largest traded contracts.

So Brian and I stayed friends over the years, and as things developed, he said, "Okay. We've got the problems solved here; we're viable. What's the next step?" I said, "Well, Brian, I think you have to have a new product." We had dinner at Wilton's, a very political London establishment. I wrote a book preface describing that dinner, during which I suggested that single stock futures was something Europe should start.

A single stock futures contract was only one portion of it, I had felt; it went back to the Berkeley study, and I said this to Brian: "Look. This is really only one part of it. You can dress it up with new products. You've made it electronic, and if you really want to grow it, you've got to demutualize it and really get rid of the member domination, and this would be the way to go through with it." So I subsequently introduced Brian to Battery and to Blackstone, and they put in, I think it was, 40 percent of $250 million. They bought a controlling interest in Liffe. By having capital at the table and being represented on the board of directors, all of the silly arguments that pitted one or another individual member's interest against the exchange no longer applied. It was impossible or at least it was very hard for anybody to sit there at the table and basically argue against shareholder value.

Thirteen months later, the exchange sold for $850 million. We originally put in $250 million. It was a nice little trade, and that began the whole demutualization and an IPO movement. I remember very specifically talking to Scott Gordon, who was instrumental in taking the CME public, and he said, "Oh. How much do you think you're going to get for that? You bought it at four pounds and you think you'll get 12." I said, "North, Scott." He said, "Fifteen." I said, "North," and we both laughed.

Sure enough, the stock traded, I think at 18 pounds and 25 tenths.

How would you apply that to the Chicago Board of Trade's IPO?

The Board of Trade's IPO again was fully resisted, and I am thankful for the clarity of Les Rosenthal and Billy O'Connor. Les very importantly led the entire battle to try to stop that ridiculous square box from being built. I mean it was just phenomenal to me to witness an exchange I loved spend $250 million to $350 million to build a single-purpose piece of concrete in downtown Chicago in the heart of the Internet revolution. You couldn't have done anything more wrong than build that building. It was only Les who basically kept the fight alive.

The other thing that was critical in the decades was that Billy O'Connor kept the vision of electronic trading alive. Billy had a nerd side to him and basically kept on driving at it, chipping away against the Luddites. And I think those people who might read this know exchanges are clubs and there are friendships involved. And unfortunately these two men took so much heat for what they did. Others became popular, were well liked, and had no problems.

If it wasn't for Les with the financial futures and just always a sober voice in the fighting over the building, and if it wasn't for Billy pushing on electronic trading, then any notion of an IPO and a vision of an exchange worth $9 billion to $10 billion would have died.

And even in spite of that, it could have been significantly larger if Les had been listened to and we hadn't built that building. If Billy had been listened to when we spent that money on electronic trading, the institution in my humble opinion could have been a $20 billion institution and not a $9 billion institution. However, Charley Carey did a masterful job in uniting a disparate membership and successfully leading the exchange to an IPO.

How about the Board of Trade in terms of the future? You've led Liffe to close its floor operation. Do you think that the Chicago Board of Trade will be able to do the same thing?

I think the trading floor is a civilization gone with the wind. And in a time of electronics, it's like saying to me, "Will there be a role for horses and buggies?" Yeah, there will be, and they're cute. They're in antique salons and things like that. Trading floors do provide a meeting place in the very thin commodities that might exist, but, by and large, they should be eliminated. They haven't a role really, and we're living in an electronic century. We manipulate genes. We communicate in thousands of ways, and we're doing this and that during the day.

I know that it isn't a well-held view. I know it may not be popular with some of the people, but I do feel that those members who facilitate an orderly transition from a floor-based exchange to a totally electronic exchange will ensure their own self-interest. If they are wise, they will be teaching their children about electronics at four years old.

Seeing that you've been so prescient about everything else, it's probably what's going to happen. But let's go back to 1992, when you addressed the United Nations Environmental Conference and you talked about the idea of emissions trading.

I got involved in the environmental movement when I was approached by a public interest group in Ohio called the Coalition for Acid Rain Equity. They approached me and said, "You know, you like to invent new products. You get blamed for being a father of financial futures. You do all of these things. You commoditize interest rates. Could you turn air into a commodity?" And I said, "Sure."

It was a far less difficult problem than turning interest rates into a commodity, because you had a notion of property rights and could always create a right to emit. Even though you couldn't divide air, you could create a secondary good called a "pollution permit" that would be a surrogate for dividing air. I wrote a position paper, which advocated it.

Again, the experience at the Board of Trade that I had as a 30-year-old chief economist was just remarkable, because I understood Congress. I understood the legislative process. I knew how to get laws passed. It was something that was in the DNA of the institution.

Fortunately, I was the recipient of that DNA. And so I advocated for the Clean Air Act. The Act got passed. Ultimately, it was the CBOT that influenced Bill Reilly in the Environmental Protection Agency's implementation of the Act. The Board of Trade was as important, if not more important, in the success of the sulfur dioxide (SO_2) program.

I was on the board of directors at the CBOT at the time, and Billy was chairman and said we ought to have a clean air committee and we ought to be trading SO_2. Basically, Jim Thompson, who was on the board at that time, said, "Come to Washington. I had been at an acid rain advisory committee meeting. They weren't going to number the permits. They weren't going to measure how much pollution was being emitted." Billy and Les said, "Hey, who's going to trade this thing without any information?"

Jim Thompson and I went to Washington and met with Bill Reilly, the EPA administrator. Bill tells me the whole basis of measuring emissions, something called the "continuous emission monitor," just like the electricity meter in your house, was placed on the stacks of utilities because of our argument. It was totally radical, but it was to measure the pollutants and the reason it's there is because speculators needed the information, not because the environmentalists wanted it. So it was this place that did it.

As a result of that meeting, I ultimately helped get the CBOT to do the SO_2 auction, which we did in combination with the EPA on a pro bono basis. We had a good run at that and ran it for quite some time. Subsequently, I ended up with the predecessor to my current employer, the Chicago Climate Exchange, traded sulfur dioxide allowances, and did the first trade ever done and registered in the EPA registry.

I got a call in 1991 from somebody who said, "Hey, we heard you did this with sulfur. Do you think that it's possible to do it for carbon?" I said, "Sure." Then I went to Geneva, met with some people at the United Nations in 1991, and subsequently in 1992 I wrote a paper called "In Search of Trees," and that paper is the basis for what I'm now doing.

Tell me more about the SO_2 program and how it worked.

The SO_2 program has turned out to be the poster child for all environmental programs. It costs probably a billion dollars to implement annually. The current estimated benefits associated with just reduced medical expenses on lung disease are estimated to be anywhere from \$40 billion to \$75 billion. We've basically eliminated acid rain in this country. We have lower electricity rates than we had when the Act was passed. It is a success.

Again, the Board of Trade was helpful. Everybody outside the industry and a few in the industry as well said, "You can't commoditize air." Okay? And they said that Treasury bonds aren't like Ginnie Maes. Then we were told 10-year notes weren't like the long bond, and that options weren't like Treasuries. Everybody thought these were unique products that couldn't be commoditized. And these arguments suggest to any student of the market that they're dead wrong, that they aren't unique. There are so many things in life, philosophically, which are the same. We all are unique, but we participate in similar processes. So, you know, just as an academic, we have to remember that. Our experiences were all unique, but are similar in terms of process.

If one looks at the world clinically, which one does as a researcher, and is able to have some clarity and look for analogies as opposed to looking at things that make something special, then finding new products and new ideas is nowhere near as radical as people suggest. The majority said carbon dioxide is different. It is a global pollutant. SO_2 is a local pollutant. With carbon, you can plant trees. With sulfur you can't use trees because they can't process sulfur. Everything was different. You couldn't measure it. You couldn't regulate it. You couldn't do it. "Orville, Wilbur, it ain't going to fly. It's going right down the drain."

From 1992 to 1997, we ended up doing what were then very radical trades. We securitized a rain forest in Costa Rica. We represented the Salish and Kootenai tribes in Montana, whose reservations had been ravished by wildfire. We basically bought the carbon that would grow in the trees planted to restore the burned forests 80 years forward.

The money that we gave to the tribes was used for fast-growing seedlings that could restore the forests even more quickly. We took garbage dumps and landfills, and tapped methane. Methane comes from decomposing organics. You sink a pipe into a garbage dump. You suck out the methane. You burn it and turn it into electricity. As a result of that, it doesn't contribute to global warming. It's 21 times more potent than carbon. So we cut our teeth on very specific projects.

Ultimately, I had the privilege of being invited to the White House in 1997, and the chair of my panel was Vice President Al Gore. Once again, everybody was saying, "You can't commoditize CO_2. It can't be done. It's not good." As a result of this event, we became friendly with the vice president. Ellen and I were at this party at Christmas following Kyoto, celebrating the advent of what we thought would be a new era. I subsequently testified before the Senate Environment and Public Works Committee, the Senate Agriculture Committee, and the Senate Energy and Natural Resources Committee, and I heard the same things: "You know it'll never work. It'll never fly. Markets can't be started."

In the year 2000, I ended up getting a grant from the Joyce Foundation here in Chicago. Paula DiPerna was president of the Foundation at that time, and she said to me, "You are the only person talking about doing something as opposed to advocating something. Do you think you could start an exchange?" The Foundation gave us a \$400,000 grant and that was followed by an \$800,000 grant. We formed an advisory committee, and here again is the CBOT message; I did what I had been doing for 30 years. I used the same methodology.

I formed an advisory committee with David Boren, the former senator from Oklahoma; Jim Thompson; Maurice Strong, adviser to the Secretary General of the United Nations; Mary Schapiro, president of

NASD Regulation; and Sir Brian Williamson. I called a bunch of friends and I said, "I need credibility. Everybody's ridiculing this idea." And fortunately, because of the friendships and whatever small success we had had, people were willing to lend their names. We worked on it. We came up with measuring, with monitoring, and with verification, and then we basically went to stage two.

Stage two was getting 30 companies involved, bringing them to Chicago every six weeks, building a consensus, and devising what would be a private Kyoto protocol. That whole notion of a private Kyoto was anathema, and everybody said, "It will never work. It will never fly. It's the stupidest idea in the world. You're never going to get it anywhere." From the moment we got the grants to the time we started the exchange, everything that could have gone wrong went wrong. I don't mean something. I mean everything. President George W. Bush refused to join Kyoto, followed by 9/11, the Afghan military operation, the dot-com bubble bursting, the stock market crashing, Enron imploding, a recession in the United States, and war in Iraq.

That was the glorious beginning. We ran out of money. I put in personal savings, and friends and family came in. Interestingly enough, our first outside investors were the Jesuits, who believed they should do something that had social impact. I told people, there's no sensation in the world like getting a call from your lead investor and saying, "Father Francis, you know this is how we're doing," and Father Francis saying, "I pray for you every day, Richard." That's quite a different attitude from most investors.

We subsequently got 14 entities to join. Mayor Richard Daley became honorary chairman. We had the city of Chicago and 13 companies. We subsequently raised 15 million pounds in London in the first round of financing. We raised another 15 million pounds a year later to start the European Climate Exchange. Goldman Sachs became an investor and took 10 percent of the exchange. We went from nothing to over 360 members, and this little Chicago company now represents 16 percent of the United States' large stationary source of emissions, all done without any federal laws or help. We went from 1.5 million tons traded in 2005 to 10.3 million in 2006. We've traded 23 million tons in the first quarter of 2007. Once again, Les Rosenthal was there to counsel and mentor. He is vice chairman of the exchange. Other CBOT members like Keith Bronstein were invaluable in making the exchange a success. He was the first market maker.

We started the sulfur futures contract based on the experience we had in the design of the CCX program and our practical experience in trading. That contract traded 400 contracts in 2005, 30,000 in 2006, and the first three months of 2007 over 30,000. We started an options contract on SO_2 and did a couple of thousand contracts. Last week Thursday, for the first time, we started an NO_2 contract, which is essentially smog, and we continue to grow. In Europe now there are seven exchanges and the European Climate Exchange is part of the CCX family. It controls more than 80 percent of the European carbon market.

We've signed a joint venture and formed the Montreal Climate Exchange with the Montreal Bourse. As soon as the Canadian government gets ready, we'll do that. We have signed up five Chinese members and two Indian members, and have seven Brazilian corporates that are emitting less, even though Brazilian companies are not required by law to reduce their emissions. So we have what we think is the beginning of what will be a multinational exchange helping to set the standards.

Again, how does this go back to the Board of Trade? Read the history of this institution. It invented grain standards in 1848. It took the federal government 50 years to adopt those standards and make them part of the U.S. Department of Agriculture.

One learns from experience that you can do it. If it was done in 1848, why not in 2000? If securities markets and regulation started with the Buttonwood Agreement in 1792, well before there was an SEC, why can't we do it now? Having the experience at the CBOT and being a student of its history gave me the courage to implement whatever ideas I had, because I had the intellectual belief that history was not an accident.

How did you come up with the idea for trading in the environment arena?

The notion of trading was totally novel when it came to the environmental arena. Previously, people thought the way to stop pollution was to put a cap on the amount anybody could emit and the cap had to be a one-size-fits-all rule. In other words, everybody had to reduce pollutants by the same percentage. That doesn't make common sense, because if your company is better at reducing emissions than mine, why can't I buy your reductions? If you can do it more cheaply, then society is better off if you do the cutting and I buy your cuts as long as there is a cap limiting the total amount of emissions.

This was a totally revolutionary concept that was first articulated by Ronald Coase. It encouraged those people who were good at cleaning to clean up more, so that they could be a supplier of environmental services to people who were less efficient at cleaning up. It's just using the markets to develop private incentives to achieve social objectives. And profit was the way to do it.

We got the sulfur exchange, the Chicago Climate Futures Exchange (CCFE), launched the same way as CCX. We got the same locals, the same names that we had before: Les Rosenthal, Keith Bronstein, Lee Stern, Brian Rico, George Haley, Mike Anderson, and quite a few of the traders in the bean pit. You find a group of people with whom you work, who lend you their names and who put their capital at work and are willing to finance the development of the exchange.

Can you explain pollution credits?

We use the term "pollution credits" when speaking of things that offset pollution from another source. For example, if you reduce emissions, that's called a "pollution permit"—you reduce the amount of pollution at the point where it's emitted. Sometimes those permits are called allowances. Environmentalists call it too many names. "Credit" is often used synonymously with "offset," because you can do things that reduce the amount of greenhouse gases in the atmosphere besides cutting them at the smokestack. You can't do that with sulfur.

With carbon, you can plant trees; you can change your crops; you can plant switchgrass—all of which hold carbon and prevent it from being released into the atmosphere. You can bury carbon dioxide geologically. There are lots of ways that you can, in effect, earn credit for preventing the release of greenhouse gases into the air in addition to reducing those gases at the smokestack. Thus the term "credit".

Can you tell me some of the exciting things you see for the future?

I really think that this world that we're living in is going to require markets to be used in dispute resolution and as a way of solving problems, and one of the critical areas is water. I spoke at a conference at the Milken Institute with some Palestinians and Israelis who recognize that they are going to either have to go to war over water or find a market solution to it. So we're looking at reserving the levels of water in the Great Lakes and developing a water market there and in the Southwest.

We think air and water are public goods that are needed for our children and our grandchildren, and how to allocate them is going to be critical. This no longer a time when students of economics learn that air and water are free—not with seven billion people, not with the growth in China and India that's taking place. I also see a time when we'll be trading futures and options on things like the spotted owl and other endangered species. And finally, I think we're going to find a way to commoditize medicine. And that's one of my great dreams: to bring down health care costs and use markets where they're not used today.

Sounds like an exciting prediction.

And I'm sticking by it.

In 1969, you said price volatility is still the most important prerequisite for markets to attract volume. Do you still believe that's true?

Price volatility is very important, because there's no need for a market unless you have a need to transfer that risk. That's for a futures market. There are things to invent where volatility is not critical, like these public goods that we've talked about. Now those are going to create volatility, but it's not the sole driver. The driver there is to invent a commodity that helps people. And the Ginnie Mae is the perfect example. When we started working on that contract, it took you three months to get a mortgage. You wouldn't get it if you were a woman; there was gender discrimination. You wouldn't get it if you were a person of different color. Neighborhoods were redlined. We commoditized mortgages, and now it takes only 24 hours to get one. It doesn't matter—white, black, woman, man, whatever other ethnic group you're in—you get it in 24 hours and it's a commodity.

And that's the critical notion here. Can you add value by commoditizing something where there are record levels of home ownership? Then the second is: Do you need a futures market to hedge the volatility associated with the market? So the first job is to commoditize and the second is to create a futures market.

Last question: What would you like your legacy to the Board of Trade to be?

My legacy to the Board of Trade is not for me to say. It's for the men and women that I've worked for to say. I just hope they view it as something positive.

CHAPTER 18

Passion for the Markets

Rick Santelli

After receiving his bachelor's degree from the University of Illinois in Champaign-Urbana, Rick Santelli worked as a trader and order filler at the Chicago Mercantile Exchange. He traded in a wide variety of pits from lumber futures and livestock to Treasury bills, gold, and foreign exchange.

By 1985, Rick was working at the Chicago Board of Trade for Drexel Burnham Lambert. He was a vice president in charge of interest rate futures and options. From that position, he went to Geldermann, Inc., where he was in charge of the Derivative Products Group. He then served as vice president in charge of institutional futures and options at Rand Financial Services, Inc.

During his tenure at the CBOT, he served on a variety of committees, mostly related to new financial products and mortgage securities.

While working in the Institutional and Financial Futures and Options division of Sanwa Futures, Rick decided to use his market experience as a veteran trader and financial executive to begin a career as a television financial analyst. In 1999, he was hired by CNBC Business News, where he worked as an on-air editor reporting from the floor of the Chicago Board of Trade. His focus was primarily on interest rates, foreign exchange, and the Federal Reserve.

Since that time, Rick Santelli has been quoted in numerous publications including the *Wall Street Journal*, *Chicago Tribune*, *Chicago Sun-Times* and *Crain's*. He continues to provide market analysis on CNBC as a bond market reporter. His coverage is always lively, intuitive, and professionally accurate. He has come to be a respected market source.

Mr. Santelli has been married for 24 years and has three daughters.

****

How did you first hear about futures exchanges?

I was on my way to law school. I had graduated from the University of Illinois in Champagne-Urbana, and I was preparing to enroll at the University of Illinois Law School. While I was thinking of getting ready for school, I made a little stop-off at the Chicago Mercantile Exchange. I had a friend whose father traded at the exchange. I went to the visitors' center, saw the activity, and was hooked. Instead of going to law school, I settled for a $60-a-week runner's job. I consider myself lucky that the rest seemed to have worked out.

How did your parents feel about that detour?

They weren't very happy. You know, between my parents helping me pay for college and Uncle Sam helping me pay for college, I did have a couple of bricks on each shoulder when I was done getting my undergraduate degree. However, at the end of the day you have to do something that you think you'll like.

When I saw all the chaos on that trading floor, and keep in mind in the late 1970s trading floors were the epicenter, it was like the Haymarket Riot going on, except it was orderly. It just seemed to call me and beckon me within 72 hours of that first visit. Before that, for the most part, I'd never even heard of futures exchanges. All of a sudden I was part of the process, but starting out at the very bottom.

And where was that bottom?

I started as a runner, wearing a yellow coat on the old CME floor. I was one of those people who took a piece of paper from a wire machine. At that time they were still printing on the old machines. I would tear it off and run into whatever pit it needed to go into. Sometimes you'd wait if they were market orders, and if they were price orders you'd hand it over and run for the next Teletype machine.

From there it started to get exciting, because I did things in a somewhat unconventional fashion. Probably within six months of my first runner job, I managed to put enough money together to lease a membership. I started to trade lumber and gold. This was at a time in 1979 when the Iran hostage situation erupted. It's kind of ironic now, because Iran is again in the headlines. The Iranian situation propelled gold from the 200s up to close to 900 before all was said and done. To go from never hearing of trading gold to within half a year leasing a membership and actively starting to trade at a time when market volatility, financial futures, and gold were really starting to come of age was just thoroughly exciting.

Can you remember your first day as a trader?

Oh, I can remember it well. Actually, my first day as a trader, I didn't trade gold. I traded a lumber contract, and the first contract I did, I was shaking so badly I could barely write on the trading card.

What happened from there?

The first trade was a very big winner, which really I think is kind of sad, because I think you never want your first trade to be a winner. It reinforces a type of behavior that might not be the best. I think I was a little too aggressive. The first time I leased a membership I did okay, but then I started to give some back, and it was a roller coaster. On Monday I'd look good. On Friday I'd look bad. But I had no kids, no mortgage, and no real responsibilities; it was a good time to be in those volatile futures markets.

Like they say in the *Star Trek* movies, all the exchanges in Chicago were like "the last frontier." Those markets were the beginning of the last frontier where an average guy could walk in, and he could potentially make a fortune, although he could equally lose a fortune.

How about mentors? Who taught you how to trade?

Actually, my mentor was a gentleman by the name of Bill Denicolo. He was a gold filler at the time, and he was filling gold contracts for J. Aron, a large metals company. J. Aron was huge in the gold market back then, and subsequently the company was purchased by Goldman Sachs.

Bill also brokered for an entity called Pacific Trading. Bill filled for both of those companies at a time when the computer was just starting to be used. The CME didn't allow computers on the floor at that point. Isn't that kind of ironic? Computers had to be off the floor. So people would do these very primitive printouts, and they would tape them on trading cards and bring them on the floor. Those were the first sheets. You know, the option guys have their pricing spread sheets. These were the predecessors to those sheets.

The thing about Pacific Trading was that it ran into some issues and ended up going broke, and when it resurfaced as Chicago Research and Trading (CRT), a lot of the original investors didn't want to get involved again. So they missed probably one of the biggest freight trains in the history of trading, because CRT was an absolute legendary organization. It really defined making money trading options, just as options were starting to get into the market.

What I remember about Bill was that he could do three things at once. He could trade for himself, he could fill generic orders, and he could deal with all these cards coming in with spread relationships. And while he was doing those three things, he could hold a conversation with you and still keep an eye on the market. You could almost see his brain click. He knew when something was getting close. He had to pay attention and fill the order. It was just amazing to watch.

I know it sounds crazy, but if you want to be a good broker, the hardest thing is being able to subtract, and I mean fast. Somebody says, "Okay. I want you to, as a customer, buy 500." Then you say, "Bidding on 500." And some guy goes, "10, 15, 11, 9." You need to subtract really quick, and you don't have time to pause, because the market doesn't wait. If that sounds simple, try putting yourself in that high-pressured situation. It is not nearly as simple as it sounds.

Tell me about the first lesson you learned at the CBOT.

I learned not to necessarily listen to people in terms of what you want to do. It's always good to listen to people to learn. Now, I'll give you an example, and I shouldn't mention any names so I won't, but let's go back to that lumber pit at the CME where I made one of my first trades. I bought lumber, and it immediately moved to limit up. Now, limit up is a great thing when you're long, because it means that everybody wants to buy it and you're already long.

I remember that one of the order fillers in the pit noticed me. I had just been there a few days. He leaned over and whispered to me, "You know, you don't want to hold that too long." But I'm thinking, "Well, hey, I just bought the lows of the day and we're limit up. What are you telling me here?" He grinned at me, and the next thing I knew, he started selling the market down. The market quickly went from limit up to limit down, and the money I had made was now a loser. That's a time I should have listened.

Back in the late 1970s, you were able to smoke on the perimeter of the trading floors. Everybody use to sit on the sidelines and smoke, and kibitz about what they thought about the market. So I guess the point of the story is everybody has an opinion, and it's interesting to listen to, but at the end of the day, it's important to formulate your own strategies, because the money you lose isn't going to be the loss of the guy who gave you advice; it's going to be yours.

How about the legendary people that you heard about or knew at the CBOT?

I think I'd have to start out with Peter Steidlmayer. The reason I say Peter Steidlmayer is not only because he is one of the nicest, smartest people to walk through the Chicago Board of Trade, but he is an avid technician. He is a man who thinks that all the answers to every market are in a chart. He believes it's just a matter of tuning in to what the market is saying. Nothing can elude the charts.

No matter how big or how small, your dot is there somewhere. Peter Steidlmayer came up with a new form of technical analysis called a Market Profile. It has morphed into so many things: capital flow and other techniques. Basically, his idea, as simple as it sounds, was revolutionary back then. It still carries amazing insight today.

He would take a bell-shaped curve and apply prices. He would apply those prices to different time frames, and he would show the way prices build, and how certain prices move away from high-volume areas or toward high-volume areas. You had point-and-figure charts, you had bar charts, and you had tick charts, but now, all of a sudden, you had this new form, the Market Profile, showing how prices are distributed over time. I think in many ways it was revolutionary, and that was all out of Mr. Peter Steidlmayer's brain.

You're right. Peter is a real genius. How about another legend?

The next person that I want to talk about is Richard Sandor. I call him "Doc." Without a doubt, he is a revolutionary individual. I was lucky to work with him when he ran a brokerage firm. He was one of the pioneers in creating interest rate futures.

John Harding also comes to mind. He helped to write the first interest rate futures contract. In today's world, if you pick up a *Wall Street Journal*, you listen to CNBC, you listen to WGN, or you read any of the magazines, it's all about derivatives. Richard Sandor and John Harding developed the original derivative building blocks in the form of the Ginnie Mae futures contract. Investment banks on Wall Street are making lots and lots of revenues on derivatives. Futures by their very definition are derivatives, so futures markets were the first derivatives, but then when you take foreign exchange or interest rates, the first contracts were really the building blocks for the complicated derivatives.

The contract that Richard wrote, with John's assistance, was truly revolutionary. That's not to say it didn't have its early flaws, but before you can run, you have to crawl. Once they figured out some of the bugs in the Ginnie Mae contract, it ultimately morphed into the bond contract. In the case of the bond contract, how the delivery process was finally determined, using the concept of "cheapest to deliver," would have never come about without the precedent set by the Ginnie Mae contract.

Richard Sandor had great foresight to see the need to apply these newfangled derivatives into the hedging process. Remember that the only reason futures contracts ever had traction to move into the mainstream wasn't for the speculators, which sounds like a negative statement or heresy when we are talking about the Board of Trade, but it isn't. You needed to find the hedgers. You needed to find the proper business channels to get the interested parties in, and that indeed was all the interest rate exposure that the world had at the time.

If you look back at that moment in financial history, you would be right before the Volcker years. You had double-digit inflation. You had huge volatility in the markets and T-bills trading in the low 80s; oh, my God, we haven't seen that in ages. When you offered the banking system, and those others that had any type of exposure to fluctuating interest rates, a new contract that would basically push the risk into somebody else's hands, that was terrific. It was also terrific for the Board of Trade, because whose hands did we push it into? Speculators'.

So it's the chicken or the egg. They finally came up with a way to answer the question. They came up with a product that had great application to industry and to hedging, and they found a group of grain traders who were willing to step out and move into the financial arena to be the liquidity to make everything work.

How about Richard Dennis?

Richard Dennis was an icon in the industry. He always hit home with people, because many remembered the story of the "turtles." It was in the early 1980s, maybe circa 1982, that Richard Dennis ran a very strange want ad in many papers looking for traders. I know it ran in most of the Chicago papers. It was his methodology that was quite different.

He didn't want anyone who already had bad trading habits. He didn't want somebody who had everything figured out. He wanted a blank page, but he also wanted a blank page that had certain personality characteristics. The early questionnaires that he sent to the people who responded to the ad had lots of questions that had absolutely nothing to do with anything about trading. They may have asked whether you picked your nose. They asked very strange things. He was looking for a certain temperament.

He must have known what he was doing, because not only did Richard Dennis make many fortunes himself, but many of those original "turtles" are still in the business, and many of those "turtles" that aren't are no longer in the business because they made so much money. So he assembled the team—blank sheet of paper, certain characteristics—and he tried to give them the wherewithal to attack the markets in the way he did. It was a very different strategy, but it worked well. People who are not traders think that this is an easy business. All you have to do is "buy low, sell high." That wasn't really Richard Dennis' philosophy.

Richard Dennis' philosophy was more like if the market is going up, buy more. Buy more! Buy more! The higher it goes, buy more. If it makes a new high, buy more, because it has a trend; it has momentum. You know, nowadays they talk about all these computer models. It's momentum models; a black box. Richard Dennis was of that mind-set decades before these models were even thought of. Another thing he said was, "Cut your losers, and let your winners run." These things sound easy, because Richard Dennis and the "turtles" put them into the whole trading vernacular.

And how about Tom Baldwin?

I came to the CBOT around 1984. I spent time at the CME prior to that, but when I met Richard Sandor, I became a believer that the interest rate futures were where you wanted to be. This was the newfangled area of prosperity and financial futures.

When I walked into that bond room for the first time, it was just amazing watching Tom Baldwin. In the mid-1980s he traded more round turns, more contracts personally, as a one-man band than Salomon Brothers did.

I can remember Tom jumping up and down with his yellow jacket on. He would just attack the market. His style, and what he is remembered for, was that he could sense when the market was a little too long or a little too short, and he wasn't one to be known for taking overnight positions. Just think about it. If the market was an hour away from closing, and Tom Baldwin looked around and had that sixth sense that the pit was just too long, he would jump up and down and offer the market down in size—hundreds and hundreds of contracts, which back then was an amazing amount, because most people were trading ones and twos. But there was Tom Baldwin doing thousands and thousands a day.

Somehow he would find those gaps where the price would fall to find value, especially in front of closes, in front of weekends, and in front of important events, and that was his knack.

And let's talk about a physical endeavor. It wasn't like he'd be buying and selling in a nice diplomatic fashion. He'd be jumping up and down, sweating, and he had things falling out of his pockets. The whole pit would become this monster wave of human flesh. The other traders would just kind of attack him, because he was the market.Some people remember Tom fondly, and some people don't, but when you're a leader, an innovator, the biggest in the pit at any given time, you are always going to find people who aren't necessarily happy about it. Maybe it's a little jealousy, but there's no dismissing that he was a legendary figure.

There's a neat story I should tell about Tom Baldwin buying the Rookery Building. Now, for those that don't know the Rookery Building, it's down the street from the CBOT. When the old financial floor was in the original grain room, there were these huge multistory windows facing LaSalle Street and which looked out on the Rookery Building. Legend has it that Tommy Baldwin use to stare out at the Rookery, which was in disrepair. He was having some good years. The story goes he bought the building so he could have something really cool to look at while he was trading. I find that so neat, and really describes his personality.

Tell me how trading impacted your personal and family life.

Well, I guess in many ways, my entire life is defined by Chicago futures. I met my wife, Terri on the floor of the Chicago Mercantile Exchange. I met her while looking for somebody to take my place holding a deck in the gold pit.

I reached a point in my career where I felt like I finally made enough chips that I had a cushion and I wouldn't have to go back to holding a deck again. I remember I saw this really cute girl and she was looking to get a job in the pit. I taught her how to hold the deck at that time, and she went on to not only do a terrific job, but be so much better at it than

I was. She was one of the first female order fillers in the futures markets. So I guess my entire life always seems to find all the good points revolving around the futures markets.

Those future markets—what did people initially think of them?

Oh, wild cowboys! There are good stories and there are bad stories. The Board of Trade hit a growth spurt with contracts that catered to the hedging community in the mortgage business. The Treasury futures caught on in a big way as the heir apparent to the Ginnie Mae contract. The Board of Trade tried for years to come back with another generation mortgage contract, but to no avail.

The point of this story is how those guys in Chicago were initially looked upon as crazy by the New York investment banking community. But over time they became viewed as major competitors. The New York financial community had witnessed the Chicago futures markets get a toehold into their cash markets. The Treasury futures market became an integral piece of the daily trading in the Treasury interest rate complex. Now, granted, it wasn't as big in notional terms, but it had a huge influence, and you could tell because whenever the Board of Trade had a holiday for whatever reason, or if the Board of Trade closed early, the cash markets were dead.

There was no doubt about the market influence. An intense rivalry grew between the cash and futures markets. Competition brings out the positive qualities, but I always thought it was one of the reasons we were never able to get another mortgage contract off the ground.

I guess to answer your question, the rest of the world looked at us as crazy, but ultimately they competed against us. They might have been a little jealous of us, and now really the truth is out there. The New York Stock Exchange has just finalized its deal with Euronext. But at the epicenter is globalization and everybody is striving to find products that will compete in the world. Guess what it is that everybody is trying to find? More derivatives. The New York Stock Exchange wants to get more into the corporate bonds, derivatives, and options markets—the same thing the Chicago exchanges have enjoyed great success with.

That is what is so interesting. The interest rate market started out as a bit of an afterthought—something with limited growth potential. It was certainly innovative, but people thought it was not really going to last. Today, in many ways, it's the epicenter of all the financial markets. Chicago style derivatives and the over-the-counter derivatives are the envy of the world. Everybody wants to be like the Chicago exchanges, because of their business model. Just look at how the stock prices have proved to be so hugely profitable.

One of the reasons it has been so successful is that the public views the CBOT as an exchange that operates with integrity.

If it weren't for integrity, you couldn't have futures open outcry. You couldn't have the Haymarket Riot effect, and I'll tell you why. Imagine a pit, like the bond pit in the 1980s, where there were probably 600 people going absolutely bonkers, and that's just in the pit. Then you have hundreds, if not thousands, more operating in all the peripheral areas. Whether they're the desk clerks or arbitrage clerks running around collecting cards or data or doing their charts, all of this couldn't work if on the simplest, bottom-of-the-food-chain level there wasn't integrity.

Why? Let's look at the trading dynamic. I am trying to sell 10 bonds to some guy across the pit I can barely see because the bodies are swaying. He says, "Okay, I'll do them with you," and that's it. Now if the market moves big and he doesn't stand up for that trade, the whole process breaks down. Trust and integrity are the fundamental cornerstones for having an open outcry activity actually work. To have that type of price discovery actually get traction, you have to trust the person you're trading with, and trust the company behind both the trades and the clearing process of the exchange. All of that trust is built on integrity.

You've described the open outcry system as a double-edged sword.

It is a double-edged sword in many ways. I personally think it's the best price discovery process there is, but, and nothing against Wal-Mart, but the world has gone into Wal-Mart mode. There's this Wal-Marting of America going on, and it's not necessarily a bad thing. It makes it so you can buy things like radios and TVs, accounting for inflation, much cheaper than in the past. If you look at what these things cost 20 years ago and you look at what they cost today, it's revolutionary. However, the point is that cheaper isn't always better.

Open outcry involves people. People are expensive. If you were to ask anybody who has ever opened a business, "What's the most expensive cost you have?" they would answer, "It's people." That brings a cost to open outcry that the computers don't have. Now, I think open outcry is the most transparent. I think it's the fairest, but let's be realistic here. The cost of a computer-driven trading platform is so much lower that at some function of price, people will settle for something that is not as good if it's cheap enough.

Now, let's add the volume into the equation. I'll give you another example. Probably by 12:00 noon, the computer matching system of the Board of Trade can do 600,000, 700,000, 800,000, maybe a million 10-year T-note futures—just the 10-year T-note futures. You could not have a pit big enough to trade those numbers. So, let's look at the facts. It's not better, but at a price that's cheaper, it could be close. The volume that has pushed the exchanges into the epicenter of the global financial community couldn't happen within the framework of an open outcry only.

The double-edged sword that I talk about is what created the whole price discovery process of futures that started the product revolution, but the fact that it was so good, and had certain costs associated with it almost by design, is one of the reasons it started to unfold. The markets were so successful, yet the process wasn't the most efficient.

As we move into the late 2000s, here we are in 2007, we can see the global competition, and all the exchanges, and all the electronic platforms. The floors in Chicago, unlike those in Europe and Asia, are still around. There are certain transactions that are so complicated that the matching systems, even at any price, aren't good enough. So even cheaper sometimes isn't the only variable.

Options and multi-leg spreads are things that the stock exchange, for example, doesn't have to deal with. When you buy or sell Microsoft, it's a bid, it's an offer. Boom, easy. If you are buying a generic futures contract, it's a bid, it's an offer. Boom. But if you call up your broker and say, "Okay, I want to do a butterfly or an iron condor," with options where there are five or six legs, those transactions are still better executed with people.

And open outcry could still surprise people and end up finding a specific niche, and that is what I think might happen. It might not be the same size as it once was, but even on a smaller scale, it might work. You could call it "the human backup." We all talk about the computer age. You have to have an off-site backup. I think people could represent that in Chicago as the merger of the Chicago exchanges still holds out the notion that a trading floor will continue to exist.

People are so important in this business, service has always been something they've prided themselves on. How does the move away from open outcry to the computer age change that?

Well, I think from a service end, computers are good. If you program in the right information and you have the right structure, computers can provide very good service. Take, for example, monitoring money in your account. If you have a large group of traders, with capital allocation to each trader, you don't want somebody losing more than they have; then these things are handled really well. So, from a back-office standpoint, computerized matching is terrific. A lot of that existed even before computerized trading; many back office operations had already moved to the computer.

One of the issues with the computer is the contrast with the floor, and I love this analogy: Just imagine a Monday night football game. Now, you can actually go to the game and watch it at the field. You're experiencing something great. Or, you can watch it on TV. Not quite as good, but still fun. That's open outcry. Now, let's go to the computer when it comes to trading. Imagine that camera on the field is only focused on the scoreboard. Just the scoreboard. All that you see is the scoreboard. That, in a way, is the way some of us look at computerized trading.

From the service side there are a lot of pluses, but the synergies of the floor, from the service of providing knowledge and insight to just the public forum to debate what's going on, will never in my opinion be replaced. They are some of the things that will disappear. Trading floors in the futures markets are second-by-second hotbeds of real-time information. That information went out to the rest of the world, as people were on phones in bygone days. A lot of that is going to be lost, and it's very hard to make up for it.

As commission prices went down, the computer looked more like a positive. But as the people disappear, many of the customers find they can't get that grassroots information like they use to. Granted, some may say, "Oh, those guys in Chicago trade second to second. None of that information is valuable. I'm a long-term player. I take a long-term view."

Believe me. Yes, maybe 20 bits of information on the floors aren't valuable to the average guy, but everything important starts out in a very small way. Some of the biggest moves and most important aspects of major changes in economies and central banking activity start out on the floors.

A lot of that will be lost, because customers aren't going to have these human brokers anymore. They're going to have toll keepers. They're going to have a person at your clearing firm that's your connection. He is going to make sure you send him the money or wire him the money. He's going to give you the passwords, and monitor your prices on his screen. In the old days, when something crazy happened in the market, you could call 50 guys on the floor, and they would give you 50 opinions, but maybe one of those was the answer. It's going to be harder to find that information in the future.

How about serving the farmers?

How ironic it is if you look at the meats at the Chicago Mercantile Exchange, and you look at the grains at this exchange, those happen to be where open outcry is lasting longer, and it's still proactive. Those were the areas everybody fled to go into the financials, where the computer diminished the body count more dramatically and much sooner.

The service side in the nonfinancial business, the agricultural business to be specific, still seems to be driven more by human relationships. All these dynamics we just talked about are disappearing much more slowly in the nonfinancial markets. I think there's more of a human element that still exists in the agribusiness community versus banking and investment sectors, which have moved quickly into the electronic trading venues.

It's like those movies when you get inside computers. A lot of the financial side is so nonhuman at this point, but it's not so true in the agribusiness. Those human relationship dynamics are alive and well. Many think that there will be a niche in the nonfinancials as well. Think regional here.

When you're talking interest rates or central banking or foreign exchange, it's more of a global perspective. When you talk about grains there are imports and exports, and there's a globalness, but everything is much more local, like real estate. They say all real estate is a local scenario. When it comes to the grains and livestock, it is true. There's a regionality to it that keeps humans, and exchanges, more in the hunt.

Where does the role of self-regulation play into all of this?

Sarbanes-Oxley. That's all I need to say. Sarbanes-Oxley is legislation that arose out of Enron, WorldCom, and some of the other corporate scandals in the early part of the new century, and this legislation was kind of rushed through because people demanded retribution. Something had to be done to stem corporate corruption.

If you look at it in percentage terms, you know there are very few bad apples in this barrel of corporations. Integrity is many thousands times bigger than the minuscule number of firms involved in corrupt activities. I'm not diminishing the Enrons and the WorldComs, but they really are the exceptions rather than the rule. Nonetheless, Congress had to rush and come up with legislation, and in hindsight four years later, they're trying to unravel much of that legislation. You have Mayor

Michael Bloomberg and some of the other big politicians, many of whom were involved in the original process, trying to backpedal.

So I think that self-regulation is different from outside regulation, because it's knowledge positive. Self-regulation means that people understand what they are regulating. They are involved in the process on a day-to-day basis. As smart as many members of Congress are, they can't be professionals and experts in every field.

I think this is particularly true in futures. Self-regulation in this industry is very important, because futures and derivatives are very complex. It is my contention that regulating something that is complex is done best by people who understand the complexities. Self-regulation is an enviable way to proceed. We now see that firsthand in the backpedaling of regulators that weren't from within the industries but had the regulatory pen.

Part of that allows the CBOT to move forward as a worldwide price discovery mechanism.

I think that what you are talking about is inspiring confidence. We spoke about the importance of integrity when the pits were the center of the world. Today the pits are no longer the center of the world, but the transactions are. So take integrity to the electronic age and inspiring confidence is hugely important.

I'll give you some examples, and I won't mention any exchanges. I will go as far as to say that they're not in Chicago. We had some periods of volatility recently. In February, the Chinese stock market had a bit of a hiccup, and everybody around the world felt that hiccup. Certain exchanges couldn't keep up with the huge amount of volume that was associated with a quick realignment of the global dynamics that connected all these markets together.

Confidence means whether it's busy or whether it's slow, whether there's a big fundamental release that's surprising or something comes out of the European Central Bank or the Reserve Bank of Australia or the Federal Open Market Committee in the United States, there has to be confidence that you can access the market. People have to know that they can get the right information. They need to feel confident that they can get their order in and get their order filled. They have to feel certain that the clearing of their trades will be performed in a logical, orderly, timely fashion.

Self-regulation gives confidence to these systems to be in place to get the job done. I think confidence globally and futures markets, which are very abstract, are some of the backbones in the Chicago futures markets, unlike the U.S. government. I don't mean this badly, but if you look at the federal government or the U.S. Treasury, you have things called "fails." It's just part of the system. You'll have a security that's on repo or you'll have special financial arrangements where that security doesn't get cleared properly, and a fail results. No futures exchange has ever had a "fail" in terms of clearing. They have been flawless. Their clearing framework is the envy of all clearing models.

Speaking of never having a "fail," tell me about the role of the Clearing Corporation.

The Board of Trade Clearing Corporation (BOTCC) was one of the triple A clearing entities on the planet. As we talked about throughout this interview, recognizing the importance of clearing, confidence, and integrity, BOTCC was the envy of the world. For many, many decades, for every trade executed, the other side of it was the BOTCC. It was the jewel in the Board of Trade's crown.

Of course, as the computer started to make inroads, especially in the late 1990s, the BOTCC ended up getting involved in issues with various mergers and other electronic platforms, so things have changed a bit; but in its prime, it was one of the premier, early institutions that was the example of how clearing was supposed to be. As I talked about, there was never a "fail."

Going forward, can you give me some idea of what products you think will have the most impact?

Products have to be designed to cater to profitability. Let's take the fear side. We talked about that on day one. Futures contracts were created because of fear that interest rates or grain prices would be volatile. The question was, "How do you hedge that?" Well, there's still a fear aspect to derivatives.

Here's a good example. Let's say you buy into automotive securities, and all of a sudden maybe the outlook for Ford and General Motors is different than for Toyota. Maybe these companies can actually go bankrupt. Now maybe they won't, but maybe they will. That fear is addressed, and how is it addressed? By creating special derivatives: default derivatives. Where's the greed? These things are very profitable. You put the fear and the greed together, and there's your answer to new and innovative futures contracts.

The exchanges are moving into those areas. They want to make derivatives that will address the more complicated needs, risks, fears, and profits of the future. You're going to get credit default swaps to guard against corporate defaults. You're going to get weather futures to help hedge global warming. Fear and greed are combined there as well.

There are people in research trying to answer the question: Is the human element really a factor? Billions of dollars are being thrown into the idea that people will buy into things to try to prevent environmental damage. Our man Richard Sandor is ahead of this curve. He is sniffing down the scent of that need. He has created the Chicago Climate Exchange to address exactly those issues. The CCX created a secondary market in pollution rights.

The need for contracts might not be as simple as it was when we had a dearth of products. You know why gold was the big volume leader in the first Iran hostage scenario? Because it was the place where people could go to lay off risk of adverse economic events. The Treasuries were relatively new and did not have the exposure and depth of market they have today. There was the Treasury complex created in 1977, but it took years before the market hit its stride.

Now I think all the easy contracts are done. You're getting into the complicated ones, but it doesn't dismiss their importance. We have new housing contracts coming on board because we all know you can't wake up in the morning without picking up a paper where there's a debate on housing. Is housing going to get better? Is housing going to get worse? There are plenty of new contracts. It's like that old story in the late 1800s when the commissioner of the U.S. Patent Office said, "Everything that can be invented has already been invented."

That certainly doesn't hold true at the CBOT, where new innovations are always popping up. Tell me about some of the best innovations that you've seen.

Well, the Dow contract provided a very exciting time, because there was a lot of competition with many exchanges jumping into the equity index game. The Dow futures contract was very important because it's one of the most recognizable equity measurements. If you stop the average person on the street and say, "What are stocks doing? What do you think of when I ask you this question?" Usually, "The Dow Jones Industrial Average" is the answer.

This is a personal question. What made you walk away from being a trader and become a reporter?

Statistics. Peter Steidlmayer thinking. Bell curves. In the late 1990s, the handwriting was on the wall that people on the floor, commission rates, the dynamics, the money, and the breakdowns were changing. You could see it from the late 1970s. You could just see how much you were paid per contract to be a filling broker, started to come down. Things like give-up fees started to come down. The amount a customer was willing to pay, whether it was retail at the bottom of the chain or the biggest institution or insurance company or pension fund, started to come down. The computer started to make a bigger presence and started to feed on itself.

I looked at it this way: In the late 1990s, my kids were still young, my mortgage was still long, and I needed to work and make some money to take care of business. So I did a quick utility function in my brain, and I thought there's a 70 percent chance that all of this will last a lot longer, and there's a 30 percent chance that my income is going to diminish.

Now 70/30 might not sound bad, but I had to think about it this way. Was I willing to take a 30 percent chance with my family that I would not be able to be the provider I'd been in the past couple of years? Even though I was having a great year in 1997, I decided I wanted to take a different route.

So I decided I wanted to do something that put my knowledge to work. I had learned all about risk and reward firsthand from brilliant, innovative people like Peter Steidlmayer and Richard Sandor. I thought, "How can I leverage my experience and my knowledge into something that involves markets, but doesn't involve being on the commission side or the trading side?" I needed to find an innovative fit with my passion for the industry.

So I thought: Doing charts is my hobby, and watching markets is my hobby, so how could I find a way to stay with the exchanges and not be on the ulcer side of the business? I still needed to profit from it. It was lucky for me that right around that time, financial news started to get a whoosh! And I just grabbed in.

As an analyst, give me an idea of what you think of the futures market from when you started to where it is now?

I can answer that with half sadness and half euphoria. I think the half sadness is: Who would have thought that in really a three-decade span, we'd go from infancy to geriatrics? I mean usually industries last longer, whether it's railroads or automobiles. The longevity going from infancy to old age should last longer. I guess that's the sad part.

I really think I was there, not necessarily from the very beginning, but from the beginning from the standpoint of when the industry was getting traction. I was there when we invented hand signals on the fly. I can honestly say I was part of that. I was there when we created symbols for companies like Refco and Goldman, so you could flash who was buying and who was selling. I was there in the beginning.

I was there when computers weren't allowed. I was there when they first made their way in. To see all of that, thinking, "Hey, I could do this the rest of my life," but then to see that it could be so successful that it morphed and ended up being taken out of the early people's hands—I mean it just did—I guess that's the sad part.

The good part is it's neat to see these exchanges rise to levels that they are at today. I mean back in the 1970s, if you had told somebody that a Board of Trade membership would be worth literally millions and millions of dollars, nobody would have looked at it that way. A membership wasn't an investment. A membership was to get into the best movie in town. That's what it was.

Tell me about a couple of struggles you have witnesses at the CBOT, like the Crash of 1987 and the importance of the Major Market Index (MMI).

You know, this is so neat because even though some people might not admit this anymore, I'm going to admit it, and I'm proud of it. I was with Drexel Burnham Lambert, and in Chicago its futures division was one of the best-run divisions on the planet. We had nothing to do with junk bonds. We had nothing to do with all the issues that eventually worked against Drexel. MMI was another one of these equity contracts that we had, and 1987 of course was the big crash.

For me it was one of the first chapters in rewriting the rules in financial markets that are in place today. When equities crash, Treasuries become a "flight to quality." Every guy running and screaming out of the turnstyle of equities is doing a U-turn and running right into the pits and buying Treasuries. That notion was cemented in 1987.

As for the MMI, legend has it that when the markets were crashing and burning in equities and nobody had a bid, we didn't have that J.P. Morgan type like in 1929. That legend goes that one day J.P. Morgan walked on the floor and said, "I'll buy everything." Now, it didn't last long and the 1929 Crash still happened, but for a couple of days everybody's headaches went away.

The MMI was not J.P. Morgan's presence, but it worked. A big order came into that pit late in the day. Many people, including myself, believe that it was an order that came from one of the Drexel offices that turned the market. It was just at the right time when a bid of any magnitude caused people to stop selling, and it brought a little order back into the market. I'm sure that the order, in terms of size relative to all the selling, was a little eyelash in an ocean, but it was important enough, at that time, to turn the psychology a bit.

So that had a big influence in bringing some order back into the marketplace. It really is a great story, and I was there when it happened. I was in the bond room when everything was going limit up, and everybody was going crazy. Then, when the bonds closed, everybody ran into the room that traded the MMIs. All of a sudden the red started to change, and bids started to come in. That one order just seemed to be at the right time to make a difference.

Can you think of other historical events that affected trading?

Well, it wasn't only the Crash of 1987; it was the minicrash in 1989, and both of those times it was kind of sad. People who had huge positions, and there were some that were legends at that time, not necessarily the ones I mentioned, but people who would carry inventories that would give me goosebumps to think, "Oh, my God! How could you sleep at night?"

When you have those kinds of shocks to the system, no matter how smart you are, your inventory has issues. You see grown men and women on the steps of the pits crying. I mean it really affected me to see the devastation of people who were at the top of the pyramid, that you aspired to be like, both from a trading aspect and let's be honest here, from a financial aspect. I wish that my bank account looked like their bank accounts. These people were devastated. Many of them lost good chunks of their fortunes. Some of them never came back, and if they did, they never, ever carried inventories again of the same magnitude. It was really earth-shattering.

The other thing I remember is the space shuttle *Challenger* in 1986. I mean it was so weird. We were all on the trading floor, and remember, this was before CNBC and CNN. We used to watch the wires come across. I remember it was one of the first times, maybe the only time, that trading completely stopped! And not because it was a moment of silence, like when President Reagan died. The floor has had respectful moments of silence, but then they passed.

In the case of the *Challenger*, the floor saw the headline that it had it exploded on takeoff, and there wasn't a sound on the trading floor. It was the eeriest thing, and that really left an impression on me. You know, I'm old enough to remember when JFK was assassinated. I can remember where I was, who I talked to, and having that really weird feeling. It was the same kind of feeling that day. I can remember that same dynamic happening and how horrible it was.

In 1997, you had the Thai baht currency Asian scenario that unfolded. The markets were very volatile. It also brings in the new aspect of night trading. Night trading evolved in the 1980s, and I was right there. I used to sometimes double shift it. I would work all day on the floors, and then come back at night. A lot of these issues, like the crashes, had night sessions. It brought a whole new dimension to trading, and I think those were times that we remember.

Tell me about some of the 'firsts' you have seen.

I remember the first night session like it was yesterday. It was really quite revolutionary. I remember the first Project A trade. Project A made the Chicago Board of Trade a pioneer in electronic trading. I've used the word 'ironic' many times, but it's ironic the way things worked out. The Board of Trade doesn't have its own electronic platform. Now it has great partnerships, and they of course have their products on Liffe Connect, but the Board of Trade was there first and actually thought about the need for an electronic matching before anyone. For various reasons that we don't have enough time to discuss, it got away from them.

Can you give me your view of the IPO?

I think that the IPO was just a tremendous thing, because you can't have the former type of management hierarchy and all the committees, and have the kind of immediacy and decision making that this institution needs. As I said, this was a little business that many never thought would get global, but as it started to get global, it kind of grew out of its own structure.

I know from personal experience, because I served as a member on millions of committees, that the joke was that in the 1980s and 1990s we were on committees because they had great lunches. I think that to some extent, for some people, that was true. You went to the committee, and they gave you great food, and you were with your buddies, and you tried to talk about new products and whatnot, but it was a very social type of arrangement.

As exchanges and products became more complicated, competition became stiffer, and the stakes became higher, you had to move to the type of structure that would allow a certain type of leadership to take the reins and lead the institution into the next field of competition.

So I think the IPO and the demutualization, moving from a not-for-profit to a for-profit, was an essential chapter. It was a hard-fought bit of ground to get there. There was a lot of inertia. You're talking about asking the same people who are going to get displaced eventually to make a decision that will ultimately be the very end of their own profession. To see floor traders, and traders who were agriculturally bound, making the decision to allow the computer to become central to their business was very tough. There was a real tug-of-war there between what's best for you and what's best for the institution.

The IPO was a great thing. It unleashed vast amounts of wealth and efficiency that had to be done, but it was a tough chapter for the CBOT. It was also a testament to the backbone of the exchange. They made it through a very tough chapter, and they came out with flying colors.

Where do you think the CBOT stock is headed?

It's going to go north. I can't throw a number on it. I think that derivatives are still in their infancy. I think there are years and years and years of new products and new synergies ahead. Just as we were amazed at the rise in value of memberships, having thought in the 1970s that they would never be worth millions, I think that the stock could be worth thousands per share and have many splits. I think in 25 years we'll look back and see that it's very cheap today, because so much is yet to happen in the industry.

Please talk about the relationship of the Chicago Board of Trade to the city of Chicago, and vice versa.

Well, the city of Chicago has a very mutually beneficial arrangement with the exchanges. We have great people in Chicago; you have great hiring by the exchanges. They really exemplify, supplement, and complement each other. I think the shift from people to computers was a bit nerve-racking, because there are a lot of cottage industries, whether it's people who print trading cards, people who put out charts, or people at telecom restaurants; but I think that what we've found is the IT personnel are making up for what we're losing in the pits, and both move on.

How do you feel about the merger of the two Chicago exchanges?

Listen, I'll go on record. There is no better, more interesting feud than the Hatfields and the McCoys. Our personal version is the CME and the Chicago Board of Trade. I think the merger of these two exchanges is destined to be a success. In my opinion, maybe someday they'll look at their struggles to make this merger happen and laugh. Why? Because they complement each other so well. People identify with each other. People have worked at both exchanges. It's an absolute natural.

CHAPTER 19

From Football to the Floor

George E. Seals

Born on October 2, 1942, in Higginsville, Missouri, just east of Kansas City, George Seals was the third youngest of 10 children. At Higginsville High School, he lettered in football and track. He was also vice president of the student council, treasurer of the senior class, and vice president of the Letterman Club. He was a natural leader among his peers.

While attending the University of Missouri, Mr. Seals majored in social work and also played football on his college team. In 1964, he was drafted out of college by the New York Giants. He was later traded in the Sam Huff deal to the Washington Redskins. His career with the Redskins was short-lived. He had a fight with one of the players and just walked out of camp. George describes this as an act of "youthful idealism."

Thinking his pro football days were over, George was considering a stint in the Peace Corps, when Abe Gibron from the Chicago Bears called him and offered him a job. Although he played for the Bears for six years, with tremendous athletic success, George retired from the sport on two different occasions. He had many different conflicts with the Bears' front office. On one occasion, he represented himself in a contract dispute. These disputes cost him both time and money.

Rather than having his fines go back into the coffers of the football organization, he negotiated for the funds to be sent to various civil rights groups. Among those were the Urban League and Operation PUSH. During this time he forged a friendship with the Reverend Jesse Jackson. Although his career in football often left him feeling angry and disillusioned, his commitment to those causes was invigorating.

In 1971, George was doing some charity work with the Better Boys Foundation. Through his volunteer work, he met Henry Shatkin, who was a member of the Chicago Board of Trade. Henry offered George an opportunity to come to the CBOT. Although he knew very little about the workings of the exchange, the idea of trading was appealing to him. He liked the excitement and the challenges that life on the floor offered him. He also liked the idea of a career post football.

The years 1972 and 1973 were important for George Seals. He signed with the Kansas City Chiefs in 1971 and bought a membership at the CBOT in 1973. He did both jobs for almost a year before retiring from his football career. He became a full-time local, trading mostly in the soybean pit but exploring other financial opportunities as well.

Being the first African-American member of the exchange was not an easy task. His early days were checkered with both cheers and jeers. Many of his colleagues were eager to lend him a hand and to guide him toward success. Many others were not happy with his presence at the exchange. They tried to run defense against his attempts to find a permanent place on the exchange floor. Determined not to let any of the negative issues stop him from achieving his goals, George created a successful career at the Chicago Board of Trade.

Thirty-four years later, George Seals is still a member of the exchange. Among his achievements was opening the door for many other minorities to find active, fulfilling lives at the CBOT. He is one of many athletes who have called on the exchange to provide them with a second career. His reputation in the industry is regarded with great respect. Since he stopped trading on the floor in 1998, George and his wife of 14 years have been living in Coronado, California.

After competing all his life in the football arena and the pits of the CBOT, Mr. Seals feels lucky now to be competing only with himself. It is a blessing for him to spend time with his family and friends. He is active in the Coronado Round Table, National Football League (NFL) Alumni Association, and National Football League Players Association. He also is an active member of the Harbor Presbyterian Church.

George is the proud father of three sons and six grandchildren.

****

How did you hear about the Board of Trade?

I remember that specifically. It was during my pro football days. I was at practice on the tackling sled and my line coach, Abe Gibron, said, "Seals, you ought to buy some pork bellies." Of course, I'd never heard of pork bellies. After practice, we talked about it. Abe said, "I do this every year before Memorial Day. I buy pork bellies and I keep them. Then, just before the holidays, when everybody is barbecuing, I sell them." That planted the seed in my mind. It introduced me to the idea of trading futures at the Chicago Board of Trade.

At the time, I was active with the Better Boys Foundation. The Foundation used to have an annual dinner where they would make awards to the statistical leaders of the NFL. It really turned out to be a huge thing, like the Academy Awards of Sports. There was a big dinner at the end of the season every year. At the time, Hank Shatkin was on the board of the Better Boys Foundation. So I knew who he was.

I was on a plane returning from the Super Bowl in Miami, the Jets versus the Colts. I saw Hank on the plane, introduced myself, and asked if he could tell me about pork bellies. He said, "Pork bellies? If I were you, I'd buy soybeans." That was during the "great grain robbery." It was a time when the Russians were buying wheat and, of course, there is that relationship between all the grains—wheat, corn, beans, and so on.

As soon as I could, I bought some soybean futures. Hank called me two or three weeks later. He said, "What do you want me to do with your profits?" And I said, "What do you mean?" He said, "You've doubled your money." I thought, "What is this? Maybe I just caught a good one. What is this Board of Trade about?" I discussed it with Hank, and he said maybe I ought to come down and take a look at it. This all happened about my eighth year in the NFL.

That's about the time in football players' careers when athletes become obsessed with making the transition from pro football into whatever they're going to be for the rest of their lives. I was a personnel counselor at Spiegel's at the time and that wasn't going too well for me.

At any rate, I came down and saw the floor. This was the early 1970s. I saw all the traders had these jackets on, and it was a kind of uniform-like look. I was active in the Civil Rights Movement at that time. I had the big Afro. I said, "Hank, I don't see any brothers with these jackets on, man. What's the deal here?" He turned a little red, and he didn't comment on that much. So we left it at that. And lo and behold, maybe it was a year or so later, I got a call from him.

He asked, "Are you still interested in the Board of Trade?" Even though I still didn't know anything about it, except from that one visit, I said, "Yeah." He told me there was a seat available and I said, "What do you mean, a 'seat'?" He explained it to me and it sounded interesting. Then he told me what it cost. At the time, $40,000 was the highest price ever paid for a seat; it was February 21, 1973, I believe. I asked him, "What kind of seat is it that costs that much?" I truly didn't know anything about it. To make a long story short, I told him I was interested.

Hank helped me through the process. I needed two sponsors to vouch for my integrity. I needed to take an exam. More important, I think, I needed to have the money. Basically, I bought a seat not knowing anything about futures trading. The Board of Trade had just created the Chicago Board Options Exchange, and they were offering those seats as a premium to guys who bought a full membership. After I bought my seat, I had only 10 grand left, but I bought that seat, too. So now I'm broke and I have two seats that I don't know anything about.

Tell me about your first day on the floor as a member.

I bet everybody remembers their first day down there. For me, I stepped from one arena to another. The difference is that I didn't know anything about this arena. Sure, there were people telling me, "You do the bid and offer." I didn't even know what "the bid and offer" was.

So here I was, standing in the pit. I was this big old guy, and by nature I'm self-conscious. I'm from a small town in Missouri. I'm here with all of these people, and I just keep thinking, "What am I doing here?" But I'm also broke, so I have got to learn this stuff. Being broke is a pretty good motivator.

I'd heard about how to "project" this outcry. I'd watched other traders. It took me a while to get up the nerve to talk out loud. Finally I get up the courage, and this little voice comes out. I am squeaking, "I want to sell five." Of course you think everybody's looking at you. I was so humiliated. I'll never forget it.

Obviously, I got better at it. For me, it was a whole new place with so much to learn. I still continued to play pro football, but now I could see an opportunity for my future. I would ask myself, do I want to play football for 15 years, or do I want to play 10 years and then step out and learn this business? Now I had some options.

How long did it take for you to make the transition from football to the floor?

It didn't take long, because at the end of my tenth year, I signed a three-year contract with the Chiefs to continue playing. Now I'm thinking, I've played 10 years already. How do you judge a pro? I mean most guys usually try to play five years. I think the average career is four and a half years. But I played 10. I didn't think there was anything to prove. I received some recognition. I knew that I could play with the best. So I just decided not to play anymore.

Most guys call a press conference and announce their retirement. I did call my new coach, Hank Stram, and said, "Hey, I hope I'm not putting you in a jam, but I think I'm going to retire and concentrate on this business." He was very supportive of that decision. That was 34 years ago and I am still here.

How did your family react to that decision?

I don't know whether they really understood it that much. What I do know is, I felt a lot of pressure and stress. I had just bought a house in the South Shore area of Chicago, and I had three boys. I'm thinking, "Golly, I've got to make this work, because I am the breadwinner." That was pretty good motivation.

Who acted as a mentor to you?

Over the years, talking with people about my career at the CBOT, I would always refer to Hank Shatkin as my mentor. For some reason, he doesn't like to get any recognition. Sometimes I don't even refer to him as Shatkin. He's "Shanklin" to me. If he doesn't want me to talk about him, okay. But golly, he's got a great big old office, with a big old, wide desk, and he's a very nice-looking man. But his door was always open.

As a matter of fact, when I started trading, I would come down and sit in his office before the open. He had this big book on his desk. He knew whether you were a winner or a loser. And he would say to me, "Winner?" He could just tell if you were a winner or not, if you were doing the right things. For example, if I made a little bit more money than I should, he knew that I was speculating and he would tell me, "You know you can't do that." He was a great spreader with huge numbers and he tried to teach me that skill, but I couldn't spread. He is just a fabulous, fabulous person. He may have started as my sponsor, but he has always been a true friend.

Tell me about the role of integrity down at the Board of Trade.

When you talk about the integrity of our marketplace, you are talking about something essential to its tradition and its character. The history of the exchange, I think, goes back to around 1848. It's important to remember all of the people who preceded you, and the integrity it has taken to preserve this institution for so many years. In a sense, it's like sports. I want guys with character on my team. Well, it's the same with the Board of Trade.

What happens with outtrades is a matter of honor and integrity. The word gets around pretty quick if a guy is not facing up to the outtrades. Think of it this way: You can have a great day and come in the next day and they say you're out five beans with Bob X and the market is down the limit. Yesterday is wiped out with a mistake made by you and whoever you did this transaction with. So you have to split this loss. That's really a tough part of the business, because you don't know until that next morning if everything cleared and you're even.

So my point is you're dealing with people. And if these people are not honorable, of the highest character and integrity, that word gets around pretty quickly. It's a very, very important part of our business. I think most of the people down at the Board of Trade have unquestionable integrity and character.

When you first came down, did people trade with you?

Actually, people were very, very kind because everybody started the same way. They would come up to me and say, "I'll buy five from you." Hank had warned me what to look for and what to be careful of. He told me to watch out for some of these guys. I said, "Oh, no. I'm all right. They were just trying to get me involved in the market, to open me up to start the process." It's the same as learning to swim; you've got to get in the water. Over the years, I saw many people standing around, not saying anything, because they were intimidated. Those people didn't do well. Hank showed me the way, and I am grateful for his advice.

Did you ever get intimidated by the market?

Intimidated by the markets or by someone?

Let's take both of those questions.

The market is very intimidating. It's really hard to explain. It is constantly moving around. They say you should never look at the trades in terms of money. But when you're broke, I'm thinking, God, if I jump in there and this thing is flying around and I'm wrong, it's going to cost me. But that's kind of fair; I mean there is no discrimination. And you've got to respect that. It's a very humbling experience.

At the CBOT, there's intimidation where individuals are concerned, too. It's a little different from football. Here there are some little guys who trade huge numbers, and their egos precede them. They might see me as this big dumb jock standing there in front of them. Maybe I look like I am trying to block what they want to do. It is something that takes getting used to. They will run over you with numbers.

The way things are played in the pit is very different from the football field. You can't respond physically. Coming from my background, that was very frustrating. Here's where my mentor, "Shanklin," comes in again. He taught me you can't afford to lose your cool here, because that would really be bad. I did all right over the years dealing with those big egos. I was familiar with those attitudes in both of my professions.

How about the responsibility of being the first African-American man on the floor? Did you feel any pressure?

I'd like to say no, but absolutely I did. I didn't know how much responsibility it was at the time. Being in the middle of something, you don't always see the big picture. I did feel a responsibility. My coming to the floor happened right after the height of the Civil Rights Movement. To come down here, buy a seat, and learn the business, everybody had to go through some type of learning process. I don't mean to pat myself on the back, but I was aware of who I was. I wanted to persevere, learn the business as best I could, and be well represented.

How did people treat you?

When it comes to trading, I prefer to think someone didn't give me that trade because he didn't see me, rather than he didn't give me that trade because I was black. There's a thousand other reasons someone might have for not trading with me. I just said, "Well, it couldn't be because of my color." Sometimes I got a pretty good chuckle about that.

There are lots of different groups at the CBOT. Did you find that you weren't the only minority?

It was kind of a microcosm of the city. In the soybean pit, it's really interesting because there would be fences, if you will. There's a group of Italians. There's the Irish. There are the Jewish guys. Before the bell rings, signifying the opening of the market, guys are all talking. It's the first place where I can remember guys coming up to me and talking about "the Jews." Before that, I thought it was just black people who were usually the butt ends of conversations. It was really interesting in that respect. So, it wasn't just about black people. I don't know what they said about me, but I can imagine.

When you bring all these different groups together, there can be challenges in the pit. That's why the self-regulatory aspect is so important. What is your take on this oversight group?

There are so many unique things about the Board of Trade. Because of the transparency of the markets, what better person to have regulating the disputes than someone who has already been there, trading over the years, who is familiar with the rules? They will know the business far better than a politician. I shudder to think what would happen if we had politicians dishing out punishments or someone who is not familiar with the rules.

There are all kinds of things going on in the market every day, and most people outside of the exchange don't even have a clue how they operate. I think that the Board of Trade has just done very well with members making up these committees and doling out the punishment or judgments on fellow traders. They do a great job with that.

Did you ever come in contact with any of the committees?

Yes, I did. I had a little confrontation. Actually, to me it wasn't so small. It happened during a lull in the grain room, where all of the grains are traded. There was not much going on. I was having a hard time making a living. I had three kids at three different universities, and book fees and tuition were due. It was a rough time.

I knew that there was more activity going on in the bond room. At first I didn't want to go there, because you get comfortable in your pit, which you shouldn't do. It was old "Shanklin" again who said, "You should be trading in the bond room. There are guys making tons of money and you're standing in the grains doing nothing." Finally I just had to go over there, and my goodness gracious, all hell broke loose.

I remember quite well; it seems like yesterday. I didn't understand the culture of that room. The traders were up in the coffee shop, and in the pit they had left their trading cards lying on the floor. This was supposed to indicate that Joe Blow is standing there and Willie Public is over here. So, I'm standing there and nobody's in the pit. I scouted the pit because I wanted to get there and get a spot.

I'm what you call a scalper. I need to be by a broker, a buyer and a seller broker, who's dispensing these orders. I feed off of that, buying and selling. These guys, they already had their little positions in the pit, just by putting their cards on the steps. I couldn't honor that, because as I understood the rules, you had to be there physically. It had always been first come, first served.

So I'm standing in the spot I have chosen. Then they come down from the coffee shop and one of them is saying, "What are you doing here? I've been standing here for umpteen years." Before I know it, it's not just this guy talking. There are cliques that have been formed in that pit. It quickly becomes an ugly situation, and it went on for weeks.

Coming from the football arena, I'm used to contact. But you see this little bitty guy coming up in your face and it's almost like they were trying to antagonize me to lose it, because then I'm up a creek. But I knew what they were trying to do and I had to stay within myself. It was a very, very difficult time. There was a lot of physical contact. There was a lot of name-calling. It was really, really ugly. I had one of my sons working down there at the time, who saw all of this. Of course we talk about it now, but after that incident none of them wanted any part of the Board of Trade. They had witnessed an ugly situation.

In the end, it worked out. We had to appear before a committee. We had to get attorneys, and eventually the situation was resolved. Everybody was fined. It was a costly resolution, both economically and emotionally. There are some scars for sure, but athletes by training are not quitters. I was going to see it through to the end. I don't know whether they realized that, but as it turned out, it was something bigger than all of us. If there was anything positive to be said of that experience, I met a lot of good people and made a lot of friends.

Did you stay in the bond pit?

I was there for a while trading the bond market. When the soybeans picked up, I went back to that pit. But I had accomplished my objective of continuing to make a living during a slow time in the grains.

You said you were a scalper. Can you explain what that is?

As a scalper, I'm in and out of the market hundreds of times during the day for the quarter, the half or the penny profit. This is different from a speculator, a chartist or a gambler. We don't like to use that term "gambler". As a scalper, I have limited my exposure to the market.

If I didn't scalp, I would have more of a risk factor by taking positions. I tried other ways of trading and I didn't do them well. It was not very comfortable for me. I am comfortable doing all the buying and selling during the day. I like knowing that I am even when I go home.

You said you don't like the term 'gambler'.

Gamblers don't do well at the CBOT. Now, the sharp speculators do very well, because they take big positions. They have a stomach for the market, and when they're wrong, just like I do with my small numbers, they know when to get out. Gamblers, on the other hand, don't know when to stop. It's an addiction and they don't usually last long. Frankly, I don't know of any gamblers at the exchange.

How about the big traders that you knew, like Julius Frankel?

When I first came down there, I think we all called him Uncle Julius. He was already in his 80s. He was all over the place. I remember him as a very warm, kind, gentle man, who came up to me and said, "You'll do all right. Don't you let them get to you." He'll never know how much that meant to me. I would see him every day and he always had nice words for me. I appreciated that so much.

Little did I know this old man was one of the biggest and best traders down there. He would just chide me in his German accent, saying, "You go over there and trade. You go ahead and buy something." A couple of times, I was so intimidated, I just kind of stopped trading. And he saw that and he would come over and encourage me, saying, "You can do this. You go on over there." And even though I was uncomfortable, I would get up my nerve and do it. He is no longer with us, but I remember him as a wonderful man. I really enjoyed being around him.

Who were some of the interesting people to watch at the CBOT?

There was a man they called "The Judge." He was probably as old as Julius. He had this booming voice. If you saw him, you wouldn't put that voice with the little man. What I enjoyed most about him were his stories. He delighted in telling me tales about his years on the exchange and the exploits of the traders that he knew.

How about some of the living legends that you knew?

Les Rosenthal would certainly fall into that category. Anytime he would walk in the pit, you watched what he was doing because he was just brilliant. You already know how much I admire and appreciate Hank Shatkin. Then there were classy acts like Red Rose and Lee Stern. I mean those guys were clean when they walked in the pit. When I say "clean," I think about the word "integrity". All of the men I mentioned did everything aboveboard. They were role models. I watched them all the time. They showed me the right way to do business.

The CBOT plays the role as the worldwide price discovery mechanism. Why is that important?

I shudder to think what would happen if we didn't have the Board of Trade, especially today with all the technology, machines and volatility of the marketplace. All of this information comes in for everybody to share equally. It comes down to the net total of one person who ultimately decides whether to buy or sell. It does a great job of that.

What does it do for the farmers?

It serves as a great hedging tool. I'm from the country, but a lot of the farmers from where I'm from feel like we don't know anything about wheat. They feel they know the crops better because they are planting them and caring for them and harvesting them. I believe in some sense that is true. I can understand that. But I think the sophisticated farmers are using the Board of Trade as a hedging tool now more than they did early on.

What was the first lesson that you learned at the CBOT?

The first lesson I ever learned down at the Board of Trade was taking your first loss. I know that sounds so simple, but it's really very difficult, because you get in the market, whether you're long or short, for a specific reason. You have to believe that when you place the trade you think you are right. By nature, it's hard to admit that you were wrong. As a trader, you've got to admit the mistake fast, because it could hurt you financially. That was one of the most difficult things I had to learn, but I did learn it very, very well.

They say in the first couple of years, you shouldn't try to make money. You should strive to just break even, meaning you know how to trade so well that you're trading the markets by taking your losses. I think that's an important foundation to have. Trading is a talent that you learn from years of experience. You can apply your skill to any of the markets. It has worked out well for me.

What did Hank Shatkin teach you?

He was a big proponent of taking that first loss, because it was important to admit to yourself that you didn't know what the market was going to do. With all of the brilliant people that we have down there, everybody's got an opinion on what the market is going to do. But at the end of the day, probably more than half of those people were losers.

It's kind of humbling to say, "Hey, I don't know anything about this. I'm just going to trade whatever the markets give. I don't have anything predetermined." I know a lot of guys who come in with an idea of how much money they want to make on a given day. I just went down there to make money and to do the bid and the offer. If it turned out I didn't make anything, really I did, because at the end of the day I hadn't lost anything. It's important to never give up the edge.

Tell me about the expression "My word is my bond."

That goes back to the integrity of the marketplace. You've got all these guys down there and you're doing all of these transactions, buying and selling all of this stuff, and there's mass pandemonium going on around you. Most of the time the orders match up, but sometimes there are outtrades.

The next day you go up to a guy and say, "Hey, we're out 25 beans and the market is 25 cents lower." And he says, "What? I didn't do anything with you." Well, the rules say that guy has to split that trade with me. So you've got to have some stand-up people and, of course, that's why integrity has been perpetuated. They've had many, many good people to keep that tradition going.

How about innovation in the business? What role does that play?

Innovation enhances the marketplace. With all the technology and the machines that we have now, and with all of this information, it's made the markets more dynamic. We used to think that only the big brokerage houses would be doing all of this business. Today, a small, sophisticated trader has all these markets open to him. It has given traders the opportunity to compete with everybody else in the market. Truly innovation has been the key.

Do you think technology has changed your business?

Absolutely. It has become a world market. One can trade 24/7. The Chicago Board of Trade has been an innovator in this process.

Can you comment on the impact of the creation of the CBOE?

As I recall, it was so new and it had such an impact that we didn't have the personnel to run it. They brought guys in from New York to run that exchange. At that time, the grains were real busy.

It's like you asked me, did I continue to trade the bond market? I said no, because I'm really a bean trader. I could look over at the bond market and see that market was huge, but I was more satisfied or content where I was and where I had been. I think a lot of CBOT members felt the same way. As a result, the CBOE took on a life of its own.

Can you comment about what's going on between the CBOT and the CBOE?

When I bought my CBOT seat, the exercise right was very important because it enabled one to trade both markets with a full membership. This privilege made it possible for many of the CBOE seats to belong to the CBOT members. So much of this controversy is over that right or privilege. I do know that the CBOE has been a tremendous success.

What about interest rate futures?

That was a huge market. I remember the "locals", guys like me who trade for themselves, would go into the pits to provide liquidity for new markets to get them going. People would look at the volume and see what was happening, and that created interest in trading those markets. Chicago, with the two big exchanges, had financial institutions worldwide using the Chicago marketplaces' instruments as hedging tools. This really propelled the exchange forward as a worldwide marketplace.

What's the significance of commodity derivative options trading?

Today, you hear that term "derivatives" a lot. But what I think has happened is that you've got the machines with the technology and the information. This has opened the market up and made it much easier and cheaper for smaller traders to participate, because there are so many derivatives involved and they can crunch all of that information. It used to be that markets were only for the big guy or the big institutions, but in terms of the world, it's made a more dynamic market for everyone to participate in.

With this dynamic market, do you think we're still going to be able to provide great service to the customers of the exchange?

You know, so far, so good. The CBOT has done a wonderful job of providing the best service for its customers. I think that is one of the things that is unique about the exchange. They always manage to do a great job for the customer. Of course, integrity remains very important.

Why do you think the exchange is unique to the profession?

I think that our commodity markets, combined with our insistence on integrity, make us unique in the business world. We're talking about a business that's 160 years old, where your word is your bond. Now, I grant you, we have computers, but there are still people behind these computers. Even with all the technological changes that have occurred since the exchange opened it doors, it is still working out well.

When you traded, what historical events affected trading?

One event that I remember is the *Mayagüez* incident. It was a really dull day in the market. I was just standing around and talking to my buddies. We were all waiting for something to happen.

Suddenly the market just trembled like an earthquake. It was like a tremendous jerk and it just took off. And I said, "What the heck is going on here?" And of course people were running to the Reuters news machines. They reported that one of our U.S. container ships, the *Mayagüez*, had been seized by the Khmer Rouge. It was the last official act of the Vietnam War. So it was really kind of hairy. I didn't trade much at that time. I just watched the market. Sometimes it's better to take a wait-and-see position and let things settle down.

Do you remember anything about the grain embargo?

Not really, except for the volatility of the market. We like all of these controversies. Usually what's bad for the world is good for us, because it's an opportunity to jump in that market and make some money.

How about the silver scandal?

That event was a little closer for me. After I'd played out my option with the Bears, I signed with the Kansas City Chiefs. I'd heard about the team's owner Lamar Hunt and what a classy organization the Chiefs were. While trading at the CBOT I also heard a great deal about his brother, Bunker Hunt, attempting to corner the world's silver market. At first, he had a huge effect on the market, but in the end, didn't succeed.

Do you think there will be a place for floor trading in the future?

I think the future is probably on the computer screen. You know, you just have to look at your grandkids and your kids and all of these computer games that they have, and how efficient they are with the little TV games. Then you look at computer trading; these markets are going to be open 24/7. I think it's just unreal. I would be more concerned about the health of people who choose to do this, because some guys are trading day and night. Maybe I've gotten old, but I don't see how they do it.

Do you remember your last day in the pit?

Not really, because it wasn't a big deal. I'd had enough of Chicago winters and had some knee problems. I knew I wanted to make a change. It was sort of like the end of my pro football career. I didn't call a press conference to announce my retirement. Once I had decided I'd had enough, I just walked away.

That's how it was on my last day in the pit. I had decided that it was probably best to go somewhere warm and let my old body absorb some sunshine. So that's what I did. Until this morning, I hadn't been back for a very long time. Coming down here today was very exciting. It made me remember how I used to feel coming into the building.

Every morning that I used to come down here, coming down that drive, it was like a kickoff. Every day was like a Super Bowl. Of course that kind of emotion and anxiety probably takes its toll on you. But I really have enjoyed the experience.

Do you like the idea of the CBOT merging with the CME?

These are very exciting times. I mean who would have thought this was possible years ago? So much has happened, and it's all good. I'm anxious to see the future with these two exchanges working together.

What would you tell someone interested in trading at the CBOT?

It's probably the most exciting business in the world, and I say that sincerely. My ignorance of the inner workings of the business when I bought my seat was a blessing in disguise. I didn't have enough sense to be frightened of what I was getting into. Now, years later and looking back on my experience, I am grateful for having had this opportunity.

Some of these guys that I worked with at the Chicago Board of Trade have become my lifelong friends. We've run with the bulls in Spain. We've rafted down the Colorado River. We've climbed mountains. But in addition to competing with these guys both on and off the floor and learning so much from them, for me it was an intimate, safe setting to learn about different minorities.

The Board has been a wonderful adventure. How special it has been to have my own business as an independent local. There's nothing like it in the world. When you want to get away, you can just go whenever and wherever you choose. You don't have to ask for permission. You don't have to find someone to cover for you in your absence. And the potential for making money is comparable to someone in the major leagues. There are many guys who could be right up there with some of the top corporations in the world. So it's just been a great adventure. It's always absolutely, unequivocally exciting every day.

Has that excitement attracted many other athletes to the CBOT?

That's interesting for me to think about, because when I first came down, I don't think I saw the connection. I didn't know enough. Now I see a definite relationship between the athlete and the market. I clearly see a very common thread between the action on the floor and the action on the field, and that can be described with the word "discipline". It is a crucial element to success in both businesses.

In times of making quick decisions, reacting to a given situation without thinking, we have some decided advantages having been pro athletes. We are able to think on our feet and execute, and that's huge.

Another advantage is our size. Of course, you can't manhandle people and be physical, but you can use that big body to shield people out of the way or use your size so they can't see around you. There are all kinds of little tricks. It's a natural business for athletes.

I was told the Board of Trade would have you and other celebrity traders represent the exchange at public events. Is that true?

From time to time, they would ask us to do things for the CBOT. They might want us to be part of a funeral contingent. One time they sent me to the "Farm in the Zoo" at Lincoln Park, and asked me to hold a pig. They thought it would be a natural "pigskin" for a football player, but I was a little skittish of the animals.

I didn't mind using my pro football career to promote the CBOT, and I know that other athletes were fine representatives as well. There was Virgil Carter, who was a Bears quarterback, and Tom Boerwinkle, who was a Bulls center. Also, there was Matt Suhey, who played for the Super Bowl Bears; Ken Gorgal of the Bears way back in the old days. Johnny Musso, the Italian stallion, was a bond trader. There were former Cubs George Altman and Glenn Beckert. A lot of athletes were here, probably many more since I retired. I like to think that's a good sign. Maybe in some small way, I helped to lead the way.

Do you think you have left a legacy with the Board of Trade?

Although it is very kind of you to ask, no, I do not. I enjoyed my experience almost every day. It's hard to believe I have spent 34 years as a member. I used to hear my folks talk about time flying by, and they were sure right. I can't believe that kind of time has gone by. But I'm very proud to have had the opportunity to be a part of the CBOT.

CHAPTER 20

My Word Is My Bond

Lee B. Stern

Lee B. Stern is a native of Chicago. After graduating from Senn High school, he attended the University of Illinois for one semester in 1945, before leaving to serve in the U.S. Army Air Force from 1945 to 1947. After returning from the service, he finished his studies at Roosevelt University.

Mr. Stern, president of LBS Limited Partnership, a member firm of the Chicago Board of Trade, has been active in the commodity industry since joining the CBOT as a member in 1949. He is a former director of the exchange and has served as chairman of the Floor Governors, Public Relations, and New Products committees. Mr. Stern was a member of the Chicago Mercantile Exchange from 1963 to 1998, as well as being a former member of the Commodity Exchange of New York.

Lee B. Stern is best known in the sports world as the founder and sole owner of the Chicago Sting soccer team, which won the North American Soccer League Championship in 1981 and 1984. He served as chairman of the Executive Committee of the North American Soccer League and the Major Indoor Soccer League. As a charter member of the World Cup Founders Club, as well as the City of Chicago 1994 World Cup Host Committee, he was active in helping to bring the event to Chicago.

At present, Lee is a member of the Corporate General Partnership of the Chicago White Sox; he has served as an owner and director since 1976 with both the Bill Veeck and Jerry Reinsdorf groups. He was elected to the Chicago Sports Hall of Fame, the Chicago Jewish Sports Hall of Fame, and the Illinois Soccer Hall of Fame. He was also selected as Father of the Year by the Chicago Father's Day Council. He was inducted into the National Soccer Hall of Fame in 2003 and currently serves as a director for the organization.

He has participated in many civic and charitable activities. Among them are the Museum of Contemporary Art in Chicago, the U.S. Holocaust Museum in Washington, D.C. and the Simon Wiesenthal Center in Los Angeles. The Stern family was instrumental in financing the lighting of the famous Picasso sculpture at Daley Plaza. Lee has been very active with the Friends of the Israel Defense Forces and was honored with their Yonatan Netanyahu Award for distinguished service.

Mr. Stern has been married to his wife Norma for 56 years. Their family includes son Jeff and his wife Linda, son Dan and his wife Robin, daughter January, son Kenny and his wife Uli, and 10 grandchildren.

****

How did you first hear about the Chicago Board of Trade?

When I was in grade school, we used to go on field trips. I went to Swift School, and among the field trips was the Board of Trade. I also visited it once or twice while I was attending Senn High School. They took us there on field trips, too. I had also heard about it from a gentleman who lived in the building above where my cousin lived, and he was a member of the Board of Trade. So I knew about the exchange, but truly very few people knew about the Chicago Board of Trade.

Do you remember what they told you about the exchange on those field trips? Why did they bring you there?

I guess they felt it was an important part of Chicago lore, and it certainly was part of the economic arena of the city of Chicago. I guess that's probably one of the reasons. It was one of the important places that represented the strength of our city.

How did you get involved with the CBOT?

You know, it was sort of an accident. After being discharged from the Air Force in 1947, my first job was with the Chicago Cubs. I worked in their front office as an administrative assistant. That job lasted only about six months before I decided to go back to school. I chose Roosevelt University because of its convenient location.

Having just gotten back from serving my country, and being a young man, I registered for late courses that didn't start until 1:45 P.M. I wanted to enjoy my newfound freedom from service and work, and that afternoon time sounded like a good starting time to go to school.

One day I was walking out of the student lounge, which was next door to the employment bureau, and I happened to see a sign: "Wanted: Runners at the Board of Trade, 9:15 A.M. to 1:30 P.M., $25 a week." That sounded pretty good, because in those days, I'm talking about 1947, $25 a week was a good amount of money, especially for those hours. We were getting $75 a month under the GI bill. If I added that to the $100 a month from the CBOT, I would be making $175 a month, and that was a lot of money. You could take your girlfriend out on the streetcar and go to a movie or have a hamburger someplace. I think pizza places were just coming into vogue in those days. So it just clicked. But had the employment bureau not been next to the student lounge, we wouldn't be talking about my career at the exchange.

So you got hired as a runner. What was it like on the floor?

I saw a lot of action. I looked at what was going on and it didn't take long before I understood what was happening. But I wanted to learn as much as I could, so I took a course that they taught here about the grain markets. It was an exciting place to see and even more exciting to feel like I was a part of it.

When I was a runner, I worked for Merrill Lynch. Initially I was one of about 10 runners on their bench. However, after only three or four months, I was the only regular left. So I decided I should go in and see if I could get a raise. I figured they would view me as a loyal employee.

My brief meeting was with a company man whose name, incidentally, was Mr. Stern. He was the manager of Merrill Lynch at the time. I gave him my pitch and he said, "Well, Lee, we appreciate your loyalty, but our runners get $25 a week. That's what they get." So with that I walked out. I said, "Thank you," and I went to find a different job.

I ended up finding a job with Clement Curtis; later the phone clerk there was handling another company, Shearson Hammill. So I was paid extra. Now instead of getting $25 a week, I was getting about $40 a week. Upgraded, right? And from that point on I made up my mind that there were good opportunities here for me. This was where I was going to make my living.

What made you want to buy a membership on this exchange?

First of all, this was the only exchange you even knew about. The Chicago Mercantile Exchange was just a small pork belly exchange at the time. And I thought it was an opportunity. I just liked it. It was something exciting and something that I felt could lead to bigger and better things. It felt right to me.

I was very fortunate to have had a couple of members at the exchange who took a liking to me as a young guy, and they sponsored me. I paid $2,250 for my membership, but I had to be guaranteed for $10,000. Two of the members volunteered to guarantee me. One was the manager for Merrill Lynch, Howard Hinman, and he guaranteed me for $5,000. And the other $5,000 came from a local trader, Lawrence "Stubby" Sachs. But the problem was that Stubby Sachs didn't have the $5,000 to guarantee me, so Milt Kirschbaum stepped in to guarantee Stubby Sachs.

John G. McCarthy, a former CBOT President, allowed me to open an account with his firm for just $500. Later when Mr. McCarthy became ill, I took over his company. In 1967, it was renamed Lee B. Stern and Company and became a CBOT clearing firm.

How did you pay for your membership?

I had a few dollars left over from what I got paid as a corporal in the U.S. Army Air Corps, but the bulk of it came from my mother. She was a buyer at The Fair Store. With my dad's encouragement, I asked her for a loan to pay for a membership. She had only one question: Did I think that if I didn't like it, I would be able to get the money back? I said, "Well, there's a market for the membership, and I think that you can always get your money back or pretty close to it."

The membership cost $2,250, and my mother had confidence and trust in me. Many years later, I gave her a check, a substantial check, figuring interest after 30 years or something like that, and she almost fell over. I still have her thank-you letter.

Would you tell me about some of the legends that you heard about at the Board of Trade?

Well, it's hard to remember some of the legends. Some of them were of course legends in their own minds, if you know what I mean. I remember reading a book called *The Pit*, by Frank Norris. It was written about 1902 or 1903. It's not easy to find, but that really covered a lot of things that happened in those early days. I don't know whether I can tell you about specific people who were legends, but I really like to look at some of the pictures taken during the early days of the exchange. I have always liked the way the members dressed. They wore top hats on the floor and they always wore a tie. Everybody, from the runners, clerks, and phone people on up, had to look presentable.

Unfortunately, today, many of them look like the cat dragged them across the carpet or something like that. And to this day, when I go down on the trading floor, I still like to wear a tie. They treat me with respect. Many people say to me, "You've been a member for over 50 years. Why do you still go to the trading floor?" I say, "They call me Mr. Stern now. They never used to call me that before. I mean, I've been called a few names, but never Mr. Stern." Now I'm older, you know, a senior member, and I get a kick out of it. I still get in the action every once in a while, just to stay active and sharp.

Can you tell me about the famous wheat corner that happened around 1897?

It had to do with Joseph Leiter, son of the founder of Marshall Fields, Chicago millionaire Levi Leiter. He had all the cash and futures cornered. P.D. Armour, the major grain elevator owner, was the big short and said, "Well, okay, put a price on it." Leiter said there was no price. Armour brought in millions of bushels of wheat from Minneapolis at a great cost, and that broke the corner.

Can you think of any time in your lifetime when other people tried to corner the market? What happened?

Yes, certainly during my career, the Chinese tried to corner the soybean market. There were a couple of attempts to corner that market. There was a famous soybean oil scandal that took place somewhere in the 1960s.

Tell me about that.

It was an interesting situation that involved Tino De Angelis. De Angelis was a big trader of vegetable oil futures contracts. He had all of these paper receipts for delivery. Unfortunately, these receipts were based on large amounts of soybean oil in his tanks. For many years he did business with the largest financiers and trading companies on the assumption he could make good on these receipts when necessary. No one seemed to question his ability to supply the oil when needed.

In 1963, the De Angelis empire came to a crashing end, as the authorities discovered that his tanks in New Jersey were not filled with soybean oil, but were in fact mostly filled with water. Perhaps this had gone on for years, but until that moment, no one had bothered to check. Now all these people were left with worthless paper. They had lent him money using his salad oil as collateral. As a result of his trying to corner the market, and then not having the soybean oil, it was a big, big mess. Eventually American Express had to pay many millions of dollars, because they were American Express receipts.

There have been a few similar things like that, but I would say, all in all, nobody has ever really cornered the market, at least in the past 100 years. Even today, with all of the big funds and large speculative limits, I think the rules and the laws are pretty good. If you violate those rules, you end up in jail. All the money in the world is not going to help you. Although cornering the market sounds very glamorous, going back to the late 1800s, I seriously don't think there has ever been a successful corner in modern times.

Let's talk about some people you knew. Did you know Joe Dimon?

Joe Dimon was quite the character. He was a big trader who did very well on the floor of the CBOT. The interesting tale about him was that he made a lot of money owning bowling alleys down in Georgia. The story was the reason his bowling alleys did so well was the bowling lanes were short the regulation distance. Needless to say, everybody who bowled there did very well, and that made his bowling alleys very popular. I don't know what happened when they found out—if they ever did!

He was definitely a character. What's interesting was that when he had a lot of money, when he was successful, he was a terrible person, really an awful guy. And when he was broke, which happened from time to time, he was the nicest guy in the world. I remember him coming into the pit one day. He was long a lot of corn, and the corn market was going down. He came in with a bunch of cornstalks that were falling apart to show how dry it was. He hoped that that would have an effect on the market. I don't think it had any effect.

I can also remember coming back from my honeymoon on a train. This was in 1951, and Joe was on the train. He said, "I'm broke." I said, "What happened?" He said, "I can't get through on the telephone. I can't get calls through to get my orders in." And he was broke. He came back and forth a few times. I think the bottle got to him a little too much, and that was the end of Joe Dimon.

How about Dan Rice?

He was one of my idols. Mr. Daniel Rice, of course, was one of the most famous people down here at the Board of Trade. He had his own company, his own brokerage and trading company, which he eventually sold many years later. At one time, he had a horse farm that raised the Kentucky Derby winner. He was quite a person.

I remember one great story. For some reason or other he blamed me for an increase in charges of some sort, and I wasn't even on the committee. It didn't matter if it wasn't me. He had decided to be angry about the situation and he blamed me.

I knew that every morning he got a shave downstairs at Vic Lala's barbershop in the Board of Trade building. One time I went to get a haircut at about 10 in the morning, and there was Dan Rice in the barber chair. He sees me and he gets up and runs away. So Vic says to me, "What goes on with him?" I said, "I don't know. He's upset with me for some reason, but I've got nothing to do with it."

At any rate, I sat down in Vic's chair to get my haircut. Just as he begins to work, the phone rings. He answers it and it's Dan Rice, who says, "I'm coming back down." Vic replies, "Well, I'm sorry, Mr. Rice, I'm giving Lee Stern a haircut." And do you know, he never came into the barbershop again.

Many years later, all of this was forgotten and we actually became very good friends. In fact, when he was dying in the hospital, my wife and I both visited him. He was very generous to many causes in the city. You'll see the Daniel and Ida Rice Foundation all over the city of Chicago in places like the Art Institute and the Opera House. The Rice Foundation is a major donor to many groups.

Why do you relate him to the origins of the Board of Trade Clearing Corporation (BOTCC)?

In the early 1920s, when you settled up your trades at the end of the day, there was no BOTCC. If I made a trade and I owed you money, I'd have to bring a check to your office. I guess once Dan didn't have a very good day and they kept trying to find him, but his office door was locked and there was a sign on it that said, "Out to play golf" or something like that. And I guess at that point in time, the CBOT decided that the system wasn't working too well, and it developed the BOTCC.

How did that clearing system work better?

Well, it worked better because the clearinghouse was the counterparty to all trades. You paid your money to the clearinghouse; you paid and collected with the clearinghouse. And if you didn't pay, you had a major problem. You were gone.

Tell me who mentored you and taught you to trade.

I was really very lucky in those early days to have people help me, like Herman Gordon. He was the head broker for Merrill Lynch. I was just getting started. I was trading odd lots of 1,000 bushels, and one day Herman asked what I was doing. I told him. He said, "Well, I need an assistant. Would you like to be my assistant?" I was a member at the time, and I said, "Sure." And he became like a father to me. We became very close. Unfortunately, he died at a young age, probably about 60. That's considered young by today's standards.

Another mentor was Bill Silverstein, who was H. Hentz and Company's top commodity partner. He was also very helpful when I was starting out. He offered me trading advice and was always open to my questions. My other sponsors, Stubby Sachs and Milt Kirschbaum, were also special to me. I was fortunate to have quite a few mentors. The one thing about the Board of Trade is if somebody got in trouble, there were usually people around to help out. That was one of the best things about the people at the Board of Trade. Someone was always there to help.

But I can tell you this: Back in the 1950s and 1960s, when you'd go to lunch, you didn't talk about how much money you made or lost; you talked about the marketplace. You talked about who bought what, who sold what, and whether there was any export business. You don't see that today at all, and that's unfortunate. I think that in today's marketplace, there are too many people who got into this business without knowing what it is all about. For them, money is their god. It's never been my god and it's never been the god of most of the people that I started with in business.

Let's talk about some of those people. Tell me about Henry Shatkin.

Henry and I went to high school together. And although we weren't close friends, we did know each other. He has always said if it hadn't been for me, he'd have never been down at the CBOT. The way he tells the story, he was working as a bartender and he heard one day that the first year I was down here I made $16,000. And he said, "If that dummy can make $16,000, so can I." And that's the reason why he came down here. I think it took him five years to reach that level!

Henry's a famous name at the Chicago Board of Trade because he has been a very successful trader and he developed a fantastic futures company. He is also a very charitable man and has helped many people get their start. Henry's been like a godfather to many, many people down here. Today we're very close friends. We just had dinner together. And guess who picked up the check?

Give me some examples of how Henry has helped people.

He's given a lot of young traders a start. I'd say that by and large, Henry is a man who is willing to take risks with people. In contrast, I'm very careful about who I take risks with, even though I've been stung a couple of times. But Henry has really been a godfather to a lot of people down here.

How about some people you palled around with in the early days?

Well, let's see. There were the Geldermanns, and there was the late Al Gruetzmacher, who was a former chairman of the board. We used to go over to the old Atlantic Hotel across the street; that's where the 111 West Jackson Building is located. We used to go and have lunch. There'd be a whole group of us, George Forbeck, Tom Geldermann, and the late Jerry Nolan, a very dear friend of ours. I like to tell the story about the times we used to have lunch together with one of the members of the Board of Trade who just passed away, former Chairman Bill Mallers.

When Bill was just out of college and came down to the floor, he was friendly with Jerry Nolan. One day Jerry invited Bill to come over and have lunch with the guys. We decided we'd pull one on him. We ordered some champagne and a large lunch and then we whispered to the waiter to give the check to Bill. So the waiter hands the check to Bill.

In those days it was probably $100. He was shocked, but tried to be calm, and he said, "Why am I getting the check?" We said, "We have a tradition. The first time that we invite a person here to have lunch with us, the person has to pick up the check." So he picked up the check. Years later he told us that was all the money he had. He said it took him over a month to make that much money. And later on, of course, he was very successful and became Chairman of the Chicago Board of Trade.

Did you have more meals together after that first time?

Yes. Those were great days without the pressure of 24-hour trading.

Pressure is certainly part of this industry, and yet people perform their jobs with great integrity.

Integrity in any business is important, but more so here because of the nature of the trading on the floor. If you try to cheat, you're going to be gone. It doesn't take long for other traders to know when you made a trade with Mr. X or Mr. Y and the trade didn't clear and the price was out; people will start to question trading with you. If it happens often, then you will be gone, because nobody will trade with you.

Integrity plays a major role in the success of trading on the floor. When there's excessive trading on the floor, our integrity enables the people who use it as a commercial vehicle to be able to understand that when they put the trades out there, they're going to get a fair shake.

Sure, we've had cases that test that thought, like the FBI sting several years ago. I think that every business has those problems. But at the Chicago Board of Trade, they're few and far between. I'd like to think in all these years, and for me it will be 58 years now on the floor of the exchange, that by and large, integrity has played the major role in the success of everybody who's successful.

What do you think makes somebody a success?

It's hard to say. You know, everybody has their own style and their own method of trading. There are some people who are naturals, and some people aren't. A few of those can be taught how to trade. But many of them don't succeed, even though they have all the integrity in the world, because pretty soon they run out of money.

Sometimes I think it has to do more with the ability to control your emotions. I don't mean your emotions by shouting and yelling, but your emotions regarding trading size: the size of your trades. Sometimes it's against human nature to take a loss. I believe that the secret to successful trading is knowing when to take a loss. Those people who don't have that ability to know when to take their losses are the ones who end up losing in the long run.

Some of my best trades were ones where I took losses and avoided disasters. I maintain that it is really against human nature to take a loss. Let me put it into the context of buying a stock. People buy a stock at $20 and it goes down to $10, and they say, "I'm not a loser. I haven't lost." I say, "Of course you've lost. Your value's down to $10 now, where it was $20." "Well, when it gets back to $20 I'll sell." To me, that's not good thinking. It doesn't make for successful trading, whether it's in grains or in stocks or anything, really.

Besides "take your losses," were there other lessons that you learned down at the Board of Trade?

That's an interesting question. The first lesson I learned was don't overtrade. Trade within your pocketbook. I think that's the best advice I could ever give anybody. You know, too many people have a tendency to go for broke. When you go for broke, that's how you end up.

Do you think that applies today?

Yes, I think it applies. The problem today is the markets are so broad. You trade 24 hours a day. I go back to when you traded from 9:30 A.M. to 1:15 P.M., and it was a different time. I find myself at 4:30 in the morning with a small position in the market, and I get up to get a glass of water, and I go over and say, "Well, I wonder where it's at?" And I don't really have any kind of position at all. My chances of losing a lot of money or losing a little money or making a little money are infinitesimal. And yet there I am.

In the old days, when trading was from 9:30 A.M. to 1:15 P.M., it allowed for a much better family life. You left the markets and had time to be with your family, and you didn't have the stress of 24-hour trading.

Was 1:15 P.M. truly the end of the workday?

The markets closed at 1:15 P.M., but it really wasn't the end of the workday. Anybody interested in the marketplace looked at the news, and would go around talking to other traders and have a luncheon with a group and discuss the markets. From that standpoint, the trading day stopped, but the news value and the information value never stopped.

I know that after the trading day ended, many people volunteered to serve on committees. Can you talk about some of the committees you served on?

I think the most interesting committee that I ever was on or ever chaired was the New Products Committee. I like to think that bringing silver and gold back in the early 1970s was quite an achievement. I went to Europe and met with people in Switzerland about the gold and silver markets there. It was most fascinating working on getting those new products started at the CBOT.

I also enjoyed my tenure as chairman of the Floor Governors Committee. I really felt it was an important committee. When you talk about integrity, that was the committee that really oversaw integrity. It was quite interesting.

You talk about bringing silver and gold back. Why weren't people allowed to have silver and gold?

First of all, the government had a limit at $35 an ounce on gold, and gold wasn't traded. Then we went off the gold standard. Gold became a sought-after commodity and New York was the major spot for gold at the Commodities Exchange (COMEX). At one time, we cleared the COMEX at my company.

Silver was another product that people liked to trade. And of course, we had the big silver market. We talked earlier about famous corners; well, there was one in the silver market by Bunker Hunt. Hunt was the son of a multimillionaire tycoon. Bunker felt that silver had a role in protecting his assets. So he attempted to corner the silver market. And he actually had it cornered until the extremely high price attracted hidden silver from India, where silver was not just for making coins, but for making vast amounts of decorative pieces. They started melting anything that they could and selling it for its bullion value.

Then people around the world started doing the same thing. People in the United States were no exception. They were lining up to melt anything silver that they had in their homes. Once that happened, there was more silver than the Hunts could handle. Silver had gotten up to around $50 an ounce and then all of a sudden the market fell apart and that was the end of the silver corner.

There's a picture of you with bars of silver. We don't know if they're coming in or going out. What was that picture about?

That picture was taken of Marvin Parsoff and me. Marvin had been living in New York and was employed by one of the major metals companies. Then he moved to Chicago and came to work for me. Together, we developed the contract for silver. In order to have a contract, you had to have a delivery.

So we brought in silver bars from New York, and they were kept in vaults down here at the Board of Trade. They had to have certain qualifications and a type that manufactured them, just like grains or other listed commodities have to possess certain qualifications to be regular for delivery. So in that photo, we were bringing in the silver bars from New York. Until just now, I had forgotten about that picture. Marvin was very important in the development of that contract.

Can you describe the character of the CBOT?

I am happy to talk about the character of the Board of Trade. The Board of Trade has been and will continue to be, no matter who owns it, probably one of the most important factors in the American economy. You can talk about trading and you can talk about the futures market, but you'll never be able to talk about the futures market without talking about the Board of Trade. Its character is beyond reproach. It is a solid, substantial financial institution. And no matter what happened in days gone by—taxes, floods, pestilence, government interference, wars—the market survived all of that.

It's a different mentality today and a different way of trading today with computers and the like, and the different investors and investments, and the funds. But all of that started at the CBOT. It didn't start anywhere else. Add to that the brilliance of people like Dr. Richard Sandor at the CBOT and Leo Melamed at the CME, and you have incredible financial opportunities right here in the city of Chicago. I call Doc Sandor the father of financial futures with the creation of the Ginnie Mae contract. I call Leo Melamed the father of currency futures.

With all this character, has anyone ever challenged you personally at the Board of Trade?

You're always being challenged to a certain extent, particularly if you happen to be a little bit better than the other guy as a trader. With any group of people, there is always the chance that jealousy will occur. It can happen at the Board of Trade. It can happen if you make a movie. It can happen if you own a sports team. There's always the chance that someone will be jealous. That just naturally comes with success.

I find the older I've gotten, the less jealousy there appears to be. As you age, people are more interested in your opinions than what you own. That makes me think about the early days on the floor. You know, we used to all wear a tan jacket on the floor. There was no differentiating between a trader and a clerk, or a phone clerk. In those early days, the phone clerks had to have a membership. If you used a pencil, you had to have a membership. You could not write an order on the floor unless you were a member. Part of that had to do with the fact that the memberships were so cheap that they were trying to support the price. If you were an assistant to a broker, you had to have a membership, because you were using a pencil. And that goes back a number of years.

The big change to our markets began in 1973. That was the time of the great Russian grain robbery. It became the subject of a book that was written about that period of our history—*The Great Grain Robbery*, by James Trager (Ballantine, 1975). At that time, the Russians out traded every major company, every major trader, and every major exporter in the world. That happened when they went to one company and they said, "We need X number of million bushels." Then they went to another company, and nobody knew they were accumulating all this incredible quantity of wheat that they needed to cover their food shortage.

That reminds me of a story about Henry Shatkin. In 1973, I went on a two-week holiday with my wife, and during that time, the wheat market started to explode. I think wheat was probably around $2.00 and it got to around $2.40. And when I came back, Henry said to me, "Boy, have you missed the market." And then I said, "Oh, my goodness."

Then Henry went on vacation and the wheat went from $2.40 to about $4.00. He came back and I said, "Boy, did you miss the market." The markets are markets. No matter who's there or who happens to be away at the time, the markets will always go on. It was very interesting. Everything happened that year. You had the crude oil situation; you had crop failures all around the world. I forget what the prices were, but record prices were set in those days. Some of those prices have been exceeded since then. Some have not.

There are many different groups of people on the floor of the CBOT. How do all these different groups of people interact?

Not very well, I'm afraid. There have always been different groups of people at the Chicago Board of Trade. That's one of the things that makes our exchange so terrific. There really is a place for everyone. Whether they're conservatives or liberals, or Jewish, Catholic, Irish, Polish, Protestants, they're all represented in our industry.

Sometimes they're cliquish, whereas sometimes they're not. Do they interact? I think basically, yes, they interact very well in the trading pits. But you know we're talking about history now. The trading pits are changing rapidly, but I think that by and large the interaction on the trading floor generally is okay. I'm not sure how well those groups interact outside the trading floor.

Let's talk about innovation in the industry. How have things changed since you started?

In terms of innovation, the biggest one for our exchange is the use of computers. Electronic trading, which has changed the world, has changed the exchanges. It's a whole different ball game today. It's difficult for a lot of people to make those changes. For whatever reason, each time something came up that might change our industry, there was always a huge fight. People here got comfortable with their way of life, and they seemed to be threatened by anything that resembled change.

I found in my lifetime that you have to make changes. Even knowing this to be true, I found the advent of electronic trading to be the most difficult change. Intellectually, I know that markets change. Supply, demand, tax changes, war, government policies, and international problems all affect trading techniques.

Now, of course, there's a different adjustment, and that's adjusting to the use of the computers in trading. And I'm finding that it's taking me a little longer to learn this new skill. As you get older, your fingers aren't so nimble. We talk about fat fingers. That's the bane of the existence of everyone, but particularly those of us who are 60 and over.

How did the CBOT react to the creation of the AMs, the Associate Memberships, and all of those different classes of membership?

When they brought in the new traders like the AMs and the IDEMs and other new membership types, I was totally against it and I was wrong. It had to be voted on by the membership, and it was a very close vote at the time. I think that Les Rosenthal was probably the one responsible for creating them and getting them passed. I said, "You have one membership, and that membership is sacred. What are all these little pieces?" I was wrong, and Les proved to be right on that one.

What happened when they were instituted?

It didn't take long before these memberships brought in more young people to specialize in certain areas. That was an important thing as far as increasing volume was concerned, and that's what we all live on as individual traders or owners of a company. If you have a company, you want volume, and if you're a trader on the floor you want volume. I can remember certain times, and 1969 stands out in my mind, when the market just stood there. Corn would have a penny range, and soybeans a two-cent range. You can't make money in those kinds of markets. From that standpoint, those were difficult times, and we needed to create more volume. It's easier to see in hindsight that these new memberships were a great way to go.

Tell me about some trading contracts that didn't last.

We traded lard. Lard was traded for many years. There was even a lard pit. I don't know how many pounds of lard were traded, but it was traded just like soybean oil. Then they developed a contract called loose lard. I don't think that lasted very long. Eventually the market closed down, because it wasn't efficient, and there was really no need for it. Soybean oil became king.

Then we traded in broilers. I think that the CME may have had a broiler contract first. I'm not sure. But we started a broiler contract, and that was interesting, except that the futures contract for broilers wasn't really needed. It wasn't like you had chickens growing out on the ground somewhere. They have major companies that deal with the chickens. Then we tried plywood, and that didn't work for us, either. The CME had a successful lumber contract. There haven't been many contracts that I can recall where another exchange has duplicated a contract and had any real success. The first contract is the winner; the second contract is the loser.

Looking back, we actually tried a cattle contract, and the CME had a cattle contract. We died like a dog on that one. This reminds me of an interesting story. I was a member of the Chicago Mercantile Exchange for a while. I was down on the CME floor when they traded their first cattle contract. They brought a steer on the floor, and I had my picture taken with that steer.

I was chair of the Public Relations Committee, and that was a lot of fun. When we decided to have a cattle contract, I suggested we do the same thing at the CBOT to introduce the contract and encourage trading. But they wouldn't let me bring a steer on the floor here. I said, "They did it at the CME. Why can't we do it?" They said, "Nope. Just because the CME did it doesn't mean that we should do it."

Tell me some other stories from your experiences with the public relations side of the exchange.

I really enjoyed being on the Public Relations Committee. I had a background in public relations and it was carried forward a little bit. One time they were doing some rehabilitation of our air-conditioning system, and people were just sweltering on the floor. It was ridiculous. Everyone was sweating and swearing. And I happened to see a sign that said, "Behind these walls is the progress for the all-new air control system in the Chicago Board of Trade for comfort year-round." Well, there was no comfort at that time! So I went downstairs and I got a bucket of ice and put the bucket of ice in front of a fan and I sat there in front of that sign and said, "This is our new air-conditioning system." I had a lot of fun with that!

That leads me to another good story. I can remember the budget for the Public Relations Committee was something like $200,000. We had to hire a new public relations director. I interviewed half a dozen people. The best one by far was the one who wanted the most money. He wanted $40,000. We ended up hiring Irv Johnson for around $14,000. He stayed with us a long time and he was a wonderful, devoted employee. He was an excellent public relations director for the farmers. But I always remembered that budget was $200,000. I think we probably pay our public relations director close to that figure now.

Tell me about the exchange's relationship with farmers.

Before I started trading, I didn't know what corn or soybeans looked like. Once I started trading on the floor, I found out. In the early days on the floor of the exchange, we had cash tables. Every carload of grain that came into the Chicago area had to be sampled. Tables were set up in the north corner of the floor and they would have open bags of grain samples on these tables. There were samples from every car of the grain that was sold, the cash grain, the actual spot grain. That's where you got to know what grain looked like.

How about soybeans?

You know, soybeans were a new product when I first started down here. We grew less than 300 million bushels of soybeans in 1948, and I can remember $3.00 was considered a fantastic price. One year we grew 280 million bushels, and then we grew some 300 million and Dan Rice would say, "Beans will never sell over $3.00."

Later on, my good friend Stubby Sachs did a lot of research on soybeans. He said, "Someday soybeans will sell at their highest price in history, with the largest crop in history." And that happened. I think we grew 1.1 billion bushels in 1972. That particular year, we grew the most soybeans in the history of the United States, and the price of soybeans went to its all-time high. Through our markets, soybeans became gold.

Today soybeans really are used for almost anything you can think of, from pharmaceuticals to paints. You take the soybean, and you crush it. It's the best feed. You get meal. You get oil, and the oil is a product that is just beginning to see many new uses. People are just finding out that certain derivatives of soybean oil might eventually help in stopping the spread of cancers. The thought of that happening is very exciting. Many of our agricultural products find uses beyond being a food product, like biodiesel and ethanol.

Speaking of derivatives, tell me about the commodity and the derivatives options markets.

I'd never heard the term "derivatives" until the past couple of years. What's a derivative? I don't know what "derivative" means. Is it a futures contract? I guess it is, but they've got a fancy name for it. I don't know who came up with this fancy name. I think it might have been Doc Sandor. I know before, we never talked about derivatives. We talked about futures contracts. And every one of these so-called derivatives is a futures contract, whether it's for options or whether it's for a regular contract itself.

Options were a different story, because I can remember that everybody was concerned about the prospect of buying options. Would they impact the volume of CBOT trading? Why would people buy a futures contract when they could buy an option and know how much they could lose and they could limit their losses? And of course there was plenty of discussion of having this type of market. As I have said, change is hard to accept at the Chicago Board of Trade. People said flatly, "We shouldn't have options." One of the reasons was because options trading was at one time banned by federal regulations.

But after many heated debates, sure enough, we had options, and options stimulated the volume of trade beyond anyone's imagination. It was really great, because anybody who sold options or bought options used futures as an offset. So if you were buying certain options, you might be offsetting a sale in the futures and vice versa. Options really were one of the big stimuli of increased volume.

How about the creation of the CBOE?

I happen to have been on the board of directors when that idea came up. I think it was 1973 or somewhere around there. It was just a brilliant idea. Henry Hall Wilson, who was out of the Kennedy White House, was the president of the exchange at the time. He hired a young man off the *Wall Street Journal*. His name was Joe Sullivan. Joe was really one of the fathers of the CBOE. He helped develop that whole exchange. There is no doubt that our Board of Trade members, Eddie O'Connor, Bill Mallers, Dave Goldberg, and a few others were very instrumental in making it happen, too. The O'Connor brothers, Ed and Billy, really backed it and promoted it, and the CBOT sold many memberships at $10,000 apiece. Pat Hennessey was also very involved in the development of the Chicago Board Options Exchange.

The CBOE became a huge success despite early problems as a newly developed enterprise. Today you have a situation that has become a major legal issue as the CBOE tries to divorce itself from the Chicago Board of Trade family. This is very unfortunate. I am confident that the Board of Trade will succeed in showing their "fatherhood" of the CBOE. Indeed, they've got the birth certificate.

I can remember when we built that trading floor for the Options Exchange on the second floor. We never shut down for a day. They brought in these huge trusses on the weekends and we actually traded with hard hats on in the pit. It was a tremendous engineering job to do that and not have to stop trading.

What was the importance of interest rate futures?

Obviously, interest rate futures are really an important part of our exchange. Interest rate futures are used by everybody, from mortgages to getting government debt financing. Today, using interest rate futures is something that nobody in finance can get along without. I don't pretend to be an expert on that. We've created bond futures. We've created other Treasury futures. It's been an exciting time watching this grow.

There are all sorts of formulas that people can use for their benefit. I had a customer who had a major building going up and he needed to protect himself. He wasn't going to get his financing for another six months. He used that market to protect himself against the fluctuation if the interest rates got too high. And it worked. He's been a good customer of mine ever since.

Do you see any new products coming that you might want to trade?

I see a lot of products being mentioned. Some of them seem ridiculous. But maybe they'll prove to be not so ridiculous after all. I think some of these products that are being mentioned are really products that are more gambling than speculating opportunities.

Almost 60 years ago I learned the difference between gambling and speculating. In gambling you create a risk. You know, if you play a baseball game, that game's going to be played whether you bet on it or don't bet on it. But the minute the farmer puts a crop in the ground, there's a risk involved. All the speculator is doing is assuming a risk that was already created. That can be for the farmer who puts his crops in the ground, or, in the case of the financial instruments, somebody who's developing a new company that needs financing. Those risks are inherent. Gambling risks are not inherent. If you are gambling, you're creating a risk that just doesn't need to exist.

Let's talk about some of the historical events that happened outside of the CBOT that affected what was happening on the floor.

The assassination of JFK took place on November 22, 1963. You remember certain dates. And the market reacted. I mean, you didn't really know what happened. I was smart enough to take the tape off the Dow Jones, and I still have the original tapes, which show he was shot. Nobody knew whether he was killed or not. And it was right near the close of the market, and I don't think it had a particularly strong effect on the market, to the best of my recollection. But it certainly had a big effect on us as a nation.

Speaking of presidents, there's an interesting story about President Dwight Eisenhower and his effect on the market. When Eisenhower first had a heart attack, the markets responded upward. There was a big upward movement, simply because he was a Republican conservative. Several months later, a friend of mine who was with Merrill Lynch in the D.C. office told me he was walking across the street in Washington when he saw an ambulance coming out of the White House. It appeared to him that President Eisenhower might have suffered another heart attack, and he said to me, "What do you think?" And I said, "I'm going to buy some beans."

I went and bought some soybeans, figuring the market would rally on this. I waited and waited for the news to come out. No news came out. Here somebody with Merrill Lynch, a top-quality, high-class man who understood the markets, was telling me he saw the ambulance come out of the White House. In the end, I think Eisenhower had an ileitis attack. But I'm waiting for the news. The market's ready to close. I bought beans, and they went down four cents. Finally, the news comes out, and the market rallies to about where I had bought them. It taught me a good lesson on trading. Sometimes trading on news factors doesn't have anything to do with the market. It's a pretend kind of a thing.

Can you think of any news that did have an impact on the market?

During the Vietnam War, almost every day there was news coming out that affected us. Is the war going to be over or isn't it going to be over? Then there was the Southern corn blight. I remember somewhere the news wasn't out, and all of a sudden the market started to understand that there was this big corn blight that was going to cut back the production. The market rallied a total of 40 cents–which had a 10-cent limits in those days–over a period of four days. Then all of a sudden it stopped when they discovered this corn blight wasn't so bad after all. The market went back down again. There are always events like that.

I think war, more than anything else, has an effect on the market. Elections certainly have an effect on the market, too. I was a runner down here when Harry Truman was elected in the big upset in 1948. He was a big underdog. President Truman was not considered a friend of the free market system. And you'd have thought the place was like a wake down here. They couldn't believe it. But you want to know something? Business went on. And Harry Truman ended up being what I consider one of the great U.S. presidents.

You mentioned that war has an effect on markets. How?

It's because of supply and demand. If you have a war, do you cut off the supply factors, such as shipping grain to different countries? The markets are also affected because of uncertainty. Anytime there's uncertainty, it's going to affect the marketplace, whether it's a market of soybeans or thumbtacks. In the case of a market that has futures contracts, the uncertainty is reflected in the future. I think it's as simple as that.

How has the war in Iraq affected this market?

That's an interesting question. Unfortunately, I'm not sure that it has affected a lot of people that it should affect. It's really affected the market in the precious metals, copper prices, platinum, and palladium. Gold has gone up because gold is a separate issue. Silver. Do we have inflation? We don't have inflation, normal inflation, from that standpoint.

I think the reason that war doesn't affect more people today is because we have too many issues that are on our radar screens.

Let's talk about a couple of other historical events. How about the crisis in Chernobyl?

I'm glad you mentioned Chernobyl, because it was a real horror. It was probably the most threatening day since I've been down here, and maybe in the whole history of the exchange. We were in the midst of a bear market. Almost everybody was short or they had their options short, because it was definitely a bear market. There were big surpluses everywhere.

Then this big explosion occurs in Chernobyl, Russia, and nobody knew what was going to happen. We hear the radiation clouds are going north over Norway and Sweden. Is this almost the end of everything? The markets took off, up the limit, and you didn't know—forget about the markets—you didn't know what was going to happen to the world.

I do remember I was short and I talked to a good friend of mine, Steve Assimos at Cargill, just before the market opened. He said, "They don't grow any wheat in that area around Chernobyl." Russia, of course, grows a lot of wheat in the Ukraine, but they don't grow wheat near there. I had an opportunity to cover my wheat position a cent higher.

Meanwhile, soybeans were up the limit and corn was at the limit, but for whatever reason, wheat was up only a couple of cents. I was able to get in my short position and eventually the wheat market went up the limit. It took a few days for this market to settle back, but eventually it turned back into the bear market supply and demand, and thank God the threat of Chernobyl didn't have an environmental or economic effect on the United States and the rest of the world.

Boy, I'll tell you, I wasn't thinking about losing money. I was thinking about living. What does it mean? You just didn't know what was going to happen. Radiation clouds were blowing, and we thought they could come here. We knew the atomic explosion had caused the leaks. And I think that that probably was the scariest time of my life, both here at the Board of Trade and just in general.

How about the Crash of 1987?

That certainly had an effect on everybody. My big concern at that time was that I had a lot of customers and I didn't know who would be affected. As it turned out, I didn't have anybody who was in the market, but certainly that was a scary time. It was a different type of scary time than Chernobyl.

In the 1990s, there was a time period for the CBOT when there was diminished interest in trading, and things weren't going very well.

There were some problems that we had, some political problems, and then the exchange itself wasn't doing well. But that's the history of the exchange. I think that right now we're at the greatest time in our history. I can say this without hesitation: I think that in my time we have had the best leadership that we have ever had at the Board of Trade. And there were some good leaders here. Up until this time, there was always this political haggling.

Of course, what's the haggling right now? Who should be our merger partner? Should we take the big money quick and run? Should we take local discounts and look at the long range future? This is something that the board of directors are going to have to decide upon, and eventually, of course, the shareholders will vote upon. As I was quoted in the paper a few weeks ago, "It's nice to be the prettiest lady at the dance." And incidentally, I'll give Dan Henning credit for originating that one.

Tell me about when you were on the CBOT board of directors.

I ran for the board of directors at a very young age, and was badly beaten. I was appointed as a director to fill an open position. I think Fred Uhlmann did that. And then I ran as a director, unopposed. I was on the board of directors when we had our first public director, so that was somewhere around 1971, somewhere between 1969 and 1973.

The first public director was Milton Eisenhower, President Eisenhower's brother. Milton Eisenhower was president of the University of Pennsylvania at the time, and it was quite a thrill to sit on the board of directors with someone as knowledgeable and as well known as him. He was a very considerate man, a very down-to-earth person. And then we also had the United States budget director.

I will always remember Milton Eisenhower. The first thing he said after the second meeting was, "I think it would be a good idea if we had an agenda of what we are going to discuss in our meetings." And I said, "What a brilliant idea." We'd never had one before. We normally just sat down and we winged it. He felt that we ought to have a formal agenda of what we should talk about. Just think, it took the president of a major university to come up with that idea.

Let me ask you a personal question. What's it like having so many family members follow your lead?

Well, I always dreamed about having my family around me. I had a wonderful dad who died very, very young, and I missed the fact that I was never in business with him. Today, of course, I have four adult children, all members of the Board of Trade. My daughter January is a member here. She was a member over at the CME for a while, and she did some trading. I don't know how well. She never would tell me.

I have three sons. Kenny doesn't live in Chicago, and is a terrific professional trader. He trades in stocks more than anything else. He is also one of the top television soccer analysts. Then there are Jeff and Dan; both of them have been members of the Chicago Board of Trade for over 30 years, which is hard to believe. They are both very good at what they do. I guess you really have to ask them what it's like to have a father in the office all the time. For me, it's fun having them around.

I think the problem is, if you're close to your sons and daughters who are traders, you have a tendency to maybe be on top of them. If they make a trade that may be long and you're short you might say, "How can they be long?" You know, those kinds of things. But it's a wonderful feeling to watch them. I think it can be difficult. It depends, really, on your children. I mean, they're not children; mine are in their 50s.

I know families that have been down there that have had major problems with their children. I've heard of plenty of problems, whether it's drinking problems or overtrading problems or stuff like that, but those problems probably would have occurred in another business elsewhere. So in some cases it can be difficult. From my own viewpoint, it's been wonderful. I am a very proud father.

What do you think will be your legacy to the CBOT?

I don't know whether there's anybody here who really leaves a legacy to the exchange. I think you'd have to have an ego that's so far up and out and away that it would be unpleasant. I'd just like to think that here I was, I worked hard at what I did as a trader, and I joined forces as a member of various committees; but so have hundreds and hundreds of members. I don't really think we leave a legacy. A legacy has to be something that is extraordinary, and I don't think I was extraordinary.

I think you are extraordinary, and I am sure your family is proud of you. Thanks for sharing your stories with me.

CHAPTER 21

Leadership Rooted in Family Tradition

Frederick G. Uhlmann

After his junior year at Lake Forest Academy in 1946, Fred Uhlmann spent his summer working as a runner at the Chicago Board of Trade. Two generations of his family were already represented at the exchange: his grandfather, Fred, and his father, Richard. After high school, Mr. Uhlmann attended Washington and Lee University, graduating in 1951, with a bachelor of arts in history.

With his degree in hand, Fred came directly to the CBOT and joined Uhlmann Grain Company, where he served as vice president. In 1952, he became a member of the Chicago Board of Trade. He left Uhlmann Grain in 1965 and worked in various capacities for many other companies. Those included H. Hentz and Company, Drexel Burnham Lambert, Bear, Stearns and Co., Inc., Rodman and Renshaw, and LIT, a division of First Options, a subsidiary of Spear, Leeds and Kellogg. In 1998, LIT was sold to E.D. & F. Man International, Inc., which is now MF Global Inc. Fred remains with that company today.

Fred Uhlmann served the exchange in various volunteer positions for many years. He was an active member of many committees, including the Membership Committee and the Finance Committee. He was a director of the exchange in 1971, and then became the vice chairman in 1972. From 1973 to 1974, he served as the chairman of the CBOT.

In 1973, Fred became a founding board member of the Chicago Board Options Exchange (CBOE). During that time, he was also a director of the Futures Industry Association, becoming the chairman of that board in 1976. From 1982 to 2000, he was a director on the National Futures Association (NFA) board and later served as its vice chairman. From 1999 to 2001, Fred was a director of the Futures Industry Institute. Currently, he serves on the Membership Committee of the NFA.

Fred was also active in the educational side of the exchange. In the 1960s, he taught the CBOT grain hedging/trading course. He taught a futures trading course at the New School in New York in 1980, and was a guest lecturer at the Wharton School of Business at Pennsylvania University and the Business School at Northwestern University.

Giving back to his community is important to Fred. He has devoted much of his time to the boards of Highland Park and Deerfield High Schools, Illinois Society for the Prevention of Blindness, Highland Park Hospital, the Sinai Community Institute, and Mount Sinai Hospital. Currently, he is a director of Lake Shore Country Club.

Married for 56 years to Virginia Strauss, they have five children: Richard, Thomas, Gina, Karen, and Elizabeth and 14 grandchildren.

****

We're going to start with some of your personal stories and talk about your family. How did you first hear about the CBOT?

It was part of our family dinner discussions every night. My father, Richard, and his father, Fred, had been members of the Board of Trade for years.

Tell me about the history of your family's business.

When my great-grandfather came to the United States, many Europeans were going to New York. For some reason, largely because of an agricultural background, he came to Chicago. Other members of the family moved to Kansas City, and for a while they were part of the Uhlmann Grain Company complex. That changed years later, when they went into the milling business and we stayed in the grain end of it.

My grandfather was the first of my family to be a member of the Board of Trade. Unfortunately, he died when I was very young. Together with my father, they started what became Uhlmann Grain Company. They had worked for another grain elevator company in Chicago and Indiana, and they decided to start a business here. It became a part futures and part cash grain business.

How did your father change the business from what his father had started?

I don't think my father changed it as much as the industry itself kept moving forward and changing. When I started in this business as a runner on the floor at age 16, it was the end of World War II. Because of the Office of Price Administration (OPA), there were price ceilings on corn and wheat. The only grains traded on the CBOT were oats and rye. At that time, the corn pit was used for poker and gin games every day.

What about the use of "privileges"?

Privileges were what today would be referred to as options, and they were traded here in the 1920s. The government eventually forced the exchange to stop trading them, because they thought they were excessive gambling. In fact, a privilege, like an option, was an option to buy or sell a call or a put, based on a price of an existing grain contract. And so they were the forerunner, and I think they became the conceptual basis, for what became options later on.

Options have been used in the securities industry for a long time as well, but they were traded over-the-counter, rather than listed on exchanges, until government regulatory agencies removed the restrictions and allowed us to trade them. We were the innovators of the CBOE, but because stocks were securities, they had to be separately regulated by the SEC (Securities and Exchange Commission).

Can you think of any other products that were traded and then were disallowed early on?

The metals market comes to mind. American citizens couldn't own gold and there was a price ceiling on silver. For a long period of time, there couldn't be public markets in either one, because we were banned as U.S. citizens from owning gold. It was a ridiculous restriction, but there it was. When it was finally lifted and the price ceilings were removed from silver, I think it was $1.29 an ounce. It was trading well above that level all over the rest of the world.

Finally these free markets were allowed to exist, and the Board of Trade wanted to get into the silver business. We tried the gold end of it, but we made a mistake by making the gold contract a kilo contract, rather than an ounce contract. That is what the New York market had. Maybe they would have been more successful anyhow, but this hurt us. We did have a good silver market for quite some time and there was a huge arbitrage business between Chicago and New York.

Is it true silver was stored at the Chicago Board of Trade building?

Somebody brought some silver in and decided to store it in the basement of the Board of Trade where we had a secure vault. There was space to store many silver bars. I have no idea how many were brought in. It came in during the middle of the night, and went out in the middle of the night. Nobody was witness to very much, but we were all aware it was happening. Their purpose was to be used for delivery.

That vault is where many of us had our lockboxes. We kept securities or family jewels or whatever there, because the banks really weren't in that sort of business. At that time, the banks didn't operate as trust companies and safekeeping companies. People had to go down to the CBOT vault and clip coupons off bonds and mail them in order to get paid. That's quite a difference from today's system.

When was the first time you saw the floor of the Board of Trade?

I'm not sure I remember the first time I saw it. I do remember when my father told me to get a summer job at age 16. I went to a few places and walked into the rooms where they were interviewing dozens of people. I decided to go over to Uhlmann Grain Company. I knew the man who was doing the hiring and was in charge of the floor runner operation. I approached him and said I wouldn't mind working there. And he told me, "You're hired, but don't tell your father I did it!"

Tell me about that first job.

I was a runner on the floor. The orders would come in by telephone, and then they'd be written out and handed to us to take into the various pits. We would read them, fold them so other brokers couldn't look over your shoulder and see whether they were buy or sell or what the price was. We learned quickly if they were market orders to wait for the fill and bring them back. We had to keep an eye out for brokers who were so busy that they were just flinging these filled orders all over the floor. Every firm had different-colored paper, so we would recognize ours by whether it was white or blue or green or brown, and we would return them to our desk. However, my most important job was getting water after the close for one of the brokers to use as a chaser, because as soon as the market closed, he'd pull his flask out and have a drink.

There wasn't much technology at the time. How were those orders handled?

Actually, orders arrived by Morse code and then were transmitted by phone to the floor booth.

And what happened at the end of the day?

The market closed at 1:15 P.M. There was a brief period when they'd extended trading, but that didn't last. As soon as the market ended, we were out of there. I would go up to the office and help clear the trades. All of this paper would go to the back office; and we had to hand-enter every trade into big ledgers. Then these sheets of trades would be carried down to the clearinghouse and matched up against the offsetting orders from the other firms. Everything was done by hand.

What happened when it didn't match up?

Those were outtrades. Even with today's technology, they still have them. But what's really remarkable is that the outtrades are well more than 90 percent resolved by the opening of the market the next day. And if a buyer and seller didn't agree, because of the inherent honesty and integrity of our industry the traders would have to work it out. Sometimes one would take a loss and that would be it.

What do you think were the business goals of Uhlmann Grain at that time?

We were handling mainly commercial hedging. The big food companies and grain elevators, whether they were country stations in the United States or subterminal markets or exporters, all passed their orders through brokerage firms. It wasn't until much later that a lot of them got into the clearing business. Also, at that time, we were in the grain elevator business as well.

Can you tell me about your mentors?

Of course my father was a wonderful mentor, but there were other people. I mean the industry was full of dedicated, really helpful people, who wanted to see more and more people come into the industry. They wanted us to survive and do well. I guess that became everybody's mantra as the years went on.

I found that the back-office people were wonderful. We had one guy named Finnegan who taught me as much as possible about the clearing end of the business. The floor people, the phone people, and the brokers were all helpful. They knew I was there to learn, not just go through the mechanics of doing a job. And I think I learned a great deal. It was better than any academic classroom scenario I can think of.

Can you remember the first lesson that you learned?

I learned when the telephone clerk got an order and slammed it down on the counter, you'd better jump and grab that order or you were in trouble! I also learned speed and efficiency have always been extremely important in this business. Value-added also comes to mind.

And how about integrity?

Integrity obviously is very important. What I mean by integrity is moral values as they relate to how people deal with other people. At the CBOT, people's reputations were built on their honesty and credibility. The integrity of the exchange became important to the outside world and the users, because if they felt that they weren't getting a fair price or good service, it would cause them to use other facilitators. The integrity of the industry and the people in it is extremely important.

Early on, was the reputation of the CBOT different than it is today?

There was a mystique and that mystique may still exist. Everybody knows something about stocks or thinks they have some knowledge about stocks. Normally when you talk about commodities or commodity futures, people may shut off a little bit. Years ago they didn't see how this fit into their lives or their way of thinking. Today it permeates so many areas of business and economics. Every day you see it on the news. There is so much media exposure that I think people have become more aware than ever before about what our industry does.

I was always mystified by the fact that schools had no classes or courses in it. We did have a wonderful course at the CBOT. I would say that almost every young person who ever came here was asked by the firm with which they were employed to take that course. I was involved in teaching it for a number of years. We had classes that met every Thursday evening and we usually had 300 or 400 people per class.

The course dealt with everything from cash grain merchandising to how elevators stored and sold their grain to exporters. It dealt with futures trading, and there was information on speculation. I thought that was an interesting topic to cover, because speculation provides the liquidity that makes these markets work.

Speculating has changed a lot, but at that time and over the years I would say that the speculators were largely the floor traders who provided the capital, and also their customers who were buying and selling futures for their own accounts. Funds were nonexistent. We dwelled on conversion of grains to food products.

How about price protection? Did they discuss that?

Price protection was also an unusual concept, almost in the category of miraculous. Instead of having insurance companies bond or write insurance policies to protect farmers, merchandisers, and consumers from price fluctuation, the market took care of it. For example, a maker of cereal, from the time he bought his wheat or corn or whatever product it was and processed it into the end product, had a market risk. But he could eliminate the vast majority of that market risk by selling or buying futures. That depended on what part of the business he was in.

So that really locked in the price.

Yes, it locked in much of the price. The big risk most commercials had to deal with was in the basis, which is the differential between the cash price and the futures price. We focused on that as well. That is a strong economic point in terms of how futures are used. If you want to take delivery of a futures contract, and you want to get it in Chicago, the price would be protected. However, if you want delivery in Texas, the price protection wasn't perfect, so the basis represented what the price differential was. During harvest, the basis is typically lower, because there is grain coming to market, whereas at the end of the crop year, the basis would get tighter. So the commercials would trade and hedge these cash and futures markets based on that differential.

How did the grain storage work?

Probably it was not too much different from today. There were country elevators, and farmers would harvest their crops and bring their grain into their local elevator. Those local elevators would, in turn, sell to either a subterminal or a terminal market, which had bigger facilities. At some point, that grain would be moved out, either to commercials or to exporters. But the commercials, take General Mills as an example, had to use elevators because they didn't have enough space in their own facilities to store all the grain they were going to need during the year. So they were paying for an elevator to store that grain for them.

Tell me about the time when there was cash grain on the floor.

There was a time when there was a cash grain operation on the CBOT floor. A number of tables were set up at the north end of the building for buyers and sellers to examine the cash grain. This inspection took place whether they were merchandisers or commercial companies, in order to do their buying and selling based on those samples. The samples came in from railroad cars sold or consigned to Chicago.

The samples were taken from these railroad cars, and they were checked by the Board of Trade Inspection Department, as well as the government. Each one made sure the other one was doing a proper job. Based on those samples, we would take the grain to the various buyers and try to get the best possible price we could. And the idea was to assign these railroad cars every day and make sure that all of them were moved to the end user.

I heard that trading was done 6 days a week.

The Board of Trade was open on Saturdays until noon in those early days. That was very painful in the summer, because everybody else was having a good time and we were down here in our sweltering offices. I think the floor of the Board of Trade must have had some type of an air-conditioner cooling system, because they had no open windows, so it wasn't as bad as the upstairs offices.

What's the difference between a chartist and a fundamentalist?

Chartists are still in existence today, but they're more under the category of technicians. In today's world, they're more computer oriented rather than using graphs and paper methods of trying to figure out whether the market is breaking out on the upside or the downside and then basing their decisions accordingly.

A lot of pit traders also knew what the chartists were apt to be doing on the basis of the same information that they read into those charts, so that they knew where a lot of the buying and selling orders would be. Fundamentalists base their decisions on supply/demand factors and also on government activity and whatever other ingredients they feel fundamentally can make the market move. In contrast, a technician probably is more short-term oriented and wants to know the immediate impact of certain market moves.

Has there ever been a chart that showed who did it better or who had a better grasp of the market?

That's a great question. Today there are trading funds, hedge funds, and other kinds of operators who have varied track records. Some have better results than others, so some investors are going to want to go with the ones who've done the best in the past. That's not always the best decision, because they run in cycles. There are no easy answers.

How about the idea of using trading models with algorithms of how the market will react?

There hasn't been a system devised that can figure out how to beat the market. Some work for a while. And there have been people here who became legends for their successful trading techniques, but later ended up in some other business.

Can you talk about some of those legends?

When I started out there was a guy by the name of Joe Dimon who was a very large Texan. He wore his 10-gallon hat and was always quite visible on the exchange floor. He was a chartist. My father used to say, "I've never seen a chartist with a clean white shirt." That meant they didn't always do so well, but this guy was a big factor in the market for a long time.

There was another man by the name of Vince Fagan who had some physical handicaps and could never get into the pit himself. He always had a way of signaling to his broker whether he wanted to buy or sell. I became very friendly with him in my early days, because I thought he was a money maker. If ever I wanted to buy something and I saw him selling, I shied away because I felt I was wrong.

How about the Gerstenbergs?

Well, there were families who had generations of people here. The Gerstenbergs were in the cash grain and elevator business. They were a dominant factor. There was another family by the name of Combs who also did futures and cash grain trading. People used to talk about the Irish Mafia on the Board of Trade, and the McKerrs come to mind. There were many successful families at the Board of Trade.

Can you tell me about a man named Butler?

Butler was a large speculator who at one time tried to corner the soybean market. For a while he was successful and then finally failed. His positions were too big and the market started to go against him and he liquidated. He disappeared like so many other large traders.

That makes me think of Ned Cook, who was a Memphis grain exporter. He was a wonderful human being. He was my friend and I had great respect for him, but he got involved in the soybean market during the time of Bunker Hunt's big trading in silver. When the Hunts were trading in silver, they were also very much involved in our soybean market. Unfortunately, Ned Cook was on the opposite end of one of the Hunts' moves in a July-November soybean spread. The spread widened about $2.00 a bushel and Ned Cook was short the market and went broke. After he got out of the spread, it went back the other way. The silver market also collapsed and the Hunt family eventually lost their fortunes as well.

Did you have any involvement with the Hunts?

We were clearing business for the Hunts. I was with Drexel Burnham at the time, and a senior executive called one day and said the Hunts had taken on enormous positions. Bunker and his two brothers also had excessive silver positions elsewhere. He told me, "You're going to have to call them and tell them that's their limit. We don't want any more." I said, "If we do that, they're going to close their accounts." He said he didn't care. So I called them and told them, and sure enough, they closed their accounts. They moved almost everything over to another firm and the Hunts just about put it out of business.

How about the name De Angelis?

Tino De Angelis was probably, in his day, the biggest crook ever to come upon the American business scene. The story is that he got into the salad oil business. He was buying, selling, and storing salad oil, which was mainly soybean oil and vegetable oil, in warehouses in New Jersey. The largest portion of those positions was held at Ira Haupt, which was a nonclearing member of the Board of Trade.

We at Uhlmann Grain Company were carrying positions for Haupt. There were two other firms as I recall, Willis and Bean and Lowell Hoit, but Haupt had the biggest positions. The positions got so big that a lawyer in Ira Haupt's office decided to go over himself to New Jersey with an inspector. When they opened up the tops of these tanks, they were really shocked. Since oil floats on water, they discovered that just below the surface of this thin layer of oil, there was nothing but water.

American Express had issued the receipts on this oil, and it turned out to be a $150 million scandal. Most of this information comes from the books I read that were written on the subject. American Express almost went out of business. It lost 50 percent of its capital. Haupt did go out of business. At that time, we had all the margin money we needed, which the banks tried to retrieve but we wouldn't give it to them. Then, all the positions were liquidated.

A group of traders at the Board of Trade were asked to go into the soybean oil pit because they knew selling orders would be coming in the next day. In order to maintain an orderly market, we needed people willing to go in there to buy all this oil. It was the lowest price at which soybean oil has ever traded.

Tell me about your relationship with Eddie Mansfield.

Eddie was the lone security guard at the Chicago Board of Trade. He was a friend to everybody here. There wasn't anybody he didn't know. He knew their family history, kids' names, and so forth. When I taught the Board of Trade grain course, Eddie was the person who used to do the facilitating. Between our afternoon and evening sessions, he and I would go to the Atlantic Hotel and we'd have dinner. He would tell lots of great stories. My regret is I didn't write them down. I should have maintained some sort of a diary of all the things that happened over the years, but my theory was who would read it?

You have a philosophy that says, "If you work hard and do a good job, the money will follow." Tell me about that.

I figured rather than putting money at the top of the list as a priority, if you work hard and are successful, the money would come. I'm not saying that money isn't necessarily a bottom-line objective, because it is, but the people I've watched over the years who've dedicated themselves to this practice have been the most successful.

What about the role of self-regulation at the Board of Trade?

The Board of Trade was established as a self-regulatory institution. The government, as it does in almost every part of our lives, decided it should have a hand in regulation. Years ago, it established the Commodity Exchange Authority (CEA), which was a small Washington operation. The CEA had small offices in Chicago and New York, to try to supervise or explore what was going on in the market.

The fact is traders dealt with each other on a daily basis. They bought and sold from each other on a platform of integrity and honesty. This was the reason that the self-regulatory process worked as well as it did. But the CEA was supposed to be the industry regulatory body. In the 1970s, when market volatility became as great as it did, the government stepped in and said, "We have to change this process and we have to have a much bigger and stronger agency." That's when it created the Commodity Futures Trading Commission (CFTC).

The CFTC was the outgrowth of the Commodity Exchange Act of 1973, establishing this government regulatory agency. The CFTC was put in charge of making sure that markets operated honorably and abuses were dealt with in a proper manner. Part of the Act involved establishing what was called a Title 13 Proposal, allowing for an industry self-regulatory agency. Several years after the CFTC came into being, a number of people in the industry got together and started the National Futures Association. This became the industry's self-regulatory body and it has been a highly successful entity.

It is my understanding that these agencies were created when you were chairman of the CBOT.

The CFTC came into being when I was chairman. Several of us in the industry were asked to come to Washington. We met with various members of Congress and we were told that this legislation was going to be developed one way or the other. We were told we could have a hand in helping to formulate it. To create this legislation, they held quite a few congressional committee hearings.

We testified before them and explained how our industry worked. Personally, I think I was involved in six, seven, maybe eight of those hearings. It was a wonderful experience. As an industry we got a reasonably objective and intellectual agency out of this process. I believe the CFTC has tried to be objective, protective, and fair with the industry and the public. You're never going to deal with government on terms that you think are 100 percent the way you would like them to be, but all in all, it has worked out well.

Also during the time of your chairmanship, the soybean embargo with President Nixon took place.

Oh, I recall it clearly. The price of soybeans had gone up so high and the Japanese and others were in the market buying. At the time, Nixon and other members of his administration decided that we should have an export embargo in order to protect the domestic markets and keep prices from going up too much higher. The unexpected result was that we encouraged primarily Brazil, and eventually other countries, to become very large producers of soybeans. Thus we lost our primary customers. It was a little lesson in economics.

You were also part of the founding of the CBOE.

I was on the founding board of directors of the CBOE. The reason that it became regulated by the SEC is because the SEC told us there would never be an options market in securities unless they had regulatory control. Well, we would have preferred having it become a total part of the Board of Trade and then been regulated by the CFTC, but we had to do it on their terms.

What do you think the impact of the CBOE has been?

It's been fantastic. It does all the things that economically provide major investment opportunities for people. I use it myself. If I own a stock and don't want to sell it for tax reasons, I may sell calls or buy puts. Also, over the years, hedge funds have developed client strategies for investment purposes. This has made the CBOE a formidable economic institution. This is one vehicle hedge funds should and do use.

How important was the development of interest rate futures?

Interest rate futures were developed in 1973, and the person really responsible for it, as far as the Board of Trade is concerned, is Richard

Sandor. He came to us from the University of California at Berkeley. I hired him when I was at Drexel Burnham, but he first went to work for Continental Grain Company. They were in the commodity futures business as Conti Commodities.

At that time, the insurance industry and the financial industry really didn't want futures contracts, nor did banks want futures in anything related to their products, bonds and government debt instruments. Richard Sandor realized that the wedge to get into the interest rate family was to create futures based on instruments of the Government National Mortgage Association (GNMA or Ginnie Mae) or some other government mortgage-backed instruments.

That clearly is one of the CBOT's greatest innovations. Can you tell me why innovations have been so important to the industry?

Innovation happens when exchanges have competition and need to develop new products and new ways of attracting public participation. We've had competing markets during my whole life here. New York markets have grown from about 10 percent of the total industry to a much larger portion, and the Chicago Mercantile Exchange (CME), which was a very small butter and egg market, became bigger than the Board of Trade, and now they are joined. That competition has certainly been the mother of invention.

What do you think will happen to the open outcry system?

I think it's going to disappear just for economic reasons, because you can't afford to have a floor with very few people on it. Perhaps some form of it will continue to exist. I can't predict that, but there are certain things, like options trading, that are handled much more easily on an open outcry basis than on a machine.

And why is that?

Because there are so many contracts listed with different strike prices and expiration time periods. There are so many strategies based on straddles and strangles and puts versus calls, which you can construct more easily when there are a group of people together in an atmosphere where they can offer different strategies to one another.

Where do you see competition coming from in the future?

All over. It's growing in Europe, where they have always had markets. Today there are exchanges in China, where they're slowly removing some of their restrictions. Japan has always been the innovator of commodity futures, and before they did it, Singapore had markets. The development of electronic markets has become a huge factor, too.

There are several that have been formed and they're backed by some of the large institutional banks.

Can you tell me any important moments in history that affected the markets?

Actually, the day JFK was shot I had left the floor to go to a lunch meeting. The waiter came over and told us, and I tore back to the Board of Trade. I wasn't on the floor; I was in our office. The markets and the stock market were very weak. Commodity markets were volatile and probably closed early that day. It was pretty hectic and unsettling.

Let's discuss the idea of the Board of Trade being a service industry. People who are outside the industry don't think of it in terms of service, but tell me why you see service as being important.

It's a good question, because too many people think that the exchanges are the makers of price, rather than the providers of a marketplace where price is determined by buyers and sellers. There have been two marches on the exchange that I recall. One was a consumer march, when prices went up during the 1973 period to levels that we haven't seen since. Soybeans were at $12.90 a bushel, and corn and wheat were proportionately as high. Another time farmer groups decided to assemble at the CBOT to protest that the Board of Trade speculators were causing prices to go down.

I always compare the Board of Trade to a supermarket. We put the products on the shelves, and people come and buy them or sell them. If there's a great demand or shortage of something, the price is going to go up, but we're not responsible for setting that price. We provide the facility for the buyers and sellers to come and make use of it.

How about the Board of Trade being a worldwide price discovery mechanism?

That's all part of it, too. Somebody described price discovery as dropping a pebble in the water and the ripples would fan out in an ever-diminishing fashion as the price was passed along to people in other parts of the world. Years ago it was by Morse code; today people are getting it so fast that floor traders don't have the time advantage they used to have.

What is your take on the merger of the CBOT and the CME?

Once again, we're in an era of competition and innovation. Investment bankers are always trying to do deals, and members are trying to capitalize on the price of memberships. Other exchanges have and will continue to come into being in order to compete with the CME and the Board of Trade. The markets, and particularly the derivatives business, are growing and becoming more competitive. The merger of the two exchanges will make it easier for them to be a stronger competitor in this new marketplace.

How will you personally participate in the new marketplace?

I still have a small business and I guess it's a disease one never gets rid of. I still enjoy what I do. I'm here for only part of the year, but I conduct some of my business from my Florida home. When I'm here, I have an office in Deerfield, Illinois, with several very competent people there. We deal with introducing brokers, some hedge funds, and a little commercial hedging. I enjoy it, but am I part of the technological revolution? No, and I don't expect to be.

You served the Board of Trade with great strength and integrity for years and years. Do you think that there's a legacy you've left this institution?

My family legacy began long ago. As I mentioned earlier, my grandfather and father started Uhlmann Grain Company. My grandfather was vice president of the Board of Trade long before I got into the business, and my father ran the business after my grandfather died in 1937. My father was a director, vice president, and then president of the exchange in 1948 for its 100th anniversary. It was a momentous occasion. He was president before they had paid staff at the exchange. The title of "president" became "chairman" when they decided to hire paid people to come in and take on the nonmembership administrative functions of the exchange.

Somewhere in the exchange's archives, or in our family files, is a film taken of the march down LaSalle Street when the CBOT moved into its new building. It speaks to the pride and enthusiasm that people have always had for this industry. I do not know the exact place this business was started or exactly who came up with the idea, but I know it has been around for 160 years. That speaks to the economic basis and integrity of the business. Our family has been a part of this industry for many, many years. We are grateful to those people long ago who devised this marketplace to serve so many people.

I was honored to have served the exchange on several committees and to have had two terms as chairman. It makes me happy that the family tradition of working at the Chicago Board of Trade has been passed on. I have a son, Tom, who's been a member for a long time. I was sorry he didn't get more into the Board of Trade politics, but I respect his reasons not to. He's still very much involved in the exchange, and that makes me very happy. I am proud of how our family has been part of this industry.